Betwixt and Between

By the same author

The Essential Wollstonecraft
Becoming Mary Wollstonecraft
Biographical Misrepresentations of British Women Writers: A Hall of Mirrors and the Long Nineteenth Century
The Life and Works of Augusta Jane Evans Wilson, 1835–1909
The Widow and Wedlock Novels of Frances Trollope
The Social Problem Novels of Frances Trollope
The Emperor's Old Groove: Decolonizing Disney's Magic Kingdom
Silent Voices: Forgotten Novels by Victorian Women Writers
Frances Trollope and the Novel of Social Change
Dissenting Women in Dickens's Novels

Betwixt and Between: The Biographies of Mary Wollstonecraft

Brenda Ayres

ANTHEM PRESS

Anthem Press
An imprint of Wimbledon Publishing Company
www.anthempress.com

This edition first published in UK and USA 2019
by ANTHEM PRESS
75–76 Blackfriars Road, London SE1 8HA, UK
or PO Box 9779, London SW19 7ZG, UK
and
244 Madison Ave #116, New York, NY 10016, USA

First published in the UK and USA by Anthem Press 2017

Copyright © Brenda Ayres 2019

The author asserts the moral right to be identified as the author of this work.

All rights reserved. Without limiting the rights under copyright reserved above,
no part of this publication may be reproduced, stored or introduced into
a retrieval system, or transmitted, in any form or by any means
(electronic, mechanical, photocopying, recording or otherwise),
without the prior written permission of both the copyright
owner and the above publisher of this book.

British Library Cataloguing-in-Publication Data
A catalogue record for this book is available from the British Library.

ISBN-13: 978-1-78527-185-4 (Pbk)
ISBN-10: 1-78527-185-7 (Pbk)

This title is also available as an e-book.

Dedicated to
Mary Ellen Hylton
(1931–2015)

CONTENTS

Acknowledgments   ix

Abbreviations   xi

Chronology of Wollstonecraft's Life   xiii

Introduction: The Betwixt and Between Life of Mary Wollstonecraft   1

1 William Godwin's *Memoirs of the Author of "A Vindication of the Rights of Woman"* (1798): A Political Philosopher's Autobiography   15

2 Mary Hays's "Memoirs of Mary Wollstonecraft" (1800): The Second of a New Genus   33

3 C. Kegan Paul's *Mary Wollstonecraft: Letters to Imlay, with Prefatory Memoir by C. K. Paul* (1879): The Victorian Gentleman   43

4 Elizabeth Robins Pennell's *Mary Wollstonecraft* (1884): A Victorian Feminist   51

5 Ralph M. Wardle's *Mary Wollstonecraft: A Critical Biography* (1951): Rosie-the-Riveter Wollstonecraft   65

6 Eleanor Flexner's *Mary Wollstonecraft* (1972): The Very Insensible Wollstonecraft   77

7 Claire Tomalin's *The Life and Death of Mary Wollstonecraft* (1974): Wollstonecraft with Sparkle   89

8 Emily Sunstein's *A Different Face: The Life of Mary Wollstonecraft* (1975): Not-so-liberated Woman   103

9 Margaret Tims's *Mary Wollstonecraft: A Social Pioneer* (1976): Wollstonecraft's Life: The Stuff of Novels   117

10 Gary Kelly's *Revolutionary Feminism: The Mind and Career of Mary Wollstonecraft (1992)*: A Literary Revolutionary   129

11 Janet M. Todd's *Mary Wollstonecraft: A Revolutionary Life* (2000): The
    "Impudent and Imprudent" Wollstonecraft 135

12 Miriam Brody's *Mary Wollstonecraft: Mother of Women's Rights*
    (2000): A Befitting Betwixt and Between Biography 143

13 Diane Jacobs's *Her Own Woman: The Life of Mary Wollstonecraft*
    (2001): Never Just Her Own Woman 151

14 Caroline Franklin's *Mary Wollstonecraft: A Literary Life* (2004): "The
    Education of an Educator" 159

15 Lyndall Gordon's *Vindication: A Life of Mary Wollstonecraft*
    (2005): Something Old, Something New, Something Borrowed,
    Something Blue 169

16 Julie A. Carlson's *England's First Family: Mary Wollstonecraft, William
    Godwin, Mary Shelley* (2007): "Con/fusions of Fact and Fiction" 183

17 Andrew Cayton's *Love in the Time of Revolution: Transatlantic Literary
    Radicalism and Historical Change, 1793–1818* (2013): "A Subject of
    George III" 193

18 Charlotte Gordon's *Romantic Outlaws: The Extraordinary Lives of Mary
    Wollstonecraft and Her Daughter* (2015): Like Mother, Like Daughter 201

Epilogue 213

Notes 219

Bibliography 233

Index 253

ACKNOWLEDGMENTS

I would like to thank Columbia University Press and Penguin, UK, who have graciously given permission to reproduce a great volume of quotes from Wollstonecraft's letters in *The Collected Letters of Mary Wollstonecraft* (2003), edited by Janet Todd, Columbia University Press. Reprinted with permission of the publisher.

I acknowledge a great debt to the biographers of Mary Wollstonecraft, in particular to those under study in this volume: William Godwin, Mary Hays, C. Kegan Paul, Elizabeth Robins Pennell, Ralph M. Wardle, Eleanor Flexner, Claire Tomalin, Emily Sunstein, Margaret Tims, Gary Kelly, Janet M. Todd, Miriam Brody, Diane Jacobs, Caroline Franklin, Lyndall Gordon, Julie A. Carlson, Andrew Cayton and Charlotte Gordon. Although chapters were not devoted to them, these biographers, too, deserve gratitude for their biographical work on Wollstonecraft: Florence Boos, Jean Detre, Clark Durant, Anne Elwood, Moira Ferguson, Henry Rosher James, Camilla Jebb, Madeline Linford, Jane Moore, Edna Nixon, George Preedy, William St. Clair, Barbara Taylor, George Robert Stirling Taylor, George Edward Woodberry and Virginia Woolf.

Additional thanks go to those scholars who have enriched Wollstonecraft scholarship with their critical treatment and insights: Sarah Apetrei, Sandrine Bergès, Pamela Clemit, Maria J. Falco, Michelle Faubert, Alice Green Fredman, Harriet Guest, Richard Holmes, Jane Hudson, Vivien Jones, Claudia Johnson, Harriet Jump, Cora Kaplan, Susan Laird, Jennifer Lorch, Anne Mellor, Ellen Moers, Mitzi Myers, Elizabeth Nitchie, Mary Poovey, Emma Rauschenbusch-Clough, Virginia Sapiro, Gina Luria Walker, Jan Wellington and Susan Khin Zaw.

Finally, I would like to thank several honors students and Sigma Tau Delta members at Liberty University who helped with the proofing of this manuscript: Erin Peters, Evelyn Jane Hylton, Wesley Pena and Hannah Underhill.

Most of all, I cannot pay enough homage to Mary Wollstonecraft, who courageously and sometimes serendipitously paddled hard against the current just to prove that a woman could do so.

Brenda Ayres
Liberty University
Lynchburg, Virginia

ABBREVIATIONS

MW	Mary Wollstonecraft
Thoughts	*Thoughts on the Education of Daughters* (1787)
Mary	*Mary: A Fiction* (1788)
Original Stories	*Original Stories from Real Life* (1796)
Female Reader	*The Female Reader* (1789)
Rights of Men	
ROM (citations)	*The Vindications: The Rights of Men and the Rights of Woman*, edited by David L. Macdonald and Kathleen Scherf (1997)
Rights of Woman	
ROW (citations)	*A Vindication of the Rights of Woman* (1792)
French Revolution	*An Historical and Moral View of the Origin and Progress of the French Revolution* (1794)
Letters from Sweden	
Sweden (citations)	*Letters Written in Sweden, Norway, and Denmark* (1796)
Maria	*Maria; or The Wrongs of Woman* (1798)
Memoirs	William Godwin, *Memoirs of Mary Wollstonecraft*, edited by Pamela Clemit and Gina Luria Walker (2001)
Paul, *L*	*Mary Wollstonecraft: Letters of Imlay*, edited by Charles Kegan Paul (1879)
Todd, *CL*	*The Collected Letters of Mary Wollstonecraft*, edited by Janet Todd (2003)
Wardle, *CL*	*The Collected Letters of Mary Wollstonecraft*, edited by Ralph Wardle (1979)

CHRONOLOGY OF WOLLSTONECRAFT'S LIFE

1688	Edward Wollstonecraft born. Married Jane (d. 1732) and they had a daughter, Elizabeth Ann (1716–1746, m. Isaac Rutson), and a son, Edward John (MW's father). The elder Edward was a wealthy master weaver in Spitalfields who, when he died in 1765, divided his property in thirds to be given equally to his daughter, his son and his son's eldest son. There was another son, Charles, who was married to Mary, but he died prior to 1765 and was not listed in the will.
1737	Edward John Wollstonecraft born.
1756	Edward John married Elizabeth Dickson, the daughter of a wealthy wine merchant in Ballyshannon in County Donegal. She died 1803 of dropsy.
1758	Edward (Ned) Bland born. Became a lawyer. Married Elizabeth Munday 1778 and had two children, Edward and Elizabeth, who immigrated to Australia. Ned died 1807.
1759	April 27, Mary Wollstonecraft born in Spitalfields of London, the second of seven children. Baptized at St. Botolph without Bishopsgate on May 20.
1761	Henry Woodstock born. Apprenticed to an apothecary-surgeon in Beverley. Presumably committed to a lunatic asylum.
1763	Elizabeth (Eliza, Betsey, Bess) born. Married Meredith Bishop 1782. Had a daughter, Elizabeth Mary Frances (born 1783 and died 1784). The MW family moved to a farm in Epping Forest in Essex. Bess died in the 1830s.
1764	Moved to another farm at Whale Bone, three miles from Epping Village.

1765	Everina (Averina) born. Died 1841 or 1843. Grandfather Wollstonecraft died leaving MW's father, Edward John Wollstonecraft £10,000 and rents for 30 apartments. Family moved to Barking, a village in Essex County then eight miles east of London.
1768	James born in Essex. Became a merchant sailor and later a lieutenant in the Royal Navy. Deported from Paris on suspicion of being a British spy. Died 1806. The MW family moved to Walkington in Yorkshire where MW attended day schools until she was 15-1/2. She benefitted from John Arden's teaching and formed friendship with Jane Arden (1758–1840) who would be a teacher for 60 years.
1770	Charles born in Beverley. Went to America in 1792. Married Sarah Garrison and had a daughter, Jane. Became brevet major in American army. Divorced Sarah for adultery. Married Nancy in 1813. Died 1818.
1774	MW family moved to Hoxton, where she became friends with Mr. and Mrs. James Clare.
1775	Through the Clares, MW met Fanny Blood (1757–1786), who would become her closest friend. Fanny's brother George (1760–1840) would propose to Everina and be rejected.
1776	MW family moved to a farm in Laugharne, Wales.
1777	Edward John returned the family to Walworth, a suburb in London, where MW's best friend, Fanny Blood, lived.
1778	MW employed as a companion to a widow, Sarah Dawson of Bath. MW met Rev. Joshua Waterhouse and exchanged love letters.
1780	MW went to Enfield, North London, to care for her mother, Elizabeth.
1782	April 19, Elizabeth died. On October 10, Bess married Meredith Bishop (1753–1835), a shipwright. Mr. Wollstonecraft remarried (Lydia, his housekeeper) and relocated to Wales. MW moved in with the Blood family and helped support them and her younger siblings with needlework. She met Neptune Blood, an Irish cousin to the Bloods, and carried on a dalliance.
1784	Bess suffered a breakdown after giving birth to a daughter, Elizabeth Mary Frances (August 10, 1783), and Bishop entreated MW to come to them. Convinced that

Bishop had been abusing her sister, MW arranged an escape, but legally Bess could not obtain custody of her child if she separated or divorced. They left without the child, after which the baby died before her first birthday. MW, Bess and Fanny Blood opened a school for girls in Islington. Failing to gain any students, the three were invited to begin a school in Newington Green. Hannah Burgh rented a building and recruited 20 pupils. MW's other sister, Everina, joined them. Wollstonecraft frequently heard Dr. Richard Price's sermons at the Newington Green Unitarian Church.

1785   Fanny Blood went to Lisbon to marry Irish merchant Hugh Skeys. Shortly afterward she became pregnant and sent for MW to help her with the birth of her child. On November 29, Fanny went into premature labor and died in the arms of her friend, and the child died soon after.

1786   Upon returning to Newington Green, MW found the school in financial trouble and closed it. Wrote *Thoughts on the Education of Daughters* while serving as a governess to three daughters of Viscount Kingsborough in County Cork, Ireland.

1787   *Thoughts on the Education of Daughters* published, and MW gave its earnings to the Blood family. Lady Kingsborough dismissed MW, and MW returned to London determined to make a living through writing.

1788   Joseph Johnson published her first novel, *Mary, a Fiction*, and her children's book, *Original Stories from Real Life*. He also paid her for translating, from French, Jacques Necker's *Of the Importance of Religious Opinions*, and she wrote reviews for Johnson's *Analytical Review*.

1789   Johnson published her anthology, *The Female Reader*. MW took the male pseudonym, "Mr. Creswick."

1790   Johnson paid MW to translate from German Christian Salzmann's *Elements of Morality, for the Use of Children*. Salzmann would later translate *Rights of Woman* into German. MW wrote a response to Edmund Burke's *Reflections on the Revolution in French*, and Johnson published it, but with no author's attribution, under the title, *A Vindication of the Rights of Men*. MW translated *Young Grandison*, Maria van de Weken de Cambon's adaptation of Samuel Richardson's novel.

1791	Second edition of *Rights of Men*, with Wollstonecraft this time listed as author. MW began work on *Rights of Woman*. She met William Godwin in November, and they shared a mutual dislike.
1792	First edition of *Rights of Woman* appeared in January, followed by a revised second edition later that year. In November, Sophia Fuseli rejected Wollstonecraft's proposal for a *ménage à trois* living arrangement. MW left for Paris in December to see firsthand what was happening in France, with its revolution. John Opie painted MW's portrait, and William Roscoe commissioned an unknown artist also to paint her portrait.
1793	Early in the year, MW met Gilbert Imlay, an American explorer, author and entrepreneur. MW registered as Imlay's wife at the American embassy, to be protected as an American citizen during the French Revolution.
1794	Joined Imlay in Le Havre in February. On May 14, their child, Fanny, was born. Wollstonecraft published *Historical and Moral View of the Origin and Progress of the French Revolution*.
1795	Imlay made several attempts to leave MW. When she became aware of his infidelity, she attempted suicide (late May). Next, Imlay sent her on a trip as his business envoy to Scandinavia, where she traveled with her child and a nurse. Upon return to London in October, she discovered that Imlay was having an affair with an actress. MW proposed that they all live together but was rebuffed. Attempted suicide again by jumping off the Putney Bridge (October 10), but she was rescued.
1796	Published *Letters Written during a Short Residence in Sweden, Norway, and Denmark*. In April she began *Maria*. She and Godwin became lovers.
1797	John Opie again painted MW's portrait. On March 29, MW and Godwin married at Old St. Pancras Church. They kept separate living quarters but visited each other every day at No. 29, The Polygon. Mary Godwin was born on August 30. On September 10 MW died of septicaemia and was buried in the churchyard of Old St. Pancras Church.

1798	Godwin published *Posthumous Works of the Author of A Vindication of the Rights of Woman*, which includes *The Wrongs of Woman, or Maria*; *The Cave of Fancy*, "Hints" and *Letters to Imlay*. He then published the *Memoirs of the Author of A Vindication of the Rights of Woman*, which made known her affairs and suicide attempts. The result was scandal and rejection of her work.
1816	October 9, Fanny Imlay committed suicide.
1818	Mary Shelley (née Godwin) published the novel *Frankenstein*.
1851	Percy Florence Shelley arranged for MW and Godwin to be reburied next to his mother in Bournemouth.

INTRODUCTION

THE BETWIXT AND BETWEEN LIFE OF MARY WOLLSTONECRAFT

If one types "Mary Wollstonecraft" as a keyword search in WorldCat, one will receive more than 17,000 hits.[1] This is not surprising, given that she was such a historically lionized individual and that she has often been credited for being the "mother of feminism."[2] Nevertheless, even as early as 1976, in her preface to *Mary Wollstonecraft: A Social Pioneer*, Margaret Tims asks why another biography should be written on Wollstonecraft. As if anticipating the plethora of biographies and criticism that would follow in the 1990s and the first decade of the twenty-first century, Tims's answer is that every biographer offers a "unique point of view" (ix).

When biographers write about a person's life, they prioritize what is important to themselves: What interests them, what resonates with them, what helps them, what teaches them, what makes sense to them and, most significantly, what advances their own political agendas, whether it is conscious or not. Their research is filtered through these lenses. Even if their biographical goal is to learn and present enough about their writers in order to better analyze a certain canon, literary critics usually begin their study from their own theoretical positions. Certainly, readers should be aware that no biographies are impartial; they bend according to their authors' psychological makeup, cultural encoding, historical agency and political penchants.[3] The survey of Wollstonecraft biographies in this volume demonstrates this.

Furthermore, biographies reflect the age in which they are written, more so than the age in which their subject lived. In studying the massive differences that exist in the biographies on the Romantics, for example, William St. Clair explains them as arising out of "cultural assumptions and aspirations of the time when they were written" ("Biographer" 221). This is not always a negative outcome, but a biography always imbues the portrait of the "biographee" with *its own* qualities so that the facsimile is never unadulterated. One can learn much about neoclassicism and romanticism by reading what Wollstonecraft's contemporaries had to say about her and her writing. The reverse is just as true: Wollstonecraft in the eighteenth century is very different from the Wollstonecraft presented by the Victorians. As Richard Holmes puts it, the truth we get from a biography "is always something of a floating currency; the exchange rates alter through history" ("Biography" 18). Biographies on Wollstonecraft carry an entirely different perspective and value system during her century and centuries after her, as this study shows and, as Barbara Tuchman has implied in the title of her well-known essay of 1986, biography is a "prism of history."

Specifically, what most people want to learn from biographies is how to overcome the obstacles in their own lives and realize their own dreams. For that reason, people are very interested in the lives of the rich, powerful, controversial and famous. Biographies allow them to fantasize about life in greener pastures. John Worthen, in his article "The Necessary Ignorance of a Biographer" (1995), writes:

> The fact that we *want* an emergent sense of the inevitable development suggests the enormously soothing quality which biographies have come to have in our age. Not only do biographies suggest that things as difficult as human lives can—for all their obvious complexity—be summed up, known, comprehended: they reassure us that, while we are reading, a world will be created in which there are few or no unclear motives, muddled decisions, or (indeed) loose ends. (231)

Park Honan sees an increase in the volume of biographies written in the twentieth century and predicts that they will continue to be popular. His theory for this trend is that "biographies bring *order* to the 'height' of accumulated knowledge, celebrate 'great' or unusual natures, counteract the insignificance of daily urban life, tell us of our 'selves,' and offer valid or convincing 'moral' exempla" (110).

Wollstonecraft did suffer, did endure and did know defeat and triumph over adversity. She was a woman determined to prove that women were intellectually equal to men and deserved ample education and opportunity to become all that they were created to be, and that gender constraints were shackles forged by men and not by God. For more than two centuries, women have taken courage from her writing and her life story by believing they could and should break the yoke of gender bondage. In her work with Wollstonecraft's political theory, Virginia Sapiro surmises that the life of Wollstonecraft "came to serve as a text for analysis by those who felt compelled to comment on the situation of women, especially those [women] who attempted to rebel against the laws and conventions that subordinated women to men" (222).

Still, how many biographies do we need of Mary Wollstonecraft? If one supposes that the most significant vantage point for any biography is that of the biography reader and what he or she needs or wants to discover about a figure, then there is great marketing potential for multiple life stories about the same person. The title of Lyndall Gordon's 2005 book, *Vindication: A Life of Mary Wollstonecraft*, states "*A Life*" and not "*The Life*": Gordon's biography is a representation of her own perception of Wollstonecraft's life, which may not be the same perception that someone else may have had or will have. The title is the recognition that none of us lives just one life. In truth, one's life and another's life are matters of perception and perspective. We are not the same person to all people. We are not even the same person to ourselves. How we see ourselves and others changes over time. If one were to write the story of one's own life today and then rewrite it in another decade, they would be two different stories. For that matter, one might write several versions of the same story today for different markets, for different effect and with a different agenda. Biographers ply life stories accordingly.

This manipulation of information raises a question, however. Is the author liable to draw a faithful, realistic, true and appropriate portrait of the subject? With the realization that biographers filter reality through their own agendas and biases, are they obligated to render a facsimile of the biographee's own psychological, cultural, political and historical constitution? In the case of Wollstonecraft, this pertains to her life's navigation through the end of the eighteenth century in dealing with issues of gender as well as class, child rearing and education, writing, marriage and religion—which inform Wollstonecraft's rhetorical themes. As this study demonstrates, many of Wollstonecraft's biographers have failed in varying degrees and times to moor their texts to these pilings. They have allowed their own value systems to sculpt their knowledge and, in turn, their presentation of Wollstonecraft.

About the "ephemeral nature of biographical knowledge," Richard Holmes raises this question:

> If no biography is ever "definitive," if every life-story can be endlessly retold and reinterpreted (there are now more than ten lives of Mary Wollstonecraft, thirty lives of Johnson, two hundred lives of Byron, four hundred lives of Hitler), how can any one life ever hope to avoid the relentless process of being superseded, outmoded, and eventually forgotten: a form of auto-destruction which has no equivalent in the novel? (Proper 15)

To Holmes, this does not pose a problem. Instead,

> it is exactly in these shifts and differences—factual, formal, stylistic, ideological, aesthetic—between early and later biographies that students

could find such an endless source of interest and historical information. They would discover how reputations developed, how fashions changed, how social and moral attitudes moved, how standards of judgement altered, as each generation, one after another, continuously reconsidered and idealized or condemned its forebears in the writing and rewriting of biography. (15–16)

Because Wollstonecraft *was* Wollstonecraft—in that she was so controversial, resolving the inconsistencies between her and her biographers, between her biographers and other biographers and between her work and her biographers' critical study of her work—this has resulted in a cornucopia of rich social, psychological, political and academic manna, not just on and about Wollstonecraft, but also on and about the times in which the biographers lived and their biases.

Tims was aware of these influences and tinctures that produce different pictures of the same subject when she wrote the preface to her biography on Wollstonecraft. With her publication coinciding with the International Women's Year (1976), she commented: "Many thousands of words have been, are being and will be written on the theme of women's liberation. It is an inexhaustible topic, as old as Eve and as new as next year's trend" (ix), an assessment that included Wollstonecraft as an icon of that liberation. As my study shows, all of the Wollstonecraft biographers viewed her as an icon for their own agenda and for their own time.

Any historiography of biography on Wollstonecraft has to begin with her husband's *Memoirs*, because every biographer since its publication has drawn material from it as if it were the gospel truth about her. On September 24, just nine days after his wife's death, William Godwin wrote in his diary that he had completed two pages of a biography.[4] Despite his own claims that Wollstonecraft wrote too quickly and without attention to detail,[5] and despite the fact that they had been married for only five months and he knew very little about her past life and had to ask her friends and family to send information, he completed what Lyndall Gordon called "his version of a life" (366) in only eight weeks; he finished it on November 15 and then took four days to revise it (C. Gordon 494). Although Godwin did not attend his wife's funeral "from grief rather than principle" (Marshall 191), by writing *Memoirs*, he effectively buried his wife for the next two hundred years by telling the world that she had attempted suicide twice and conceived two children out of wedlock. As Robert Southey put it, Godwin showed "the want of all feeling in stripping his dead wife naked, as he did."[6]

Therefore, the starting point for this analysis of the diverse biographical representations of Wollstonecraft will be Godwin's *Memoirs of the Author of*

A Vindication of the Rights of Woman. Indeed, Godwin's *Memoirs* are not really his memories of his wife, since he did not have many of them, but it was a rendition by a political philosopher of his wife as a political figure. However, it was neither accurate nor politically efficacious.

A more credible attempt at portraying Wollstonecraft can be found in an obituary published in the *Monthly Magazine* a few days after her death. It was written by her protégé, Mary Hays, whose purpose was to memorialize Wollstonecraft. After the appearance of Godwin's *Memoirs,* Hays was the first to try to exonerate her in "Memoirs of Mary Wollstonecraft," published in *The Annual Necrology* in 1800. When discussing this portrait of Wollstonecraft, Andrew McInnes (2017) refers to "Hays's Wollstonecraft" (2017, 57). Biographers have constantly taken possession of Wollstonecraft and remade her in their desired image. Hays advances her own rebellious agenda by attributing the following to Wollstonecraft: "Vigorous minds are with difficulty restrained within the trammels of authority; a spirit of enterprise, a passion for experiment, a liberal curiosity, urges them to quit beaten paths, to explore untried ways, to burst the fetters of prescription and to acquire wisdom by an individual experience" (411). Wollstonecraft's *Rights of Woman* certainly does argue passionately for men and women to "quit beaten paths," but she also urges them to become more modest and virtuous. Hays's implication is that Wollstonecraft was a rebel who defied social conventions. Hays's rhetoric and sympathy toward Wollstonecraft provoked an outcry by several reviewers who accused Hays of being a whore, just like Wollstonecraft. Therefore, by the time Hays was writing her six-volume *Female Biography* that, as her subtitle demonstrates, was supposedly to include "Illustrious and Celebrated Women, of All Ages and Countries," she omitted Wollstonecraft.

Although in the next century Wollstonecraft was becoming widely quoted and was embraced by American suffragists, her reputation became more shocking and unacceptable. Still, a few Victorians attempted to reinvent her as the weaker sex who had been mistreated by ungentlemanly men, beginning with her father, and her life story became a cautionary tale.[7] Her major champions were Anne Elwood, C. Kegan Paul and Elizabeth Robins Pennell.

Elwood's account in *Memoirs of the Literary Ladies of England* (1854) is sympathetic, except that Wollstonecraft has to be criticized for lack of Victorian propriety, even if she was not a Victorian. For example, she was not just victimized by Imlay; she exhibited a "violence of conduct [...] far more like to estrange than to restore the affections of Mr. Imlay" (149). Therefore, Elwood's final assessment is appropriately censorious for a Victorian lady:

> It is lamented that Mary Wollstonecroft [*sic*], whom nature, when she so lavishly endowed her with virtues and talents, evidently mean should

be a bright pattern of perfection to her sex, should, by her erroneous theories and false principles, have rendered herself instead, rather the beacon by which to warn the woman of similar endowments with herself, of the rocks upon which enthusiasm and imagination are too apt to wreck their professor. (152)

Just as Elwood uses Victorian rhetoric and mores to chastise Wollstonecraft, Paul uses Victorian rhetoric and mores to defend Wollstonecraft (*Mary Wollstonecraft*). He was Wollstonecraft's first real advocate, defending her against most accusations, assumptions and presumptions, especially in regard to her sexual conduct. He dismisses the Fuseli affair as a malicious rumor spread by Fuseli himself and his biographer. To Paul, she and Imlay were married, and her behavior was either very proper or understandable: Any decent, delicate woman scorned as she was by Imlay would take it hard and might find herself on Putney Bridge.

Pennell, however, was not interested in defending Wollstonecraft's behavior. She first identified it as defiant, and second applauded it for its defiance. Wollstonecraft was Pennell's heroine, one who challenged social conventions and chose to live and die by her convictions. Pennell saw Wollstonecraft as a reflection of herself, a self-reliant woman who jumped over the hurdles meant to keep her and any other woman from running the same race as men. Wollstonecraft gave all of herself to the race. By the 1870s, Pennell believed that history vindicated Wollstonecraft, as symbolized by the replacement of the "willowed trees" by her gravestone with "trees [...] of goodly growth and fair promise. And, like them, her character now *flourishes*, for justice is at last being done to her" (1890, 11). It is telling that Pennell uses the word "character" because, indeed, Wollstonecraft had primarily suffered character attacks. Pennell declares that it is not just her works that have been vindicated, but also her character.

Except for the significant inclusion in Virginia Woolf's 1929 *Common Reader*, not much was written about Wollstonecraft—nor was much read of the work from Wollstonecraft's own hand—until the 1950s, when Ralph Wardle exhumed her. As is well known, Woolf was a suicide victim and, during the Great Depression of the 1930s, suicide rates were up 65 percent (Baudelot and Establet 92). Woolf's understanding of the mental anguish that Wollstonecraft suffered throughout her life was very keen. Katerina Koutsantoni's analysis of Woolf's essay on Wollstonecraft greatly supports my theory that biographies are often more about the biographer than they are about the biographee or that their identities are so enmeshed, they are inseparable. Koutsantoni observes that Woolf's narrative technique is "free indirect discourse" wherein "Woolf mixes her own thoughts with those by Wollstonecraft in order to convey to the reader the sense of despair that overcame her character, and also to accomplish her intersubjective vision" (164). Koutsantoni demonstrates where and how Woolf "intentionally blur[red] clear distinctions regarding the identity of the speaker" (164).

Not surprisingly, with the surge of feminism in academe, the 1970s ignited a renewed interest in Wollstonecraft. Seven biographies were published in that decade. Janet Todd makes the point—as I am doing here—that Ralph Wardle created "another image of Wollstonecraft suitable for the modern era," meaning the 1950s, but even by the 1970s, his "assumptions about women appear[ed] dated" ("Biographies" 728). To Todd's disdain, two biographies appeared, in 1970 and 1971—Margaret George's and Edna Nixon's, respectively. They are not much more than a retelling of Wardle's, and Nixon's is guilty of replicating some errors that Wardle corrected, although Todd does not tell us what these are ("Biographies" 729).

On their heels appeared analyses by scholarly reviewers who compared these biographies to each other and to those that preceded them: Florence Boos, who published in the newly established *Mary Wollstonecraft Journal* (1973); Alice Green Fredman (1976), who taught at Columbia University,[8] and Janet Todd (1976), who would become the foremost scholar on Wollstonecraft, beginning with publication of four different articles on Wollstonecraft during the 1970s. Todd published in the first issue of the *Wollstonecraft Newsletter* (1973),[9] and by 1976, she had produced an annotated bibliography for Routledge. Boos reviewed George, Wardle and Flexner. Fredman reviewed Flexner, Tomalin and Sunstein. Todd's article, "The Biographies of Mary Wollstonecraft," is a history and a comparison/contrast of Wollstonecraft biographies, which include Hays, Polwhele, Godwin, Paul, Pennell, Emma Rauschenbusch-Clough, G. R. Stirling-Taylor, Henry. R. James, George R. Preedy (or Gabrielle Long), Wardle, Flexner, Tomalin and Sunstein, with particular attention paid to the last three.

Fredman refuses to give credence to Detre's 1975 biography. In her renunciation, she misrepresents Detre's own publisher when he asked if it were biography or fiction.[10] What the publisher said in an advertisement is "how to classify it? Is it biography [...] ? Or is it fiction [...] ? Perhaps it is neither, or both" (quoted in 136). Surely the publisher wrote this to market the biography as a book that is as enjoyable to read as is fiction. Nevertheless, or as a result of Detre's fictionalized biographical account of Wollstonecraft, Fredman decries it as "ludicrous and appalling" (137).

Boos, Fredman and Todd dismiss the biographies by Nixon, George and Detre, taking seriously only Flexner's, Tomalin's and Sunstein's (Tims's was published after their reviews). Fredman actually discounts Nixon's biography as "unreliable, factually inaccurate piece of shoddiness" (136).

Todd criticizes Nixon's biography for, besides being drawn primarily from Wardle, as being marred by "excessive generalization, rhetorical questions, winking asides about future events and by rather glaring inaccuracies" (*Annotated* xxi). Todd complains that many popular biographies have omniscient narrators, and so does Nixon's, which Todd considers to be unacceptable. Another issue for Todd is Nixon's assumption that Wollstonecraft has her mature ideas in her early years, which does not take into account that they evolved as Wollstonecraft matured grew (xxi). Given these great deficiencies, my biographical study does not include a chapter on Nixon, George and Detre.

Academe discovered Wollstonecraft in the 1970s. In the fourth edition of *The Norton Anthology of English Literature* (1979), Wollstonecraft appears for the first time, but she is placed in the Romantic period, listed as 1798–1832, which is an incongruity in that what Norton excerpted was Wollstonecraft's *Rights of Woman* published in 1792. She has remained as a Romantic, but in 1993, Norton expanded the date of romanticism to run from 1785 to 1830. As this maneuvering suggests, placing Wollstonecraft in a literary age is a slippery task. Is she Neoclassical or Romantic or both? Many scholars, including Gary Kelly, have identified her Enlightenment theories and have placed her writing conventions squarely in the Neoclassical Age, but then there were her Romantic tendencies that compelled Elizabeth Denlinger to identify her as a British Romantic.[11] As Barbara Kanner muses in her review of Kelly's book, despite the outpouring of scholarship on Wollstonecraft, she "still awaits definitive placement in the canon of modern British history" (229). Virginia Sapiro would not agree with such a statement because she was uncomfortable with trying to force Wollstonecraft into an arbitrary dichotomy between neoclassicism and romanticism that has been constructed by scholars so that they can manage the eighteenth century. "Our modern intellectual heritage," according to them, as Sapiro critically describes it, "often seems anchored by two overdrawn figures. On one side is the rationalist Enlightenment thinker who emphasizes reason and mind to the exclusion of emotion, passion and body. On the other side is the romantic who intuits the mysteries of the world through the senses and passions and who knows that the intelligence of reason is only illusory" (xx–xxi). Sapiro sees—as do I—Wollstonecraft sometimes betwixt and between the two literary periods and sometimes solidly in one of the other or both.

The 1990s was the apex of literary scholarship. Those were exciting times to major in English, when academe was producing literary scholarship from every angle, across disciplines and through a bewildering array and depth of theoretical approaches. In its midst, Kanner heralds Gary Kelly's 1992 book in its contribution to the "continuous flow of modern studies on Mary

Wollstonecraft [, which] has created a virtual subfield in English literary history and a category for analysis in feminist critic and gender theory" (229).

The 1990s were like an oil gusher; biographies and criticism of Wollstonecraft have been published nearly every year ever since. However, in part due to the technological advancements that make publications more readily accessible, and in part due to the rise of literary theory that has since framed and propelled scholarship, literary criticism of the twenty-first century is much more diverse, interdisciplinary, multicultural and revisionary, so that the first decade and a half have produced a smorgasbord of information and disparate perspectives on Wollstonecraft. Thus, George Robert Stirling Taylor's interest in Wollstonecraft was economics, Andrew Cayton's was revolutionary politics and Wendy Gunther-Canada's was Enlightenment politics. Julie Ann Carlson focuses on Wollstonecraft as a writer; Mitzi Myers as a children's-story writer; Harriet Jump as a Romantic; Christina Nehring as a romantic; and Susan Laird as an educator. Susan Khin Zaw approaches her understanding of Wollstonecraft through psychology; Barbara Taylor as a feminist democrat who hoped for radical egalitarianism (*Eve*); and Sarah Apetrei through religion. Thus, I say again that the biography is just as much about the biographer as it is about the biographee. Yet the reader expects to learn about the biographee and not the biographer. How then does the reader separate one set of information from the other?

Untangling this Gordian knot is one of the tasks of the present study. I ask questions like these: What do we know about Mary Wollstonecraft that is Godwin's version, which is radically different from Barbara Taylor's? How is the eighteenth-century Wollstonecraft different from the nineteenth- and the twentieth-century versions? How does she change from the first to the second to the third waves of feminism? How is the neoclassical Wollstonecraft different from the Romantic and then, again, the Victorian? How do people perceive an anti-Jacobin Wollstonecraft and revolutionary Wollstonecraft existing at the same time in history? What do we learn about Wollstonecraft from a biography driven by psychological analysis of her versus a biography with a Marxist approach? The questions are as varied as the biographers who wrote her life story, as are the readers, and they are as paradoxical as Wollstonecraft was herself.

I also highlight and analyze the contradictions presented by the biographers and critics. These might be mistakes resulting from poor research or from lack of resources available at the time of the research. Some are interpretations based upon biases. All biographical accounts are a fusion of a repository of information regarding the biographee, biographer, other biographers and the reader. To dismantle this amalgam is an invaluable exercise toward separating the creators of the biography from the biographee. Such analysis requires identification, correction and resolution of inconsistencies and errors. These are not mere mental isometrics; they force us to search for truth and reality, realizing all the while that truth and reality are often quite arbitrary. Still, we owe it to people like Wollstonecraft to know and understand them as honestly as we can. Especially with Wollstonecraft, who so valued reasoning, we ought to strive to be as rational as we can and gain a faithful replica copy of her. But she never lived in a vacuum. She was, has been and will always be defined by the people who want to know her in their own particular way.

This is a valid characteristic of any form of writing. It is a product of the writer. The two are inseparable, even with the most objective report, newspaper article or textbook. How it is written is more or less dictated by the personality and priorities of its writer or writers. But many biographies are riddled with gaps of knowledge, often concealed, plastered in with fiction or ignored. The most frequent culprit is missing documentation. Some oversights I suspect to be deliberate as well, such as when biographers do not want to deal with issues like religion. These gaps contribute to the "betwixt and between" composite that they construct of Wollstonecraft.

The phrase "betwixt and between," which I have borrowed for this volume's title, comes from Wollstonecraft in describing herself. In writing about her situation as a governess for Viscount and Lady Kingsborough, Wollstonecraft defines her station and herself as "something betwixt and between."[12] The allusion is to a common plight for unmarried women of her rank, with the only employment opened to them being someone's companion (which Wollstonecraft was with Mrs. Dawson from 1778 to 1789), or teaching in a girl's school (which Wollstonecraft did when she created two schools that could provide employment for herself as well as for her sisters and Fanny Blood from 1784 to 1786), or working as a governess (which Wollstonecraft did in Ireland from 1786 to 1787) or by writing (which Wollstonecraft began to do in 1787). Wollstonecraft yearned for women to be allowed to exercise their talents and gifts and to earn livings that exceeded the limitations of "betwixt and between"; yet, "betwixt and between" were parameters that have historically enclosed women.

Wollstonecraft recounts what it was like to be a governess: She was treated like a gentlewoman but was frequently reminded by her employers that she was of an inferior station (Todd, *CL* 88). In *Thoughts*, she complains that a teacher at a school was nothing more than an upper servant strapped with performing multiple menial tasks. If a woman were a governess, the mother would constantly look for her faults so that she herself would not feel ignorant, and the charges would complain to their mother if they were asked to do something they did not want to do or were disciplined. The children often treated the governess with disrespect and insolence. Then, when the governess was no longer young or genial, she would have no way to support herself because over the time of her service, she would have made very little money (71–72).

Paradoxically, Wollstonecraft perceived the aristocracy to be vulgar; all the while the aristocracy looked down upon governesses like Wollstonecraft as if *they* were vulgar. But a governess, because of her own class, desired polished society (73). Thus, she was "betwixt and between." The governess hungered for love and friendship, but because she was poor among the rich, she was not to expect this from them (74). Again, she was "betwixt and between."

Then there was the matter of falling in love. If she were "a beauty without sentiment," she was a prime target for being seduced. Men of higher station would flirt with pretty governesses, might make love to them, as George Ogle did to Wollstonecraft, and the woman would anticipate marriage, thereby to escape from their financial and employment woes (75–76). In reality, there were very few Rochesters who would marry their Janes. Wollstonecraft and her sisters were "betwixt and between" love and hope.

To be a woman and to be in the middle class of an "emergent class society" that characterized the eighteenth century was to be in a "position of agency and influence in the formation of social relations" (Sutherland 25). Women like Wollstonecraft, who were middle class and intelligent were poised in an ideal place to "balance the extremes" of the class structure and reinforce a "prescriptive force of a set of mental and emotional qualities culturally defined as 'feminine': sympathy, decorous accomplishment, chastity" (25).

According to Jan Wellington, during the last half of the eighteenth century the British perceived themselves in terms of men who were "rational, active, purposeful, and dominant." In contrast, they saw the French as womanly or "emotional, trifling, passive, and submissive" (35). Wellington supports this with a quote from Wollstonecraft's *French Revolution*, in which Wollstonecraft attacks her perceived effeminacy of Frenchmen and lack of character: "A variety of causes have so effeminate reason, that the French may be considered as a nation of women." To Wollstonecraft, the French were effeminate in these ways: "More ingenious than profound in their researches; more tender than impassioned in their affections; prompt to act, yet soon weary; they seem to work only to escape from work, and to reflect merely how they shall avoid reflection." Wellington attributes this "self-negating weakness, shallowness, and lack of fortitude with which conservative polemicists of the day characterized women," which included Wollstonecraft in her salvo at upper and middling classes of women of her day.[13]

In the eighteenth century, "woman," so Gary Kelly theorizes, came to represent a "vessel of feeling" (14), but with her confinement in a domestic, private world, she also became, like France during the Revolution, the critic of the "Old Regime" that was being perceived as corrupt and immoral

(15). But Wollstonecraft was betwixt and between femininity and masculinity and also sensibility and reasoning. Referring to Samuel Johnson's definition of "sensibility" as "quickness of sensation; quickness of perception; delicacy" (*ROW* 140; ch. 4), Wollstonecraft was dismayed that such sensibility entrapped women into behaving and being treated as if they were the "weaker vessel" (78; introd.) because "their conduct is unstable, and their opinions are wavering" (137; ch. 4). Thus, Wollstonecraft would like to become more "masculine" and encourage other women to be likewise (76, 79; introd., 16).[14]

Psychologically, Wollstonecraft was betwixt and between in other ways. Kelly thought she had a divided personality. Sometimes she felt and acted superior to others. At other times, she was consumed with self-blame (25). Her letters alone testify to Kelly's observations. About Lady Kingsborough, she writes: "Her conversation is ever irksome to me as she has neither sense nor feeling. [... A]nd the rest of acquaintance so very fashionable and insipid they *annoy* me" (Todd *CL*, 114), which is just one of many letters that make the same complaint. But in other letters she admits that Lady Kingsborough treated her like a gentlewoman (88) and invited her to join her company in the drawing room and to attend balls (108); nevertheless, Wollstonecraft was expected never to forget her "inferior station."

In her relationships with men she constantly vacillated between asserting herself as their superior and subordinating herself so lowly that her needs and opinions were moot. Enthralled by Henry Fuseli, she proposed to "unite" her "mind" with his. She "was designed to rise superior to [her] earthly habitation," but if she thought that the passion she felt for him was "criminal," she "would conquer it, or die in the attempt" (205). With great authority and firmness, she frequently warned Imlay about being "too anxious about money" (235) and that commerce "debases the mind, and roots out affection from the heart" (277), but then declared her stupidity and her inability to comprehend him because he wanted her to join him in England but also said that he planned to return to Paris (281). With frustration, she asked, "Pray Sir! When do you think of coming home?" (235), but in the same month wrote: "I am glad to find that other people can be unreasonable, as well as myself [...]. Yet I am not angry with thee, my love, for I think that it is a proof of stupidity, and likewise of a milk-and-water affection [...]" (234). Finally disillusioned by Imlay, she charged him with treating her "ungenerously" and warned: "Beware of the deceptions of passion! It will not always banish from your mind, that you have acted ignobly—and condescended to subterfuge to gloss over the conduct you could not excuse" (333). Just as often, she was full of self-deprecation, asking him to put up with her and assuring him that he was "one of the best creatures in the world. Pardon then the vagaries of a mind," she pled, "that has been almost 'crazed by care,' as well as 'crossed in hapless love,' and bear with me a *little* longer" (231–32). She was ambiguous to Godwin as well, as evident by these statements: "I am glad that you force me to love you more and more, in spite of my fear of being pierced to the heart by every one on whom I rest my mighty stock of affection" (369). Wollstonecraft was emotionally and psychologically torn between her desperation for security and happiness and her disposition toward self-destruction. As a woman, she was emotionally and psychologically torn between wanting to be independent and to be treated with respect and equality by men and negotiating with a culture that approved of her only if she played the part of a needy, dependent woman who required the protection of some man.

Arguably the two dichotomies that gave her the greatest trouble were being a Christian devoted to living a life pleasing to God and being a lonely woman who was driven by her desperation for earthly love. It is very difficult to trust a "Heavenly Father" (92) when one has known only abuse from an earthly father. Throughout her life, she was mostly betwixt and between these two fathers, and it was there, in the middle of the two poles, that she clung to love she thought accessible in the men she met, even if to do so, was immoral. The result placed her betwixt and between grief and happiness; her median was melancholy that wearied her to death.

The entire history of biography and literary criticism on Wollstonecraft seems itself to fall betwixt and between: biography and literary criticism are often pathographic or hagiographic, written by friend or foe.

However, when Sapiro, a political scientist, wrote *A Vindication of Political Virtue: The Political Theory of Mary Wollstonecraft*, she complained that although 23 books were published on Wollstonecraft's life (by 1992), very little analysis had been done on her work, especially beyond *Rights of Woman* (xxii). Today, if you type in "Wollstonecraft" at *Google Books*, you get 281,000 results.[15] It is *not* the purpose of the present book to provide a map to help readers through such a minefield. Janet Todd—one of the undisputed experts on Wollstonecraft—published an annotated bibliography on Wollstonecraft in 1976. It a very useful book—for works published before 1976—beneficial enough for it to have been republished by Routledge in 2012 and digitized by Taylor and Francis in 2013. Obviously, it cannot be considered a comprehensive source in that an avalanche of publications on Wollstonecraft appeared after 1976. If one attempted to supply a useful bibliography today on Wollstonecraft, it would be woefully out of date by the time it rolled off the presses.

My treatment of the major biographies includes, by necessity, some description of them; however, it is not an annotated bibliography nor is it just a review of those biographies, although that is also integrated. The primal drive of the present volume is to identify and analyze the vast incongruities that have been published on Wollstonecraft's life.

This is the reason I like Wollstonecraft's phrase "betwixt and between" for the title of this book. It seems an appropriate metaphor for what biographies have attempted, what with their prejudice, contradictions, gaps, as well as significant insights, accurate and credible information and memorable tributes to her life and works—but all according to their own individual agendas.

The present volume investigates these aspects, found in what I consider to be the benchmark biographies of the period in which they were written. Because the 1970s were a key decade for Wollstonecraft scholarship inspired by the sexual revolution, I investigate four of this decade's biographies. With the rise in the 1990s of third-wave feminism, which challenged any and all attempts to universalize what women should be and do and can be and do, of course there would be a torrent of biographies and critical studies on Wollstonecraft. I include six biographies from that decade. Near the end of this study, Andrew Cayton's 2013 biography fine-tuned his lens to zoom in on Wollstonecraft's love for Imlay and Godwin, and on how that love changed the world. Perhaps we can expect future biographies to be similarly streamlined to focus on more narrow aspects of Wollstonecraft's life and works. There also needs to be continued effort to correct mistakes and misinformation from what is in print.

"There is no such thing as a definitive biography," Stephen Oates has stated. A prolific biographer, himself, who wrote a brief overview of the biographies on Lyndon Johnson for the *Texas Observer*, Oates explains his statement: "The nature of life-writing and reminiscence, the process by which one human being resurrects another on the basis of human records, memories and dreams, precludes a fixed and final portrait of any figure" (18).

Therefore, the purpose of my book is to provide a tool to help readers navigate through the muddy but delightful waters of text about Wollstonecraft. In this effort, I am not immune to making the same mistakes and creating new holes, the very enterprises for which I have indicted the biographers. There is so much material available on Wollstonecraft that synthesizing and managing it can be overwhelming, as one ends up having to layer information until it is nearly unreadable at times. Regardless, it is my hope that this study will prove worthwhile to readers in educating them as to the flaws, disparities, biases and ambiguities of this body of scholarship and advise them to make their own investigations about one of the most remarkable women who ever lived—to extrapolate what is valuable and true about her life and works that will lead them to their own liberty and virtues. If they do this, they will be readers ever faithful to Wollstonecraft's own heart, and will honor what she bequeathed to posterity. Devoney Looser was absolutely right when she wrote in her 2016 article: "Wollstonecraft has long been described as a figure who cannot be laid to rest, an active presence among the living" (61).

Chapter 1

WILLIAM GODWIN'S *MEMOIRS OF THE AUTHOR OF "A VINDICATION OF THE RIGHTS OF WOMAN"* (1798): A POLITICAL PHILOSOPHER'S AUTOBIOGRAPHY

Most scholars agree that Godwin's biography of Wollstonecraft is biased and unreliable.

In 1981 Mitzi Myers notes this and also observes that, even after two centuries, his biography "remains the substratum on which even the newest lives erect their varying portrayals" of Wollstonecraft ("Godwin's" 299). It continues to be so; *Memoirs* is quoted more than any other source for information about Wollstonecraft as if it is the definitive biography. Since Godwin was Wollstonecraft's husband, the assumption is that he knew her better than anyone else, but the truth is the time that Godwin spent with Wollstonecraft was very short and sporadic. Furthermore, as Myers argues, the biography is more an autobiography by Godwin than a biography of his wife (310, 313).

Godwin joined Joseph Johnson's coterie on November 13, 1791, having received an invitation to a dinner party to honor Thomas Paine. From all accounts, he and Wollstonecraft struck an instant dislike for each other.[1] They might have seen each other on a few additional occasions at Johnson's table, but they were barely acquaintances before Wollstonecraft left for Paris and fell in love with Gilbert Imlay. Wollstonecraft does not mention Godwin in any of her extant letters prior to their sexual relationship. After Wollstonecraft returned to London with Fanny, Mary Hays schemed to get her two friends together and finally convinced both Godwin and Wollstonecraft to come to her home for tea on January 8, 1796. That setting proved to be more successful than earlier meetings.[2] By February 13, Godwin was romantically interested in Wollstonecraft as he called upon Rebecca Christie in the hopes of finding Wollstonecraft there, but she was out of town visiting a friend (L. Gordon 291). After taking new lodgings close to him in Somers Town, now known as King's Cross, Wollstonecraft called on him at his home on April 14 (293). That a single woman alone would visit a single man at his home, who was also alone, was a brazen act. Was it her experience with the French Revolution "that made it seem a matter of no importance whether she put on her cloak and went to visit Godwin in Somers Town, or waited in Judd Street West for Godwin to come to her?" Woolf wonders (198). This reflects a similar suggestion printed in the *Anti-Jacobin Review*, except that the latter is full of sarcasm and accuses Wollstonecraft and Godwin of "Jacobin morality" (178). "The fate of the *Vindication*," Jean Grimshaw theorizes some seventy years after Woolf,

> cannot be separated from views of Mary's personal life, nor from the fate of radical political ideas in the wave of repression and political reaction that dominated English politics in the years after the 1792. Mary's name and her work were tarred with the brush of French-style liberty, free thought, free love, irreligion, the undermining of family life, and all those things that were anathema both to conservative political orientations and to nineteenth-century evangelicalism. (9)

After Godwin made public his wife's private life, she became considered: a Jacobin in the eighteenth century, a fallen woman in the Victorian period in England, a champion of women's rights to the American suffragettes, perhaps a historical footnote during the first half of the twentieth century, an advocate of free love in the 1970s, an icon for feminists after that and whatever-you-want-her-to-be ever since. Whatever she was and is, very few readers and scholars are willing to separate Wollstonecraft from Godwin's image of her.

They became a couple, and their "intimacy increased, by regular, but almost imperceptible degrees," writes Godwin (*Memoirs* 103).[3] He went on a short excursion in July, at which time they both realized that they could no longer bear to be parted. By the following January, she was pregnant, and they decided to get married. They exchanged vows at St. Pancras Church on March 29, 1797, and shortly afterward set up an unconventional living arrangement: They took a three-story house, known as the Polygon, on Werrington Street, but Godwin rented separate quarters for himself some twenty doors away. They would live separately through the day, with Godwin returning to the Polygon by four or five, when they would dine together or spend time with other people, but they did not live as a couple. Thus, they kept their distance so that they could each work and avoid what Godwin referred to as "excessive familiarity" (110).[4] After five months of "married life," Wollstonecraft was dead. They "knew" each other as a couple with well-defined boundaries that separated them, for only 18 months.

There was so much that Godwin did not know about Wollstonecraft that after her death, he had to write letters of inquiry to her friends and relatives in order to amass enough information to write his brief biography. Nonetheless, Harriet Jump calls his research "meticulous," as he "numbered letters and contacted friends" ("Fond" 6). Florence Boos considers *Memoirs* "an excellently written tribute to his wife's character which combines his own recollections of her with what she had told him of her childhood and whatever information he could gather from friends and contemporaries" ("Biographies" 6). She also thinks that *Memoirs* is "a beautiful work in itself"—the memoirs "narrate an unconventional life with remarkable honesty, and very nearly preclude the need for any additional biography of Mary Wollstonecraft" (6). However, Boos also thinks that what Godwin had learned about Wollstonecraft from Wollstonecraft was "incomplete" and "inaccurate" because of her own questionable recollection of the past and because of Godwin's access to only a minimal number of his wife's voluminous letters. Boos concludes that there is more to say about Wollstonecraft (6). This was Boos's assessment in 1973. Because of the gaps in biographies and criticism to that point, scholarship on Wollstonecraft would burgeon afterward, but most of it would repeat Godwin's inaccurate statements.

When Haskell House republished *Memoirs* in 1927, the brilliant W. Clark Durant offered a preface that includes something of an apology for Godwin's rendition of Wollstonecraft: "Give this lady's brilliant genius a possible chance to arise from those dark troubled waters of the River Lethe in which it has been for so long undeservedly submerged. Remove that false label!" (xi). He also makes a point to refer to Wollstonecraft as Wollstonecraft instead of Mary Godwin and attacks those who did and do otherwise (xi).

Indeed, *Memoirs* is drastically flawed by errors and incomplete data. Janet Todd's research revealed that although there were many letters between Wollstonecraft and Fanny Blood, none were preserved. Most likely Everina destroyed letters that might have contained revealing information (x). The lack of availability of such letters accounts for some of the misinformation in *Memoirs*, but the greater problem is that Godwin often manipulated what information he did have to further his own agenda. Pamela Clemit, who co-edited the Broadview edition of Godwin's *Memoirs*, concurs, arguing in her article on Godwin's autobiographical writings that much of Godwin's writing was autobiographical (including his *Memoirs* of Wollstonecraft) and for the purpose of "the commemoration and vindication of his social and political ideas," which he felt increasingly compelled to proclaim after the disappointing outcome of the French Revolution ("Self-Analysis" 176). His objective for writing *Memoirs* was not to present a fair and accurate portrait of Mary Wollstonecraft.

Supposedly Godwin was shocked by the acerbic and vehement outrage that followed his publication (Jenkins 405). Was Godwin really so naïve to think that society was going to tolerate such blatant defiance of social conventions? Did he really have no idea that by proffering his own agenda in writing Wollstonecraft's story the way he did would effectively bury Wollstonecraft's work with her, which is exactly what happened? His own public defiance of social and moral conventions expressed in *Memoirs* also "led to a concerted campaign to discredit his ideas" (Clemit, "Self-Analysis" 174).

Several critics have absolved Godwin of any complicity in damaging Wollstonecraft's reputation. One defender is Tilottama Rajan (2000), who argues that Godwin's *Memoirs* is not about Wollstonecraft. Instead, Godwin is deliberately working out what Rajan terms, his own "historiography" about her life, but in so doing, contemplates his own genius and what it means to be a genius (512). Equally conciliatory, Jane Darcy (2013) considers *Memoirs* an experiment in biography: Godwin "earnestly attempts to present Wollstonecraft's powerfully intuitive nature as an exemplar for a new post-revolutionary age of openness and equality" (2). Clemit theorizes that his "innocuous" exposure of himself and Wollstonecraft came out of his Calvinistic upbringing, which encouraged public "self-scrutiny" (166–67), but after the fallout from *Memoirs*, he became "skeptical about the political efficacy of universal truth-telling" (174).

However, Myers (1981) emphasizes that *Memoirs* was not the first biography Godwin wrote, so he ought to have known what private information should have been kept private ("Godwin's" 307). Furthermore, Godwin expresses in *Memoirs* his awareness of how scathing society's opinion was about Wollstonecraft's illegitimate pregnancies (Godwin 105–6), so he could not have believed that his exposé would escape censorship (Myers, "Godwin's" 309). How ironic that, of all the men in her life, the one Wollstonecraft found the most congenial with her worldview and aspirations to change the world was the most efficacious in silencing her voice, devaluing her work and erasing her identity.

Godwin did this not only by publishing information about her alongside his social subversion, but also by overriding her belief systems with his own and by flagrantly disregarding facts about her life, which resulted in debasing it and her works. A Victorian who reviewed Paul's *Letters to Imlay* questions "the peculiar constitution of mind which induced Godwin to lay bare to the world the wrongs and agonies of his wife," and in 1879 was grateful for Kegan's more informed and sympathetic treatment of the "unfortunate writer."[5] Jump (2000) supposes that twentieth-century readers would think Godwin's "tender, frank and lucid" account is a "model of all that a biography should be" ("Fond" 6).

Godwin does try to honor his wife. His first attempt is by describing her as "distinguished in early youth, by some portion of that exquisite sensibility, soundness of understanding, and decision of character, which were the leading features of her mind through the whole course of her life" (45). How does he know this? He did not know her in her youth. His statement is followed by the since widely referenced, "She was not the favourite of either of her father or mother" (45), as if her childhood experience of rejection was what produced her "exquisite sensibility, soundness of understanding, and decision of character" (45). However, he does not explain how one resulted from the other, nor does he explain how he knows this about Wollstonecraft. Is it something she shared with him? Or does he simply deduce it from his reading of *Mary*, a novel to which he refers immediately afterward, saying, "The mother's partiality was fixed upon the eldest son" (45), which is nearly a quote from *Mary* (87)? This statement established a precedent for future Wollstonecraft biographers and critics—that is, the free application of details from Wollstonecraft's fictional works to her life, as if both novels were copiously autobiographical.

Godwin continues with more commentary about Wollstonecraft's childhood. Nearly every biographical work on Wollstonecraft, whether blurb, sketch, essay or book, hereafter includes this anecdote about Wollstonecraft's father:

> Mary would often throw herself between the despot and his victim, with the purpose to receive upon her own person the blows that might be directed against her mother. She has even laid whole nights upon the landing-place near their chamber-door, when, mistakenly, or with reason, she apprehended that her father might break out into paroxysms of violence. (46)

Although Godwin does not have much to say about Wollstonecraft's father, Edward Wollstonecraft did uproot his family many times due to his chronic business failures. That he might have vented his frustrations on the women in his life, who could not fight back, is credible. From Godwin's perspective, to publicize the father's abusive treatment of his family was an advantageous allegation in the hands of a social reformer who was, as the *Anti-Jacobin Review* worded it, "anti-hierarchical."[6]

Since the father was ineffective as a reliable provider or leader for the family, "Mary was ever ready at the call of distress," Godwin assures his readers, and "to promote the welfare of every member of her family" (53). Again, her entire family would not have agreed with this statement. Bess had very little to say to her sister once Wollstonecraft began making money from her writing—after she had promised her sisters that they would be able to quit their positions as governesses and come to live with her. Once Bess learned that her sister was apparently married to Imlay, she expected that he would take care of her as well. Although it was Wollstonecraft's dearest dream that Imlay and she would have a new beginning in America, and that Wollstonecraft's siblings would join her and no longer have to suffer from the class divide in England, it just did not happen (Todd, *CL* 243, 282). However, Wollstonecraft did manage to set up her brother Charles on a farm in America and acquire a commission at sea for her brother James. She also paid for Everina to live in Paris for a year so that she could become proficient enough with French to be able to teach it as a governess. All of this was confirmed in a letter to Godwin from Johnson on the day that Wollstonecraft was being buried at St. Pancras. Johnson speculated that Wollstonecraft had spent at least £200 on her brothers and sisters, and that she was always sending money to her father.[7]

Wollstonecraft's father died in 1803, leaving a horse and some cows, but also an old will that asked his eldest daughter to pay off his debts (Tomalin 254). Her brother, Ned, died in 1807, and the only comment about the effect of *Memoirs* on him was written by Claire Tomalin. Apparently, the notoriety was so bad for his children that they "grew up into strait-laced conservatives" and resettled in New South Wales (255). When *Memoirs* went public, Everina and Bess were terrified that their association with a scandalous sister would lose them their positions at schools in Dublin. Everina was running a boarding school for girls, and Bess was running one for boys (L. Gordon 414). Everina wrote to her sister that she was suffering a "paroxysm of despair" and proposed that they both emigrate to America to escape the publicity (Sunstein 350), but both weathered the storm and kept the schools until Bess died in the early 1830s. After that, Everina lived in London and "continued to denounce Godwin whenever she got the chance, up to her death" (Jacobs 287) in 1843 (Tomalin 255). Wollstonecraft's daughter, Fanny, committed suicide when she was 22, leaving behind a letter that clearly evidenced that she had suffered immeasurably because of the public exposure of her mother. Fanny writes:

> I have long determined that the best thing I could do was to put an end to the existence of a being whose birth was unfortunate, and whose life has only been a series of pain to those persons who have hurt their health in endeavouring to promote her welfare. Perhaps to hear of my death will give you pain; but you will soon have the blessing of forgetting that such a creature ever existed as [...]. (quoted in Dowden 328)

Although Godwin would share what details he knew about his wife's two failed suicide attempts and two out-of-wedlock pregnancies, he was strangely reticent about other matters that would have been considered scandalous. He alludes to Wollstonecraft's "attendance" to her sister, Bess, who had a "dangerous lying-in," and that "Mary continued with her sister without intermission, to her perfect recovery" (54). There is no mention of Bess's great depression after giving birth, or of Wollstonecraft's estimation that Bess was in an insufferable marriage and needed to be rescued. Wollstonecraft helped Bess escape from Bishop, leaving behind a child who would die shortly thereafter. Whether or not Wollstonecraft had judged Bess's depression and marital relationship correctly is another issue. That one woman would defy social custom and insist that another woman who was oppressed by a marriage should be free from it, and that the oppressed woman would also defy a legal system that would never grant a divorce in such a situation was an act of feminist bravado. Therefore, it is strange that the social-reforming Godwin chose not to include this story. Miriam Brody congratulates Godwin's omission as a deliberate act of protecting Bess's reputation (41, 138). Myers deduces that the withholding of the Bishop story indicates that Godwin is making conscientious and calculating decisions on what to include ("Godwin's" 310), which furthers the theory that Godwin's selection is being driven by his own personal and political agenda.

When Godwin summarizes Wollstonecraft's caregiving of Bess with her delivery as "perfect recovery," perhaps this is a gloss for more than a physical and mental recovery. Even though he does not detail the "escape," the next episode he describes is Wollstonecraft's endeavor to start a day school to support her two sisters, Fanny Blood and herself. A discerning reader can connect the dots: If Bess needed to be supported and would participate in teaching at a day school, obviously she was no longer living with Bishop. It is possible that Godwin spares the details of Wollstonecraft's involvement in order to veil Bess's separation from her husband. Otherwise, Bishop might have been pressured to take legal action against Bess.

The biography moves on with Godwin's conviction that she possessed an extraordinary proficiency in teaching. He does not relay that her first school failed and that her second school floundered. After Wollstonecraft returned to the school, which was being run by her two sisters while she tended to Fanny in Lisbon, she "was dissatisfied with the different appearance it presented upon her return, from the state in which she left it" (63). Godwin implies that the school could not run without her and that her sisters were incompetent.

Godwin presents very few details about her experiences with the Kingsboroughs other than to compliment her for liberating the children and "govern[ing] them by their affections only" (65) He also recognizes her victory in regarding herself as an equal to the Kingsboroughs instead of a dependent, even though she was a governess (65). These are too simplistic statements about her actual experiences, but they certainly make room for subsequent biographers to elaborate. They also illustrate Godwin's own philosophies about education and equality of the masses.

Godwin handles the Fuseli and Imlay experiences circumspectly. He never mentions Wollstonecraft's proposal for a *ménage à trois* in both situations, which she did make. Godwin projects her behavior with Fuseli as always pure, innocent and uncompromising (79). More of an endorsement of himself as a lover, Godwin asserts that Wollstonecraft "set a great value on a mutual affection between persons of an opposite sex" (79) but always wanted "domestic affection" (81). That is his answer to the accusations that his wife was "masculine," "celibate," "amazonian," "homosexual or bisexual" (hinted by many biographers regarding her relationship with Fanny Blood[8]). It also answers the accusations that she was licentious. Whether the object of her desire was Fuseli, Imlay or Godwin, her motivation, as portrayed by Godwin, is that she always wanted a permanent domestic situation. As soon as she realized this was not possible with Fuseli, she bravely distanced herself from him by going to France, so Godwin explains (82). Once she realized that Imlay was not going to commit to a permanent domestic arrangement, the disappointment was so great that she did not want to live anymore and thus twice attempted suicide (about which Godwin expresses his disapprobation). The only reason she did not want to marry Imlay, according to Godwin, was because she was afraid that her family's pecuniary situation would cause a hardship for him (86). However, Godwin does not mention that she considered herself his wife until she realized that he would never be faithful to her and take responsibility for their child.

Coupled with the distortion and paucity of facts, *Memoirs* is deficient as a biography when Godwin uses it as a forum to inflate his own ego at the expense of his deceased wife. He does this by demeaning her work through his reviews, which are inappropriate when telling the tale of her life. In regard to *Rights of Men*, Godwin says she "was in the habit of composing with rapidity," although he had never been physically present with her when she wrote. Furthermore, just because someone writes rapidly does not necessarily mean that the work is going to suffer the worst for it. Voltaire wrote *Candide* in just three days. Godwin considers Wollstonecraft's work marred by being "too contemptuous and intemperate" in her attack against "the great man" (73). He does not consider the piece as being professional enough to be a credible attack on Edmund Burke's ideas and not on the man himself. Whether Godwin realized it or not, he seems to have been threatened personally as a man that a woman dared to take on a man of such stature as Burke. Although Godwin praises her for being ardent with *Rights of Woman*, he thinks that being "contemptuous and intemperate" are undesirable comportments. Are they undesirable only because she is a woman? His own passage below and his statements against marriage in *An Enquiry Concerning Political Justice* have been considered contemptuous and intemperate by many critics:

> We did not marry. It is difficult to recommend any thing to indiscriminate adoption, contrary to the established rules and prejudices of mankind; but certainly nothing can be so ridiculous upon the face of it, or so contrary to the genuine march of sentiment, as to require the overflowing of the soul to wait upon a ceremony. (105)

Godwin calls marriage "evil." Two people "see each other for a few times and under circumstances full of delusion [...] vow to each other eternal attachment"; that is, if they marry for love and become "the dupes of falshood" [*sic*]. Further, "marriage is an affair of property," and to expect "two human beings" to live together for any great period of time is "to subject them to some inevitable portion of thwarting, bickering, and unhappiness" (*Memoirs* 136–37). The *Monthly Review* concludes its shocked response with: "No evil may result from recording the vow of love; but *many* evils *must* result from a contempt of marriage. It is one of the first institutions that are essential to social order" (181).⁹

As for *Rights of Woman*, Godwin tries to pay tribute to its merits. It is "bold and original" (74), he concedes, but the remaining comments are tinted with arsenic: *Rights of Woman* has "strength and firmness with which the author repels the opinions of Rousseau, Dr. Gregory and Dr. James Fordyce, respecting the condition of women" and it "cannot but make a strong impression upon every ingenuous reader" (75). Why "ingenuous"? Did he mean "innocent and unworldly" and that Wollstonecraft's argument is not sophisticated enough for more educated and logical minds? Or does he mean "honest"? He is not surprised that her criticism of men for their wanting "pretty, soft creatures" in women received hostile defense. At times her "passages" are "of a stern and rugged feature" that "did not belong to her fixed and permanent character" (75). It is as if he wants Wollstonecraft, herself, to be a "pretty, soft creature" in her writing and avoid "this rigid, and somewhat Amazonian temper"—a trait of which he does not approve (75). But he reassures his readers that her book is remarkable in its "luxuriance of imagination" and its "trembling delicacy of sentiment, which would have done honour to a poet, bursting with all of the visions of an Armida and a Dido" (75), two women who destroyed themselves for the sake of love. Undermining her political and philosophical credibility, he is saying that Wollstonecraft is not in his league as a political philosopher; however, she is indeed championing a political philosophy of equality for men and women in *Rights of Woman* and would be long remembered for it before Godwin's own ideas would be carried into posterity.

Instead, Godwin reduces *Rights of Woman* to the little lady's work full of "trembling delicacy of sentiment."

He must have thought he was praising her work by crediting it with "trembling delicacy of sentiment" and that he was doing her a favor by telling readers that, in her "fixed and permanent character," she was not as "masculine" and "rigid" and "amazonian" [*sic*] as she appeared in her writing. It is doubtful if Wollstonecraft would have been flattered by his efforts, judging from this passage in *Rights of Woman*:

> Dismissing then those pretty feminine phrases, which the men condescendingly use to soften our slavish dependence, and despising that weal elegancy of mind, exquisite sensibility, and sweet docility of manners, supposed to be the sexual characteristics of the weaker vessel, I wish to show that elegance is inferior to virtue, that the first object of laudable ambition is to obtain a character as a human being, regardless of the distinction of sex; and that secondary views should be brought to this simple touchstone. (14; introd.)

Is this a woman who would have appreciated Godwin's condescending tribute, his nod to her femininity, his act of making her dependent on him for validation? She conveyed her indignation about his criticism of her writing in *Wrongs of Woman* in a letter of May 16, 1797 (Todd, *CL* 414–15). Godwin not only destroys her reputation, but he belittles her writing and theory, pitching her as a "woman of feeling" in contrast to the "man of reason" (Caine 41).

Such comments represent the "positive" treatment of Godwin's review of *Rights of Woman* inside *Memoirs* before he discredits it as "undoubtedly a very unequal performance, and eminently deficient in method and arrangement. When tried by the hoary and long-established laws of literary composition, it can scarcely maintain its claim to be placed in the first class of human productions" (76). But Wollstonecraft's ambition was not to imitate the kind of "masculine" style considered as "long-established laws of literary composition." Neither was it her goal to be number one nor to produce "first class of human productions." With "a disinterested spirit," Wollstonecraft writes to Talleyrand, "I plead for my sex—not for myself" (dedication 2). Her purpose for writing *Rights of Woman* was to persuade the new French government to provide equal educational opportunities for females.

Toward that end, she articulates her "rough plan": She will not organize her thoughts and write in a linear progression. Instead, conscious that she is defying established rules of rhetoric, she is going to experiment with an unconventional style. She is a woman and is about to demonstrate that women can write effectively and argue logically, but in their own way. That is, in itself, a display of equality (*ROW* 78; introd.). If Godwin truly understood Wollstonecraft or her writing, he would have been aware of what she was trying to achieve with her subversive rhetoric.

Godwin is right, though, in predicting that because of the importance of what she wrote, her work would "be read as long as the English language endures" and that she "performed more substantial service for the cause of her sex, than all the other writers, male or female, that ever felt themselves animated in the behalf of oppressed and injured beauty" (76)—despite his misdirected efforts that would compromise her literary presence.

The next book Godwin critiques in *Memoirs* received his absolute encomium, but this too is chauvinistic. "If ever there was a book," commences his eulogy for *Letters from Sweden*, "calculated to make a man in love with its author, this appears to me to be the book" (95). In it Wollstonecraft "speaks of her sorrows, in a way that fills us with melancholy, and dissolves us in tenderness, at the same time that she displays a genius which commands all our admiration" (95). What does he mean by "genius"? He does not elaborate. He gives her no credit for the substance of the book—only for her feminine emotion, as he continues in the same vein: "Affliction had tempered her heart to a softness almost more than human; and the gentleness of her spirit seems precisely to accord with all the romance of unbounded attachment." It is a lovely way to describe her "romance" with the wildness of Scandinavia, but it neglects the serious and critical things she had to say about it as well. For example, she warns travelers not to be critical of other countries just because they do not resemble their native country. If they want sameness, they should just stay at home (*Sweden* 59). Some travel writers have perceived people in other countries as being "stupid by nature." Wollstonecraft muses that nature and governments have much to do with developing the work habits of people. If obtaining the "necessities of life" are too difficult or too easy, natives are not going to be very passionate about industry. A case in point are slaves, she says. Why would they be industrious if they have no self-interest? How can people excel in the arts and sciences if they are treated as brutes? (52). There is more in *Letters* than just feminine "softness."

The last book Godwin discusses is *Wrongs of Woman, or Maria*. Not surprisingly, he has nothing but complimentary things to say about this book, including a comment about Wollstonecraft's taking her time in writing it (111). After all, he edited, rewrote and published it after his wife's death. Rajan's theory is that he preferred Wollstonecraft's fiction to *Rights of Woman* because of its originality and, in particular *Maria*, because it was unfinished like her life and ideas (514–16). Rajan believes Godwin saw *Maria* as "another side" of

Wollstonecraft (516), a "corrective" to *Rights of Woman*, a realization that not much had changed for women since 1792 (516).

Another theory Rajan posits is that Godwin perceived Wollstonecraft as a genius (512), but with personal "tendencies" to sabotage her "performative power" to contribute in the construction of utopia (512–15). Godwin insists that her behavior and thoughts are not to be measured by any gauge of morality (512) or English set of propriety (515). This is similar to Harriet Guest's observations that Wollstonecraft was "endowed with the physicality of sensibility and imbued with its implications of utopian projection or desire" (96). Quoting from a poem by Charles Lloyd, she interprets the lines as depicting Wollstonecraft with "exceptional status" as if "she were a figure of superhuman, sublime, or heavenly powers, raised by her suffering sensibility above the judgements of ordinary mortals" (106).[10] Although Rajan understands that Godwin and others believed genius could find a home only in certain people with high sensibility like Wollstonecraft ("Framing" 513–15), there can be a breach between the spirit and the body preventing genius from having its full sway and effect, which was the case with Wollstonecraft, according to Godwin (522). Godwin does not present her as "stereotypically perfect," to use Rajan's words, but as a "project-in-process"—unfinished, fragmented, not always effective, debilitated because of the gap between theory and practice, whether the gap is caused by her own frailties or because of society's resistance to change or a combination of both (528–30). With both Wollstonecraft and Godwin, their integrity "licensed [their] unconventional morals (108)— Rajan infers that it was Wollstonecraft and Godwin's integrity that gave them the license to practice "unconventional morals" (18). She also deduces that Godwin "deangelicizes Wollstonecraft by stressing sensibility rather than propriety" (514).

However, Godwin was in denial about his wife's religious convictions. Perhaps the most serious irreconcilable presumption Godwin makes— regardless of his motive—one that in succeeding biographies has become repeated as fact, based only on his statements—has to do with her religion. It is as if he had a personal agenda as he purposed to prove that while he lived with her, he succeeded in making her wise and reasonable to the point of denying that there is a God. Godwin states:

> Mary had been bred in the principles of the church [*sic*] of England, but her esteem for this venerable preacher [Dr. Richard Price] led her occasionally to attend upon his public instructions. Her religion was, in reality, little allied to any system of forms; and, as she has often told me was founded rather in taste, than in the niceties of polemical discussion. (56)

How can he say that her religion was not "allied to any system of forms" when *Rights of Woman* has so many references to the King James Bible? How can a woman who translated Jacques Necker's *On the Importance of Religious Opinions* and Christian Gotthilf Salzmann's *Elements of Morality*, fail to engage in "polemical discussion" with Dr. Price, especially since she attended his sermons and spoke to him often at Johnson's house?

Godwin maintains that Wollstonecraft had had very little religious instruction from her parents (56). How does he know this? If he would have claimed this knowledge by declaring that she had told him so, then his statement might have more credibility. Her parents did see to it that she was christened at the Church of St. Botolph without Bishopsgate on May 20, 1759, a detail that Godwin neglects to mention. He does report that she regularly attended church until 1787 but not constantly after that, until "in no long time" she discontinued. How does he know this? Regardless of her adherence to the COE and attendance in a church, the astounding volume of references to the King James Bible in *Rights of Woman*, published in 1792, does not refute Godwin's claim, but it does question his inference that she had very little training and that she had lost faith in God by 1787.

Godwin further denigrates her faith by declaring "her religion was almost entirely of her own creation," and implies that it was either pantheistic or panentheistic (56). How could this be so when she constructed arguments as to the rights of women almost entirely out of building material from the Bible? He claims that she did not accept "the notions of judgment and retribution" (56). How could a Christian write about "the conduct of an accountable being" and "the throne of God," as Wollstonecraft does in *Rights of Woman* (109, ch. 2), and not believe in the Great Judgment as it is prophesied throughout the Bible and mentioned frequently in *The Book of Common Prayer*?[11] Since Wollstonecraft demonstrates a thorough knowledge and trust in the Bible in her extensive references to it in *Rights of Woman*, then Godwin's statement that she rejected the "notions of judgment and retribution" reflects his own challenges with Christianity.

Furthermore, in *Rights of Woman*, Wollstonecraft refers to Christ's parable of the talents (125; ch. 378; ch. 4), which closes with this judgment: "For unto every one that hath shall be given, and he shall have abundance: but from him that hath not shall be taken away even that which he hath. And cast ye the unprofitable servant into outer darkness: there shall be weeping and gnashing of teeth" (Matt. 25:29–30). She uses the word "talents" 27 times in *Rights of Woman*. Judgment—whether active in the individual or through God—was important to Wollstonecraft. "Judge" and "judgment" appear a combined 46 times.

As previously mentioned, Godwin maintains that Wollstonecraft ceased attending church after 1787. Caroline Franklin reminds us that 1787 was "coincidentally" the same year that Godwin purportedly turned his back on "High Calvinist beliefs." He wrote a letter to Joseph Priestley that he was "not a complete unbeliever till 1787" (quoted in 14).[12] Wollstonecraft, herself, gives us the strongest reason to doubt Godwin's assessment of her attitude toward religion. She writes in a 1796 letter to him, "I do not intend to let you extend your scepticism to me" (Todd, *CL* 356). We do not have the letter that he sent that provoked this response, but Todd reasons that the skepticism to which Wollstonecraft refers is religious, that when she mentions that she sent him a "family present given to me, when I was let loose in the world," she is probably referring to "a religious work received in childhood" (Todd, *CL* 356n748). It is very likely that this "family book" was some form of religious instruction for children, a genre that dominated the market of juvenilia (Grenby 86). An educated guess is Sarah Trimmer's *Fabulous Histories*, later known as *The Story of the Robins*, first published in 1786. Wollstonecraft left home to be a companion to Mrs. Dawson in 1788, so the date is correct. Trimmer (1741–1810) wrote over 50 books for children and about educating children. She was a High Church Anglican, and all her tales are morally didactic, both of which would have appealed to Wollstonecraft. Samuel Johnson was a mutual friend, and since Trimmer lived in London, she and Wollstonecraft might have known each other. With Wollstonecraft's passion for education reform, no doubt she would have been familiar with this book, and it may have inspired her in 1788 to use animals in her *Original Stories from Real Life*, especially the robin in chapter 3. In 1796 she was revising *Original Stories* for another edition, and this may have been part of the discussion in the 1796 letter to Godwin.

Godwin's strongest statement concerning Wollstonecraft's state of mind toward religion, a statement repeated over and over, concerns her last days when septicemia set in after the birth of the child: "Her religion, as I have already shown, was not calculated to be the torment of a sick bed" (*Memoirs* 118). This is an avowal of a man who saw religion as struggle with guilt. However, Wollstonecraft writes over and over in her letters that she looks forward to death. For example, in 1785 she says that the "prospect of death" cheers her, that she is not of this world and longed to be called home (Todd, *CL* 65). In 1786 she writes that she "long[ed] for eternal rest" (90) and for her warfare to be over (92, 93). Most of her letters to Everina identify this world as a place in which a Christian is an alien (149, 99), echoing 1 Chronicles 29:15: "For we are strangers before thee, and sojourners, as were all our fathers: our days on earth are as a shadow, and there is none abiding." Wollstonecraft's contempt is for the "forms of the world" to which she "should have bade a long good night" (409). On her death bed, Wollstonecraft would have taken comfort in knowing that she was soon to be with the "tender father" (121). As I note in the next chapter, Mary Hays claims she was with her during those last hours, and that Wollstonecraft was at peace because of her faith.

Instead of believing this, Godwin states: "In fact, during her whole illness, not one word of religious cast fell from her lips" (118), but by his own detailed accounts of those final days, especially after the birth on Wednesday, August 30, and through Sunday when he thought all danger was passed, he spent very little time with her (112–15). Once he was aware that she was in great danger, a string of doctors attended her, and he was out of the room, and even retired (117–20), much of the time. He was not with her during her final hour (120), 11 days after Mary's birth. So how did he know what Wollstonecraft said during his absence or even what she thought once she was no longer capable of talking?

In his article, "Mary Wollstonecraft's Religious Characters," Simon Swift blames Godwin for "marginaliz[ing]" Wollstonecraft's religion, which set a pattern that was not broken until Barbara Taylor began publishing her scholarship on Wollstonecraft. Godwin represented her faith as a "process of secularizing interiorization whereby religion becomes a sentiment for the sublime, under the sign of melancholy." Those who did have anything to say about her religion, regarded it as her "sublime introspection" (135).

Godwin really knew so very little about his wife, so to consider him an authoritative source is imprudent. One example demonstrates his lack of knowledge of her life. In a paragraph on page 57, he mentions two of Wollstonecraft's friends, Hannah Burgh and John Hewlett. There are only a few comments about Burgh—that she was the widow of the author of *Political Disquisitions*, that she was known for her "warmth and purity of her benevolence," and that Wollstonecraft spoke of her with great honor for her virtues. How disconcerting it would have been had Wollstonecraft read that her friend was identified only paternally. Burgh was a person in her own right; she did not exist only in the identity of her husband which can be implied by the address of "Mrs. Burgh." She was not just a widow of a man whose achievement is mentioned, but not hers. She was Hannah Burgh. Godwin offers no discussion about how important this woman was to Wollstonecraft. Burgh not only convinced her to start a school and provided its funding, but also in fact, constantly loaned her money for both the school and her personal needs, such as when Wollstonecraft required funds in order to travel to Lisbon to be with Fanny.

James Burgh had already published *Thoughts on Education* (1747) and *The Dignity of Human Nature* (1754), but Wollstonecraft disagreed with many of his ideas, such as his insistence that boys be sent to boarding school so that parents cannot indulge their "childish follies" (154–56). Wollstonecraft was against both boarding schools and tutoring at home. At the former, children became "gluttons and slovens"; at the latter, they develop "a too high an opinion of themselves" as they are "allowed to tyrannize over servants." Instead, she would have both boys and girls attend, together, a day school (*ROW* 252; ch. 12). Despite their not agreeing about pedagogy, The Burghs gave Wollstonecraft her full support. Furthermore, regardless of what others might have thought of Wollstonecraft when she helped her sister leave her husband, Hannah—a devout Dissenter—stood by her. Burgh ensured that Bess would be part of the teaching team at the new schools. After they failed, Burgh secured for Bess another teaching post (L. Gordon 72) at a time when most people—including Wollstonecraft's older brother—and the legal system would do nothing to help a woman who had left her husband. In fact, the usual practice was to try to persuade or even force the woman into returning to him. Bess not only left her husband, she left her infant child who would die a few months later. Yet Burgh showed her nothing but kindness and material aid.

As for Reverend Hewlett—whose name Godwin misspells (as he did frequently in *Memoirs*)—he deserves credit for suggesting, encouraging and facilitating Wollstonecraft's publications. If not for Hewlett, would have she come up with the idea and confidence that she could earn a living from writing? He was an Anglican priest who lived not far from Newington Green, where Wollstonecraft had her school. He was running a boarding school while working his way through Magdalene College, Cambridge (L. Gordon 58). With Wollstonecraft's devotion to education reform, they must have had numerous invigorating conversations. The interaction Wollstonecraft had with religious men and women throughout her life contravene Godwin's notions that she had very little religious training or religious interest after any particular date.

Besides being a male friend to her, Hewlett introduced her to Samuel Johnson (58), the first of many intellectuals who would accept her into their community. Feeling she belonged was crucial to this young woman, who had felt so rejected in her own family. She had low self-esteem as well, but now she was hobnobbing with some of the most brilliant people in London, such as Joseph Priestley, Richard Price, Thomas Paine, John Horne Tooke, William Blake, Anna Laetitia Barbauld, Henry Fuseli, Thomas Holcroft, Thomas Malthus, William Enfield, Gilbert Wakefield, Priscilla Wakefield, Erasmus Darwin, William Cowper, Johann Reinhold Forster, John Newton, Mary Hays, John Hewlett, William Nicholson, John Bonnycastle, Thomas Percival, Thomas Henry and William Godwin.

Hewlett gave Wollstonecraft the encouragement to write her own book, *Thoughts on the Education of Daughters*, and he showed it to Joseph Johnson (Todd, *CL* 68–69), who would become her publisher, best friend and father figure (173). In addition to making a path for her financial independence and opening the door for her to become a literary tour de force, Johnson gave her a position on his new magazine, *Analytical Review*, by which she might earn regular income from writing reviews and translating articles. She was hired to be a hack reader and translator (Braithwaite 94). Perhaps even more significant than this point is that she was, as Lyndall Gordon reminds us, "the first woman to take up short-notice professional reviewing as a substantial part of her income" (137), making way for such female writers as Edith Simcox, Fanny Fern and George Eliot to launch their literary careers.

Godwin's omissions of Burgh and Hewlett should raise questions as to what he knew and what he did not know about Wollstonecraft, as well as his discernment as to what he should say and what he should not. *Memoirs* does give us some glimpses of Wollstonecraft, but the book is mostly about Godwin and only negligibly about some pearl of a woman who delighted and disappointed the men in her life. What *Memoirs* does prove, however, is that this particular biography is more about the biographer than it is about the biographee. Jackson Benson, in his "Defense of Biographical Criticism," charges the biographer and the literary biographer with this responsibility: He or she

> must struggle in his relationship with his subject with recognitions of sameness while trying to comprehend an otherness that may be disturbing and nonsensical to his own sensibilities. He, also, is involved in a risky transaction at a distance which requires both identification and objectivity. This is a balancing act difficult to maintain and one at which any number of biographers have failed. (113)

With Godwin's inability to separate his own priorities and perceive Wollstonecraft as an identity distinct from his own, his *Memoirs* is not a trustworthy account, neither of her life nor her works. Therefore, scholars and other readers would be well advised to cease quoting him as if his information is factually accurate. Readers should question those biographies and critical articles that base their renditions on Godwin's narrative. Just because the same statements from Godwin's *Memoirs* have been repeated in texts for the past two hundred years does not make them true. Norman White came to a similar conclusion when he was working on his biography of Gerard Manley Hopkins. He discovered: "The fact is that biographical untruths are accepted by audiences if they have been said two or three times and fit in with expectations" ("Pieties" 214).

A reviewer for my book *Wollstonecraft's War with Religion* took issue with my challenge to Godwin's statements about Wollstonecraft's apostasy. This was her accusation: "Godwin states very clearly in the *Memoirs* that Wollstonecraft was not a practicing Christian of any stamp in her later years and that she uttered 'not one word of a religious cast' on her deathbed, and this assessment of Wollstonecraft's religiosity has been repeated in many subsequent biographies of her." This logic—that the sheer repetition of information makes it true—amazed me, especially that it came from an academic. Since when do three men make a tiger? She was not finished with her diatribe however: My "refusal to recognize the widely held opinion of Wollstonecraft's abandonment of Christianity in her later years appears, at best, to demonstrate the author's self-deception about this topic, and, at worst, to show the author's desire to mislead the reader." That the reviewer felt so strongly about this subject caused me to wonder about her own agenda. It also caused me to remember what White said in defense of biographers: "What often gets in the way of telling truths about someone's life is not the biographer's distortions or myopia, but the reader's reconceptions about what should be there, the way it should be told, and the conclusions which should be drawn" (214).

Regardless of the perpetuity of Godwin's claims about Wollstonecraft, the most immediate impact his book had on Wollstonecraft's reputation was that it effectively entombed her books for decades that followed. Too many readers have fallen into the same trap as did the writer for the *British Critic*, who begins his 1798 review of *Memoirs* with: The "authenticity of the tale no doubt can be entertained." After all, "the author was the husband of the heroine" (228).

Chapter 2

MARY HAYS'S "MEMOIRS OF MARY WOLLSTONECRAFT" (1800): THE SECOND OF A NEW GENUS

With vision, intention, determination and focus, Wollstonecraft announced to her sister Everina that she would become a different kind of writer, what she termed, a new genus.[1] Even though she published for only nine years before her untimely death, her aspiration was *fait accompli*, so much so that many scholars and biographers credit Wollstonecraft for being a pioneer as a political thinker, an unconventional woman, a reformer and a writer with innovative narrative technique and theory. Wollstonecraft successfully broke new ground that would make way for the appearance and growth of new kinds of people—especially new women who could be freer, more virtuous, more productive and happier. Her innovative writing techniques also launched a new school of women writers, who would imitate her style and then mature it.

Perhaps one can make the claim that Mary Hays, who revered Wollstonecraft as one would a guru, should be considered as the first fruit of Wollstonecraft's labor, thus the rationale for the subtitle to this chapter. To be so recognized was quite an honor to Hays until Wollstonecraft's "sins" were exposed to the public, and then Hays denounced her. After the publication of Godwin's *Memoirs*, being associated with her and attempting to defend her could only besmirch her own reputation and destroy her literary career. As a single woman depended upon the income from her writing, Hays could not afford to share Wollstonecraft's ignominy. After a valiant attempt to redeem Wollstonecraft in a short biography published in the *Annual Necrology*, one that triggered blistering attacks, Hays severed her relationship with Godwin.

Before that, Hays arguably had been Wollstonecraft's closest female friend in the last days of her life, staying next to her through the labor and deathwatch. Todd asserts that Hays visited every day (*Revolutionary* 455–56), and Godwin's biographer Peter Marshall says she attended through the end and afterward (191). However, Gina Walker records that Godwin barred her from the death chamber beginning September 5, 1797 (*Idea* 249, "Two" 61) but does not document this information. Lyndall Gordon describes the row between Hays and Godwin and states that the two had very little to do with each other after Wollstonecraft's death (365), but Gordon likewise offers no documentation. Finally, Charlotte Gordon repeats this claim (485) and documents a letter from Hays to Godwin that October.[2] But then Charlotte Gordon makes the mistake of saying that Hays "remained loyal to Mary's memory," which if true, raises the question why Hays did not include Wollstonecraft in the *Female Biography*. According to Kegan's Paul's copy of Godwin's diary, Hays visited on September 1st, 4th and 5th (275). Wollstonecraft died on the 10th. Regardless, as indicated above, Godwin did not remain in the house throughout the entirety of Wollstonecraft's sickness and therefore could not know if Hays had come at other times.

Apparently Godwin had an altercation with Hays and demanded that she leave when she was there trying to comfort her friend. He said there were too many people in the house. Hays retorted that she was "not altogether insignificant," meaning that she believed herself to be a close friend to Wollstonecraft. Godwin's response was, "To speak frankly, I think you have forgotten a little of that simplicity & unpresuming mildness, which so well becomes a woman."[3] Godwin's statement to Hays speaks volumes of his own gender definitions that help explain his efforts to depict his wife in *Memoirs* as a victim, especially in her relationship with Imlay; but Godwin's *Memoirs* also was an attempt to protect her by depicting her femininity when, in fact, he could not have done more to inflict damage to her reputation and to discredit her writing.

Wollstonecraft did mentor Hays. After reading *Rights of Woman*, Hays wrote Wollstonecraft compliments on the book and requested to meet her.[4] In November 1792 she gave Wollstonecraft a copy of the preface to *Letters and Essays* with the hope that she would recommend publication by Johnson. Wollstonecraft responded with constructive criticism. Johnson did not publish this book,[5] but later would publish Hays's *Appeal to the Men of Great Britain* (1798). Johnson hired Hays to write reviews for the *Analytical Review*, and after Wollstonecraft returned from France, he put Hays under Wollstonecraft's tutelage (Kelly 109). Working as Johnson's editor, Wollstonecraft assigned her to write a review of Jane West's *A Gossip's Story* (Todd, *CL* 392–93). It appeared in the January 1797 issue of *Analytical Review*, signed "V. V."

Also attributing Wollstonecraft as Hays's mentor, Mary A. Waters analyzed the literary advice she gave Hays about how to avoid being discarded as a mere woman writer and to write "credible […] masculine discourse addressing a broad audience" (424). Not only did Wollstonecraft help Hays publish for a living, Hays passed on some of the same advice she received when she reviewed *The Castle on the Rock* for the *Analytical Review* (Waters 424). This novel was the second published by the female Gothic writer, A. Kendall.[6] Apparently in an advertisement for the book, Kendall apologized for her own writing and called it "bantlings," which means a brat or a small child.[7] She was the first author I could find to refer to her own creation with this word. Byron would follow suit, calling his poetry "bantlings" (10), and then it would appear often as a metaphor for one's writing or art.[8] Hays figured that Kendall did this as a form of posturing, as if to say, "Be gentle with me, male critics, because I am just a little lady." However, if this were truly Kendall's reasoning, why did she disguise her first name and gender by giving just an initial?

Regardless, Hays did indeed chastise Kendall for humbling herself just because she was a woman. Besides, Hays had learned that critics were "little given to gallantry: their 'tribunal' is erected for the purpose of administering impartial justice, from which they ought not to be turned aside by flattering speeches, or *lady-like* blandishments" (Hays, Rev. 418). She strongly encouraged Kendall as a writer to avoid being so timid and beguiling and concealing "less agreeable subjects" (419). In other words, Hays rejected the idea of gendered text: Women should not hide behind the use of "lady-like" rhetoric for fear that they would be called masculine or that their writing would be considered inappropriate for their sex or that they would bashed in the way that men bashed men.

Kendall did not take Hays's advice. Her next book, *Tales of the Abbey*, offers this humble advertisement: "Again an adventurer presents a trifling offering at the shrine of public opinion, whose former awards she gratefully acknowledges exceeded her most sanguine expectations. In the following work, though Criticism may find much to condemn, she flatters herself Candour will see something to approve" (A2).

Female flattery was something Wollstonecraft abhorred. She compared women to "obsequious slaves" (81; 127; ch. 4) who "hug their chains, and fawn like the spaniel" (126; 163). She would have been proud of Hays's advice to Kendall. "My own sex, I hope, will excuse me, if I treat them like rational creatures, instead of flattering their fascinating graces, and viewing them as if they were in a state of perpetual childhood, unable to stand alone," Wollstonecraft began with her own counsel to her sex. In *Rights of Woman* she continued:

> I earnestly wish to point out in what true dignity and human happiness consists—I wish to persuade women to endeavour to acquire strength, both of mind and body, and to convince them that the soft phrases, susceptibility of heart, delicacy of sentiment, and refinement of taste, are almost synonymous with epithets of weakness, and that those beings who are only the objects of pity and that kind of love, which has been termed its sister, will soon become objects of contempt. (77; introd.)

If to be rational was masculine, then let women be masculine, she added (80). She wanted an equal playing field where reason would rule, and she did not believe that reason was exclusively a masculine quality (35–80). Wollstonecraft admired those who were able to write without the appearance of gender, as did Catharine Macaulay, and she refused to label that ability as "masculine" (176; 188). It was an effective form of writing that was strong, clear and honest; and she would have all women communicate in such a manner.

Hays did echo Wollstonecraft's narrative theory to Kendall and in her own writing. Several scholars identified additional influences. Margaret Sloan highlighted the similarities between *Maria* and Hays's *The Victim of Prejudice*, published one year later. Sloan noted that critics regarded Hays "as a less talented version of Wollstonecraft" and the *Victim* "as a derivative of Wollstonecraft's earlier novel," *Mary* (233). This was followed by Sloan's identification of the similarities and the differences between the three novels, with frequent references to *Emma Courtney* (233–40). Gina Walker described *Emma Courtney* in this way: "Hays's 'fiction' blasted the hypocrisy of masculine promises of Enlightenment freedoms, documenting the apparent impossibility of extending these to women" (17).[9] Sloan supplied convincing evidence that Hays's *Female Biography* of 1803 was possible only because of Wollstonecraft's penchant in prioritizing information about women, highlighting their education and abilities (240–42). Walker claimed that Hays formatted her biographies after Godwin's *Memoir* (253), which is ironic in that *Female Biography*—all six volumes—excluded Wollstonecraft despite that it was supposed to be about "Illustrious and Celebrated Women, of All Ages and Countries." What Walker meant by "format" is "the development of her intellectual, religious, and/or political beliefs" (253), an approach Godwin took in writing *Memoirs*, which she considered to be historically innovative.[10]

Many scholars compared *Rights of Woman* to Hays's *An Appeal to the Men of Great Britain* and claimed that Wollstonecraft inspired her to write it.[11] But Anne Mellor argues that Hays wrote it before reading *Rights of Woman*, even though she did not publish it until 1798 (144). Regardless, the similarities between the two are striking.[12] Not deterred by Godwin's *Memoirs*, Hays writes that Wollstonecraft aspired "to awaken in the minds of her oppressed sex a sense of their degradation, and to restore them to the dignity of reason and virtue,"[13] (and in another periodical) "to advance on the scale of reason half the species, is no ignoble ambition."[14]

Immediately following Godwin's *Memoirs*, Hays wrote a biographical essay on Wollstonecraft for the *Annual Necrology for 1797–1798*. In it she elaborates with more sordid details about Wollstonecraft's life than did Godwin. Although Hays did remind readers that we all make mistakes, most readers continued to believe that Wollstonecraft was licentious and brazenly defiant of morality and social decorum. In her article for *British Women's Life Writing*, Amy Culley concludes that both Godwin and Hays used Wollstonecraft for their own political agendas, and their—what Culley calls—"slippage between writing about the self and writing about the other" to do so (173).

After describing Wollstonecraft's harsh childhood, Hays writes very little about Wollstonecraft's love for Fanny Blood and her sorrow when Fanny died. Hays skips over the Bishop affair and lingers over Wollstonecraft's stint at being a governess but does not say why she left; Hays sets her in London to work with Johnson and then puts her on common ground with the biographer. Hays empathizes with Wollstonecraft's "dejection of spirits" brought on by intense labor, but also by "the mechanical nature of her occupations" of reviewing—which Wollstonecraft taught Hays to do in order to earn a living (420). What drove Wollstonecraft, Hays adduces, was her commitment to provide for her siblings (420). Although Miriam Wallraven describes these years as rich for Wollstonecraft as she enjoyed the intellectual exchange and support from her intellectual friends in Johnson's circle (53), Hays emphasizes her loneliness and "an unfortunate attachment" in September 1791 (most likely Fuseli, but Hays does not identify him; 423).

By the time Wollstonecraft arrived in Paris, she was like "the stricken deer" with a "barbed arrow" in her heart (425). Alone, in a country of a strange language and manners, with violence around her, "a cruel languor took possession of her spirits, while the melancholy tenor of her mind gave a jaundiced hue to the objects that surrounded her" (425). Hays is preparing the reader for Imlay; she means to make it clear that Wollstonecraft was not the profligate that others had painted her to be. It was because of Wollstonecraft's vulnerability and loneliness that she fell "into an intercourse of the most tender and interesting nature. To this attachment reason and duty, as in a former instance, no longer seemed to be opposed. In the indulgence of a sentiment that soothed and flattered her heart, she was led to a connexion, that, without the forms, had with her all the sanctity and devotness of a matrimonial engagement" (427). Hays believes Wollstonecraft perceived herself to be married: With their American certificate, "having thus publicly avowed their attachment, they thought it most eligible to repair to Paris, and reside under the same roof" (430). Hays indicates that they were sexually pure before this, and because of the American certificate that testified to Wollstonecraft's marriage to Imlay, their relationship should have been considered legitimate.

"Till the present period her life had been a series of difficulties, sorrows, and disappointment" (430), but being in love and being loved transported her into a woman of great "confidence, and her tenderness was unbounded, lavish, ineffable, combining the force, the devotion, the exquisite delicacy and refinement" (430). This was not the affair of a street woman. Instead Hays affirms that Wollstonecraft's youth was chaste and now, naturally, she was fully satisfied as a woman, especially when she was with child (431). Hays includes many excerpts from letters to demonstrate how much in love and how devoted she was to Imlay, followed by the letters of despair as Imlay vacillated in his commitment and finally abandoned her. No reader—especially a woman— could blame her for wanting to die. Considering the emotional power of the letters, Hays argues that Wollstonecraft was exceptional in her sentiments and passion and followed the suit of others who experienced

> that enthusiasm which constitutes the grander passions, is founded on *illusion*: stripped of the glowing colours in which fancy decks them, what are the objects for which ambition wades through seas of blood, for which martyrs, in all causes, for all opinions, braving destruction, press forward to the scaffold or the stake? (438).

Thus Hays portrays her as a martyr to something so grand as love and describes the first failed suicide attempt as her having been "[s]natched from the desperation of her own purposes" (439). Then, roused by love to be of further "service of the man for the man who had transfixed her heart with an envenomed arrow; the man for whom *she had dared to die!*" she bravely went to Norway for him, attended only by her female servant. She took little Frances with her because "she could not resolve on separating herself" (439).

Hays's description reads like a period novel. All Wollstonecraft did, even her suicide attempts, were done for love, a passion so powerful that even though she was also a loving mother, she could relinquish her child for him by killing herself. For no other reason would she leave her child behind, as demonstrated in her journey to Norway, which would be dangerous for both her and the child and even more cumbersome because of the child—so Hays recounts.

Pages of excerpts follow from her letters that are full of anguish for Imlay, but his "promises were faithless." "*Hope*," Hays writes with melodrama, "a thousand times frustrated, at length seemed extinguished; fortitude was exhausted by suffering; the tone of her mind destroyed (as she believed) for ever. Once more *she resolved to die*. She addressed on her knees the man to whose libertine habits she had become a victim," and then Hays excerpts Wollstonecraft's suicide letter (447–48). Unlike Godwin, Hays gives us some of the realism of the emotional and psychological journey that took Wollstonecraft to Putney Bridge. Even if critics treated Hays's rendition with ignoble disdain, surely there were many women who read her account of what they had previously regarded as the scandalous portion of Wollstonecraft's life and, afterward, had an entirely different understanding and perception of a pure heart betrayed.

Still, Hays is aware that by the time Wollstonecraft and Godwin became a couple, many in their circle were full of reproach (455). In her biography, Hays quotes from *Rights of Woman*, emphasizing that Wollstonecraft violated her own moral code and suffered the consequences as a result. But in Godwin, Wollstonecraft found peace, and her heart was ready to receive and give love again and "her genius resumed its tone and vigour" (456).

Hays claims that she was with Wollstonecraft until the very end of her life and attests that she died in peace. "The religious sentiments she had imbibed in her youth," Hays comments, "had in them no terrours that could discompose a dying hour; her imagination had embodied images of visionary perfection, giving rise to affections in which her sensibility delighted to indulge" (457). According to Hays, Wollstonecraft died with the assurance that she was leaving to be united with her Lord.

In summarizing Wollstonecraft's life, Hays admits Wollstonecraft made errors that were "eminently her own," but that she also suffered much from "the vices and prejudices of others" (460). Before closing the memoir, Hays apologizes both for Wollstonecraft's behavior and for the grammatical errors Wollstonecraft made in her writing (460). Prior to writing this entry, Hays always defended Wollstonecraft and her right to sexual freedom and to challenge social mores. But by 1800, she realized that it was wise to depict Wollstonecraft's behavior as a cautionary tale (458–59). On the other hand, Hays thinks she has served Wollstonecraft well with her "Memoirs," asserting in the preface to a later edition that would include supplementary material, "I think I may claim to be the most faithful, constant, and unfailing lover Mary Wollstonecraft ever had," and believing that Wollstonecraft sat in the very room in which Hays wrote the biography, "looking over my shoulder every now and then, to discover whether the paragraphs then visible were pleasant or painful reading to her" (1927 xlv).

Therefore, Hays's disclaimer was not enough to convince one anonymous reader for the *Anti-Jacobin Review* that Hays does an adequate job in making Wollstonecraft's "real history [...] short and simple." In fact, before he begins to fume, he assures the reader that it degrades him to even deal with "the tainted name of Mary Wolstonecraft" [*sic*], and then he alludes to her as a whore (93). This is his explanation for the epithet:

> Mary Wolstonecraft [*sic*], alias Imlay, alias Godwin, in the course of three years conceived an adulterous passion for one man, which she could only cool by flying from the kingdom, made two attempts to commit suicide, and lived in a state of prostitution with *two other men*, the last of whom became her husband, and published this story, her amours, or at least of as much of them as she thought-fit-to entrust to him; for many

still remain untold, which, if faithfully related, would make a book, in comparison with which the adventures of *Moll Flanders* would be a model of parity. (93)

This reviewer is so irate at the biographer's sugar-coated revision of Wollstonecraft's life, that he calls "him" "infamous and blasphemous [...] when he tells us, 'that she believed in her own conformity to the Supreme Being.'"[15] Interestingly, the critic regards the biographer as a male, which may have given him the freedom not to mince words, but by the next-to-last paragraph of the letter, he does state that he assumes the biographer was Mary Hays.

It is amazing how often people misspell Wollstonecraft's name, especially the ones who are angry at her. It strikes me that the misspelling is emblematic of the propensity to misquote, misalign, misunderstand and misrepresent Wollstonecraft. The quote above is a perfect example. The critic misquotes Hays, who quotes from a letter that Wollstonecraft writes to Everina shortly after she extricates Bess from the Bishop marriage. The correct verbiage is: "Don't suppose I am preaching when I say uniformity of conduct cannot in any degree be expected from those whose first motive of action is not the pleasing the Suprem Being—and those who humbly rely on Providence will not only be supported in affliction but have a Peace imparted to them that is past all describing" (Todd, *CL* 47–48). Neither Hays nor Wollstonecraft mentions "conformity." The context is that Wollstonecraft is trying to explain to Everina that she does believe in the sanctity of marriage. She writes, "I hold the marriage vow sacred" (48). Society expected a "uniformity of conduct," which in this case would be that Bess should remain in her marriage even if she were miserable. She declares that no one can endure the unbearable who does not prioritize pleasing God, but life is hard, and it is full of warfare (48), recalling 2 Corinthians 10:4 and Ephesians 6:12: "The weapons of our warfare are not of the flesh [...]. For we wrestle not against flesh and blood, but against principalities, against powers, against the world forces of this darkness, against the spiritual forces of wickedness in the heavenly places."

Wollstonecraft's religious convictions about the sanctity of marriage need to be weighed against her life experiences that would prompt her to refer in *Rights of Woman* to "the slavery of marriage" (248; ch. 11). Too many of the marriages she knew, beginning with her parents', had turned women into "convenient slaves" and men into "tyrants" (9–10; ded.). If both husband and wife were not living according biblical precepts, then the marriage covenant was broken. Wollstonecraft felt at "peace" with her intervention to extricate Bess from a bad marriage (Todd, *CL* 48). The critic completely ignores the struggle Wollstonecraft describes in this specific letter as well as the previous ones, and ignores her assertion that she has arrived at an understanding with God that her rescue of Bess was His will. Others might criticize her; Wollstonecraft despised the "cant of weak enthusiasts," who follow the law of religion but never think of trying to please God where there is grace, mercy, forgiveness and peace.

The critic is so indignant at the biographer (Hays), that he says "it was impossible for a good man to copy such passages without trembling, and it is impossible not to observe, that the 'virtue' of such 'heroines' is prostitution, and that their deities are impure and malignant daemons" (94). To prove his point, he accuses Wollstonecraft of having sexual relationships with Fuseli and Opie (94) and deduces that the moral of *Maria* is that marriage is wrong and adultery is right. For him, the character Jemima connotes "that nauseous description of the amours of the gin-shops, which contains the collected essence of all the hottest and rankest obscenity that ever smoked from the stews of Hedge-lane" (94). In the next paragraph, he abuses Mary Hays by name and accuses her of having written "licentious novels and lying necrologists," which makes her "perfectly well qualified" and "in all respects fitted to be the biographer and successor of Mary Wolstonecraft, F—I, O—e, Imlay, Godwin, &c. &c." (94). He signs it MISOSPLUDES, alias for John Giffard of Dublin.

By 1803 Hays had disassociated from Wollstonecraft by excluding her from the six-volume *Female Biography* (Jump, "Fond" 6). Kenneth Cameron defends her against those who strongly criticized her for this by reminding us that she also left out Catharine Macaulay, Hester Chapone, Anna Laetitia Barbauld, Elizabeth Inchbald, Maria Edgeworth, Amelia Opie, Anne Radcliffe and Hannah More (161). One *has* to wonder what Hays's criteria were for successful women. Regardless, the reality is that Hays's reputation was tarnished by her association with Wollstonecraft, a situation she could not afford as it impacted the sale of her books and therefore her ability to support herself through her writing. Why else would she have omitted such an "extraordinary woman, an able champion" as Hays described in *Necrology*? (459). To protect herself further, she asked Godwin to return her correspondence with Wollstonecraft, but he refused (Walker, *Idea* 190–91). In April 1836 she asked Mary Shelley to return all letters between Wollstonecraft and herself, which Shelley did.[16] But Hays could not take back the true words of her testimony to Wollstonecraft's legacy: She left us with "the spirit of reform," and it continues "silently pursing its course. Who can mark its limits?" (Hays 459).

Chapter 3

C. KEGAN PAUL'S *MARY WOLLSTONECRAFT: LETTERS TO IMLAY, WITH PREFATORY MEMOIR BY C. K. PAUL* (1879): THE VICTORIAN GENTLEMAN

Sir Percy Florence Shelley, the son of Mary Godwin Shelley and Percy Bysshe Shelley, and his wife Jane attempted to redeem the reputations of their parents and grandparents. They destroyed papers and letters that contained anything that could be considered scandalous, and they commissioned official biographies that would present their famous progenitors in only a positive light. One such task was given to their neighbor, a vicar by the name of Charles Kegan Paul. In 1876 he first published *William Godwin*, which gave a more suitable Wollstonecraft than the one drawn by Godwin. This was followed three years later by Paul's brief biography of Wollstonecraft and the publications of her letters to Imlay (Jump, introd. xxiii).

C. Kegan Paul begins his preface to his Wollstonecraft biography with:

> The name of Mary Wollstonecraft has long been a mark for obloquy and scorn. Living and dying as a Christian, she has been called an atheist, always a hard name, but harder still some years ago. She ran counter to the customs of society, yet not wantonly or lightly, but with forethought, in order to carry out a moral theory gravely and religiously adopted. (v)

Soon after Paul's biography, Elizabeth Robins Pennell gives a similar attribute: "Few women have worked so faithfully for the cause of humanity as Mary Wollstonecraft, and few have been the objects of such bitter censure." In addition: "She devoted herself to the relief of her suffering fellow-beings with the ardor of a Saint Vincent de Paul, and in return she was considered by them a moral scourge of God" (1). This introduces the biography Pennell wrote for "Eminent Women," a series that included Wollstonecraft as the ninth entry and was preceded by articles on George Eliot, Emily Brontë and George Sand. In that introduction, Pennell praised Paul for "vindicating [Wollstonecraft's] character and reviving interest in her writings [...], re-establish[ing] her reputation" (10).

Paul makes a statement that all biographers who read Godwin's *Memoirs* might bear in mind: "But in fact Godwin knew extremely little of his wife's earlier life, nor was this a subject on which he had sought enlightenment from herself" (xxxi). As I pointed out previously, they were married for only five months and they had separate residences. Furthermore, as I have also noted, Godwin spent very little time in the room where Wollstonecraft lay dying.

Although many of the biographers of the twentieth century would depict Wollstonecraft as a neurotic, self-centered, love-starved, erratically emotional creature from the past, Paul—ever the Victorian gentleman—portrays her as a selfless person who was always thinking of "others rather than self" (v) and as "one of the martyrs of society" (vi). He does not explain why he saw her as a martyr, but without a doubt, most Victorians extolled the virtue of paying selfless duty to others. In her was "real enthusiasm of humanity before the words were known which designate a feeling still far from common" (v). This is Paul's understanding of Wollstonecraft's expansiveness. When Godwin alludes to her generosity, he pitches it in pathological terms; she was "the victim of a desire to promote the benefit of others" (55). However, such a "diagnosis" also portrays Wollstonecraft as sensitive and ingenuous to a fault, someone who was constantly disappointed and hurt at the way people treated her in return and failed to show their gratitude (55).

Wollstonecraft's motivation for giving to the point of sacrifice was to win desperately needed approbation and love. Early in her childhood she learned from her parents that the only love she was going to get was based conditionally on her behavior. So, by the time she was in the most intimate relationship of her life, with Imlay, she complained that he did not write often enough (Todd, *CL* 268), that he spent too much time away (271) and, when he did write, it was too brief and obviously written in haste (277). At times, she wanted to rebuke him for his bad behavior (276) and a few times actually gave him ultimatums, threatening to leave him forever (308), but then she would rescind, apologize and blame herself. Wollstonecraft needed more from him emotionally than what he was willing or able to give (258). "Do not suppose that I mean to allude to a little reserve of temper in you," she wrote obsequiously. She reminded him that she "sometimes complained" of this "little reserve of temper," which was her confession that the problem was with her complaining and not with his temper. "You have been used to a cunning woman, and you almost look for cunning [in me]," she wrote to reassure him that she would never be like those cunning mistresses he used to know and despised (259–60), as if to say, "It's okay with me that you are a womanizer; I am just so grateful that you chose me to be one of your women, and I am going to try to avoid annoying you so that you will want to keep me around." In that same letter, she felt she must tell him that he broke her heart with his reserve, but it was okay for him to wound her, for she would love him no matter what. The very last letter we have from her to Imlay continues to say goodbye and says something like: "You hurt me, but I still love you." She does say, "[Y]ou are not what you appear to be"—This is it—"I part with you in peace" (Todd, *CL* 339).

Before Wollstonecraft met Imlay, she wrote in *Rights of Woman* with great disdain: "Whilst [women] are absolutely dependent on their husbands they will be cunning, mean, and selfish, and the men who can be gratified by the fawning fondness of spaniel-like affection, have not much delicacy" (231; ch. 9). Ironically, Imlay would later relate his history of living with women. In Wollstonecraft's words, he would get rid of them once they became "cunning," so Wollstonecraft intends to avoid that. However, she muses that Imlay seems to be cunning toward her in "*managing* [her] happiness" (Todd, *CL* 259–60).

According to the "moralists" of her day, women were meant to be toys for men (53; ch. 2), and they were expected to speak with "childish expressions" (106; ch. 2) and "childish simper" (293; ch. 13). Although Wollstonecraft criticizes her fellow women for being puerile in their behavior toward men and criticizes her fellow men for wanting women to act like affectionate spaniels, within only a year after the publication of *Rights of Woman* she behaved in the manner she absolutely derided two years previously, writing in a letter to Imlay, "Do not call me stupid, for leaving on the table the little bit of paper I was to inclose.—This comes of being in love at the fag-end of a letter of business." And then she childishly begged him not to scold her (Todd, *CL* 250–51). "Cunning is a natural gift of woman," so claimed Rousseau, one that should be cultivated, but they should also be taught not to use cunning to take advantage of men (348). From *Rights of Woman*, we know what Wollstonecraft thought of Rousseau's advice.

Paul is too polite to intrude into the inner sanctuary of Wollstonecraft's heart and to deal with such delicate matters mentioned above. This is a concern that Paul Murray Kendall expresses about Victorian biographies. He likens them to whiskers that "hid the Victorian face no more securely than pseudobiography hid the Victorian heart" (105). Kendall theorizes that more biographical information can be found in the novels written by Victorians (like Dickens), albeit disguised, than in biographies that are expected to be mannerly and not to expose that which is too delicate to discuss. Thus, Victorian biographies are "hobbled" and "taken into the protective custody of the age"

(105–9). Although he does not mention Wollstonecraft's biographies, he would not have put much stock in C. Kegan Paul's depiction.

Ever her champion, Paul laments that she is not being recognized for her literary and social contributions. One example he gives was a slight by Charlotte Yonge who, in a reissue of *The Elements of Morality*, which had been translated by Wollstonecraft from the German, Yonge misspells her name as Wolstonecroft and Wollstonecroft (vii).

About Bess's marriage, Paul speculates that Bishop was a clergyman, but he does not say why he thinks this. He deduces that the marriage from day one was unhappy, and he supposes that the fault lay on both sides. Of Bishop, he is sure that he was a "man of furious violence" and, as for the "Wollstonecraft sisters," they were "enthusiastic, excitable, and hasty tempered, apt to exaggerate trifles, sensitive to magnify inattention into slights, and slights into studied insults" (x). Writing in the nineteenth century, Paul can make such statements as if they are fact without backing them up with convincing argument, evidence or testimony. The Bishops had trouble with their nerves, says Paul, which to every Victorian signaled that of course they had marital trouble because of their nerves or because of their marital trouble they had bad nerves. Paul paints Wollstonecraft as a heroine who "considered no sacrifice too great" for her sister and willingly gave up "all hopes of an independent career" in order to provide for Bess (xi).

It is amazing that a Victorian male is so supportive of Wollstonecraft and sympathetic to an unhappy young bride during a period when not only was marriage considered a holy sacrament, it was the pillar of Victorian society. But the chivalrous Paul assures his readers that Bishop "dissolved" his marriage when he treated his wife with brutality. Paul offers no proof of this brutality, as if he cannot conceive that there would have been any other reason possible as to why Wollstonecraft would intervene. He adds his indignation that laws continued to bind a woman to remain married to "a brutal, loveless savage" (xii). Paul provides no details about what the Bishop household was like before or after Wollstonecraft's visit, nor does he describe the women's flight.

About *Rights of Woman*, Paul again defends her against accusations: "For Mary Wollstonecraft did not, as has been supposed, attack the institution of marriage; she did not assail orthodox religion" (xxvi). To support these claims, he does offer some quotes from *Rights of Woman*. Regarding her belief in the value of marriage is this statement: "I respect marriage, as the foundation of almost every social virtue" (149; ch. 4). Regarding religion: "What would life be without that peace which the love of God, when built on humanity, alone can impart?"[1] Wollstonecraft's book is not about those two things anyway, he assures the reader; it was an argument for national education that would allow co-education (xxvii). The only problem he has is that she wrote with an unsettling "plainness of speech" (xxvi)—not considered a desirable trait to most Victorians—to deal with such volatile subjects as "greater freedom of divorce" and a denial of "the eternity of the torments of hell" (xxviii). What plain statements he has in mind he does not say, nor does he suggest what he would have had Wollstonecraft write instead. Nevertheless, although others were spouting terms such as "sacrilege" and "preposterous" in response to Wollstonecraft and her work, Paul is concerned about plain statements that were "grave faults" (xxix). Yet he is too much of a gentleman to point them out.

Strangely, Paul expresses his opinion that it was "singularly unfortunate" that Wollstonecraft "was fated, as it were, to see the unattractive side of almost all of the great institutions of society" (xvii), such as education, marriage and aristocratic life, because they "coloured" her judgment when she wrote about them in *Rights of Woman* (xvii). Yet, had she not seen the dark side of these aspects of her world, she would not have been motivated to write about them and initiate the changes that did eventually come about. In another act of chivalry, Paul wants to address the slander leveled against her that she corrupted the minds of her pupils. He reminds his readers that her letters reveal that she practiced an "earnest orthodox piety" and "high morality" (xx).

Regarding the Fuseli slander, Paul questions Godwin's judgment about this. According to Paul, Godwin understood that, had Fuseli been free, "Mary might have been in love with him." These are Paul's words about Godwin's presumptions, yet Paul charges Godwin with knowing very little about his wife's earlier life and having learned very little about it from her (xxxi). To Paul, the entire scandal was nothing but a "preposterous story," for Wollstonecraft continued to be a correspondent and close friend to Mrs. Fuseli for the rest of her life (xxxii). Furthermore, Paul confidently asserts that Wollstonecraft arrived in Paris at "the age of thirty-five without, so far as I can discover, any trace of romance such as comes into most women's lives at a far earlier period" (xxxii). The point is not clear with that statement alone, but as we often read in Victorian novels, Paul prepares us for what would transpire in Paris. He points out that she was a woman who went to Paris alone without any father or elder brother or elderly gentlemen friend to guide and protect her (xxxii). It is reminiscent of Dickens's *Oliver Twist* when the prostitute Nancy tells Rose, "Thank Heaven upon your knees, dear lady [...] that you had friends to care for and keep you[. ...]" (3:158; ch. 3). Likewise in Jane Austen's *Pride and Prejudice*, a novel closer to Wollstonecraft's time, when Lizzy has to tell Darcy that her youngest sister "has left all her friends" and eloped with Wickham (240; ch. 13), again the suggestion is that the bonds of friendship will keep a woman chaste, but a woman without a male protector is nothing more than bait for ever-circling sharks.

Once in Paris, where she met Imlay, Paul writes, "she soon gave him a very sincere affection, and consented to become his wife." Paul emphasizes that he uses the word "wife" deliberately, acknowledging the legal difficulty of their getting married when France was at war with England. Otherwise, she would have to make known that she was a British citizen, which would have put her in grave danger (xxxviii). Even if there had been a civil wedding ceremony, it would not have been recognized in England. To protect her, Imlay called her his wife (xxxix). Additionally, Imlay sent her off to do business for him in Scandinavia with a legal document declaring her to be his wife (xxxix-xl). Her letters, according to Paul, reassure the reader that Wollstonecraft considered herself, in the eyes of God, Imlay's wife. Then Paul blames Imlay for his fickle affections and for deserting her (xxxix), charging him with lacking the loyalty and exercise of self-denial that characterized Wollstonecraft's behavior (xl). Believing herself a "devoted wife" (in Paul's words), she gave birth to Fanny (xli). Once she realized that Imlay was keeping a mistress, she attempted suicide from Putney Bridge. Paul does not pass judgment; he merely remarks that only George Eliot could have described such a painful experience, as she did in *Daniel Deronda* with Myra's attempt at suicide (xlviii).

By the time Paul describes the Godwin/Wollstonecraft relationship, he totally glosses over any impropriety, saying only that they "held the same views on marriage," but he does not explain what those views were. He adds with equal vagueness that they "felt the need of being inconsistent" (liv). He makes no attempt to reconcile their living together outside the bonds of matrimony, and claims that only for the sake of the child to be born, they married. This news was "cordially received by all but Mrs. Inchbald" (lvii), which was not true: There were many friends and acquaintances who snubbed them once Mrs. Imlay became Mrs. Godwin.

As for Godwin's misunderstanding of why Mary said when she was dying, "Oh, Godwin, I am in heaven," Paul reasons it was because Godwin refused to deal with the issue of heaven and that she was dying (lix-lx). Godwin's response was: "You mean, my dear, that your physical sensations are somewhat easier" (quoted in lx), which he assumed because the doctor had given her a medicinal draught. Paul speculates that had Wollstonecraft lived, Mary's "calm faith" might have converted Godwin to her faith (lxii), like a good Victorian who believed that women could make their husbands more religious. Paul may have hoped for this but in so doing, he is forgetting that it was probably this very hope that got Wollstonecraft in trouble with Imlay in the first place, and that she was no more successful in transforming him than was

Helen in Anne Brontë's *The Tenant of Wildfell Hall*, who married the handsome but profligate Arthur Huntingdon and believed she could reform him. Paul puts forth no reason for supposing that Wollstonecraft would have been any more successful with Godwin. However, she did succeed in getting him to the altar (*Memoirs* 105). No doubt, religious differences would have taken a toll on their marriage had she survived, as indicated by her letter of August 31, 1796 in which she wrote to Godwin, "I do not intend to let you extend your skepticism to me" (Todd, *CL* 356).

Several reviews of Paul's biography praise his work and his tactful treatment of a woman who, as a writer described her in the *London Quarterly Review*, had "bitter early trials which swayed her judgment" (257). "Without extenuating Mary Wollstonecraft's [notice the correct spelling] errors," the reviewer continues, "he does justice to her fine qualities and great talents, and his careful research into the melancholy story of her life—many important incidents in which he has been the first to make known—justifies his eloquent championship" (257). In contrast the reviewer criticizes Godwin for "lay[ing] bare to the world the wrongs and agonies of his wife" and expresses gratitude for Paul's "throwing new light on the character of their unfortunate writer" (258).

The *Examiner* appreciates the letters Paul published, asserting that after reading them no one could deny that Wollstonecraft "was a good, pure, and religious woman" (147). In very strong words for a Victorian, the reviewer praises Paul, who "has done good service in clearing her memory of the stain which narrow-minded bigotry and dull stupidity had cast upon it" (148).

Paul's biography did not sit well with all Victorians. Edmund Gosse mocks it, describing it as "The old melancholy story of feminine devotion and unselfish love driven by cold looks and distracted thoughts to a despair which is almost hatred" (573). Gosse states that, although Paul deserved credit for his "invaluable *Life of Godwin*," the preface to his letters of Wollstonecraft to Imlay was written in "the most pathetic style" (573). However, Gosse thinks that the letters are invaluable and, by the end of the review, congratulates Paul for "his successful rehabilitation of a maligned and unfortunate woman of genius" (574).

Perhaps Paul's conventional style of writing did not appeal to Gosse, but Gosse highly esteemed Wollstonecraft's work. In *The British Quarterly Reviewer*, another writer—of the anonymous variety—eulogizes Wollstonecraft as "one of the most remarkable women England has produced" (495), but in appropriate Victorian fashion, the reviewer finds in Paul's précis, a warning of "how defiances of the law of social morals and decorum are inevitably linked with unhappiness and misery" (495). This reviewer's assessment of Paul's memoir was that it exhibited "great self-control"—one of the most highly prized of

Victorian virtues. The memoir also possesses "lapses only by the use of one or two phrases," but the reviewer is too proper to say what those might be, and had Paul supplied them, she would have been outraged that he spoke the unspeakable. Joseph Conrad did not explain what the "unspeakable rites" were in his *Heart of Darkness* (1899)—one referred to undergarments as unmentionables, and the privy was known as the necessary. Quite right, too: some things are better left unsaid in Victorian biographies.

Chapter 4

ELIZABETH ROBINS PENNELL'S *MARY WOLLSTONECRAFT* (1884): A VICTORIAN FEMINIST

In 1884 Elizabeth Robins Pennell (1855–1936) produced the first book-length biography of Wollstonecraft since Godwin's notorious *Memoirs* (1798). As discussed in the previous chapter, five years earlier Kegan Paul wrote a preface to *Mary Wollstonecraft: Letters to Imlay* that was a noble effort to retrieve Wollstonecraft's reputation from the pyre; it was an act of a gentleman who reintroduced Wollstonecraft to the world, giving her always the benefit of the doubt, not mentioning the unmentionables, and extending chivalrous sympathy toward all the miseries in her life. Pennell had primarily only Godwin and Paul from whom to draw—along with some letters that had been stored in the British Library. She tried to get help from Paul, but his response was: "My strong impression is that you will find no more to be said on Mary Wollstonecraft than has already been said." And then he added this shocking comment: "No one of course, except really students of Mary's character, read her writings."[1]

Pennell must have been an extraordinary person in her own right, one who found a kindred spirit in Wollstonecraft. She was born in Philadelphia and, like Wollstonecraft, suffered a miserable childhood in that her mother died when she was quite young. Not wanting to be saddled by children, the father packed off Pennell and her sister to a convent school, where Pennell stayed until the age of 17.[2] In the meanwhile, her father remarried (as did Wollstonecraft's father), so that when she came home, she felt awkward living under the governance of a stepmother. As John Hewlett encouraged Wollstonecraft, so did a kindly uncle—Charles Godfrey Leland, a folklorist—who suggested she might gain her independence through writing.[3]

The man who would become her husband, Joseph Pennell (1857–1926), was born into a Quaker household that disapproved of his pursuing a career in art. Nonetheless, that is exactly what he did at the age of 25 after attending the Pennsylvania Academy of the Fine Arts in Philadelphia ("Joseph

Pennell").⁴ Before long, he was a highly successful magazine illustrator. He was commissioned to illustrate an article on Philadelphia for *Century Magazine* in 1882. The article was to be written by Leland, but he turned the opportunity over to his niece, Elizabeth. She came to know what it was like to be a writer and to fall in love with an artist, as did Wollstonecraft with Fuseli. The difference for Elizabeth, though, was that the artist was a single man, and she did marry him (June 1884).

Theirs must have been the kind of marriage of which Wollstonecraft dreamed. As described in a short biography at the University of Pennsylvania's Penn Library, which holds most of their work, the "marriage [...] was one of equals and complements, bringing together two talented individuals with keen minds, ambition, and a love of work" ("Pennell Family"). Between the two of them, they produced over 230 books and hundreds of articles ("Pennell Family").

Elizabeth Pennell begins her biography of Wollstonecraft with this homage:

> Few women have worked so faithfully for the cause of humanity as Mary Wollstonecraft, and few have been the objects of such bitter censure. She devoted herself to the relief of her suffering fellow-beings with the ardor of a Saint Vincent de Paul, and in return she was considered by them a moral scourge of God. Because she had the courage to express opinions new to her generation, and the independence to live according to her own standard of right and wrong, she was denounced as another Messalina. The young were bidden not to read her books, and the more mature warned not to follow her example, the miseries she endured being declared the just retribution of her actions. Indeed, the infamy attached to her name is almost incredible in the present age, when new theories are more patiently criticised, and when purity of motive has been accepted as the vindication of at least one well-known breach of social laws. (*Life*, 1)⁵

When Pennell had only two chapters finished, Thomas Niles, Jr. (a partner in the Boston publishing house, Roberts Brothers) expressed his approval of them but warned: "You will however be getting into delicate ground soon[; ...] her course of life requires deft treatment."⁶ As Pennell herself notes: "Probably the article which was most influential in perpetuating the ill-repute in which [Wollstonecraft] stood with her contemporaries, is the sketch of her life given in Chalmers's *Biographical Dictionary*" (1814) (6). The dictionary lists her as "Godwin (Mary)," never a good start, but it gets worse: she is "better known by the name of WOOLSTONECRAFT." Chalmers recognizes her as "a lady of very extraordinary genius," followed by a "but": "whose history and opinions are unhappily calculated to excite a mixture of admiration, pity, and scorn" (51). He finishes his biographical entry with the opinion that the posthumous works and memoirs Godwin published after her death "had better been suppressed, as ill calculated to excite sympathy for one who seems to have rioted in sentiments alike repugnant to religion, sense, and decency" (55).

After Pennell's book was released by Roberts Brothers as part of their Famous Women Series, another was released as a British edition by John H. Ingram, but he slashed the book by a third and changed the title from *Life of Mary Wollstonecraft* to *Mary Wollstonecraft Godwin*, both of which infuriated Pennell (Clarke 118–19).

Nevertheless, it was instantly successful on both sides of the Atlantic and republished five times before 1910 (Clarke 119). *Fortnightly Review* asked Pennell to write an article on Wollstonecraft, which she did, and she also expanded the topic to cover "A Century of Women's Rights." In her prefatory notes to its 1892 Walter Scott edition of *Rights of Woman*, Pennell writes that Wollstonecraft "saw the evils in the conception of the woman's sphere and duty" and "had the courage to say what she thought and knew at a time when women were not expected to think or to know anything" (vii).

Working with only sparse biographical material, Pennell nonetheless produced an edition of 209 pages, because she took a skeleton and added interior and exterior parts to make it alive and visible to her readers. Whether or not she was always accurate with her assumptions is another issue. Regardless, her book demonstrates great empathy for Wollstonecraft. Here is an example of how she takes one detail (Wollstonecraft's life at age five, when the family lived in Barking, Essex) and fleshes it out:

> This place was the scene of Mary's principal childish recollections and associations. Natural surroundings were with her of much more importance than they usually are to the very young, because she depended upon them for her pleasures. She cared nothing for dolls and the ordinary amusements of girls. Having received few caresses and little tender nursing, she did not know how to play the part of mother. Her recreation led her out of doors with her brothers. That she lived much in the open air and became thoroughly acquainted with the town and the neighborhood, seems certain from the eagerness with which she visited it years afterwards with Godwin. This was in 1796, and Mary with enthusiasm sought out the old house in which she had lived. It was unoccupied, and the garden around it was a wild and tangled mass. Then she went through the town itself; to the market-place, which had perhaps been the Mecca of frequent pilgrimages in the old times; to the wharves, the bustle and excitement of which had held her spellbound

many a long summer afternoon; and finally from one street to another, each the scene of well-remembered rambles and adventures. Time can soften sharp and rugged lines and lighten deep shadows, and the pleasant reminiscences of Barking days made her overlook bitterer memories. (*Life* 15–16)

The only facts with which she had to work were: (a) in 1768 the family moved to Barking (*Godwin* 48), and (b) in 1796 Wollstonecraft and Godwin visited the area (48). All of Pennell's embellishment seems credible, but it is fiction. However, since her book is a biography, readers accept the fiction as fact.

How did Pennell know that Wollstonecraft "cared nothing for dolls and the ordinary amusements of girls"? She did not have access to all the letters that we now have; regardless, in none of the letters does Wollstonecraft ever state this. It is not in Godwin's *Memoirs*, and neither is the information that she played in the open air with her brothers, nor that when they visited the homestead, she reminisced about playing in the open air. Pennell's hypothesis is that because Wollstonecraft did not have a good mother model, she may not have known how to play mother to a doll; however, most psychologists and counselors—perhaps postdating Pennell—find that girls who have been physically abused or who had poor mother figures in their lives, still do play with dolls, even if they act out on the doll the abuse they received in the home.

Probably Pennell inferred Wollstonecraft's distaste for dolls and her preference for playing outside with her brothers from *Rights of Woman*, in which Wollstonecraft is critical of making girls play with dolls. When they do, they focus on dressing up the dolls (160; ch. 5) and then grow up to be themselves dolls who prioritize how to dress (264; ch. 12). Instead, they should be allowed to exercise in the open air as do boys in order to strengthen muscles and relax nerves (115; ch. 3). Wollstonecraft might have disliked it that girls focused on dressing and ornamenting dolls, but perhaps she did like the idea of girls pretending the dolls are their babies. If girls practiced taking care of dolls as if they were real infants, this could prepare them for motherhood. One might recall that Wollstonecraft strongly valued motherhood, and that a driving force behind *Rights of Woman* and its argument for good education was so that girls could grow up to be "more observant daughters, more affectionate sisters, more faithful wives, more reasonable mothers—in a word, better citizens" (*ROW* 241; ch. 9). Also, by Godwin we are told that Wollstonecraft "found an inexpressible delight in the beauties of nature" (*Memoirs* 56). By 1768, Wollstonecraft had two younger sisters. Would have she not been playing with them? It was customary for girls to play with dolls, and most likely the five-year-old Wollstonecraft would have comforted her baby doll in the way she wanted to be comforted, in the way Dickens portrayed Esther Summerson and her doll in *Bleak House*. One fiction is as valid as the next, but both are fiction.

Furthermore, Pennell's understanding of gendered baby dolls comes from the Victorian period. We need to keep in mind that the eighteenth-century doll in Wollstonecraft's youth was not designed to be like a baby. For 400 years, dolls had been imported from France. She was intricately and elegantly dressed in courtly fashion (Mennell 129–30) and, as Wollstonecraft described it, girls spent their time dressing and redressing their dolls, which further inculcated their priority of dress instead of learning about other virtues. Childlike dolls and the baby doll did not appear until the mid-Victorian period. If dolls had been imitations of babies that would have given children practice in tending to one, perhaps Wollstonecraft would have seen some value in them as a toy for either girl or boy.

Ever since Pennell asserted that Wollstonecraft never played with dolls, every biographer who followed her stated the same thing, as if Pennell's statement were fact; for example, Miriam Brody's text (2000): "Rather than playing inside with dolls, Mary loved to join her brothers in the merry sports of outside play" (15)—no documentation, no citation, but surely Brody is paraphrasing Pennell. The same appears in Lyndall Gordon's biography (2005): "There [in New Farm], she preferred outdoor games with Ned, aged six, and Henry, aged two, to girls' games with dolls and baby Bess" (8). The latest biography on Wollstonecraft by Charlotte Gordon has her despising dolls (14).

When Godwin wrote *Memoirs*, he took the license of drawing details from Wollstonecraft's fiction and treating them as biographical certainties. For example, he claimed that Wollstonecraft's mother preferred Ned over her, because he was male, and treated her eldest daughter with severity (45). Pennell echoes this detail (8). The source is not from any statement that Wollstonecraft made about herself, as far as I know. Godwin pulled it out of *Mary, a Fiction* (87) and, as a result, every biographer has treated this as fact. Diane Jacobs (2000) enhances the detail even more by saying that, on her deathbed, Wollstonecraft's mother still "preferred Ned" (30). If I understand her syntax correctly, Emily Sunstein (1975) went even further in her suggestion that Wollstonecraft's brother Henry was so mentally ill that he had to be committed to an insane asylum, and the reason for this illness was because his parents gave preference to Ned (147).

This is the kind of detail—the preference for the eldest son, and the drama that can arise in families as a result—that Victorians loved. Especially because of primogeniture, trying to get one's daughter married to the right son created much comedy in Elizabeth Gaskell's *Wives and Daughters* (1865), when Mrs. Gibson is determined to have her Cynthia marry the bachelor who is to become the heir of Hamley Hall. She overhears that the eldest is dying of a fatal affliction, so she manages to arrange an engagement between her daughter and the second son; however, the men just cannot seem to cooperate with her when it came to dying.

Pennell pitches her biography in terms that her late Victorian contemporaries would appreciate. About Wollstonecraft, she writes: "She was, like Carlyle's hero of *Sartor Resartus*, one of those children whose sad fate it is to weep in the playtime of the others. Not even to the David Copperfields and Paul Dombeys of fiction has there fallen a lot so hard to bear and so sad to record, as that of the little Mary Wollstonecraft" (9). This illustrates how a biographer rewrites history for her own age. In this case, Pennell is accurate; Wollstonecraft did suffer from chronic depression as she discussed often in most of her extant letters, and we do know that her suffering began in her childhood with a very unstable and violent father.

It is to be hoped that biographers are so immersed in information, awareness and intuition for their subject that they can offer some insights that are not apparent from simple facts. Pennell does this when she reminds us that Wollstonecraft learned from Fanny that a woman can earn enough money from her talents to support not only herself but her family. Pennell bestows on Fanny Blood the honor "of having given the first incentive to her intellectual energy" (25). Another insight Pennell offers is Godwin's "what if" he and Wollstonecraft would have met when he was a student in Hoxton, and her family was living there. Pennell must have thought to answer this in her later 1890 version, proposing that "He would never have become a cold, systematic philosopher. And Mary, had she found a haven from her misery so soon, would not have felt as strongly about wrongs of women. Whatever her world's work under those circumstances might have been, she would not have become the champion of her sex" (26–27).[7]

One might not be so sanguine about the projected outcome for both. Godwin did attend Hoxton Academy with the intention of following his father and grandfather into the ministry. Supposing he had met Wollstonecraft, it is possible that her faith and her strong conviction that reasoning and faith should go hand in hand, might have helped counter the doubts that he amassed while a student. Without her, he still managed to graduate and enter the ministry, but only at that time did he become overwhelmed by questions about Christianity, and stirring inside were drives to become a political activist. After reading Peter Marshall's biography on Godwin, one will find it difficult to believe that Wollstonecraft could have managed to keep him "in the faith." After all, she was unable to convert him during their relationship.

Then, too, Wollstonecraft proved with Imlay that she was powerless to change a man, which also was a lesson she should have already learned from her parents' relationship. She saw from her mother how vulnerable women were in relationships. They had no legal, political, social or financial recourse to get themselves out of a bad marriage in which they were being abused. Wollstonecraft already understood female entrapment. She experienced how the Blood women had to work until they were bone tired with their stitching in order to keep their family afloat financially. She was aware that there were not viable opportunities for women to earn a living for themselves and for their families, nor for them to develop their God-given talents. She knew all of this before she was seventeen years old. Had she married Godwin, as she did later, she would also have faced the dilemma of providing financially for the family because Godwin seemed incapable or disinclined to prioritize solvency. As soon as they married, the first thing Wollstonecraft did was set out to write *Maria* for the purpose of bringing in money (L. Gordon 340–42).

The condition for women had not changed much by the late Victorian period, and Pennell was certainly aware of it. Pennell was like Wollstonecraft with as much fire and indignation, but without the same negative experiences with men. From all evidence, the Pennells were extremely well matched and happy with each other, but that did not deter Pennell from fighting on behalf of other women. As she describes Bess's marriage to Bishop, trying to be equal minded in attributing faults to Bess's disposition, she agrees with Wollstonecraft that women are human beings, too, and should have a voice. Pennell writes about a situation that took place in 1783 as if it could and did take place a hundred years later in her own time:

> The general belief then was, as indeed it unfortunately continues to be, that women should accept without a murmur whatever it suits their husbands to give them, whether it be kindness or blows. Better a thousand times that one human soul should be stifled and killed than that the Philistines of society should be scandalized by its struggles for air and life. [Bess's] happiness might have been totally sacrificed had she remained with Bishop; but at least the feelings of her acquaintances, in whom respectability had destroyed the more humane qualities, would have been saved. (*Life* 43–44)

Pennell is sympathetic to both women when Wollstonecraft helped Bess escape from her husband. Although Wollstonecraft would be censured for breaking a biblical law about marriage,[8] Pennell uses language that Victorian readers would have appreciated to describe how they should feel about this. I have italicized the diction below that represent sentiments held near and dear by most Victorians:

> No one can read the life of Mary Wollstonecraft without loving her, or follow her first bitter struggles without feeling honor, nay reverence, for her *true womanliness* which bore her bravely through them. She *never shrank from her duty* nor lamented her clouded youth. *Without a murmur* she left Walham Green and established herself as *nurse and keeper* to the *poor mad sister*. There could be *no greater heroism* than this. With a *nervous constitution* not unlike that of *poor* Bess, she had to watch over the frenzied mania of the wife and to confront the almost equally insane fury of the husband. (*Life* 38)

None of this portrays a woman in defiance of social conventions and godly ordinances. To make her point even more emphatic to Victorian readers, Pennell supposes that Meredith Bishop's temper was so bad that Wollstonecraft advised Bess to flee from him even if it meant leaving behind the child (41). Whereas the twenty-first century reader would be skeptical about Pennell's reasoning, to the Victorians it would have been inconceivable that any woman would give up a child, so that since Bess did leave behind her child (in the eighteenth century, women had no legal right to their children), her situation must have been extremely intolerable.

Pennell is equally sympathetic to the plight of Fanny Blood for similar reasons—reasons that would strongly resonate in the Victorian period. By 1780 Fanny was showing symptoms of the dreaded disease, pulmonary tuberculosis, better known as consumption at the time. It was already the number-one killer in England. By the early nineteenth century, approximately half the population in England had the disease (Dubos and Dubos 9). Also called the "white plague," consumption was "unquestionably the greatest single cause of disease and death in the Western world" (10). Although the later Victorians had learned much about the disease, how it spread and how it could be cured, a lot was still a mystery when Pennell wrote her biography, and consumption deaths were still numerous, reaching a peak in 1870 in England (and in 1890 in France) and only by 1921 dropping by 50 percent (Harrison 129).

Nearly incomprehensible today, it was the disease that was romanticized. "Consumption had a romantic quality," Mark Harrison observes. It was "widely associated with etiolated young women and delicate, artistic young men" (124). Therefore, Pennell's romantic account of the Fanny Blood/Hugh Skeys story was tailor-made for a Victorian audience prepared to respond with appropriate sensibility to the consumptive Fanny. Pennell's prose reads like a summary of a Victorian novel. Skeys was in love with her but was disinclined to marry her, understandably so, because of the embarrassment and burden of her family's chronic impecunious situation. From Fanny's and Wollstonecraft's points of view, Pennell describes this vacillation as "torture[d] by the unkindness of an uncertain lover" (*Life* 35). And here is a positively Victorian pièce de resistance: "Instead of resenting his unpardonable conduct, as a prouder woman would have done, [Fanny] bore it with the humble patience of a Griselda" (24). The suffer-in-silence, self-denying, obedient-to-the-husband-no-matter-what dream girl of Chaucer's fantasy could have been the poster woman for the Victorian era.

Pennell's recounting of the period when Wollstonecraft was the governess to the Kingsborough girls would have also been read as a Victorian cautionary tale. Pennell employs biblical language that would have resonated with the Victorians to encourage them to sympathize with Wollstonecraft, "as a child of Israel among the Philistines" (*Life* 73). Earlier in the nineteenth century, the middle class imitated the upper class in hiring governesses. Being a governess was one of the few occupations deemed suitable for daughters of middle- and upper-class families. But by the 1880s, most of the middle-class children were going to school, and only the upper classes were employing governesses. Still, with the popularity of *Jane Eyre* and *Agnes Grey* (both in 1847) and a plethora of other governess novels,[9] the Victorians had been well educated as to how difficult it was for governesses to fit, as Wollstonecraft put it, "betwixt and between" the classes. By no means a laborer or a servant, yet not a member of the family, but raised middle or upper class and therefore worthy of respect and privileges, governesses often felt isolated and barred from forging any close relationships with anyone within their employer's home. So, readers could empathize with Wollstonecraft's trials in that area.

Pennell alludes in biblical rhetoric to Wollstonecraft's "follies" with men— that she "was also peculiarly susceptible to the many slings and arrows from which those who live in the world cannot escape" (*Life* 111). This reminded her readers that they were sinners too, and that young women especially could easily end up like Little Em'ly in *David Copperfield*, a good girl who was beguiled by the handsome but unscrupulous Jay Steerforth. Unlike the portrait Victorians had been given of Wollstonecraft as a heathen and a hussy, Pennell depicts her as extremely sensitive in the Christian vein, loathe to cause anyone pain by speech or actions: "The thought that she had added to a fellow-sufferer's life-burden cut her to the quick, and she was unsparing in her self-reproaches"; she often "reached the very acme of mental torture" (*Life* 112). Pennell demonstrates this point with a letter that begins, "I am sick with vexation, and wish I could knock my foolish head against the wall, that bodily pain might make me feel less anguish from self-reproach" (quoted in *Life* 112).

Pennell's empathy for Wollstonecraft and her advocacy of opportunity for women are clear as she echoes Wollstonecraft's motivation for writing *Rights of Woman*: "She saw that women were hindered and hampered in a thousand and one ways by obstacles created not by nature, by man" (116). For a Victorian this is definitely a feminist statement that flew in the face of the Victorian fundamentalists. The Church was fond of reminding its congregants that women were the "weaker vessel." It is true that 1 Peter 3:7 refers to a wife as a weaker vessel, but it does not refer to all women as "the weaker vessel." Still, Wollstonecraft tackles this phrase insofar as it did become a common designation of women (*ROW* 78; introd.) and concedes that women are physically inferior to men (75), but that has never given them the right or reason to "morally and physically" degrade the sex (147; ch. 5).

Pennell believes that the theories of *Rights of Woman* were more acceptable during the 1880s, and that Wollstonecraft "lived a century too soon" (269). Although Wollstonecraft's reputation continued in Pennell's time to carry "a mark for obloquy and scorn," Pennell is determined to vindicate her. She borrows Kegan Paul's words[10] in her declaration to "to clear her memory of stains" by rendering "impartially the facts of her case" (122). She reminds her readers that when Britain was at war with France during the French Revolution, it was very dangerous for a British citizen to be in Paris. If Wollstonecraft would have married Imlay, she would have had to make her presence known, and the guillotine might have been the consequence. That, plus the pecuniary embarrassments and burden of her family and that Britain would not have recognized the marriage—were the three reasons why Wollstonecraft could not marry Imlay (199–204). Were these not noble reasons? Emily Sunstein titled her chapter on Wollstonecraft's willingness to go to Scandinavia at Imlay's request, "Leaning on a Spear." The image one gets is a woman gripping with both hands a spear pointed at her heart, and leaning into it, a modified form of seppuku. How did one persuade a Victorian audience that "living in sin" instead of cohabiting under the sanction of holy matrimony could be acceptable? One way was to suggest female seppuku, leading others to believe that the woman did it for the sake of the man. Then, if there are any stones to be thrown, they would be directed at the man. After all, Pennell suggests it was Imlay's idea for them to live this way and "Because she loved him she could not think evil of him, nor suppose for a moment that his passion was not as pure and true as hers" (*Life* 201).

Furthermore, Pennell takes pains to describe Wollstonecraft as an upstanding moral woman whose conscience before God was clear (202). Pennell adds Paul's approbation: "No one can read her letters without seeing that she was a pure, high-minded, and refined woman, and that she considered herself, in the eyes of God and man, his wife."[11]

Pennell's Wollstonecraft was no Mrs. Robinson or Mrs. Jordan, even though she was often compared to them (*Life* 202). Mary Robinson was a married actress who left her husband to be mistress to the Prince of Wales, who became King George IV of Great Britain and Ireland. After the prince ended the affair, Robinson had several other liaisons, including with Banastre

Tarleton, a hero of the American War of Independence. Championing women's rights, she wrote several feminist articles, distinguished herself with her poetry, was called "the English Sappho," and wrote three plays and eight novels. Dorothea Jordan (1761–1816) was also an actress and mistress of the prince, who became King William IV, and had ten illegitimate children with him. Before this relationship, she lived with several other men at different times and also bore children. Both women died in poverty. Both were considered "fallen women" in the Victorian period. From a Victorian perspective, they were held up as models of the unspeakable immorality that plagued Britain before a God-fearing monarch assumed the throne.

Wollstonecraft was not as controversial as George Sand, who was "masculine by nature as by dress, love was of her life a thing apart, and a change of lovers a matter of secondary importance" (*Life* 202). Instead, for Wollstonecraft "love was literally her whole existence," Pennell explains, in a way that would resonate with her female readers (202), and Imlay was the Prince whose kiss saved Sleeping Beauty, "awaken[ing] her heart to happiness," which she had always sought but never known (207). Furthermore, Pennell emphasizes that Wollstonecraft believed "fidelity a virtue to be cultivated above all others" (202). So, Wollstonecraft was different from those scandalous women who hopped from one bed to another.

Wollstonecraft is further exonerated by Pennell's depiction of Imlay. Although at first he was a "devoted" husband (210), it did not take long for his true colors to show. He was a cad who "had forgotten love and honor, and had virtually deserted her" (218). Pennell's chapter 9 is titled "Imlay's Desertion." Pennell blames money-making for enticing Imlay away from love and honor. This would have resonated with a lot of Victorians. In all his novels Charles Dickens warns against the fanatic obsession with "making one's fortune" that drove his age. "*Wealth, wealth! Wealth! Praise be to the god of the nineteenth century! The golden idol! The mighty Mammon!*" so John Sterling writes in 1848. He perceives that these "are the accents of the time, such the cry of the nation" (25). Novels, plays and essays alike reminded the Victorian of 1 Timothy 6:10: "The love of money is the root of all evil."[12]

Imlay was the villain in this melodramatic reenactment of Wollstonecraft's life. Pennell runs through the two suicide attempts very quickly, focusing mostly on Imlay's culpability. He left her to live with another woman in Paris "for whom he had sacrificed wife and child." The tender Wollstonecraft "renewed her excuses for him [...]. Here it may be said that, though Imlay declared that a certain sum should be settled upon [Fanny], not a shilling of it was ever paid" (*Life* 245). In the 1890 version, Pennell closes this chapter with "And so ends the saddest of all sad love stories" (247). Pennell assumes the customary Victorian didactic mode of warning young women about reprobates such as Imlay. Pennell has nothing approbative to say about Imlay, not even that he was tall, dark and handsome. Her agenda is purely to give a sympathetic account of Wollstonecraft in a way that said to Victorian ladies, "There, but for the grace of God goeth thee."[13]

Pennell is ever careful to restore Wollstonecraft's reputation from the damage that men did to it—and not just her lovers but also biographers like Godwin and John Knowles (Fuseli's biographer). Pennell introduces the subject by describing Fuseli as "one of her dearest friends" (180). Pennell equates Wollstonecraft's friendship with him to the innocuous relationships she held with George Blood and Joseph Johnson (180). Wollstonecraft was never a coquette. In fact, as made clear in *Rights of Woman*, she disdained flirting and instead was spontaneous and transparent. By the same token, Pennell asserts that Wollstonecraft lived in a state of celibacy at this time, restrained by the fact that Fuseli was married, that society frowned on adultery (180) and that she believed in the sanctity of marriage, a prevalent theme in *Rights of Woman*.[14] As for Fuseli: "He, like her, was an enthusiast. He was a warm partisan of justice and a rebel against established institutions. He would take any steps to see that the rights of the individual were respected" (180), which is to say that he was not the sort of man to allow Wollstonecraft to compromise herself.

To Pennell, both parties were innocent of the charges made by Knowles, "so prejudiced a writer that his words have but little value" (*Life* 181). In Pennell's 1890 edition, she adds another paragraph in her attempt to combat the negative press resulting from the portrayal by Knowles. The story about the proposed *ménage à trois*, Pennell disputes by quoting Kegan Paul, who said that he was unable "to find any confirmation whatever of this preposterous story," and that Wollstonecraft remained a close friend to Sophia Fuseli until her death.[15] Pennell agrees with Paul and insists that Wollstonecraft "never played fast and loose with her principles" (184) and adds this argument:

> Her character is the best refutation of Knowles's charges. She was too proud to demean herself to any man. She was too sensitive to slights to risk the repulses he says she accepted. And since always before and after this period she had nothing more at heart than the happiness of others, it is not likely that she would have deliberately tried to step in between Fuseli and his wife, and gain at the latter's expense her own ends. She could not have changed her character in a day. She never played fast and loose with her principles. These were in many ways contrary to the standard of the rest of mankind, but they were also equally opposed to the conduct imputed to her. The testimony of her actions is her acquittal. That she did not for a year produce any work of importance is no argument against her. It was only after three years of uninterrupted industry

that she found time to write the "Rights of Women." On account of the urgency of her every-day needs, she had no leisure for work whose financial success was uncertain. Knowles's story is too absurdly out of keeping with her character to be believed for a moment. (184)

Pennell also disputes the first time Godwin wrote that Wollstonecraft suggested a *ménage à trois* with Imlay and his mistress:

> There is not a word in her letters to confirm this extraordinary story. It is simply impossible that at one moment she should have been driven to suicide by the knowledge that he had a mistress, and that at the next she should take a step which was equivalent to countenancing his conduct. It is more rational to conclude that Godwin was misinformed, than to believe this. (244)[16]

In her tenth chapter, Pennell gives an overview of Wollstonecraft's works. I found her description of *Maria* to be a perfect example of my premise that Pennell's biography is uniquely Victorian. The novel teaches that committing great sins always brings about terrible consequences, and thus it is a tale of redemption and warning. Pennell continues her assessment of *Maria*:

> It is an astonishing production, even for an age when Fielding and Smollett were not considered coarse. But, as was the case in the "Rights of Women," this plainness of speech was due not to a delight in impurity and uncleanness for their own sakes, but to Mary's certainty that by the proper use of subjects vile in themselves, she could best establish principles of purity. Whatever may be thought of her moral creed and of her manner of promulgating it, no reader of her books can deny her the respect which her courage and sincerity evoke. One may mistrust the mission of a Savonarola, and yet admire his inexorable adherence to it. Mary Wollstonecraft's faith in, and devotion to, the doctrines she preached was as firm and unflinching as those of any religiously inspired prophet. (274–75)

This passage is rife with religious jargon: "impurity," "uncleanness," "purity" "religiously inspired prophet." Pennell evokes biblical language to persuade that Wollstonecraft's last novel was morally beneficial, and that Wollstonecraft died a "religiously inspired prophet" (275). Pennell's concluding remarks about Wollstonecraft's works are "Whatever may be thought of her moral creed and of her manner of promulgating it, no reader of her books can deny her the respect which her courage and sincerity evoke" (276).

Chapter 5

RALPH M. WARDLE'S *MARY WOLLSTONECRAFT: A CRITICAL BIOGRAPHY* (1951): ROSIE-THE-RIVETER WOLLSTONECRAFT

Aside from appreciative references to her, especially by American suffragists, and a fictional account by George R. Preedy (Gabrielle M. Long),[1] the nineteenth- and twentieth-century periodicals were silent about Wollstonecraft until 1947, when Ferdinand Landberg and Marynia F. Farnham published a bestseller, *Modern Women: The Lost Sex*. They accused Wollstonecraft of encouraging women to be more like men, which resulted only in increasing men's and women's neuroses because, according to them, women cannot be happy outside of their domestic sphere and men cannot be happy when women are competing with them for jobs and not supporting them at home, where women belong. Lundberg was a journalist, but Farnham was a psychiatrist who had her own private practice and worked for the New York State Psychiatric Institute. Despite the fact that Farnham was a professional who worked outside the home, they both criticized postwar women who wanted to continue to earn a paycheck "in an era that enshrined home, family, and motherhood in public discourse, but the social reality was often quite different" (Sigerman 8). The book is now considered "a classic in the genre of antifeminist psychoanalytical literature" (Buhle 174).

By the end of that year, 1947, a professor at the University of Omaha, Ralph M. Wardle, rose to Wollstonecraft's defense and published a sympathetic article about her for the *PMLA*. It focused on her employment as a reviewer for the *Analytical Review*. Four years later, he wrote the first comprehensive and first scholarly biography of Wollstonecraft.

It is in his biography that we not only perceive an attempt to depict Wollstonecraft's life without moral censorship, but we also find explanations for the behavior of most of the people in her life—explanations that are more plausible and credible than those that would follow during and after the great age of literary theory of the 1990s. For example, most biographies depict Wollstonecraft's father, Edward John Wollstonecraft, as a reckless dreamer whose wanderlust caused immeasurable and irreparable damage to his family. But Wardle's portrait seems much more realistic because of its historical context.

Edward Wollstonecraft was born to a father who had known humble beginnings but worked his way up to be a master weaver who set up a highly lucrative industry in Spitalfields. He did this with the hope that his son could be a gentleman. He left that son £10,000, which made him a millionaire. Wollstonecraft's father was handed the much-cherished English dream of being born wealthy and able therefore to spend the rest of his life in relative ease, being the squire or lord of a manor on a sprawling working farm that would provide for him and his. And to his credit, as Wardle understands it, he wished to raise his children in the healthy countryside (4). This is the first statement of anything positive about Mary's father to be found in the biographies.

He took his young wife, their two-year-old presumptive heir, Ned, and newly born Mary to a farm in the Epping Forest (4).[2] The later biographers claimed that he did not know what he was doing, that he was a novice at being a gentleman farmer, bungled it, and would repeat the experiment over and over as if he could not accept his failure. Barbara Taylor describes his experience this way: "Unlike his father, however, Edward Wollstonecraft had little taste for the commercial life, opting instead to become a gentleman farmer. [...] Edward, it seems, had no talent for farming, nor for anything else" (5). Jennifer Lorch says that he "lacked the staying power for lasting success" (7). Elizabeth Denlinger makes this clever statement: "Edward Wollstonecraft had been a gentleman farmer, but he was a bad manager as well as a bad father, and the family fortune dwindled as his seven children grew" (26).

However, Wardle reminds us that Wollstonecraft's father had to contend with the effects of the Enclosure Acts, when large farms were being created to ensure that land would remain intact within families. Larger farms could sell produce and grain at lower costs, which forced the small and independent farmers like Wollstonecraft out of business. Thousands of small landowners lost their farms (4). Therefore, the struggle that Mary Wollstonecraft's father endured was not necessarily due to his inaptitude or lassitude, and his failure to make his farm succeed was not unique. And then, it was only logical that when the farm at Epping Forest failed to be profitable with no prospects of improvement in sight, that Wollstonecraft should try another farm, and another and another. What else was he expected to do? A gentleman did not labor for a living, and he had been brought up with the expectations of being a gentleman. It is no wonder that he became so angry, although there is no excuse for turning his frustration into abuse of his wife and children, even if he was legally permitted to do so.

Still, according to Wardle's reasoning, it was that abuse that made Mary Wollstonecraft write *Vindication of the Rights of Men* and *Vindication of the Rights of Woman*. Having to endure the tyranny of the primary man in her life, namely her father, she formed an early impression of the capacity and liberty of men to oppress and control women. It bred in her an "abiding hatred for tyranny of all sorts and fearlessness in fighting it," which would erupt passionately in the two *Vindications* (7). Alongside forming her perception of eighteenth-century patriarchy, she also cultivated a disdain for women who passively accepted it. "By witnessing her mother's abject servitude, she acquired a resentment of the conditions that kept women in a state of submission." It was while guarding her mother's bedroom door from her father's violence that Wollstonecraft "developed a passion for freedom and a dauntless courage which did much to shape her later career" (7).

To frustrate her even more and force on her the realization that she had no legal recourse because she was only a woman, her father took money that was bequeathed to the Wollstonecraft girls and squandered it (344–45n6).

Wardle describes Wollstonecraft as full of "self-dramatization and self-pity, and more than a hint of her lifelong neuroticism" (97). How could she not struggle with neurosis after her traumatic childhood? On top of that, she was heavily burdened to provide for herself and her family while severely restricted with opportunities to do so simply because she was a woman.

Otherwise, Wardle is mostly ostensibly kind and sympathetic in his assessment of Wollstonecraft's behavior. One can tell this from the chapter titles: "Education of a Rebel," "Brief Triumph," "Return to Bondage," "New Directions," "Success," "*A Vindication of the Rights of Woman*," "Theories on Trial," "Frustration and Despair," and "Fulfillment." One might say of Wardle's biography that it was written by a polite gentleman. George is right when she describes Wardle's treatment of "Mary" as if she were "someone to whom he is attracted across the years" (12).

Cora Kaplan, in 2003, also notes Wardle's chivalrous treatment:

> And Wardle, who had himself objected that earlier champions had made her unrecognizably into a "saintly lady" (339) sums her up, equally incredibly, in the soft-focus language of idealistic postwar Hollywood heroines, who, "once she had rid herself of the brashness displayed in the years of her first successes" became, "above all, a woman of personal charm [...] not the placid charm which rises from beauty and graciousness alone; it was the positive, energetic charm of a courageous woman eager to serve humanity" (341). ("Reception" 253)

With confidence in Wollstonecraft's judgment, Wardle asserts, "Soon she had penetrated to the root of Bess' trouble and concluded that it stemmed from a profound aversion which she had taken to her husband." And then Wardle does not even hint at Wollstonecraft's behavior as being neurotic because of her father's treatment of her mother; instead, she had become familiar enough of Bishop to believe that he was a villain and that she needed to rescue her helpless sister (26).

To the contrary, writing in 2000, Janet Todd considers Wollstonecraft's involvement with the Bishop marriage as meddling, impulsive and domineering. Often critical of her, Todd charges Wollstonecraft for having to be "centre stage" in every crisis (*Revolutionary* 46). In fact, Todd also suggests that when Bess showed signs of recovering from postpartum depression, Wollstonecraft interfered and whisked her out of the marriage against her will (49). Todd's analysis is that Wollstonecraft overreacted, thinking only of "her parents' unsatisfactory union" and the "'lingering' illness of her mother" (45).

As for the unhappy time Wollstonecraft spent as a governess with the Kingsboroughs, Wardle sides with her in condemning Lady Kingsborough as a terrible mother, and he expresses his understanding that Wollstonecraft could not, in the short time she was with the three girls, undo all the damage done to them by their mother over the years (63). But it was this experience that exposed her to the lifestyle of nobility, which appears under her critical eye in *Rights of Woman*. Wollstonecraft told her sister that women spent five hours a day with their dress.[3] Lady Kingsborough was the very type of woman in *Rights of Woman* who could not be bothered by her children but lavished all of her affection instead on her dogs.[4] Wardle is certain that the reason Lady Kingsborough fired Wollstonecraft was because she was jealous of the love her daughters felt for their governess (78).

Wardle thinks that Reverend John Hewlett introduced her to Johnson (37), but Hays, before him, was the first to give Hewlett credit for suggesting to Wollstonecraft that she could support herself with a literary career (417–18). Wardle also suggests, without knowing for sure, that Hewlett introduced her to Reverend Joshua Waterhouse (38), one of a number of men who fell in love with her. More likely she met Waterhouse in Bath while he was living there. It may have been when she was there with Mrs. Dawson—who had hired her as a companion. This would have been in 1778 and may have brought on the disappointment, the afflictions, phantom, the storm and indolence she described in letters to Jane Arden.[5] Todd theorizes that the 1781 letters were about her morose realization that she could not marry Waterhouse (*CL* 28n66). Elizabeth Nitchie thinks the romance happened later, when she accompanied the Kingsboroughs to Bath in 1787 (167–69). Regardless, Wardle is convinced that she loved Waterhouse (38) and notes that their relationship ended abruptly in 1785 (43) but later claims that it was Wollstonecraft who called it off (171).

Wardle downplays the Fuseli affair but does mention it, finishing with Wollstonecraft's proposed *ménage à trois*, which was received by an expulsion by Sophia Fuseli. Wardle's opinion is that Wollstonecraft felt her behavior had been justified, and that she followed "the rules of her own morality, if not the world's" (177).

With Imlay, Wollstonecraft at first was not interested in him, but according to Wardle, he pursued her (185), and it was he who called her "wife" (225). Wardle's assessment is that, after the baby was born, Imlay had become bored with her but was too much of a coward to end the relationship (221).

Wardle is always Wollstonecraft's champion. He will bring up unpleasant situations, but he never accuses Wollstonecraft of wrongdoing. With very little information, he alludes to Ann, the child Wollstonecraft adopted (178). He is not the first; Godwin mentions her (71) and so does Elizabeth Pennell (*Life* 76), but no biographer, including Wardle, reveals what happened to her—that Wollstonecraft could not cope with having a little girl around, so she gave her up.

Wardle does not mention the baby Fanny at all, nor does he mention Mary, daughter to the Godwins. He does focus on Godwin's expressed disdain for marriage before getting involved with Wollstonecraft (259–60) and then points out that Godwin wrote his sister in 1784 to find him a "proper wife." When she presented a Miss Gay, Godwin felt she would suffice, but after two months of getting to know each other, he ended the relationship (260). In his forties, he apparently felt that a female companion might be desirable. He was attracted to Mary Reveley but at a time when she was married. After the two became widows, he thought he would marry her. But before Wollstonecraft, he flirted with Elizabeth Inchbald, Amelia Alderson and Mary Hays (261). In fact he was still pursuing Inchbald romantically while he was involved with Wollstonecraft (288). So, Wollstonecraft's two major lovers do not come off well in Wardle's book.

Why did Wollstonecraft and Godwin not marry before having conjugal relations? Wardle's theory is that Godwin had debt and could not support a wife. He was also attracted to Inchbald, and rumor had it that Wollstonecraft and John Opie, the artist who would paint two portraits of Wollstonecraft, were engaged (271). Once Wollstonecraft learned she was pregnant, then, according to Wardle, she persuaded Godwin to marry her because she was afraid of social ostracism (286).

Wardle does go into detail about her birthing and the problem with the placenta, which led to her death. He thinks Godwin's *Memoirs* was the work of a man who dearly loved his wife and wanted her to be recognized for her achievements, and that he naïvely revealed everything (314). The problem, to Wardle, was with timing; Godwin published the biography during the severe Anti-Jacobin Movement in England, in reaction to the anarchy in France when Wollstonecraft "became a symbol of the hated Jacobinism" (317). She was denounced for all manner of immorality and unethical behavior by the *Anti-Jacobin Review and Magazine*. As if two suicides and two illegitimate children conceived out of wedlock were not scandalous enough, the reviewer accuses her of showing no respect to her parents, when the truth is that she spent the last moments of her mother's life comforting her and spent most of her life bailing her father out of debt. She was charged with neglecting her pupils, but she had to go to Portugal to be with her dying best friend, Fanny Blood. She apparently concocted a plan to emigrate to America to escape her creditors, when she constantly paid her debts as well as those of her father and brother, Ned. She did hope to immigrate to America—it had been her mother's dream (6). They both held romantic notions of a simpler life there, and when Wollstonecraft was sure that she and Imlay would marry, he had promised to take her to America, where they would live on their own farm. The review ends with a smug declaration that Godwin's *Memoirs* was at least a warning to people as to what lifestyles to avoid (318).

"Such abuse," Wardle, the gentleman of the 1950s, declaims, was "abominable taste when applied to a person able to defend himself," but it was "unforgivable when written for a dead woman and her grieving husband" (321).

As his title implies, Wardle's book is not just a biography; it is a critical biography. He was the first to offer criticism of Wollstonecraft's books. Because he also published a collection of her letters, he drew from them in order to make some observations about her literary production—observations that were not as kind and generous as were his comments about her life. It was one thing to be a gentleman and condescend to champion the little lady against attacks; it was another thing to deal with a woman who encroached upon a man's profession. Wardle calls *Thoughts on the Education of Daughters* a "potboiler scribbled for the sake of ten guineas" (52), and he more than once makes it clear that *Maria*, even had it been finished, would never have made a "great novel" (298).

In his analysis of her canon, Wardle attempts to situate it in both sociohistorical and literary-historical contexts. He argues that there were "Devout Christian gentlemen" in Wollstonecraft's day who could easily find biblical support for the subjection of women "as a means of atoning for their share in man's fall from grace" (135–36). Men perpetuated stereotypes of women, as Wardle demonstrates by discussing Samuel Johnson. Hewlett introduced Wollstonecraft to Dr. Johnson in Newington Green and, according to Godwin, Wollstonecraft was quite in awe of him and hoped to get to know him better, but he was ill and died shortly after their one and only meeting (Godwin 60). Surely Wollstonecraft must have been familiar with the following quote from Johnson that Wardle reproduces to illustrate the bias against women that provoked Wollstonecraft to write *Rights of Woman*: "Nature has given women so much power that the law has wisely given them little."[6] Johnson claims that men married ignorant or foolish women thinking that they were manageable and that they would not be afraid that their wives would be smarter than themselves. Of this kind of woman, there are two varieties: the spaniel fool and the mule fool. The spaniel fool might be managed by beating her, but eventually she would turn into a mule fool who will cause her husband no end of trouble. "Men know that women are an over-match for them," says Johnson (257). It was just such a portrayal of women, whether stereotypically, partially or generally true, that Wollstonecraft disdained in *Rights of Woman*. It was disgusting to her that women believed they had to be manipulative and obsequious like spaniels in order to get what they wanted from men (231; ch. 9). She criticized both genders for their complicity in demeaning the female and fostering such dishonest and ignoble behavior.

Wardle next provides an overview of the portrayal of women in eighteenth-century literature (137–42). In 1951 this was very progressive work for anyone, but especially for a man. The decade following World War II was one of the most antifeminist periods of history in both England and the United States. During the war, women went to work in the factories, took positions of high authority in business, were the heads of their families—in short, had to do the work that was traditionally done by men. Not only did they learn that they were capable of doing this work, but many of them liked doing it, and even more liked the independence and financial benefits that came from it. Yet, when the men returned, the women were expected to vacate these positions, return to the kitchen and have babies, and let the men be men again on the home front. The movies, advertisements, magazine articles and books were rife with propaganda aimed to return civilization to definite divisions of labor defined by gender.

Wardle continued to be actively engaged in his research on Wollstonecraft. His 1951 biography would be followed by another edition in 1967. In 1966 he published the letters between Godwin and Wollstonecraft. Wardle reviewed Tomalin's biography in 1975, beginning with a comment that only three biographies had been published on Wollstonecraft in the first 69 years of the century, and they were written by men. Between 1970 and 1974, he said, there were four new biographies, all by women: George, Nixon, Flexner and Tomalin (147). He must not have been aware of Detre's, or perhaps Detre's was not in print by the time he was writing his review. His was an important point, that feminism had now arrived, women were becoming political activists through their positions in academe and scholarship, and they reclaimed Wollstonecraft. "No pioneer in the cause of women's rights has profited more from the Women's Liberation movement than Mary Wollstonecraft," Wardle observes, adding, "All of her works which have been out of print for two centuries are now published or being prepared for pub" (147).

In 1971 Margaret George would be the first to write one of the seven biographies that would appear in the 1970s, reflecting the first serious reclamation of Wollstonecraft since Wardle. Nevertheless, in 1976 Wollstonecraft critic Alice Green Fredman expected more from scholars. Wollstonecraft, "has not, on balance, been well served by her biographers," she charges at the beginning of her review of George's biography. The reason behind this accusation, Fredman states, comes from a "variety of impedimenta, including personal and sexual prejudice, misunderstanding of her mind and personality, as well as rapidly shifting socio-historical tides" (135). The major deficiency is "the kind of scholarly editing and informed introduction which would situate her properly in *her* times for an intelligent reading in *our* times" (135).

Fredman praises George's treatment of Fuseli and Imlay as "unsurpassed" (143).[7] She also thinks George's discussion of Wollstonecraft's religion is worthy of attention (143).[8]

Florence Boos rates George's biography as a "highly idiosyncratic essay" replete with inconsistencies ("Biographies" 8). One example she offers to support her harsh appraisal pertains to George's contradictory treatment of Wollstonecraft. George calls Wollstonecraft a "pre-historic woman,"[9] which Boos explains from her reading of George as referring to "an exception to but also part of the 'history of the "passive and negative"' which constitutes the story of women before their own history can be worked out."[10] Whether or not this is a good thing or a valid consideration, Boos does not say, but in the next sentence she illustrates George's condescension to Wollstonecraft with several examples that are not only condescending but contradictory: "But any sort of introduction would insist on *the certainty of Mary's historical reputation*," Boos continues in her quote from George, adding emphasis. This reputation was "based on her stunning contribution to liberal ideology, indeed to general modern consciousness."[11] Boos compares that to a statement George makes nearly 170 pages later: "Because she hadn't solved her most pressing problems, hadn't worked anything out for herself, *she could hardly be an historical force*, could hardly lead or guide others. Her story is an illumination, a mirror, of the others, in its incoherence, confusion, and indecision a magnification of the others."[12] In a bibliographical note, Flexner writes: "Margaret George, while adding no new facts to Mary's life, interprets them from the viewpoint of today's feminists" (286), but Boos emphatically disagrees with Flexner about George's "feminist" interpretation (8).

Insofar as George based much of her work on Wardle, it is not surprising that she applauds Wardle for his "careful work," but then, as Boos points out, George criticizes Wardle for not taking seriously Wollstonecraft's political views on gender.[13] Boos counters this as a false claim. Although acknowledging some sexist attitudes in Wardle, Boos appreciates his presentation of the "heroic qualities of her resistance to eighteenth century misogyny, and lists the repressive circumstances she overcame with thoroughness and distaste" ("Biographies" 7).

Nearly all of the biographies since Wardle, cite Wardle. His book continued to be reprinted through 1967, and his collected letters were published under the title of *Godwin and Mary* in 1966, then as *Collected Letters of Mary Wollstonecraft* in 1979.

The preface to *Godwin and Mary* shares credit for the book's production with his wife, Mary E. Wardle. She was a graduate of Radcliffe College and may have been the inspiration that piqued his interest in Wollstonecraft.[14] Even so, 1951 was not a popular time for someone like Ralph Wardle to be critical of gender divide. The title of his collection of letters (*Godwin and Mary*) is, however, somewhat problematic in that it follows the old convention of referring to men by their last names and the ladies by their first. Maybe he chose "Mary" in honor of his wife and, in the 1950s, people simply did not refer to women by their last names unless they were servants.

In the postwar climate, Wardle must have felt compelled to provide a literary history about feminists earlier than Wollstonecraft (143–44). As for *Rights of Woman*, he observes how ungenerous Wollstonecraft was toward her sex but comments that she would have had trouble pointing out many distinguished women because women had acquired very little education and had few opportunities (153), a hint he is making about what would happen to women if they were forced to accept eighteenth-century sexual ideology.

On the other hand, when Wardle examines *Rights of Woman*, he highlights that Wollstonecraft argues that women ought to be better educated for the purpose of being better wives and mothers, which is an accurate assessment of part of what Wollstonecraft does write. Wardle reassures his readers that Wollstonecraft believes that women, once they receive a good education, would continue to prioritize their "domestic pursuits" and not aspire for "distinction in the world" (153). It seems that he wanted Rosie the Riveter to return to the kitchen after all.

Oddly then, Wardle concedes that Wollstonecraft does contest for political and economic equality, and in this he is very supportive (154). In this position, he was not too different from Benjamin Heath Malkin, a close friend to William Blake and a frequent visitor to Joseph Johnson's dinners, but while Wollstonecraft was in France. Later, Malkin would get to know Godwin through dinners at Horne Tooke's and therefore probably never talked to Wollstonecraft, although he must have wanted to for their shared interest in educational reform. He would become the headmaster of Bury St. Edmunds Free School and then, in 1828, first professor of history in the new London University. In 1795 Malkin wrote "On the Female Character," published in *Essays on Subjects Connected with Civilization* in which he praises Wollstonecraft for criticizing "those prejudices [...] which have prevailed to the exclusion of half our species from the common rights of humanity, and the unfettered exercise of reason" (257). He agrees that boys and girls should be educated together and taught to be virtuous. However, Malkin felt compelled to warn against Wollstonecraft's "extravagance" (263) in encouraging women to pursue those subjects of study that might make them too pedantic (274) and thus "carry them too far from the sphere of domestic concerns" (278). He is right that Wollstonecraft valued domesticity, but he disagrees with her that women should be circumscribed by it. She poses this question: "How many women thus waste their life away the prey of discontent, who might have practised as physicians, regulated a farm, managed a shop, and stood erect, supported by their own industry, instead of hanging their heads surcharged with the dew of sensibility" (*ROW* 217; ch. 9). Again, she is betwixt and between affirming women's talents and duties in the home but, at the same time, advocating women's talents and duties in the world outside the home.

Fraser Neiman, of the College of William and Mary, reviewed Wardle's book for the school's quarterly and gave it a mostly favorable response. He recognized it as a "scholarly and illuminating account of the life of a pioneer in the emancipation of women" (434). He would have liked more historical context of the period, in particular, how Wollstonecraft fit into the "vigorous intellectual life of the period" (434); further, he was dismayed that the book lacked a bibliography (435). Neiman did not recognize—or at least did not address—any relevance that the book might have had for the 1950s.

There were not many reviews written on Wardle's book that I could find. It was not until he published the collected letters of Wollstonecraft and Godwin in the late 1960s when work about Wollstonecraft began to receive serious notice. The 1960s gave rise to the second wave of the woman's movement in the United States and England and in many of the Western countries, and the terms "feminism" and "women's lib(eration)" became household words. In 1966 NOW (the National Organization of Women) was created for the purpose of fighting for equality in all areas of life for women, with the major focus on getting Congress to pass the ERA (Equal Rights Amendment), which never happened. It was also the beginning of the birth-control movement. Betty Friedan published her landmark *The Feminine Mystique* in 1963. The time was ripe for the resurrection of the eighteenth-century feminist. Because of feminism, Richard Holmes muses, "we now have admirable lives of Mary Wollstonecraft as well as her husband William Godwin" ("Biography" 19). The *Mary Wollstonecraft Journal* was created in 1973. In the second number, Florence Boos reviewed Wardle's biography (along with other biographies to date) and pronounced it "an official version," meaning "Wollstonecraft's life as seen by her herself and Godwin."

In that same year (1973) Ellen Moers helped introduce Wollstonecraft to a new generation. She acclaims Wardle's 1951 biography of Wollstonecraft as "the first and still the most important scholarly" work on her and states she prefers it over Eleanor Flexner's, primarily because of his guide to Wollstonecraft's writing (n.p.). She writes that he was correct in his reminder that she was not the first woman to earn her living through writing. But Moers wants readers to know that "she may well have been the first to fight for a place on Grub Street in this solitary fashion, to set up her own home in London without family support or companionship, without husband or lover, without any defense against inevitable sexual insult but her own pride" (n.p.).

In 1976 Janet Todd launched her long career of scholarship on Wollstonecraft. In her review of the biographies published by that date, she identifies Wardle's treatment of Wollstonecraft as "an heroic woman." His "enthusiasm and respect for her added to her stature," Todd claims. He traced her intellectual growth as it evolved "from orthodox to liberal to radical" ("Biographies" 728). I do not see this in Wardle, but it would be her theory in the Wollstonecraft biography she would later write.

Additional observations Todd makes on Wardle's work are not altogether positive. She notes that he follows Pennell's lead in addressing the critical reception of Wollstonecraft's books by her eighteenth-century contemporaries (728). Todd also attributes Stirling Taylor's 1911 biography as providing literary antecedents and the social setting of *Rights of Woman*, and theorizes that Wardle follows his cue (728–29). Finally, she considers Wardle's to be a scholarly remake of Godwin's *Memoirs*, with both men being overly complimentary of Wollstonecraft as a person (729) and with both accounts being faulty, containing historical errors (728).

As Todd and Moers remark, Wardle contributed much to the re-emergence of Wollstonecraft by undertaking a serious study of her works and identifying the biographical elements in them. For example, he makes the observation that when she went to Lisbon to tend to Fanny Skeys, she thought Portugal filthy and immoral (Wardle 46). Later, in *Mary*, she describes it as "the most uncivilized nation in Europe […] due to Romish ceremonies […]. Religion […] has never humanized their hearts" (quoted in 45).

Wardle is critical of the quality of Wollstonecraft's writing in *Rights of Woman*, suggesting that she should have invested six years instead of six weeks in writing it (156). Wollstonecraft did not have the luxury of six years. She knew that Charles Maurice de Talleyrand-Périgord was one of the writers of the Declaration of the Rights of Man. He was greatly instrumental in recreating the French government, and it was her hope that she could persuade him to grant equal educational opportunities to women and consider them in other reforms (Bergès 22–24). She felt that if she succeeded in doing this, since the eyes of the world were on France because of its revolution, if France adopted her recommendation, perhaps other countries would follow suit. Besides, she had the burden of the ever-haunting impetus to earn her living and support her siblings and father from her publications.

Regardless of why she wrote it so quickly, Wardle faults *Rights of Woman* for being full of clichés and "far-fetched metaphors." The work also lacked organization, and Wollstonecraft "could seldom round off a subject without a high-sounding peroration, seldom relax into simple, direct language when her subject required it" (156). Even though she wrote or translated seven books and reviewed over 200 more, Wardle complains that she "had much to learn about the craft of writing" (156). However, he does praise *Rights of Woman* for being "new and original. It was so new, in fact, that nearly a century elapsed before its tenets were applied and when later, feminists formulated their bill of rights, they introduced no points which Mary had not anticipated" (157).

As for the broader picture—the important work Wollstonecraft accomplished in *Rights of Woman*—Cora Kaplan makes these observations of Wardle's assessment: He perceives that she

> was never "mean" or "dull," but *Rights of Woman*, Wardle implies, is still a daunting, difficult read—while the life has the appeal of popular film or genre fiction, but with an improving political message. Yet his biography does highlight Mary's intellectual and political trajectory. Rather like Woolf, Wardle celebrates Wollstonecraft's fusion of political, social, and emotional rebellion; like Woolf it is the persona that he in part invents rather than the texts before him that stirs his imagination. ("Reception" 253)

Wardle closes his biography with this memorial to Mary Wollstonecraft:

> It is, however, Mary's personality that has kept her memory alive. Surely dozens of readers have thrilled to her history or been fired by her example for every one who has read his way through *The Rights of Woman*. There was indeed, as she said, something residing in her heart that was not perishable; and it was her heart, more than her mind, that made her a great woman […] a courageous woman eager to serve humanity. (341)

Chapter 6

ELEANOR FLEXNER'S *MARY WOLLSTONECRAFT* (1972): THE VERY INSENSIBLE WOLLSTONECRAFT

Flexner's research is mostly impeccable, painstaking, thorough, thoroughly documented and soundly applied. Usually she makes clear when she is posing a deduction or is filling in a gap with creative research or backing up an assumption by drawing from Wollstonecraft's fiction. For example, in describing Mary's paternal grandfather, Flexner surmises that he began as a tradesman with the ambition of becoming a gentleman (19–20). Although the other biographers—before and after the 1970s—mention that he was a weaver in the Spitalfields district and that he did well financially, they do not provide the kind of specifics that qualify these generalizations as does Flexner. She recounts that between 1753 and 1755 Edward Wollstonecraft leased land on Primrose Street in Spitalfields in London, an area that was the center of the silk-weaving industry (20). She found this information in the parish registers and poor-rate books of St. Botolph without Bishopsgate, records of which she located in the London Guildhall Library (287n1). On three blocks, he built houses from which rent would be collected from about 30 tenants for 60 years (20). The lease was to the Worshipful Company of Goldsmiths, and additional specifics are documented in Appendix A. Flexner recounts that the grandfather also owned shares in an East India Company merchant ship, *Cruttenden*, and she lists the voyages in Appendix A. Mary's brother inherited these shares. The evidence of the grandfather's purchase and development of land supports Flexner's assertions that he was not just a tradesman but also a man who was ambitious enough to invest his money in property that would place him and his heirs in the gentry.

When Flexner knew that she could not validate a claim from her research, she let the reader know it. Still, she did make some unsubstantiated claims, whether accurate or not, such as: "At some point Mr. Wollstonecraft had become so badly entangled financially that he used part of the money settled on his daughters to extricate himself. Mary's statement, in a letter to Jane

Arden, is forthright: he took it, and she agreed to relinquish her share" (28). Surprisingly, Flexner neither cites the letter nor the source of the money.

Flexner is very critical of *Rights of Woman*, expressing her doubts that Wollstonecraft ever read the works she cited by Swedenborg, Monboddo, Adam Smith, Bacon and Leibneith (164), but Flexner does not say why she thinks this, other than that she doubts that Wollstonecraft could have read all of these books during the short four years she was in London. Flexner tempers her statement by crediting Wollstonecraft's having read tidbits here and there and gleaning from reviews in the literary journals. Flexner quotes Ralph Wardle's calculation that Wollstonecraft wrote a total at 412 reviews. She also lists Derek Roper's count of 204 plus 208 of "varying degrees of authenticity ("Analytical" 1003).[1] After Flexner, Margaret Tims figures that Wollstonecraft wrote 19 review articles during the first six months of the *Analytical Review*'s existence and 153 during the second year (91). George Eliot also earned a living from writing reviews, during which she "read over 166 books in two years" (Hughes 167), and Geraldine Jewsbury reviewed over 2,300 books between 1850 and 1880 (Onslow 70).[2] All three (including Wollstonecraft) were voracious learners; it is not inconceivable that these women digested such a great volume of writing in such a short period of time.

Furthermore, even though Wollstonecraft worried that her French was not fluent enough to teach the Kingsborough daughters,[3] she translated Jacques Necker's *Of the Importance of Religious Opinions* (1789). She taught herself Italian, and translated from Dutch Berquin's translation of Richardson's *Young Grandison* (Godwin 39). While she was just beginning to learn German, she translated Salzmann's *Elements of Morality for the Use of Children* in 1791 (Lucas ix), and she considered it an "exercise" to translate it (Rauschenbusch-Clough 28).

The reviews were essential for her livelihood. Johnson paid very well; when she published *Thoughts*, she made ten guineas, which was higher than any other publisher would have given (Tyson 6, 8). Johnson was such a generous publisher that, even though he contracted a certain amount to publish *Tales of Fashionable Life* for Maria Edgeworth, he doubled the amount because of its sales (8). To Wollstonecraft's brother Charles, he wrote in 1796 that she deserved to be paid "more than most women, & cannot live upon a trifle."[4] Indeed, at that time a woman could expect to pay about six pounds a year for clothes, five pounds a year for a maid, twelve pounds a year for a cook, two shillings for a chicken and eight pounds a year for coal. Wollstonecraft sometimes rented in St. Paul's and sometimes about Bloomsbury, both considered expensive neighborhoods. The better houses cost £150 per year, but she probably rented a house for about £50 per year, which would require another £25 for taxes (Besant 305). Wollstonecraft was so financially stretched that when Talleyrand visited her, he drank wine out of a cracked teacup (Brody 86). If it had not been for Johnson's generous advances and loans, she would have never survived. As it was, at her death, she owed him £75.[5]

Beginning with having access to the library of Jane Arden's father (Todd, *CL* 17) and then the Clares' (Godwin 49), Wollstonecraft was extremely self-disciplined and an avid learner, reading everything she could get her hands on. Julie Carlson claims that Wollstonecraft was autodidactic, as were other intellectual women of her time: She taught herself (222–23). Eager to learn, she probably devoured every book given to her to review.

But it was a deficient educational background, which accounted for the poor organization in *Rights of Woman*, supposes Flexner. This is the reason Wollstonecraft was unable "to follow a consistent train of thought, or to avoid digressions when they are largely irrelevant and in her habit of loose generalizations. She is incapable of the coherent organization of ideas or of avoiding repetition [...]" (164). What Flexner fails to consider is that Wollstonecraft was being deliberate in her style; she was determined not to write in linear order. In *Rights of Woman* Wollstonecraft presents a "rough sketch" of proposed rhetoric:

> and should I express my conviction with the energetic emotions that I feel whenever I think of the subject, the dictates of experience and reflection will be felt by some of my readers. Animated by this important object, I shall disdain to cull my phrases or polish my style;—I aim at being useful, and sincerity will render me unaffected; for, wishing rather to persuade by the force of my arguments, than dazzle by the elegance of my language, I shall not waste my time in rounding periods, or in fabricating the turgid bombast of artificial feelings, which, coming from the head, never reach the heart.—I shall be employed about things, not words!—and, anxious to render my sex more respectable members of society, I shall try to avoid that flowery diction which has slided from essays into novels, and from novels into familiar letters and conversation. (33–78; introd.)

In this introduction, Wollstonecraft warns the reader that her style of writing is going to be radically different from what was conventional. The energy of emotion will drive what she writes, and she will not polish it. Her thought will be spontaneous and honest without fear of social scrutiny. The rhetoric would approximate what has since come to be known as a stream of consciousness. It would become a prototype for organic writing that would be welcomed in the Romantic period. Her rejection of a linear progression in her rhetoric was a rejection of the order that was paramount to the Age of Reason, and it was a rejection of the masculine standard of the day.[6]

Flexner also criticizes Wollstonecraft for her portrayal of female socialites of her time: "She never really substantiates her basic assumption that all women, or even most women, are as she describes them: trivial, deceiving, pleasure-loving, and weak in character, morals, brain, and body" (164). This is an ungrounded accusation. In chapter 9 of *Rights of Woman* Wollstonecraft positively describes an ideal woman, the kind one would expect to find among the rustics and the middling classes. This woman suckled her babes, kept a "clean hearth" and clean husband and children, and tended fastidiously to every aspect of her household (232–31). Wollstonecraft did not condemn the entire aristocracy either. In chapter 5 she extolled such women as the Baroness de Staël, the Comtesse de Genlis, Hester Chapone and Catharine Macaulay. Flexner questions why Wollstonecraft did not mention the women of her acquaintance who did not fit the stereotypical mold of being shallow and materialistic. The women omitted were Mrs. Clare, Mrs. Burgh, Jane Arden and Fanny Blood (164). However, these names would have meant nothing to Wollstonecraft's readers. It is true that Wollstonecraft did generalize about women of the middle and upper classes, but her complaint was legitimate: As mentioned previously, the majority of women were expected to behave like coy little girls, spaniels or toys. The perception that women were created only to be man's object of desire is as old as the ages, and it was prevalent in Wollstonecraft's time and has not disappeared yet.

Wollstonecraft did view the majority of the women of the upper classes as hedonistic, manipulative and anti-intellectual—as Flexner surmises and questions—but with what Wollstonecraft witnessed when living with Mrs. Dawson in Bath, the playground for the eighteenth-century rich and famous; with what she observed through her association with Lady Kingsborough and being exposed to the upper crust of Irish society and travelling again to Bath; and with her acquaintances among the wealthy in London after she became famous—all experiences that Flexner recounts in her biography—how can one doubt that Wollstonecraft's generalizations are inaccurate and needed to be substantiated? Despite these indictments of *Rights of Woman*, Flexner concedes that "Wollstonecraft wrote a classic whose seminal influence on the social history of women has no equal" (165).

A good point that Flexner makes that is not noted in other biographies is how brave Wollstonecraft was to write *A Historical and Moral View of the Origins and Progress of the French Revolution and the Effect* while she was still living in France. The book conveys her disappointment with and criticism of the French Revolution. Several of her friends were incarcerated for much less and were even executed while she was in France.[7] Aware of the danger she was in, she warned Everina that, when writing letters to France, to never mention anything about politics (195).

Another unique contribution to Flexner's credit is that she references John Adams's response to Wollstonecraft's book on the French Revolution:

> This is a Lady of a masculine masterly understanding. Her Style is nervous and clear often elegant, though sometimes too verbose. With a little Experience in Public Affairs and the Reading and Reflection which would result from it, she would have produced a History without the Defects and Blemishes pointed out with too much Severity perhaps and too little gallantry in the Notes.[8]

Adams was not yet president; nevertheless, as Flexner puts it, his "estimate [...] was not unflattering to Mary," except that Flexner fails to relate whether Wollstonecraft was aware of what Adams wrote. The quote was published in a journal in 1923, according to Flexner. Here she might have done more research. Zoltán Haraszti records that Adams read *French Revolution* twice, in 1796 (prior to Godwin's *Memoir*) and 1812 (186–87). G. J. Barker-Benfield argues that Godwin's *Memoir*, which Adams also read, influenced the way he read her book and his response to it in a 12,000-word commentary (432–34). Barker-Benfield identifies the sexist language in Adams's response and such disparaging remarks that could have come only after reading *Memoirs*, such as: "this weak woman," "this mad woman" and "this foolish woman" (433). Still, these comments were not available to Wollstonecraft; they were written in the margins of Adams's copy of *French Revolution*. The book was placed in the Boston Public Library in 1893 (Cary 35). I found no evidence of letters that passed between Adams and Wollstonecraft, so Flexner's comment that Wollstonecraft was flattered by his attention must have been only theoretical.[9]

However, Flexner does try to correct earlier theoretical statements about Wollstonecraft's "sweetheart": In a letter to his wife, Joel Barlow describes Imlay as "the very sensible man [...] of Kentucky,"[10] But Flexner asserts that he was "neither sensible nor from Kentucky. Today we know a great deal more about Gilbert Imlay than Mary ever did" (181). Flexner tints her language with acrimony as she explains that the man "posed as a frontiersman, a useful role in Europe at the time," suggesting that he was both an opportunist and imposter. Flexner writes that "he maneuvered himself into an important position in the French scheme to attack the Spanish colonies of the Mississippi Valley and win them back for France" (181–82). His negotiations were not state sanctioned, and, as Flexner correctly deduces, his parleying could have embroiled the United States in a war with Spain. He was part of a "treasonable conspiracy" (182) is her conclusion. Unfortunately, Flexner did not have available, as we do now, Joseph Fant's dissertation on Imlay, although she was aware that he was working on it (298n23). Flexner's biography was published in 1972, and Fant's dissertation was defended in 1984. Neither did she have W. M. Verhoeven's *Gilbert Imlay: Citizen of the World* (2009), which sheds much more light on Imlay's schemes and business and political intrigues, which were extremely risky and volatile. Although a very clever man, most of Imlay's enterprises, like Mr. Wollstonecraft's, left him the poorer and Wollstonecraft the sadder.

Despite Flexner's hostility toward Imlay, her research was resourceful and is still valuable. She cites Emerson's and Rusk's scholarship, both performed independently at about the same time. She notes that most of their material came from the *Annual Report of the American Historical Association* (1908, vol. 1), the *American Historical Review* (vols. 1 and 3),[11] and books by Frederick Jackson Turner.[12] Flexner also interviewed a distant relative of Imlay, Admiral Miles Imlay, USCG, retired, in order to ascertain Imlay's service in the Continental Army. She also consulted the National Archives and land grants in the State Library in Richmond (insofar as Kentucky was once part of Virginia).

In all her comments about Imlay, Flexner is ever the defender of Wollstonecraft. She wonders how much if anything Wollstonecraft knew about the Louisiana scheme. According to a letter of April 22, 1793, from Brissot de Warville (a member of two French committees, Public Defense and Foreign Affairs) to Pierre Leburn, Minister of Foreign Affairs, Imlay was to leave in two weeks for a secret military operation in America, while Wollstonecraft's friend Joel Barlow wrote to his wife on April 19 that Wollstonecraft was leaving shortly, getting married and going to America with Imlay (183). How could Imlay carry a wife to America if he were preparing to engage in a war against the Spanish? Flexner gives this as one example of Imlay's deception (183).

Several biographers make it a point to quote Wollstonecraft, in a letter to William Roscoe, that she "might take a husband" while she was in Paris.[13] Flexner refers to the letter twice (175, 280) but, unlike the other biographers before and since, she does not believe that it explains the motivation that took Wollstonecraft to Paris. Instead she contends that Wollstonecraft was driven by political curiosity and hope to witness the birth of a new republic, one that would grant equality to all people. Once there, though, Wollstonecraft was met with disillusionment, not only because of the violence and anarchy of the Revolution but also because of a relationship with Imlay that she embraced with equal impulse, only to be grossly disappointed. Flexner expresses the opinion that Wollstonecraft should not have been surprised that coupling with Imlay was a bad idea. "From the outset there was doubt and friction between them," Flexner states (188). She quotes from a letter to Imlay about their moving in together for the first time:

> You can scarcely imagine with what pleasure I anticipate the day, when we are to begin almost to live together; and you would smile to hear how many plans of employment I have in my head, now that my heart has found peace in your bosom. Cherish me with that dignified tenderness, which I have only found in you; and your own dear girl will try to keep under a quickness of feeling, that has sometimes given you pain. But good-night! God bless you! Sterne says that is equal to a kiss—yet I would rather give you the kiss into the bargain, glowing with gratitude to Heaven, and affection for you. I like the word affection, because it signifies something habitual, and we are soon to meet, to try whether we have mind enough to keep our hearts warm.[14]

This passage is full of anxiety: Wollstonecraft will try to "keep under a quickness of feeling, that has sometimes given you pain." Although having "quickness of feeling" might be interpreted as being spontaneous and transparent, both positive qualities that were lauded by the Romantics in Wollstonecraft's day, according to the *Oxford English Dictionary (OED)*, "quickness" in regard to emotion carried negative connotations in the 1700s. One example given in the *OED* was from Richardson's *Clarissa*, "This quickeness upon me [...] is not to be borned" (1.15.105). Also helpful is the *OED*'s explanation of "keep under": "to hold in subjection or under control; to keep down," drawing from the Authorized Version of the biblical 1 Corinthians 9:27: "I keep under my body, and bring it into subjection" (1611).[15] Wollstonecraft's statement implies that there had already been words exchanged about her being too tender and affectionate, that she needed to be more "dignified" and exercise more self-control.

From the original letter, Flexner omits a sentence after "pain," without ellipses. It reads, "Yes, I will be *good*, that I may deserve to be happy; and whilst you love me, I cannot again fall into the miserable state which rendered life a burthen almost too heavy to be borne." There are two important points about this omission. First, Flexner claims that Wollstonecraft lost her faith over the Fuseli affair (176), but here we find Wollstonecraft's promise to be good, and if she is, she deserves to be happy. This philosophical axiom has been a part of her theology as conveyed in *Rights of Woman*, in which she says more than once that virtue will be rewarded (174; ch. 5).

Additionally, Wollstonecraft asks God to bless Imlay. She is thankful to "Heaven," which was a traditional way for High Church people to express gratitude to God. They did not say "Thank God" or "Thank the Lord," as did/do Evangelicals because they thought those expressions were too familiar and not reverent enough. Neither was the reference to "Heaven" (with a capital "H") a secular expression; Wollstonecraft thanks God for Imlay's love.

The second important point about the omission is that Wollstonecraft is placing a very heavy "burthen" on Imlay; it is a veiled threat that if he proves to be unfaithful to her, she will not be able to cope with the pain of life. She places her happiness and peace solely on him, and this is a responsibility he has never wanted. In today's lingo, she is "too needy." She must have sensed, even if she assumed herself married to him, that his love was temporary as she signifies with "whilst you love me." When she has to face the end of their relationship, she does make good her word with her double attempts to commit suicide.

Flexner is most likely accurate in her assessment of Imlay, that he "was not the man to find anything 'habitual' necessarily attractive" (189). Wollstonecraft made this an accusation in a letter: "I have found out that I have more mind than you, in one respect; because I can, without any violent effort of reason, find food for love in the same object, much longer than you can."[16] Here, Flexner offers another astute point although she does not explain why she thought it: "The insoluble conflict lay in the fact that the eternal lover would soon have bored Mary" (190). They had been together for only 15 months, and sporadically at that, before Wollstonecraft attempted suicide the first time. She let go of the relationship six months after that, so there may not have been enough time for Mary to get bored, but why Flexner thinks this is uncertain for, as she later argues, Wollstonecraft attempted to receive from Imlay the love and security that she was denied from her own father (192). Flexner draws parallels between the two men: Her father "was easily angered, restless, and dissatisfied with his occupation and place in society, who wanted wealth and position but lacked the capacity to work slowly and steadily for the realization of his ambitions" (192). Although Imlay did not have the same temper, and as far as we know, he never beat women, the rest of Flexner's description of him seems plausible. Flexner theorizes that Wollstonecraft was trying to "mold" Imlay into the man she needed, and that she "was still trying to resolve the failures of past relationships, of daughter with father, and wife (her mother) with husband" (192). Paradoxically, she must have been attracted to Imlay because she knew she could not change him, nor did she want to—except for his lack of constancy to her. His intrigue and unpredictability must have been appealing to a woman as unconventional as she was. She was so greatly enamored with the idea of sharing adventure with him by starting anew in America (Todd, *CL* 277). Wollstonecraft readily agreed to travel to Scandinavia on Imlay's behalf, undaunted by being a woman, travelling only with a maid and taking an infant with her. She was not only unafraid of adventure and the unknown, it energized her. She describes Imlay to Everina in these idealistic terms: "Having been brought up in the interior parts of America, he is a most natural, unaffected creature" (Todd, *CL* 249).

Flexner figures Imlay to have been the kind of man who detested routine and stasis. He was also extremely ambitious, and "wounded her[. ...] The insoluble conflict lay in the fact that the eternal lover would soon have bored Mary, yet a man who was active and ambitious wounded her each time he disengaged himself, while he became more and more irritated by her efforts to absorb him completely" (190). Flexner is probably right as well in her speculation that the great attraction was the similarity between Imlay and her father—such as their rootlessness and restlessness. Since she never had a healthy relationship with her father, which caused an emotional hole, she tried to fill it with Fuseli, then Imlay and finally Godwin (192).

They were not together long before Wollstonecraft was aware that Imlay was fickle with his love for her. A few months into the relationship, she writes, "I do not know why, but I have more confidence in your affection, when absent, than when present."[17] Already Wollstonecraft must have been trying to sort out what about Imlay was real versus fantasy/wishful. Once she was thoroughly convinced that the relationship was over, the man she regarded as her husband, the father of her child, who had had bodacious and unabashed affairs with other women while they were together—after all of that—she still held to a belief and understanding of him that was only fantasy, but which she regarded as real. The very last extant letter we have from her to him concludes with: "It is strange that, in spite of all you do, something like conviction forces me to believe, that you are not what you appear to be."[18]

The relationship had not been totally one-sided; neither was it only Wollstonecraft who desired domestic bliss. She responds to "a picture" that Imlay apparently shared with her of a happy couple surrounded by happy children in front of a fireside.[19] As Flexner puts it, Imlay "made promises and broke them, prevaricated, ran away, and often misled her; but he also reaffirmed his love for her on countless occasions, renewed his commitment, and declared that their lives were inextricably interrelated, and each time he did so, he revived her hopes and faith in him" (191).

Such revelations, not found in previous biographies, led most reviewers to be pleased with Flexner's work. Alice Green Fredman pronounces it the best "level of informed appreciation" for Wollstonecraft written to date, barring Wardle's (137), and that Tomalin's and Sunstein's, which followed after, made no improvements. Todd describes Flexner's biography as "smoothly readable" and was pleased with its "original scholarship," which corrected some of Wardle's and earlier biographers' errors, but she does not say what these errors were (*Annotated* xxi). Unlike Wardle, Flexner is critical of Wollstonecraft's behavior and contradicts specifically Godwin's depiction of the relationship between the sisters, according to Todd. She also comments that Flexner thinks Wollstonecraft was "tactless" in the dealings with her sisters (xxii).

Agreeing that Flexner's research was extensive and more accurate than Wardle's, Boos observes that the research was directed more on Wollstonecraft's family and associates (8). Where Wardle sympathizes with the burden Wollstonecraft had to bear in taking care of a family that would not accept responsibility for itself or each other, Flexner is more critical of Wollstonecraft's attitude toward the family, claims Boos (9). Flexner clarifies and corrects Wardle about the family legacy with the assertion that Wollstonecraft's father did steal his daughters' legacies (8). Boos feels it is obvious that Flexner admires Wollstonecraft's mother, whereas Flexner thinks that Wardle and Godwin were condescending and regarded her as "supine" (9). Throughout Flexner's evaluation of Wardle's work, Flexner stipulates when and where she believes Wardle is giving an opinion that he presents as fact. Despite many positive comments about Flexner's biography, Boos continues to regard Godwin's and Wardle's works as official versions, noting that unlike most biographers of any biographees, Flexner offers criticism on Wollstonecraft's work, but it does not compare to Wardle's insight which, to Boos, is "one of the best features of this book" ("Biographies" 9). Boos suggests that Wardle and Flexner be read together (9).

The reviewers had some issues with Flexner's views. Todd, for instance, observes that Flexner does not like Wollstonecraft's "rhetorical and diffuse polemical style" in *Rights of Woman*. Neither does Flexner like Wollstonecraft's bitter tone in the Imlay letters, but she is sympathetic to the Godwin–Wollstonecraft relationship (*Annotated* xxi–xxii). Fredman censures Flexner's criticism of *Rights of Woman* and *Maria*. She thinks that Flexner judges Wollstonecraft's work by her knowledge of later novels instead of realizing that the novel was a new development in the eighteenth century. To Fredman, Flexner should have given credit to Wollstonecraft for being innovative (139).

Nonetheless, Fredman considers Flexner's biography exceptional for its "synthesis of both psychological and social history" (137), and Todd concurs that Flexner focuses on Wollstonecraft's childhood rather than on philosophical movements of the period (*Annotated* xxi). Todd recognizes that Flexner uses "modern psychiatric evidence" to diagnose Wollstonecraft's "repressed anger," initially caused by an abusive father and exacerbated by every man she became entangled with. However, Todd rejects Flexner's psychological reading but does not explain why (xxi).

In Boos's words, Flexner complains that "Wollstonecraft's emphasis on duty, God, religion, and motherhood were ignored by later feminists" (9). Boos objects to this claim by arguing that the Victorians had already dealt with these subjects to the point that they distorted Wollstonecraft's life and works (9). As evidence, she suggests Millicent Garrett Fawcett's introduction to the 1891 edition of *Rights of Woman* (9). Besides, "some allowance must be made for cultural relativism" in that "many who were devout in 1790 might not be so if living today" (9). Her point is not clear here unless she is implying that later feminists would not be interested in these aspects of Wollstonecraft because they did not share the same value system. If this inference is accurate, her definition of "later feminists" is reductive and biased.

Flexner herself makes an interesting, accurate and peculiar statement about what the "later generations of feminists" thought about Wollstonecraft's extramarital relationships. Concerning Wollstonecraft's sexual engagement with Imlay and then Godwin outside the sanction of marriage, she noted that they "hailed" the affair as a stand that Wollstonecraft made that she had the right to live life on her own terms (192); but still other feminists, or maybe the same ones, criticized Wollstonecraft for wanting domesticity at the same time (192). Flexner does not list any specific feminists or cite any sources, but her regard of Wollstonecraft is one of psychological analysis and sympathy. Instead of seeing her as part of a political machine or considering her religious convictions, Flexner interprets Wollstonecraft's actions from a psychological perspective, that she was a broken individual who was incapable of embracing happiness, even if it would have come her way:

> Over and beyond any immediate causes for depression such as Fanny's absence, her family problems, and the life of Bath, there is already evident a deep-seated malaise, a chronic depression which made Mary Wollstonecraft unhappy in every situation in which she found herself during the greater portion of her life. (34)

Her need for relationships with Fuseli, Imlay and Godwin were born out of insecurity, desperation, incompleteness and pain; but no man could satisfy the lack that she felt.

Despite her inability to be happy or even to make her own happiness, Wollstonecraft left us an important legacy that, as Flexner argues, was invaluable in the 1970s and, one might argue, is still invaluable today:

> Mary Wollstonecraft had justified—and encumbered, in the opinion of the later reformers—the demand that women must be trained to use their minds to achieve their highest possible development by arguing that, because woman was a creature—the work of a divine creator—her right to self-development was also a religious and moral responsibility to herself and to society, that rights *and* responsibilities (to herself, her community, and to her husband and children as well) were indissolubly linked. (266)

Flexner is only partly correct though. Wollstonecraft insists that men need to be thinkers as well. Society will never improve if only one gender becomes rational. "What is the hardest thing in the world?" Ralph Waldo Emerson asked. The answer is "to think." He also warned, perhaps hopefully: "Beware when the great God lets loose a thinker on this planet." Emerson's own mother and aunt were greatly influenced by *Rights of Woman*.[20] Maybe the problem is not when there is just one thinker let loose on the planet, but that there must be other thinkers before thoughts can have effect.

Chapter 7

CLAIRE TOMALIN'S *THE LIFE AND DEATH OF MARY WOLLSTONECRAFT* (1974): WOLLSTONECRAFT WITH SPARKLE

As highlighted in the chapters in Flexner, second-wave feminists enthusiastically appropriated the works of women in the past, especially of Wollstonecraft, to support their causes during the turbulent, antiestablishment decade of the 1970s. Academe was beginning to reassess literature by women that previously had been stigmatized, marginalized and largely ignored. In 1985 Jane Tompkins challenged a traditionally patriarchal system in academe and in the publishing industry, one that dismissed women's writing and refused to include it in "the canon"; therefore, it was not printed in anthologies that were taught in colleges and universities. Tompkins analyzed the bias and the value system that was in place that negated nearly all literature not written by white, Anglo-Saxon, Protestant males. The 1990s would see the beginnings of a recovery movement when people such as Angela Leighton wrote *Victorian Woman Poets: Writing Against the Heart*, which reclaimed many female poets who had been excluded from anthologies. I published *Frances Trollope and the Novel of Social Change* in 2001 and *Silent Voices: Forgotten Novels by Victorian Women Writers* in 2003.[1]

In the 1970s and the decades that followed, the market called for republication of women writers and biographical information about them. The political demand sometimes outdistanced the attention to quality literature and rigorous writing and research. However, Claire Tomalin focused on facts, and instead of embellishing them with unsupported suppositions of Wollstonecraft's interiority to advance a political agenda, Tomalin was a more reliable detective with the nose of a historian, even if she studied English literature at Cambridge. After her work with Wollstonecraft, she would devote her life to journalism and biographies. As a journalist, she would have disciplined herself to stating facts that could be proved, and avoided assumptions that could not be proved, but in her biography, at times, she does not provide enough documentation. Still, she tries to form her assessments as an objective journalist. For example, she declares *Rights of Woman* "a book without any logical structure" (105). She does not evaluate it as a good or bad thing; it is what it is. She adds: "It is more in the nature of an extravaganza." Again, she does not comment on this aspect. "What it lacks in method," she suggests, "it makes up for in élan, and it is better to dip into than to read through at a sitting" (105). However, Alice Green Fredman, who wrote a severely critical review of Tomalin's book, attacks her treatment of *Rights of Woman* as being "thin and misconceived"—a "reductive reading" (144). As is the case for nearly all the Wollstonecraft biographies of the 1970s, their publishers were mainstream: Detre with Doubleday, Flexner with Penguin, Nixon with Dent and Tomalin with Harcourt. That is no excuse for shoddy scholarship, but at that time the kind of rigor that Fredman wants to see, especially regarding literary criticism, was not required for a general audience. A good question to ask is why the university presses were not publishing biographies on Wollstonecraft.[2] Given the political climate of the women's movement, mainstream publishers such as Harcourt knew the public was ready to be introduced to Wollstonecraft, and so it published Tomalin's biography.

Tomalin had an intuitive sense of what would interest a general audience, and she was an excellent researcher who found information that had never been published on Wollstonecraft before. As Ralph Wardle observes, she contributed new information about the Wollstonecraft family through searching parish records and the Public Record Office (147). She also studied surveys, historical archives throughout England and France, the Abinger microfilms, letters (published and unpublished), diaries, interviews, family papers, museum manuscripts and many books with titles that seemingly have nothing to do with Wollstonecraft.

Tomalin became a literary biographer extraordinaire. Following her biography on Wollstonecraft, she wrote *Shelley and His World* (1992) and, in 1995, *Mrs. Jordan's Profession: The Actress and the Prince*. In 2007 she published an excellent biography on Jane Austen, as well as biographies on Samuel Pepys and Thomas Hardy. In her 2011 *Charles Dickens: A Life*, she found some things to say about Dickens that had not been written before, and if that was not enough, the next year she focused on the relationship between Nelly Ternan and Charles Dickens, which was also when she was publishing *Katherine Mansfield: A Secret Life*. In 2000 Tomalin wrote about her own life in *Several Strangers: Writing from Three Decades*, in which she included many of the reviews that she had written for the *New Statesman* and *Sunday Times*. Her interest in exceptional men and women from the sixteenth through the twentieth centuries and her courage and curiosity have given her a breadth and depth as well as an objectivity that have made her work more trustworthy than some of the other biographies on Wollstonecraft.

Into the bargain, much of her prose reads like a novel. For example, other biographers simply stipulated that the Wollstonecrafts made their money in Spitalfields; however, Tomalin's discussion opens with a setting:

> At the ragged eastern edge of the City of London is a district known as Spitalfields. Today it is very sparsely peopled; wave after wave of immigrants has come and gone, leaving a few sad Indian faces on the streets and a floating population of tramps who build bonfires at the deserted corners on winter Sundays. The buildings are a mixed lot also: Victorian breweries and factories tower over tiny almshouses, whole streets are near derelict and the Georgian church has an even more theatrical and misplaced air than most of its fellows. Such eighteenth-century terraces as still stand are decayed and covered in grime; they have not housed families for years. (1)

This is a perfect illustration of not only Tomalin's style and ability to embellish facts with facts, but it shows how her details enable the reader immediacy and realism, which ensures a more ready access to Wollstonecraft, the people in her life and the time in which she lived.

The predominant immigrants in Spitalfields in the 1960s and 1970s were Bangladeshi who worked in the textile industry that characterized Spitalfields. The Irish—which may have included the Wollstonecrafts—settled there first and began the silk-weaving business, and then were joined, as Tomalin explains, by the Huguenots, who fled from France in the 1680s because they were banished by King Louis XIV in the 1680s. They brought their textile skills with them (1). In between Wollstonecraft's time and Tomalin's, the area lost its edge in industry when an 1860 treaty with France allowed cheaper importation of French silks. A quarter called "the rookery" declined into a dangerous slum, the site of the mutilation of Mary Kelly by Jack the Ripper and the fictional stomping ground for Bill Sikes and Fagin. In the 1960s Spitalfields was undergoing urban regeneration and gentrification, and a move was under way to preserve the historic Georgian architecture.

When Tomalin describes Wollstonecraft's residence in Newington Green, Richard Price becomes a real person who greatly influenced Wollstonecraft in ways not mentioned in any of the other biographies, as demonstrated in this excerpt:

> As a neighbor, he was kind and particularly responsive to the young, the vulnerable, and those in difficulties. He always had time for children and

there were many stories current concerning his humanity to animals that must have appealed to Mary: he was said to free netted birds when he found them on his long country walks, and set upturned beetles carefully back on their legs. This was exactly the sort of quixotic goodness she liked, and though as an Anglican she was not officially one of his flock, it made no difference to his interest in her or her response to him. (31–32)

From this information, one can clearly see Price's influence on Wollstonecraft's creation of Mrs. Mason in *Original Stories*, who attempts to teach two little girls what is meant by "goodness." "It is, first, to avoid hurting any thing; and then, to contrive to give as much pleasure as you can," she says (4–5). After the lesson, Mrs. Mason and the little girls are delighted by two singing larks and then, to their horror, they see an "idle boy" shoot them with a gun. They find the birds, and Mrs. Mason has to kill the male with her foot, to put him out of his misery. His pain is graphic: "Its little eyes seemed starting out of their sockets, it was in such exquisite pain." The female has a broken wing, and the girls will nurse it back to health. They will also have to take care of her nest of chicks. Mrs. Mason praises them for "doing good" in imitation of God. Man "feels disinterested love; every part of the creation affords an exercise for virtue, and virtue is ever the truest source of pleasure" (9).

Tomalin's narrative regarding Price also enriches the reader's understanding of Wollstonecraft's moral system. Because of Price's unconditional love, which he practiced and preached, Wollstonecraft perhaps became less dogmatic about Anglican doctrines and integrated some of the Unitarian philosophy and tenets from other Dissenting religions into her own worldview.[3] Todd would probably not agree with me on this, in that she has already argued that Tomalin's treatment of Price and Johnson's circle is very "poor" in light of the importance they played in Wollstonecraft's life (*Annotated* xxii–xxiii).

When Tomalin addresses Wollstonecraft's temperament, it is within a context. Wollstonecraft is like a character in a novel. However, there is enough evidence subtly provided to assure us that the depiction is not just a figment of Tomalin's imagination. Janet Todd praises Tomalin's "urbanity of style," which she thinks outdistances Flexner's and Sunstein's, and at the same time, evidences effective research except for a few areas (*Annotated* xxii–xxiii). Here is an example of what Todd must have meant by "urbanity of style"—about Wollstonecraft when she lived in Newington Green:

> A network of men and women with ideas and ambitions a little outside the common run clustered about Price; Mary found herself made welcome on the Green by many Dissenting households. They included the large family of the banker Thomas Rogers, whose son Samuel was a poet. (32)

Flexner also mentions Thomas Rogers, but not his son. Their presence shows Tomalin's and Flexner's diligence in finding specific people at the Green who may have contributed to the construction of Wollstonecraft's theology as well as her interest in pursuing writing as a living. Flexner provides a little more description of Thomas that makes him more significant to Wollstonecraft. He had "benevolent sympathies," but Flexner does not explain to whom and in what way. It could mean that he helped her father through his myriad crises with debt. Also, he was a "keen student of theology, literature, and philosophy" (48). For a woman who had felt so rejected while growing up, being welcomed into a community of intellectuals who were also devout Christians surely began a healing process. Some of the relationships forged at the Green would sustain her later, after she quit being a governess and assumed responsibility for the support of her sisters and Fanny Blood. The acceptance she felt in this community among Dissenters who had the courage to follow the dictates of their consciences and hearts, and with religious convictions that caused them also to be deprived of many rights they would have enjoyed had they been Anglicans, must have given Wollstonecraft the courage to pursue her own convictions, including writing a book on the rights of women.

Although other biographies do discuss Wollstonecraft's acquaintance with Richard Price and acknowledge Mrs. Burgh's financial assistance to her, especially in the setting up of a school, Tomalin identifies her as a well-learned woman. She and her husband helped Wollstonecraft find employment for George Blood in the Green. Tomalin acknowledges another strong woman of high intellect and the widow of a schoolmaster, and that is Mrs. Cockburn, who is not mentioned in the other biographies (32). So, Wollstonecraft was exposed to godly women who were very different from the aristocratic and vain women she criticized in *Rights of Woman*. From the women of the Green, Wollstonecraft formulated her ideal woman: virtuous, well educated and capable of having effect in the public area.

Still, more information about Mrs. Burgh would have been useful here. All Tomalin says is that she was "energetic and cultivated" (32). Emily Sunstein tells us that she was Sarah, and not just the "widow of James Burgh" (95), an important feminist distinction. Sunstein gives Mrs. Burgh this credit: "Without Mrs. Burgh's connections it is unlikely that Mary could have become what she did, no matter what her talents and motivation. Call it luck, that sometime reward for spirit, drive, and readiness, which attracted and attached Mrs. Burgh to Wollstonecraft like a veritable fairy godmother" (95). Tomalin does, however, make a similar point, although it is not as much in the foreground. These people in Newington Green formed a tight network of helping each other. Tomalin might have provided more detail about them because they were so important to Wollstonecraft, a deficiency that is mentioned in the review written by Fredman Green (138).

Tomalin's description of George Blood as a pet is a credible and clarifying description of the relationship Wollstonecraft had with him. Otherwise, with a few of the other biographical accounts, it is difficult to understand why Wollstonecraft took it upon herself, not only to support her own family and other women, but also to take charge of a full-grown man who had privilege and opportunity due to his sex, but denied to Wollstonecraft.

Details are what make a person and setting come to life for a reader, and Tomalin is one of the best biographers to do this, as demonstrated in this excerpt:

> There was none of the usual village domination of squire or parson at Newington, but a more equal sort of society in which Mary, her sisters and Fanny could take their place with some dignity. Still, in any village day-to-day life is largely a matter of petty interests, quiet friendships, small irritations; if it is to be enjoyable there must be the temperament and the leisure to relish small change and a jog-trot pace. But Mary's temperament was geared to drama, violent emotion and struggle: when she was angry with Mrs Cockburn it was (temporarily) a boiling hatred; when she defended George from attack it was without reservations. She had no nuance or irony; and then she was always busy, too busy to pause and smile. (32)

Although documentation to support this depiction would add to its credibility, Tomalin has taken facts from previous biographies, such as those about Wollstonecraft's temperament, and made her a knowable character in realistic fictive world.

Ralph Wardle poses an objection to the license Tomalin took in describing Wollstonecraft. In his review of her book in *The Wordsworth Circle*, he quotes Tomalin: "It was soon observed that whereas Bess was nice-looking and polite, her elder sister was sharp in manner and often angry in appearance: her eyes bulged, the corners of her mouth turned down."[4] Although J. Chapman's masculine portrait of Wollstonecraft, which is reproduced on Tomalin's book cover, does present Wollstonecraft with bulging eyes and turned down mouth, Wardle finds such details inconsistent with Opie's portraits (147).[5] The description supports Tomalin's inclination to portray Wollstonecraft as bossy, domineering, judgmental, contemptuous and quickly angered. Wardle argues that this is an unfair and inaccurate understanding of Wollstonecraft's personality and behavior, with the only support being lines pulled out of context from letters (147–48).

Tomalin's biography does make some politically feminist comments about details in Wollstonecraft's life, and her selection of information is obviously feminist, but not militantly feminist. For example, when Wollstonecraft conveys in a letter that she wants to remain in France with her daughter rather than join Imlay in England,[6] Tomalin interprets her as an independent woman who was determined to support herself and her child. The rationale that Wollstonecraft gives in the letter is, however, that she is afraid that in England Fanny will be ostracized as a natural child.

This is how Tomalin relates Imlay's recruitment of Wollstonecraft to take care of business for him in Scandinavia:

> There is an almost sublime effrontery about sending off a discarded mistress, newly recovered from a suicide attempt and accompanied by a small baby, on a difficult journey into unknown territory, to recoup your financial disasters for you and leave you free to enjoy the company of her rival without reproach: in his own way, Imlay was a man of resource. (179)

Despite Tomalin's apparent perspectives that are politically feminist, notably she organized her biography primarily around the men in Wollstonecraft's life. Here are some of the titles of her chapters: "Joseph Johnson and St Paul's Churchyard," "Fuseli," "Imlay" and "Godwin." An appreciable exception is the chapter on Bess's marriage, titled "Eliza" instead of "Bishop." Aside from that chapter, there is very little information about the women in Wollstonecraft's life; there are no chapters titled "Elizabeth" for Wollstonecraft's mother or "Everina," for her other sister or "Fanny" for either Fanny Blood or Fanny Imlay. Were Wollstonecraft's life and death, according to Tomalin, defined by the men she knew?

Nonetheless, the elegy Tomalin offers is very astute and worth repeating here:

> Her death coincided with the falling-off of many things she had believed in. She had embodied the spirit of the age faithfully, its political optimism, its faith in willpower, self-improvement, education. She had hoped that courage and good intentions might triumph over dead convention, and that the whole structure of society might be reformed and renewed by philosophers. She had imagined generously that what she wanted for herself might be welcomed by all her own sex and at least understood by the other. She had hated prudence, bigotry and cant. Had she lived on [...]. (226–27)

And then Tomalin reminds us what was yet to come in the Victorian period that would have been very painful for Wollstonecraft, so that Tomalin's last word is: "It may have been almost as well" that she died when she did (227). She may have been right, but if Wollstonecraft could have continued to write and advocate for women's equality, perhaps she could have helped accelerate change for women. At the end of her life, to Victorians she would have been a respectable, married woman, and she might have had a larger audience for her work. If the history of her life had not been made public by her husband, which Godwin most likely would not have written if she had not died when she did, her works would have had greater, and sooner, effect.

Tomalin does not end her book with Wollstonecraft's death. Her last chapter is titled "Aftermath and Debate" (followed by an epilogue). In this chapter she provides a very brief and incomplete history of the reception of Godwin's *Memoirs*, with her own comments about its "omissions, inaccuracies and misrepresentations" (231). This is followed by an also-brief address of the betrayals of friends after *Memoirs* became public, such as Amelia Alderson, who married John Opie. Tomalin records that in 1799 Godwin told Holcroft that John Opie was no longer his friend (245). John Opie was a divorced man when Amelia Alderson married him. After that she wrote several novels, beginning with *Father and Daughter* (1800), which attempted to establish her own respectability and discredit Wollstonecraft (235).

Then there was the Kingsborough scandal that was blamed on Wollstonecraft because the youngest daughter, Mary, had been one of her charges. Mary eloped with her illegitimate half-brother. Her brother Robert killed him. Mary bore a child, but it was taken from her. This all came out at the time of *Memoirs*, and an Irish bishop preached a sermon that placed the responsibility for the Kingsborough tragedies on Voltaire and Wollstonecraft (237–38).

Tomalin follows this by another brief overview of literary works that continued to fight Wollstonecraft's causes, such as Mary Hays's attempt to write the sequel to *Rights of Woman*, which Wollstonecraft had intended to produce. Hays's book was *Appeal to the Men of Great Britain in Behalf of the Women*, but Tomalin believes that Hays's defiance of social mores of sexual behavior did more damage to Wollstonecraft's reputation (239–42). A number of women took up the mission to promote better education for females—such as Maria Edgeworth, with her *Practical Education* (1798; 242–44), and Hannah More with her *System of Female Education* (1799; 244–45). Additional works promoted similar feminist arguments for women's rights, including Elizabeth Hamilton's *The Modern Philosophers* (1800; 245), Priscilla Wakefield's *Reflections on the Present Condition of the Female Sex, with Suggestions for its Improvements* (1798; 246), Jane West's *Letters to a Young Man* (1801; 246–47) and Fanny Burney's *The Wanderer, or Female Difficulties* (1813; 248–50). These, in turn, says Tomalin, influenced arguments for the equality of women in William Lecky's *History of Morals*

(1869) and John Stuart Mill's *On the Subjection of Women* (1846). Tomalin also demonstrates Wollstonecraft's influence in the creation of strong women who appear in William Thackeray's *Vanity Fair* (1847), Elizabeth Gaskell's *Ruth* (1853), Charlotte Brontë's *Shirley* (1849), Charles Dickens's *David Copperfield* (1850) and George Eliot's novels (252–53). Tomalin is the first biography to include a discussion of Wollstonecraft's impact, effect and legacy.

It is a contribution that Fredman—in her very critical review of Tomalin—acknowledges, but she also faults this biography for being "little more than a hurried survey" (140) and, worse, it reflects "the peculiar taint" that Fredman finds permeating Tomalin's work on Wollstonecraft. She is more specific; Tomalin's tone is "scornful and hostile" toward Wollstonecraft (140), and in her discussion of the Imlay affair she produces "undercurrents of disapprobation which find their expression in such descriptions as this of Mary's long suppressed sexuality" (143). To support this assessment, Fredman quotes from Tomalin: "She knew that depravity could exist in women, but found it hard to believe that it might be enjoyable, or that she might be capable of anything like it herself; and it certainly never occurred to her that what she felt for Gilbert was the simplest of physical yearnings" (149). To Fredman, Wollstonecraft must not have been sexually emancipated enough and therefore must have been a disappointing role model for what many women demanded in 1976—namely, not only equality in the public arena, but also in the sexual arena, so that they could have as much sexual freedom as they thought men practiced.

Tomalin's understanding of Wollstonecraft's sexual attraction is apparent in this passage:

> If you believe, as she did, that love derives first of all from a mental and spiritual sympathy, it becomes very difficult to acknowledge to yourself that you have been wrong in your estimate of your partner. Mary could not say to herself that although Gilbert was physically attractive and delightful to her, he was not really very clever, congenial or interesting once the excitement of hearing his stock of ideas and experiences was complete. He had to be idealized into a worthy recipient for her love. (149)

When she continues her analysis as to what attracted these two strong personalities, she is very insightful in suggesting that Imlay was equally excited—even sexually excited—about the "triumph about transforming a clever and strong-willed woman who did not normally suffer fools gladly into a creature eager, dependent and trembling" (149–50). These excerpts demonstrate that Tomalin attempts to see the world through Wollstonecraft's eyes and still tries to be objective enough to analyze why she had this perspective. But there are times when Tomalin can be abrupt and judgmental without explanation—for example when she writes that Bishop lent money to Wollstonecraft to give to the Bloods because he thought she was a "reliable and obliging woman, a decision that probably wrecked his chances of happiness in life for good" (23). Later, Tomalin says that Wollstonecraft, "as a schoolmistress [...] was a failure" (33). Perhaps this is the journalist in her to be too succinct.

To the contrary, Fredman censures Tomalin's "stance" as "complete with gratuitous digressions and interpolations," which "constantly intrudes extrabiographical matter into the account and unavoidably calls into question even those passages of straight-forward discussion and sound judgment which happen to circumvent the author's partiality" (140). Tomalin's inclusion of research leaves much to be desired, complains Fredman, and "if the biographer has dismissed a priori, as it were, serious consideration of alternative approaches to her subject matter, then she will not find it useful to study the several sides of an issue before coming to a conclusion" (140). Tomalin does include a list of sources and even claims that every entry in her bibliography "illuminated" her knowledge of Wollstonecraft, but as Fredman points out, there's "little correlation" between these entries and her narrative (140). Albert Goodwin's review of Tomalin also notices "several inaccuracies," but does not say what they are, but like Fredman, criticizes Tomalin for "total absence of detailed sources" (110).

To Fredman, more troubling than the poor documentation, "Tomalin's tendency is to ignore, or reduce to its most superficial aspect, the contextual dimension for situating and understanding Mary Wollstonecraft's thought" (140). When Tomalin does refer to Wollstonecraft's letters, especially the Arden correspondence, she "misreads the implications [...] as well as their cultural context" (141–42). Instead of reliable research, credible use of it and documented apparatus, Tomalin furnishes "surface sparkle" (142).

An example that Fredman provides is one that has raised a number of scholarly eyebrows; it is a statement that, if true, has significant consequences in how we are to understand Wollstonecraft's conduct with the Bishop marriage. Fredman quotes Tomalin as having written that Bess married Bishop in October 1782, with this description: "Within a month pretty ladylike [Bess] with her beautiful brown eyes and Chelsea boarding school manners was pregnant."[7] But, according to Eleanor Louise Nicholes (38), Flexner, George and Wardle, within weeks of the 1782 wedding, Bess had her child (142), implying that Bess married Bishop because she was pregnant. Fredman is inclined to disbelieve Tomalin because of Tomalin's many "deviates" and because Fredman does not account for the differences between her timeline and those of two recent predecessors. "It is this sort of scholarly irresponsibility," Fredman rails, "coupled with Tomalin's frequently denigrating comments about her subject, that damages her reliability as a biographer" (142).

Todd argues that the dating of Bess's pregnancy factors into the biographers' attitudes in recounting Wollstonecraft's "rescue." Flexner's date implies that the Bishops had a "have to marry marriage," but Tomalin's suggests that Bess chose to marry (*Annotated* xxii). Tomalin is not very supportive of a Wollstonecraft "rescue" and depicts a dubious Bess, who was not convinced that leaving her husband and child was the right thing to do. Bitter at her sister's interference, Bess then would refuse to let Fanny Imlay come to her after Wollstonecraft's death (Todd xxii).

Fredman offers another example of Tomalin's failure to follow through with critical biographical information. Tomalin barely mentions the Dissenters of Newington Green and Johnson's circle. The one group prepared Wollstonecraft for the other, claims Fredman, and both catapulted Wollstonecraft's personal and intellectual growths. Flexner supplies two chapters to this experience within a cultural context (138).

Fredman grants that Tomalin offers more literary analysis of Wollstonecraft's work than does Flexner (139). But Fredman is less than impressed with Tomalin's critical eye: "Given the nature of Tomalin's bias and her disinclination to penetrate Mary's work, it is no surprise that her four-page selective précis of *A Vindication of the Rights of Woman* is thin and misconceived. It is a shame, however, that Mary's greatest work should receive such perfunctory and superficial treatment" (144). An example is Tomalin's abrupt comment, which lacks development and support: Wollstonecraft's "book remains remarkable both in its scope and tone."[8] This is an irreconcilable conclusion to her preceding complaints that *Vindication* fails to have a "logical structure," that it is "an extravaganza," that instead of method it has "élan," and in Fredman's paraphrase of Tomalin, "the best way to absorb it is by dipping into it rather than by sustained reading" (144). Indeed, Fredman summarizes all of Flexner's "hurried comments" about Wollstonecraft's work and condemns them as full of misunderstanding, shallowness and inaccuracies. The only credit Fredman gives Tomalin is that she recognizes Wollstonecraft's innovation in *Wrongs of Women* in addressing the problems of women of the working class, but then Tomalin also reduces the novel to an autobiography (144).

Whatever her reasons for accusing Tomalin of hostility toward Wollstonecraft, Fredman emphasizes that it is a serious charge: "Such behavior in a biographer can only be counterproductive: it calls attention to itself; it distracts the reader into speculating on the reasons for its being, even on the rationale for writing a biography about a figure and subject which appear so disconcertingly antipathetic to the biographer" (140).

These are Wardle's last comments in his review of Flexner's biography: "Mary had her share of failings: years of insecurity and frustration had left her high-strung and irritable. But she was blessed with a warm heart and a courageous spirit; she was, beyond question, a truly gallant woman actuated by generous motives, and she deserves more tolerant treatment than Miss Tomalin has accorded her" (150).

Todd acknowledges that Tomalin did some good research, albeit unevenly. In discussing Wollstonecraft in Ireland and her experiences with the "feminist movement" during the Revolution, Todd describes Tomalin's work as "illuminating," and, as of 1974, of all of the biographies, Tomalin's is the "wittiest and most fluent" (xxiii). She does not identify hostility in Tomalin, but she herself expresses plenty of it when writing her own biography of Wollstonecraft.

Fredman, Godwin and Wardle all make the following observation, and it is a fair and serious criticism: Although Tomalin provides a research apparatus, very little of it correlates with her claims. Fredman, an English professor at Columbia, disparages Tomalin: "The level of scholarship permitted by editors or publishers [...] is astonishingly casual and slipshod, its practitioner remarkably unaware of basic procedures" (148). As if chastising her students, Fredman complains that Tomalin and Sunstein do not follow any rules for documentation, and the result is "a veritable mare's nest of totally useless, since incomplete, citations. There is no excuse for such amateurism" (149). Goodwin voices a similar lament: The "total absence of detailed sources [...] makes her researches inaccessible to other students" (110). Although Wardle comments that "Miss Tomalin's" bibliography and notes are praiseworthy and that she "approached her task conscientiously," she supplied a "surprising disregard for the exact detail" (147), did not support her claims, and when she did, she pulled information out of context (148). Fredman likewise accuses Tomalin of misreading "the implications of the letters as well as their cultural contexts" (141). Fredman's final verdict is that Tomalin substituted "surface sparkle for hard research" (142).

Albert Goodwin wrote a review on Tomalin in a 1975 issue of *Literature and History* that was more a diatribe against Wollstonecraft than it was about the biography. For example, he endorses Fuseli's quip that she was "the assertrix of female rights."[9] His introduction states: "Even the later leaders of the feminist movement were often too embarrassed by her efforts to establish ménages à trois with the lovers who had discarded her to recognize her services as an innovator" (108). He does not identify who were the "later leaders" of which "feminist movement." Neither does he provide a source that documents this supposed embarrassment, which is ironic because he criticizes Tomalin for not documenting her sources (110). It is also ironic because many in the second-wave woman's movement would claim Wollstonecraft as an early advocate for free love and would tout her two proposals of *ménages à trois* (first to Fuseli and second to Imlay) to be very progressive, open-minded, antiestablishment and sexually liberating.[10] They "adopted Wollstonecraft as foremother and sometime heroine" (Kaplan, "Reception" 253). She was their "icon" and "origin and avatar of western feminism," because of her fight for women's rights, but also her "sexual difference" (247). In her 1975 introduction to *Rights of Woman*, Miriam Brody asserts that Wollstonecraft's name [...] became virtually synonymous with free love and Jacobinism" (lx). But John C. Hampsey rejects this claim, stating that Wollstonecraft was "against the kind of free love that Oothoon expresses in [Blake's] *Visions*. With free love, Wollstonecraft believed, women would only end up pregnant and abandoned—"I cannot discover why [...] females should always be degraded by being made subservient to love or lust."[11] By 1983, Barbara Taylor was calling Wollstonecraft "an irritating little saint" (98).

Of all the reviewers of Tomalin's biography, only Goodwin has something positive to say. He thinks she succeeds in presenting Wollstonecraft within her contemporary setting of the eighteenth century (110), but he does not support this claim. In fact, immediately after the compliment, he decries her lack of research and documentation. But any concession about Tomalin's being culturally true to Wollstonecraft is disavowed by Fredman, who identifies the major deficiency of Tomalin's work as "the kind of scholarly editing and informed introduction which would situate her properly in *her* times for an intelligent reading in *our* times" (135).

Preceding his review, Goodwin makes this strange comment about Mary Hays, Wollstonecraft's "contemporary female disciple and continuator": She

> besmirched not only her own but her friend's reputation still further by her unseemly and unsuccessful pursuit of acquaintances like the Cambridge radical, William Frend and later the young poet, Charles Lloyd. Feminism of that kind could be and was easily equated with the desperation which unattractive women were then supposed to undergo in their search for husbands or lovers. (109)

Goodwin's theory clearly bears his prejudice against feminists as well as a popular stereotypical notion that all feminists were physically undesirable women who preyed on men, especially young ones.

Before attacking Tomalin, Goodwin concludes his invective of Wollstonecraft with: "Though she was a good daughter, a fond sister, a passionate lover and a devoted and tender mother—these domestic and family virtues did not compensate for her prima donna disposition, her blithe immodesty or her pathetic attempts at suicide" (109).

Giving Wollstonecraft "sparkle" instead of a more accurate rendition is not always a negative thing, however. After all, Richard Polwhele, one of Wollstonecraft's severest detractors, criticizes intelligent women for their "sparkle." He writes, "Yet alas! The crimsoning blush of modesty, will be always more attractive than the sparkle of confident intelligence."[12] There is plenty of sparkle in Tomalin's biography that is appropriate and well deserved.

Chapter 8

EMILY SUNSTEIN'S
A DIFFERENT FACE: THE LIFE OF MARY WOLLSTONECRAFT (1975): NOT-SO-LIBERATED WOMAN

For her biography's title Emily Sunstein borrows from "Mary" (1801–3), a poem written by William Blake,[1] which she also uses to introduce chapter 1. The first stanza of Blake's poem clearly alludes to the perception that many had of Wollstonecraft after they read Godwin's *Memoirs*. The second stanza contains the phrase in Sunstein's title:

> Some said she was proud, some call'd her a whore,
> And some, when she passed by, shut to the door;
> A damp cold came o'er her, her blushes all fled,
> Her lilies & Roses are blighted & Shed.
>
> "O why was I born with a different Face?
> Why was I not born like this Envious Race?
> Why did Heaven adorn me with bountiful hand,
> And then set me down in an envious Land?" (17–24)

Published in 1975, Sunstein's biography is driven by this poem's representation of how some people viewed Wollstonecraft as "whore" and "different." Sunstein reintroduces Wollstonecraft as the nearly perfect icon for the women's liberation movement of the 1970s, a woman who was sexually free of social restraints and who was unconventional and walking to the beat of her own drum.

Britain and the United States were greatly impacted by the antiestablishment decade of the 1960s, with its revolt against social conventions and institutions. *Rhinestone Cowboy* and *Poetry Man*, *Boogie on Reggae Woman* and *Lady Marmalade*, *You're No Good* and *Mandy* were some of the billboard hits of 1975; the titles themselves, their subject matter, their unique rhythms all testified that the

West had finally realized its diversity, and a "love-in" generation celebrated it. In 1971 Canada made multiculturalism its official national policy, followed by Australia. In the United States in the 1970s the New Left adopted the term "political correctness," Edward W. Saïd published *Orientalism* in 1978, and the world was ready to lionize the woman from the eighteenth century who dared to be different. Sunstein prioritizes this aspect of Wollstonecraft.

Before addressing the political bundling implied by the word "whore" in Blake's poem and then reappearing in Sunstein's book, please let me say that her biography is eminently readable and engaging, but its scholarship lacks documentation for many of the claims. It was published by Harper & Row and not a university press, so it was not written for a scholarly audience even though it attempts to speak with absolute authority. Many of the books published in the 1970s and earlier, whether academic or not, did not provide scholarly apparatus. Writers and scholars must have felt they had the freedom and authority to make statements without evidence or support to back them up, and that they could express their opinions as intellectual experts and ultimate authority simply based on their PhD or other credentials at a time when few attained higher degrees and when scholars were an elite minority. As a result, many of the early biographies and books on literary criticism are rife with unsubstantiated deductions, sweeping generalizations, evaluations and conclusions without documentation. Access to material was also an issue, so instead of being able to read original sources, many biographers repeated the mistakes of the earlier biographers.

Since the 1990s, literary criticism and theory have become demanding and unforgiving disciplines. Without convincing argumentation and support, a statement is only an opinion and has very little credibility. Sunstein's biography does contribute to our knowledge of Wollstonecraft, but it must be read with a critical eye.

Sunstein did not have an advanced degree, but she was considered an independent scholar. She married a stockbroker in 1943, which thrust her into high society in Philadelphia (Baltzell 38–39). While married, she earned a bachelor's in art history in 1944 from Vassar. That she did not quit her dream just because she was married demonstrates how remarkable she was. That she earned a college degree in 1944 and one at such a prestigious school is quite an accomplishment for anyone, but especially for a woman at that time. An obviously strong, independent woman, she became the first woman to chair the Philadelphia chapter of the American Jewish Committee (Fox n.p.).

Regardless of Sunstein's credentials, Janet Todd also detects the lack of research and scholarship in her biography and states that it falls short of Flexner's and Tomalin's biographies (*Annotated* xxiii). In 1989, when Sunstein wrote her next biography, *Mary Shelley: Romance and Reality*, she did a lot better on this score, so much so that she won the prestigious Modern Language Association Prize for Independent Scholars. Her Shelley book is widely quoted, which is no wonder when such a statement as this introduces the text: "It is one of biographical history's more remarkable miscarriages of justice that Mary Shelley, a legend in her own time, came to be misunderstood, or belittled, or maligned in specious comparison to Shelley. Her life has been collapsed into his" (6).

Sunstein is also widely cited for one item that she contributed to the Wollstonecraft discourse. She is the first to theorize that Wollstonecraft's brother, Henry, was committed to a madhouse, and she inferred that this is why he is rarely mentioned in any letters or biographies (36–38). One logical support is Sunstein's deduction that the reason the Wollstonecrafts moved to Hoxton in the first place was because it had three insane asylums. In the eighteenth century, "'Hoxton' was synonymous with lunacy" (35). Lyndall Gordon notes that Godwin states in *Memoirs* that one of her brothers had died before Wollstonecraft's death, and then Gordon repeats Sunstein's theory in a lemma.[2] John Hostettler, in his 2012 work, apparently does not accept this theory because he claims that Wollstonecraft had only five siblings and not six (141). The fact is that there were seven children born to Edward and Elizabeth Wollstonecraft (Ned, Mary, Henry, Bess, Everina, James and Charles), but what happened to Henry remains a mystery. Sunstein's theory is plausible, but it is theory and not fact; it is speculation without supportive evidence.

Still, she is to be commended for her investigation of this missing brother, and as Todd emphasizes, even if Sunstein lacks in research and contexts, she is very sympathetic and "does not seek to avoid the raw pain of Wollstonecraft's life," unlike Flexner, who treats it with too much irony. Sunstein portrays Wollstonecraft as a "dignified woman, worthy of respect" (*Annotated* xxiii).

The first page of Sunstein's first chapter establishes that Wollstonecraft was born at a time when women were considered "inferior morally and intellectually, and into a class whose ideal women were the sheltered, submissive, lifelong wards of fathers or husbands—decorative, domestically useful *sex objects*" (4; emphasis added). "Sex object" was a contentious subject in the mid-1970s. An interviewer asked Miss America 1974, Rebecca Ann King, how she felt about being a "sex object." She replied that she did not understand the term, but that she was "very proud of being a woman" and did not feel "exploited." If she had to appear in a swimsuit in front of millions of ogling viewers in order to win a scholarship, she did not see anything wrong with it (Riverol 91). In 1972 "Ms." was born. Comparable to "Mr." in that it does not designate marital status (unlike Miss or Mrs.), "Ms." became the title of an overtly feminist magazine. The first issue sold its 250,000 copies in eight days (Farber 69). Kate Millett published *Sexual Politics* in 1970; and Germaine Greer, *The*

Female Eunuch in 1971, both denouncing patriarchy and capitalism for treating women only as sex objects. And then in 1975, drawing from Freudian and Lacanian psychoanalysis, Laura Mulvey wrote her seminal essay "Visual Pleasure and Narrative Cinema," introducing the "male gaze" and voyeurism into our vocabulary and critical processes.

Sunstein's first page ends with: "Mary Wollstonecraft was particularly modern in another sense: she demanded happiness. At thirty-three, when she was at last able to free herself of personal and social inhibitions […]" (4). Sunstein remodels her for the 1970s. The "pursuit of happiness" speaks to the reader of the 1970s. America was out of Vietnam. Harvey Ross Ball invented the Smiley Face, and then Bernard and Murray Spain came up with the slogan, "Have a nice day," and 50 million Smiley Face buttons were sold in one year.[3] On the other hand, with nostalgia for a simpler time when supposedly Mom always had freshly baked Tollhouse cookies to hand to her kids in person when they returned home from school (while she was still wearing her neatly ironed and spotless apron with starched ruffles) and Dad could always be found in his favorite chair reading the newspaper, the TV hit series *Happy Days* began its ten-year run.

The ideology for the 1970s was, however, that happiness was possible only if one became free, as Sunstein implies, of "personal and social inhibitions." In 1972 birth control pills became available to all women, even the unmarried ones, in all states in the United States. Country music star Loretta Lynn celebrated its availability in her song, "The Pill," recorded in 1972 but not released until 1975 because of its controversial message. Lynn recounts how the men who ran the radio stations did not want to play it. She says, "It's like a challenge to the man's way of thinking. See, they'll play a song about making love in a field because that's sexy, from a man's point of view. But something that's really important to women, like birth control, they don't want no part of, leastways not on the air" (62). The year 1975 saw the release of *The Stepford Wives*, making the not too subtle statement that women refused to be restricted and defined by patriarchal stereotypes.

Sunstein sets her framework of telling Wollstonecraft's story in ways that appealed to the readers of the 1970s, but in doing so, was she honest to Wollstonecraft's story? Was Wollstonecraft's priority to be happy when she helped Bess leave her marriage? In the letter Wollstonecraft writes to Everina about her internal struggle over the intervention, she says that the "first motive of action" must be to "pleas[e] the Suprem Being and then to rely upon Him" (Todd, *CL* 48). Time and time again she writes in her letters that it is very unlikely that a Christian is going to be happy in this life, and this is not due to religious restrictions. Instead, she views this life as a preparation for the next, which required her to allow God to correct and improve her toward perfection, but perfection is not possible in this life (48). One day, but not in this life, "every creature about us [will be] happy" (48). To George Blood she says that she longs for "this warfare" to be over and that her "soul will not vainly pant after happiness" (93). She believed that happiness was an impossible dream: "we declare in general terms that there is no such thing as happiness on Earth" (47). However, a year before her death, she advises Mary Hays to "extract as much happiness" as possible "out of the various ills of life" (344). So, she was not optimistic about situations in this life that could make someone happy, but she did believe that one has to create happiness; the alternative is to be miserable because of miserable thoughts (344).

As for discarding "personal and social inhibitions," in *Rights of Woman* she is very critical of those ruled by "adulterous lust" and "promiscuous intimacy" prior to marriage. Those who are so, treat love only "as selfish gratification" (260; ch. 13). Sunstein's description of a 33-year-old woman finally having an affair with a man, which was obviously sexual in that it produced a child, reads more like a novel for the 1970s, declaring that freedom was all about having sex, and sex outside of marriage was socially acceptable and healthy. Sunstein's statement is more accurate for the sexual revolution of the 1960s and the sexual permissiveness that followed it, but it is not an accurate estimation of the sexual ideologies Wollstonecraft had embraced as evident in her frequent statements in *Rights of Woman* that endorse sexual purity, modesty and conjugal fidelity. Sunstein later refers to the author of *Rights of Woman* as a sexual prude (60), and inserts her own value system again by asserting that Wollstonecraft "was a long time outgrowing a sense of shame about sex" (59). Later, about the Imlay affair, Sunstein again applauds Wollstonecraft for casting off moral restraints:

> As the Imlay trauma lost its power to hurt her, Mary Wollstonecraft was able to build on it. If in modern eyes the Fuseli-Imlay period can be seen as a delayed and protracted identity crisis for Mary, a breaking down of internal and external repressions to a full comprehension of herself, Mary Wollstonecraft then proceeded, as exceptional spirits must, and within the limitations of her insight, to act on this discovery with integrity, initiative, and certainty. (305)

By "modern," Sunstein is referring to her own time of 1975, but even so, to assume that Wollstonecraft's rejection of Christian morality regarding extramarital sexuality awarded her the accolade of "integrity, initiative, and certainty" is extremely problematic. What happened to the author of *Thoughts on the Education of Daughters* (1787), which tells adults to teach young girls to regard "religion over sensual pleasure" (Jacobs 42)? Wollstonecraft's "unsanctioned sexuality" outside of marriage resulted in her two suicide attempts and ultimately the successful suicide of Fanny, the illegitimate child born because of it, a child who felt that stigma all her life as she mentioned in her suicide note. Sunstein herself reproduces the note's last statement close to the end of the biography: "I have long determined that the best thing I could do was to put an end to the existence of a being whose birth was unfortunate."[4] Where is the "integrity, initiative, and certainty" in that regret?

Based on an excerpt of *Maria*, Sunstein claims that Wollstonecraft placed the blame for what happened to her with Imlay squarely on the shoulders of society: "Mary had not acted her age with Imlay and she blamed part of her immaturity on current mores, which limited women's experience, retarded their development, distorted their judgment, and let them unnaturally, sometimes painfully vulnerable" (306). Throughout her biography, Sunstein relies too heavily on Wollstonecraft's fiction to explain her behavior and psychological states. How could Sunstein arrive at such a verdict? After having been on her own as an adult for 14 years earning her own living and realizing fame as an author, why would Wollstonecraft have thought that her "development" had been "retarded"? Why would a devout Christian have blamed society's mores for the reason she decided to have an illicit sexual relationship? And after that, with its devastating consequences and its learning experience, why did she enter into another one with Godwin? Where is the logic appropriate to historical context? Where is the documentation?

Nevertheless, Sunstein's understanding of Wollstonecraft's sexual repression is something to consider. Sunstein engages in a short but candid discussion about Wollstonecraft's puberty and menstruation, a subject avoided by all the other biographers, male and female alike. Sunstein figures that Wollstonecraft began to menstruate at the age of 15 because that was the average at that time. Most historical sources put the age at 16, between 15.5 and 17.[5] Sunstein assumes it unlikely that Wollstonecraft's mother advised or helped her through it, which may explain, as Sunstein thinks it does, why in *Rights of Woman* Wollstonecraft thinly disguises a topic that she knows cannot be discussed in public, but believes it necessary to address all the same (24–25). One statement in *Rights of Woman* to which Sunstein refers is "How can *delicate* women obtrude on notice that part of the animal economy, which is so very disgusting?"[6] Wollstonecraft wonders how any "delicate woman" could allow herself to see (and be aroused by) female genitalia, which she euphemistically encodes as "that part of the animal economy" (*ROW* 215; ch. 7).

Another time, Wollstonecraft refers to "nasty customs, which men never fall into."[7] In addressing the same kind of euphemisms, Mary Poovey does not speculate as to what Wollstonecraft refers but assuredly supposes the repulsion has to do with "female bodies and female desire—and all the ramifications of sexuality that she does not want to think about here" (76–77). It is apparent that Wollstonecraft implies women's exploration of each other's bodies and the resulting sexual pleasure. She is concerned that this homoeroticism will result in the loss of "maidenish bashfulness" and will form "old habits" which then will result in the loss of respect for "the mere difference of sex in their husbands" and cause women to "treat their husbands as they did their sisters or female acquaintance" (*ROW* 216; ch. 7). Unless she was unfamiliar with human anatomy, the only thing she could mean is that women will become so desirous of sexuality with the same sex that they will reject sexuality with their husbands in preference to sex with other women. She did not exempt men from homoeroticism either, referring to it in biblical language as "unnatural crimes" (*ROW* 86; ch. 1).

Sunstein is correct that, at some point, Wollstonecraft surmounted her sexual reticence and abandoned her religious restraint to be sexually active outside the bonds of matrimony. Sunstein identifies its origins when Wollstonecraft was introduced to high society through Lady Kingsborough in Dublin. She attended a masked ball, and from the letters to her sister Everina about the event, Sunstein infers that it was a *coup de foudre*. Was it George Ogle who had been mentioned with great pleasure in her letter and the object of jealousy between her and Lady Kingsborough or was it with Henry Gabell if one assumes that he is the model for Henry in *Mary* (Sunstein 135)? Sunstein is probably correct in describing Wollstonecraft at the age of 28 as being "a strongly sexed woman of rigorous morality, pleased in a provocative atmosphere: elegant women, vital young people, seductive men like Ogle, sympathetic men like Gabell. No wonder she had to deprecate flirtations, languishing and frank sexuality, at the same time she felt their appeal" (137). Wollstonecraft certainly is vitriolic in describing such dynamics in the fashionable salons of her time, with women "tainted by coquettish arts to gratify the sensualist" (*ROW* 103; ch. 2).

Otherwise there are many gaps in Sunstein's biography that are troublesome. An example is this early statement that is far-reaching: Wollstonecraft "produced what one historian has called perhaps the most original book of her century" (3). Sunstein provides no citation for this, and ever since her publication, Sunstein—and not the mystery historian who supposedly made the claim—has been cited multiple times as its source.

There are other sweeping statements with meanings that Sunstein must have assumed the reader would understand without explanation. One example is this: Her "whole existence was an attempt to make life conform to her needs, and her expectations and demands were so unrealistic as to be self-defeating" (4). Sunstein adds that she "sought ideal men and women, individual and systemic justice" (4) but does not define that ideal and does not explain the kind of justice. This is not provided anywhere in the biography.

Another sweeping statement that she does not explain, but it does become clearer later in the biography is this: "One must work backward at least from *A Vindication of the Rights of Woman* to see the layers of profound resentment as they were uncovered, and to understand the extreme conflict between young Mary's awareness and actions and the anger she actually felt" (17). Sunstein is right in this assessment, but when critiquing *Rights of Woman*, it would have been helpful had she provided an example or two to support it or at least reminded the reader of Wollstonecraft's familial disappointments.

Neither does she explain this significant statement: "Mary gave her money to her father not only as a duty but also as a down payment on her freedom" (55). Why did Wollstonecraft feel it was her obligation to give money to her father? To the contrary, Lyndall Gordon argues that Wollstonecraft's grandfather left money to Mary Wollstonecraft, but her father appropriated it as only a loan.[8] Furthermore, Wollstonecraft continued to try to pay off her father's debts the rest of her life. Joseph Johnson, who was frequently loaning money to Wollstonecraft, testified that she paid over £200 to her family (quoted in Gordon 132). In fact, as mentioned earlier, Godwin writes that the reason Wollstonecraft did not marry Imlay was because she did not want him to be burdened with her family's debts (*Memoirs* 68–70) and that is the same reason she did not want to marry Godwin (Sunstein 321). Why would she let her family's financial difficulties stand in the way of the pursuit of having her own family? And why does Sunstein think Wollstonecraft could purchase freedom from her father in this way? What kind of freedom? However, Sunstein does make a valid point that it was fortunate for Wollstonecraft that her father decided to remarry. Although the second marriage probably only aggravated his financial difficulties, and Wollstonecraft continued to send him money, Sunstein reminds us that it was the custom of the day that the eldest daughter would have been expected to become her father's household manager if he became a widower (72). Wollstonecraft became free to pursue her own life once he remarried.

Sunstein wrongly represents Wollstonecraft's belief that "most women were indeed innately inferior to men" (211). She tries to support this claim with quotes from *Rights of Woman* that do not support it, and she lifts these quotes entirely out of context. The only concession Wollstonecraft makes in *Rights of Woman* to the innate inferiority of women is physical strength (76; introd.). Nearly forty pages later, after decrying the social conditions that have caused so many women to be insipid and less than what they could be does she assert that which Sunstein quotes, that she knew only a "few extraordinary women" who seemed to have "male spirits [...] in female frames."[9] The only reason they had "male spirits" is because they were as Wollstonecraft would have all women, and that is "more masculine" intellectually, possible only if they were to receive education that would allow them to become so. There is nothing innate about their inferiority outside of physical strength.

Sunstein pursues her argument with Wollstonecraft's claim by demonstrating that Wollstonecraft represented only a minority of "distinguished women"[10] as if she is the exception to the rule, and maybe she was; however, Wollstonecraft was ambitious for all women to be distinguished; she did not believe intellectualism had sex. Wollstonecraft bemoaned the loss of "human discoveries and improvements" to civilization simply because historically men have suppressed women's talents, abilities and intellect (*ROW* 107; ch. 2). She did not believe that women were "innately inferior to men" as Sunstein states.

When Sunstein relays the incident of Wollstonecraft's "rescue" of Bess from her marriage with Bishop, she devotes to it an entire chapter that begins with a reminder of the relationship of Wollstonecraft's parents. This is important to Sunstein's project because she reasons that Wollstonecraft's haste in removing her sister was because she immediately compared Bess's marriage to her parents' and was determined that Bess would not share the same fate as her mother's. Sunstein writes, "Mary's predilection for the role of rescuer had its origins in her childhood. […] Bess'[s] choice of a man so similar to Edward John Wollstonecraft, and Mary's ambivalence toward that man, make the family connection complete" (88). This is a logical deduction, and it suggests why Wollstonecraft was so quick and drastic in bringing her remedy to Bess's trauma. But rather than applaud Wollstonecraft as a deliverer, one might agree that her motives were activated by her parents' bad marriage, but her reaction was extremely premature, impulsive and dangerous.

Of all of the biographers, Sunstein extends more care in painting portraits of Bess and Bishop, and her interpretation of them is very different from her cohorts'. Sunstein contends that Bess's "temperament was similar to Mary's, but even more unrestrained—hypersensitive, moody, ambivalent, and highly emotional, without reticence or self control" (*Mother* 79). She claims that when Bess married Bishop, she was "pretty, spoiled, thoughtless, irresponsible, and pleasure loving" (79). Wollstonecraft had been often hurt by petty, thoughtless, capricious comments Bess had written in letters to her, so she might have hesitated to interfere. After all, the Bishops had been married only one month before Bess became pregnant, so surely they needed more time to work out conflicts after Bess's emotional turmoil wrought by pregnancy. But Sunstein also deduces that Bishop's behavior and lack of maturity, even if he were thirty, was not much better than Bess's, describing him as "emotional, childish, domineering, erratic" and "irrationally jealous" (82). Obviously Sunstein formed a dislike of him without much evidence, asserting that he insisted upon resuming intercourse with his wife "instead of acting with patience and self-constraint," and Mary "held [him] off." This is written by the same biographer who asserts that Wollstonecraft was sexually repressed (60) and that she "was a long time outgrowing a sense of shame about sex" (59). Instead of concluding that Wollstonecraft came to her sister's rescue and protected her from unwanted sex, Sunstein might have remembered her earlier assessment of Wollstonecraft's attitude toward sex and considered that her action was motivated by her own sexual anxieties in the situation. There is no indication that Bess refused Bishop or that she wanted to refuse him. There is only a suggestion that when Wollstonecraft writes to Everina saying Bishop "cannot behave properly" (Todd, *CL* 41), she means that he wanted to resume intercourse with his wife, and Wollstonecraft resents it.

We do not learn about how Bess felt about it. Janet Todd suggests that it might have been Bess who was sexually repressed or else that Bishop suspected that that was the reason for her "female hysteria," given that physicians connected the two (*Revolutionary* 45). Brody perceives Meredith Bishop as a "robust and self-confident man, fierce about having his way but also affectionate and kind" (*Mother* 41). His inviting his sister-in-law to help with her sister was not the act of a bully. Brody writes that Wollstonecraft liked him (41), that she considered him "unsteady and self-indulgent, like her father, but still a good man, even a generous one." At her request, he gave her 20 pounds to give to the Bloods (41); "He lent it very properly without any parade" (quoted in Sunstein 83). In a letter to Jane Arden, Wollstonecraft seems glad when she heard that her sister had married Bishop because he "was a worthy man whose position in life is truly enviable."[11] So when and why did Wollstonecraft turn against him?

Sunstein mentions Wollstonecraft's belief in the sacrament of marriage, held dear by Anglicans such as herself, but Sunstein does not develop this idea. As would Brody, Sunstein focuses more on the lack of options for women, which compelled them to enter into and remain in undesirable marriages in the eighteenth century (89). She also points out that Wollstonecraft and Bess were in peril of being imprisoned for their daring escape (41). And, as did Brody (*Mother* 42), Sunstein underscores how controversial Wollstonecraft's action was, so controversial that even Godwin, who seemed otherwise oblivious to what caused controversy in his time, omits it from *Memoirs* (89). Sunstein considers the episode "one of the most controversial" in Wollstonecraft's life, and maybe she was right—not because Wollstonecraft committed a crime and violated a number of social mores during the late eighteenth century—but because none of her biographers empathizes with Bishop and none of them wants to criticize Wollstonecraft's precipitous behavior. In fact, Sunstein surmises, "Mary Wollstonecraft's part in the separation therefore can be justified.

She acted with cause and in character" (90), despite the fact that Bess lost her hearing again after her rescue, continued with her depression, and lost her daughter who would die a few months later.

Sunstein provides an ample discussion of Joseph Johnson, Wollstonecraft's publisher, and fittingly so. She also includes a list of women and their publications at the time Johnson was encouraging Wollstonecraft to write, as well as a brief history of the condescension male critics showed women writers (153–54). That Johnson treated Wollstonecraft in the same way he treated his male writers was revolutionary and well worth noting (154), although Sunstein might have added the details from Godwin's *Memoirs* that Johnson told her that she could "make his house her home" and stayed with him for two or three weeks (*Posthumous* 1:63). Albeit the son of a Baptist and a devoted Unitarian, Johnson seemed to fear no scandal or moral impropriety in providing shelter for an unmarried woman when he himself was a bachelor. Nor does Sunstein mention that he paid the rent for her at 49 George Street (Todd, *Revolutionary* 123) and, again, feared no accusation of having a "kept woman."

A situation that Sunstein does not have straight was how Wollstonecraft got her literary start. Sunstein does not give John Hewlett the credit due to him for his part in convincing Wollstonecraft to become a professional writer; she simply states that he "had suggested to her previously that she might make money by writing" (107) and that he gave Wollstonecraft's first manuscript to his publisher as "an act of disinterested kindness' (114). Sunstein thinks that the idea originated with Wollstonecraft: "She told Johnson she wanted to be a full-time writer and asked for his advice and help" (152), and pronounced to her sister that she was going to be the "first of a new genus" (quoted in 152).[12] For that matter, Janet Todd gives all the credit to Johnson and does not mention Hewlett (*Revolutionary* 117).

Wollstonecraft would pioneer the professional writing career for a woman. Astutely, Sunstein makes this claim: "As no other woman of her generation had yet done, without supplementary job, income, genteel shelter, or attending family to lend respectability, Mary Wollstonecraft now set out alone to earn a living by her pen" (160). But more than that, Wollstonecraft proved a woman could have the talent and intelligence to write professionally (Paul 1876, 191). And as noted by Brody, she was a "new genus" in being a woman who infiltrated the political arena through her writing ("Writes" 106).

A final point to be drawn from Sunstein is that she claims Johnson told Wollstonecraft to stop working on *The Cave of Fancy*. This is a detail that, if true, has been omitted in the other biographies—others do say she gave up on it, but not why. Jacobs relates that Wollstonecraft stopped at the third chapter and theorizes it was because Wollstonecraft "lost either interest or conviction in the genre" (61). It would have been very useful to have documentation as proof, but also to know why Johnson told her to quit.

A Different Face does fill in some gaps left by other biographies, with historical context that makes Sunstein's inductions plausible if not convincing. Perhaps the most crucial is that she was the first to offer the likelihood that Wollstonecraft's brother Henry was institutionalized for mental illness. Sunstein also offers a historical side note that helps the reader understand Wollstonecraft's relationship with Fanny Blood. In her explanation of "elevated friendship," Sunstein reminds us that the sexes were strictly separated once they reached puberty. She refers to a popular advice book by Hester Chapone, *Letters on the Improvement of the Mind* (1790),[13] in which the author encourages the formation of deep friendships between girls; however, she also warns that same-age relationships are not productive because the girls might be blind to each other's faults and thereby reinforce weaknesses (76). A girlfriend eight to ten years older is the ideal because she has the maturity to improve the younger (77). With Fanny's being only two years older than Wollstonecraft, and with Wollstonecraft's disposition to take the lead in all things, their relationship is not what Chapone has in mind as an ideal, but Sunstein is right in quoting Chapone about encouraging intimacy between women, intimacy so significant that it would, one hoped, extend "beyond the grave" (80).

Like Tomalin, Sunstein is "equally guilty of biographical distortion by way of another version of posterity's condescension" (Fredman 144). Sunstein revises Wollstonecraft as a woman transplanted from the eighteenth century into the 1970s (144), which Fredman declares to be a defect.

Also like Tomalin, Sunstein demonstrates an "incapacity for illuminating the pivotal phases in Mary's intellectual growth" (147). Sunstein often introduces a major incident in Wollstonecraft's life but then does not follow through with it (147); Fredman expects Sunstein to have a better background in the sentimental novel or literary history of period (148). Whether or not a valid criticism for Sunstein's agenda, Fredman demands more rigorous scholarship and accountability, a trend that found its genesis in this decade. Both Tomalin and Sunstein followed no apparent system for documentation (149).

Todd also has problems with Sunstein and echoes Fredman's criticism that Sunstein tends to summarize incidents in Wollstonecraft's life without giving necessary detail (xxiv). In general, Sunstein's research was faulty and not as accurate as Flexner's. However, both were often guilty of "simplistic psychologizing" of Wollstonecraft's character and motives. For example, they avoid dealing with Wollstonecraft's pursuit of Fuseli. Todd does credit Sunstein for explaining Wollstonecraft's involvement with Bess's "escape" from Bishop. With Sunstein's theory that Wollstonecraft's brother Henry was committed to an asylum for the insane and that most people in the eighteenth century believed that insanity ran in the family, Wollstonecraft feared Bess had succumbed (xxiii). Perhaps Todd's theory also deduces that Wollstonecraft was thinking that Bess, like Henry, had to be removed from the home that either triggered her episodes of insanity or would have been endangered by them.

As with Tomalin, Fredman's response to Sunstein's critical treatment of Wollstonecraft's works is that it is "quite disheartening" (147). Of *Rights of Woman*, Sunstein affords "some half-dozen pages of superficial review and 'critical naiveté' (147). She rambles instead of developing a "thematic structure which would give a summary such as hers the focus it requires to raise it above an elementary exercise in précis-writing" (147). Fredman's assessment is harsh: Sunstein

> seems generally ignorant of tides of cultural sensibility and taste, and particularly unprepared to deal with the vogue for the sentimental novel. There is no evidence of any extensive reading in the various kinds of fiction being written in England in the last quarter of the eighteenth century; nor is there any indication whether Sunstein is even aware of the classic study of the subject for this period. (148)

All these comments are exacting but appropriate criticism. They point to the direction scholarship had to take and would take, demanding scholars be cognizant of more than just the life and works of an individual, but also to know the culture, the history, the society, the economics, the literary history and to have read the reviews and critical history already published on the subject. The biographies after the 1970s would contain many more reliable facts, credible theories and interpretation, and most critical of all, documentation.

Sunstein had been politically active up until her death in 2007. Her biography absolutely contributes to our knowledge of Wollstonecraft, but much of it was written with a 1970s agenda, touting Wollstonecraft as a trailblazer of sexual liberation at a time in our history when "sexual liberation" was the modus operandi and would not be curtailed—but then only stalled—by the Aids panic of the 1980s. One must read it through these lenses and be critical of many of the assumptions and deductions Sunstein proffers that cannot be accurate to the period in which Wollstonecraft lived or accurate to the religious morality Wollstonecraft once held sacred.

Furthermore, when one reads *Rights of Woman*, one needs to pay attention to what Wollstonecraft says about the liberation of not only women but of men as well. Wollstonecraft makes clear that one cannot be free when the other is not free. Arvonne Fraser claims her as "the first to put her theories in the context of a broader liberationist, modern human rights theory" (863). Wollstonecraft wanted liberation for all people.

Chapter 9

MARGARET TIMS'S *MARY WOLLSTONECRAFT: A SOCIAL PIONEER* (1976): WOLLSTONECRAFT'S LIFE: THE STUFF OF NOVELS

Margaret Tims wrote her biography on Wollstonecraft during the 1970s, before she had the advantage of the collection of Wollstonecraft's letters that Janet Todd edited and annotated although, like Todd, Tims did have access to the original source in the Abinger collection at the Bodleian Library. It is obvious from Tims's writing, that she organized those letters chronologically and read closely Wollstonecraft's works, and then wrote her biography from them, constantly quoting and foregrounding them and filling in the gaps between them. The end result is a quilt of nonfiction and fiction. Sorting out which is which, though, is no easy task.

Unique to Tims's biography is an extensive treatment of all of Wollstonecraft's works as well as works written by contemporaries relevant to Tims's discussion. Her biography contains a lot of excerpts from the letters and from Wollstonecraft's works, and it includes much critical treatment of the works. Unlike other biographers, however, Tims does not presume that what Wollstonecraft wrote in her books and stories were autobiographical.

She acknowledges that her major biographical source was *Memoirs*, which is unfortunate, as I have argued elsewhere, because it is severely flawed with misinformation and bias. Also used were two biographies published in the 1970s, Flexner's and Tomalin's, but Tims's is not a rehash of theirs. She often disagrees with their information. Aside from these sources, she relies upon W. Clark Durant's introduction to *Memoirs* and Ralph Wardle's *Mary Wollstonecraft*. She did much original research that took her to record offices and libraries. Even so, much of her information has since been disputed by biographers. Regardless, she furnishes many ideas unique to the other biographies that have not been disputed, affirmed or embellished. She has made several astute observations from what little information she had to work with. In addition, her prose is enjoyably lyrical.

Tims (1915–2005) was married, but spent the last 27 years of her life a widow.[1] Judging from the titles of her books, I assume that she was a feminist as well as a poet. In addition to her work on Wollstonecraft, she wrote *Jane Addams of Hull House, 1860–1935; a Centenary Study* and co-authored with Gertrude Bussey *Pioneers for Peace: Women's International league for Peace and Freedom 1915–1946*, both of which are widely quoted.[2] Her other books are out of print. I was unable to find reviews and references to her biography on Wollstonecraft.

The first sentence of her first chapter does not bode well. It is Tims's assertion that Wollstonecraft "was born and died a feminist although she did not always live as one" (3). She adds that Wollstonecraft was a "'feminist' by force of circumstance—both personal and historical—rather than from any natural inclination of temperament, as her life-pattern clearly demonstrates" (3). Such a pattern is not clear to me at all. Presumably Tims understood "feminism" to mean the advocacy of equal rights, but to Tims, that must have precluded a woman's desire to be a wife and mother and it might have precluded being a Bible-believing Christian. However, feminism must be broad enough to respect the rights of those women's who, like Wollstonecraft, chose equality and appreciated the value of woman's work within domesticity.

This assertion does date Tims. The 1970s was a clamorous time for women to sort through exactly from what they desired liberation, but in their zeal for freedom from traditional patriarch restraints, many of them seemed to want to throw out the baby with the bath water. It was a time when it was "unacceptable" for women to want to stay home and raise their children. Paradoxically, the very women who were fighting for freedom for all women were often at the same time determined to deny other women the freedom to choose their own priorities. The freedom to choose should have been at the heart of women's liberation, but it frequently was not.

Tims next goes through the usual details of Wollstonecraft's early life, but she also mentions that when Wollstonecraft's father received £10,000 upon the death of his father, the Wollstonecraft family was doing very well. By today's standards, this amount would equate to over a million dollars.[3] By the time the family moved to Barking, they were still doing very well and deserving of the respect of their neighbors, the very wealthy landowners Bambour—an MP—and Joseph Gascoyne (5). But when the family left Beverley, they went with very little wealth and much disgrace, according to a letter Wollstonecraft wrote to Jane Arden.[4] Wollstonecraft's father must have had to resort to the "fortune that was settled on [his] children" (Todd, *CL* 24) in order to appear to be of good standing to the Allens and Wedgwoods in Cresselly (Tims 10).[5]

Tims does not list Henry as a possible brother to Wollstonecraft. She did find a record of Henry Woodstock Wollstonecraft's being apprenticed to Hewitt, a surgeon and apothecary. However, she lists David John Wollstonecraft (gent.) as his father with the only documentation being the "Beverley Corporation Apprentices Register" (6, 359n8). Strangely, Sunstein already wrote about this, and Tims apparently was familiar with her account. Sunstein looked at the same register and quoted it without any mention of David John Wollstonecraft, arguing that Henry was one of Wollstonecraft siblings and that he most likely was committed to an insane asylum in Hoxton (35–38, 361n1).

Tims accepts without question Godwin's statements that Wollstonecraft was not a favorite with either parent (7). It is possible, even likely, given the attitudes of the times, that Wollstonecraft did feel a "second-class status" as a daughter, and this did have a lasting effect on her attitude about love and acceptance as Tims argues (8–9), but Godwin is not a reliable source for this as fact.

Regarding her relationship with Fanny, Tims cautions us not to "dismiss" it as "a sentimental, schoolgirl 'crush.'" Nor should we consider it an "unnatural fixation." Instead, we are to believe that Wollstonecraft simply gave and received love, which was the "deepest need of her being" (11), an evaluation that is less than satisfactory compared to the in-depth consideration offered by other biographers.

What Tims does offer about Fanny is quite interesting, although unsubstantiated and highly speculative. Most biographers agree that Fanny's health deteriorated because of financial stress, overwork and emotional struggle as a result of Skeys's inconsistent regard of her. Certainly, Wollstonecraft's scathing letter blames Skeys for Fanny's sinking health, which could never be restored, and Tims quotes from this letter.[6] But Tims argues that the exacerbation of her bad health (consumption) was not caused by Skeys but by some other lover for whom she pined (24, 33). Tims supports her theory by Fanny's less than passionate description of her new husband, that he is "a good sort of creature, and has sense enough to let his cat of a wife follow her own inclination in *almost* everything."[7] The letter refers to some picture of Skeys that Fanny says is a fair likeness, but in reality Skeys was heavier and looked at least ten years older. Of course, photography had not been invented yet, so this picture might have been a painted portrait or a sketch. Tims uses it as an argument that when Skeys and Fanny married in Portugal, they had not been previously acquainted, and that the match was a marriage of convenience instead of love. Whether a portrait or a sketch, it was an artist's practice to portray the subject in the most flattering prospect possible or else he would not have been paid for his labor. Probably this was the point that Fanny was making. Curiously, Diane Jacobs would reproduce the same excerpt of the letter as support that "no mistaking it," Fanny was supremely happy (40). To me the letter reads with the rhetoric of an eighteenth-century woman who was more than content. It seems like the playful banter of a satisfied wife. Not all women were as ebullient in describing their feelings for their lovers in the way Wollstonecraft was. To show uncontrollable emotions was not considered proper, so Tims may not have a case here that argues that Fanny was not in love with Skeys and that she desired someone else.

With regard to the "rescue" of Bess from an undesirable marriage, Tims imparts some fresh insights. She suggests that Bess traded the schoolroom and her unbearable father's household for a worse evil, and that Bishop was just as "brutal and dominating as her father—or perhaps he was just the average man of his time, who viewed his wife as his chattel and gave scant consideration to her feelings" (23). We do not know what Bishop was truly like in this marriage, but Tims reminds us that Wollstonecraft instantly, irrationally opted to remove Bess permanently from her marriage situation rather than thinking about a temporary rest cure. "Her motives in mounting this rescue-operation must be viewed with a little suspicion" (23), Tims warns. She quotes from a letter that demonstrates Wollstonecraft's resentment and jealousy of her sister that she was married and therefore of higher standing than herself: "You remember Bess; she was a mere child when were together, and it would have hurt our dignity to have admitted her into our Parties, but she must now take place of us, being of the most honourable order of matrons."[8] Tims also quotes from another letter to Arden in which Wollstonecraft says that when couples settle into matrimony, they remember the joys and delights of their honeymoon with only disgust. She also rejoices that she is single and therefore free to "pursue one's own whims [...] without having a husband and half a hundred children [...] to control a poor woman."[9] This was written by a very young Wollstonecraft who was just 23 and would write only days later, as Tims points out with irony, "I almost wish for a husband, for I want some one to support me."[10]

Referring to Bess's extreme behavior of biting her wedding ring to pieces, Tims wonders if Wollstonecraft's reaction to Bess was predicated on fear of her sister's "mental instability" (26). Tims does not pursue this, but it ties into my theory that one of the fears that vexed Wollstonecraft was that insanity ran in the family.[11] If this is correct, Wollstonecraft knew Bess was suffering from something more desperate and permanent than postpartum depression. Physicians did not know much about the depression that afflicts many women after giving birth, but they, and especially women, knew that it often occurred.[12] If Wollstonecraft assumed Bess was temporarily depressed, she would not have taken such long-lasting measures to resettle her away from her husband.

Tims asks very good questions that seem to have eluded other biographers: "Did Mary really imagine that she was setting her sister's mind at rest by snatching her away from her child? And that in doing so she was acting in [Bess's] interest rather than her own?" (27). Indeed, Tims's assessment of Wollstonecraft's attitude seems correct, that they were "devoid of concern for the abandoned baby": "Bess is tolerable well; she cannot help sighing about little Mary whom she tenderly loved; and on this score I both love and pity her. The poor brat! It had got a little hold on my affections, sometime or other I hope we shall get it."[13] It is true that it was illegal to take the child, but it was also illegal for a wife to leave her husband's house without his permission (Skinner 92). Tims mentions this and also reminds us that if Bishop were "half the tyrant he was painted," he could have had Wollstonecraft thrown into jail and her sister forced to return (25). Tims's treatment of the Bishop escape is critical: "Mary is shown here at her worst. It is quite clear that she had exerted a dominating influence over her weaker sister and allowed her judgment to be warped by her own dislike of [Bess's] husband" (28). Although Wollstonecraft believed in the "marriage vow, she could not accept its consequences" (28).

As for her own love affairs, Wollstonecraft very well may have loved Joshua Waterhouse, but there is no proof. Tims suggests places and times that they might have met each other, but Tims is not persuaded that Waterhouse would have been the kind of man who would have been attractive to Wollstonecraft; he would not have been intellectually stimulating (35). On the other hand, Tims hints that it was because of a foiled romance that Wollstonecraft was suffering from the depression she writes about in her letters, a depression to which she never attaches a specific cause (35).[14]

Then enters the mysterious "Neptune," which has evoked much speculation. Tims says that Wardle thought Neptune was a pun on Waterhouse (46). Regardless of who Neptune was, Tims believes Wollstonecraft was in love with him and fell into deeper depression because she could not have him (46–47).[15]

Henry Gabell may have been another contender for the mysterious Neptune, although Tims does not suggest it. Wollstonecraft stayed with Gabell and his wife for three weeks and at first was extremely impressed with how happy they seemed to be (101). Lyndall Gordon, too, notes this (174). Unlike Gordon and any other biographer, Tims notices something about this experience which is very important. Wollstonecraft recognized that the two were very happy together, but theirs was not a marriage she wanted. Wollstonecraft's letter to Everina does not make this clear, but we can deduce that she reasoned the Gabells were unequally yoked intellectually. To her sisters, she wrote, the "Goddess of this place" (Ann Gabell) is insipid (Todd, *CL* 178), but according to the letters she wrote to Gabell, he was very well educated and was a philosopher. Strangely, she seemed to begrudge their happiness. "My die is cast!" she announces, "I could not just now resign intellectual pursuits for domestic comforts" (Todd, *CL* 178). It sounds as if she declares that she will never marry, preferring a life of intellectual pursuits instead. Perhaps she contemplated marrying a man like Gabell, but when she realized that he fell in love with someone who was not his intellectual equal, she became indignant and assumed that most men do this, as she laments in *Rights of Woman*: "Do passive indolent women make the best wives?" (106; ch. 2). For the Gabells, the answer may have been in the affirmative. Otherwise, we might assume that Wollstonecraft was jealous.

Tims's critique of *Rights of Men* is useful. She corrects some of Wollstonecraft's mistakes about Burke, agreeing with her advertisement that she did not have the "leisure or patience" to read through Burke's work as closely as she needed to do.[16] Tims argues that *Rights of Men* is unique in Wollstonecraft's canon because she uses "personal invective," which Tims thinks is neither effective nor accurate. By attacking Burke as a vain man, Wollstonecraft ignores that he "upheld the American claim to independence, abhorred slavery, attacked the harshness of the penal system and caused the impeachment of Warren Hastings for alleged ill-treatment of the native people of India" (106).

Tims makes an observation that could be applied to *Rights of Woman* as well, when she claims that Wollstonecraft strikes against the very thing of which she is guilty, even in the very act of striking. Here is an example Tims gives: Wollstonecraft criticizes his "sensibility" by insisting that his "petty flights arise from your pampered sensibility [...] you foster every emotion till the fumes, mounting to your brain, dispel the sober suggestions of reason."[17] It is obvious to Tims that this is the very "echo of herself" and finds it quite comical that even as Wollstonecraft attacks his feelings going amuck, the invective rhetoric she uses to check his exudes emotion—and often to the exclusion of reason (106–7).

After that, however, Tims finds plenty to recommend Wollstonecraft in an extensive review of *Rights of Men* (106–20). The next chapter focuses solely on *Rights of Woman*, but instead of offering a critical treatment, Tims contextualizes the work, describing the literature of Wollstonecraft's contemporaries, both of men and women who were writing on similar subjects.

When she returns to biography, Tims does something uncommon among the biographers; she trails Bess and Everina,[18] and then she pauses to tell us what little she can figure out about the mysterious Ann whom Wollstonecraft adopts.[19] She rehearses the then usual theory that Ann was a niece of Hugh Skeys and the daughter of a friend who died, but then she tells a story that was being spread by an American, Mrs. Mark Leavenworth. The details are too bizarre to be worth repeating here, but not too bizarre for Tims and later for Janet Todd, who would include it in a footnote to her 2003 collection of Wollstonecraft letters. It impresses upon one the notoriety that Wollstonecraft was receiving for such a story to originate and circulate. And it is like a synopsis of the orphan girl novel that was popular at the time. The wording in Tims is verbatim from *The Literary Diary of Ezra Stiles* (1901): Ann was "an orphan girl, which the dying mother of the Child an East Indian gave her to bring up, and which she is educating she says as a child of nature."[20]

Ezra Stiles was one of the founders of Brown University in Providence, Rhode Island; President of Yale College (1778–95), a Congregationalist minister, theologian, writer and American Revolution hero. In his diary, he records that he had just finished reading *Rights of Woman* and recalls that Mrs. Leavenworth—wife of one the pastors—had just returned from London, where she had met Wollstonecraft. She described Wollstonecraft as being about 32 or 35, with "the same middling or smallish Stature of Mrs. Jno Sherman." This is what else he knows about her: "Was born in Wales, where her father now lives in ordiny circumstances. Her mother died young. She has been a Governess in Families & had the Educa of Children. First published small Books for Children. Devoted to Reading" (502). Then he writes about Ann. This is the rest of the entry:

> A Publisher of one of the Magazines employs her in compilg & correctg for the press. She by her writg gets a good subsistence. Mr Joel Barlow became acquainted with her, & he & his Wife now in Lond. often visitg, brot with them Mrs Wolst. To vist at Mrs. Leav. so she became intimately acquainted with her. She was writg the Rights of Women when Mrs Macaulay died, & before Payn wrote his Rights of Man. Mrs W. was intimately acquainted with Mr Payne. (503)

Unfortunately, Tims does not include this excerpt because it is very telling. Stiles was the first honorary member of the Society of the Cincinnati (Loomis 17), devoted to the preservation of the ideals of the American Revolution, so he was impressed with Wollstonecraft because of her friendship with Thomas Paine.[21] Rev. Mark Leavenworth, a Congregational minister in Waterbury, Connecticut, was ordained by Stiles. Leavenworth's wife visited the Barlows, where she met Wollstonecraft. Did one of the Barlows fabricate the story about the orphaned Ann? Did Wollstonecraft make it up? It is very doubtful that Leavenworth would have just invented it, and she certainly believed it or else why would have she repeated it to Stiles?

The only thing Tims can say about the story is that "the experiment proved short-lived."

Wollstonecraft's behavior toward the girl—if we have all of the facts—is certainly not the responsible conduct of a visionary feminist who ended a book on education with "I have indeed so much compassion for those young females who are entering into the world without fixed principles" (*Thoughts*

135). Wollstonecraft had an opportunity to put her theories on education into practice on a girl who desperately needed her help, and unless there are other facts to the case that we do not know, she abandoned the child because Ann worked on her nerves and because Wollstonecraft was busy writing, ironically, *Rights of Woman*, and mostly because Wollstonecraft was having a crisis of her own that distracted her from her experiment of being a mother and educator. The crisis's name was Henry Fuseli.

Tims provides a lot of information about Fuseli (154–57) for a biography on Wollstonecraft. Her theory is that the reason for the mutual attraction was opposites: her "humane, open eyed vision" versus his "nightmare fantasies" (160). Robert Browning's clever poem "Mary Wollstonecraft and Fuseli" emphasizes similar differences between the two but also the mad courage Wollstonecraft had to do the very thing that terrified her, for the sake of love—but, alas, unrequited love unnerves Wollstonecraft:

Oh but is it not hard, Dear?
    Mine are the nerves to quake at a mouse:
If a spider drops I shrink with fear:
    I should die outright in a haunted house;
While for you—did the danger dared bring help—
From a lion's den I could steal his whelp
With a serpent round me, stand stock-still,
Go sleep in a churchyard,—would will
Give me the power to dare and do
Valiantly—just of you!

Tims also makes some interesting observations about the kind of changes Wollstonecraft experienced while living in London, while being independent, while not having to live with a family to take care of. She also charts the changes she goes through in her relationship with Fuseli (158–68), reminding us of something Godwin writes: "I believe Mary came something more a cynic out of the school of Mr. Fuseli, than she went into it."[22]

There is no consensus amongst her biographers as to why Wollstonecraft left for Paris on December 8, 1792. Yes, she was escaping from the negative experience she had had with her pursuit of Fuseli. Yes, she wanted to see what was going on in France with its revolution. But Tims offers this point as well: Because she stayed with Mme. Aline Fillietaz in Paris, she must have been serious about finding teaching posts for her sisters. Mme. Fillietaz was the sister of Mme. Bregantz who employed Bess and Everina in her school in Putney (172).

Tims's rendition of Imlay and the affair does not exceed in depth or accuracy that found in most biographies. She considers Wollstonecraft's "crime or folly [...] not that she had become the mistress of the man she loved, but that the object of her love fell so far beneath her own previous conception of what such a man should be" (185). Although she follows this with a strong case that Wollstonecraft had had a history of being unable to "read" a man correctly and that she carried around with her an "ideal" that her man would be the "embodiment of all the virtues that flowed from reason, chastity and compassion," and in Gilbert Imlay, she thought she had found him (185–86). While true that, throughout their relationship, Wollstonecraft hoped Imlay was better than what he actually was, he did nothing to delude her. From the very beginning he made it clear that he was not the marrying kind. He had had affairs already and relayed that he had been involved with a "cunning" woman (Todd, *CL* 259–60). Chaste, he was not. Neither was he transparent and honest and immaterial. She knew that in France he was involved in an illegal and unethical trade of items that were stolen from aristocrats who had been imprisoned, exiled or guillotined. He was trading silver plating and the like with the Norwegians for flour and other items needed in France and making a hefty profit (Verhoeven, *Imlay* 186–99). Attracted to what she believed was a man of the wilderness, she did not contemplate the sort of independence such a man would want from any commitments that tied him down.

As usual, Tims has her own unique take on what happened and does not assume that Imlay was a tragedy for Wollstonecraft. Instead, Imlay was an "essential process in her development" (187). What she means by this, she does not say however. Tims does not develop ideas, but she does develop scenes with exquisite detail. For example:

> During her first few weeks in Paris Mary found the streets so "disagreeable"—and the weather so bad—that, as she described it in a letter to Ruth Barlow, "I half-ruin myself with coach-hires." Her lodging at No. 22 Rue Meslay was in the north-eastern Gravilliers section (the house still stands, although sadly derelict: a gaunt, six-storey building with an inner courtyard). Nearby lived Tom Paine, in a former residence of Madame de Pompadour at No. 63 Rue du Faubourg St Denis. Thomas Christie also is said to have stayed here. Travelling a little west [...]. (187)

With her skill in giving immediacy and creative description of scene and action, Tims would have produced a much better historical novel about Wollstonecraft instead of a biography.

There is a question as to whether Wollstonecraft wrote or co-wrote *The Emigrants*, but not to Tims.[23] She is convinced that Wollstonecraft should have read it and then she would have known that Imlay was not her intellectual equal (186) and that he did not admire women for their minds. Tims supports this with an excerpt from *The Emigrants*: "The lovely Caroline's face diffused the soft effulgence of an opening rose when heaven impearls it with the morning dew."[24] Although she has a point, this and another excerpt do not make her case. The style of writing with its metaphors is exactly the style that Wollstonecraft chose in all of her works when she wanted to wax eloquently on subjects dear and near to her heart, as if the lyrical embellishment made the concept even more important or divine. Without a metaphor, the concept or object was to be considered more mundane. Here is an example from *Rights of Men*:

> Sacred be the feelings of the heart! Concentrated in a glowing flame, they become of the sun of life; and, without his invigorating impregnation, reason would probably lie in helpless inactivity, and never bring forth her only legitimate offspring—virtue. But to prove that virtue is really an acquisition of the individual, and not the blind impulse of unerring instinct, the bastard vice has often been begotten by the same father. (63)

Wollstonecraft probably would have approved Imlay's description of Caroline's bosom that "disclosed the temple of bliss."[25] What she would not have appreciated was the obviously voyeuristic description of Caroline after she has been rescued from the Indians, that she was "torn into shatters by the bushes and briars, with scarcely covering left to hide the transcendency of her beauty, which to be seen by common eyes is a profanation" (198). This would have been a better excerpt to make Tims's point.

Significantly, Tims devotes ample time developing Bess's story of her leaving Upton Castle with the hopes that her sister would get her a job in Paris, all of which she conveys in two pages (241–42), but about Wollstonecraft's first attempt at suicide, we get just a few sentences, and they express doubt as to whether or not Wollstonecraft was serious about dying (243), although Tims has more to say about the second attempt (273–80).

Rather romantically, Tims provides a paragraph about Joshua Waterhouse as if he never recovered from his blighted love with Wollstonecraft (354–55). The rest of the story follows in quick order, including Godwin's second marriage, George Blood's marriage and subsequent loss of his wife during childbirth, Fanny's suicide and, briefly, the Shelleys.

Appropriate to 1976 when she published this biography, Tims makes the statement that Wollstonecraft could not have known that it was neither education nor occupational opportunities that would emancipate women, but contraception (357). Had contraceptive devices been available to Wollstonecraft, her life would have been vastly different and most likely prolonged. In the

1970s, the birth control pill was a hotly contested item, with its legalization for single women in 1972. Wollstonecraft would have been pleased, however, to learn that the enrollment of women increased in colleges and universities because of the availability of the pill—and because women had more control over their bodies, more of them were entering the job force.[26]

But Tims's final assessment of Wollstonecraft's philosophy is an invaluable thought to leave with her readers of the 1970s as well as today: "The two sexes mutually corrupt and improve each other—and society" (357).

Chapter 10

GARY KELLY'S *REVOLUTIONARY FEMINISM: THE MIND AND CAREER OF MARY WOLLSTONECRAFT* (1992): A LITERARY REVOLUTIONARY

Gary Kelly's 22-page introduction, titled "Gender, Class and Cultural Revolution," is brilliant. However, it in no way lets Wollstonecraft take center stage, even though the book is supposed to be about her. Although the subsequent chapters do focus on her works and a little on her life, she seems supplementary and only marginally convenient for his Marxist theory on the "Cultural Revolution," which was led, he argues, by the professionals in the middle classes bent on changing the behavior and perspectives of the classes above and below them. By "Cultural Revolution," he means the reaction of British intellectuals to the French Revolution and their political theories to divert a physical revolution in Britain through bringing about social reform. These ideas, to Kelly, "founded the modern state of Britain." Debate through writing instigated reform, and it included Wollstonecraft's "revolutionary feminism." However, if Wollstonecraft had been interviewed by Kelly, based upon his questions to her, she might have said, "Do I need to be here?" Kelly's theory is what is important. He describes Wollstonecraft's mind and career only as they fit into his theory.

In her review of Kelly's book, Barbara Kanner conveys similar concerns and adds that it is "not an innovative historical biography" but is only a synthesis of "literary and feminist scholarship produced over the past two decades," and which borrows from Wollstonecraft scholars Mitzi Myers, Janet Todd, Cora Kaplan, Mary Poovey and Moira Ferguson (229). This criticism is severe, for surely Kelly does more than that. On the other hand, he barely gives a nod to any Wollstonecraft scholarship other than Mitzi Myers. One footnote lists all of the biographers to date (233n1), but other than Godwin, he rarely cites them. Nevertheless, Kanner praises Kelly for "his rendering of Wollstonecraft as a historical figure" (229). However, Kanner describes his work as "weav[ing] together her life experiences and her literary productions within the socioeconomic and cultural contexts of the time" (229). I do not find many "life experiences" in Kelly's work; Wollstonecraft's life is peripheral.

Here is one example of how Kelly subordinates information. He first provides a helpful overview of the production of "conduct books" by women and argues that they were efforts to train other women to raise their daughters with the same values and opportunities available to men (17–33). To Wollstonecraft's credit, Kelly says that her *Thoughts* "attempted the most thorough feminist transformation of the cultural revolution of her time" (21), but she failed as did her cohorts in envisioning any "real social roles for women" (31). They could become like men, but men were not going to make room for them in the public sphere. Thus, Kelly places *Thoughts* in the subgenre of conduct books. In the process, he calls the Apostle Paul "the biblical conduct writer" (31).

It is true that much of the content and purpose of Paul's letters to various churches and leaders of churches was to chastise their conduct. But to label him as a conduct writer distinctly exposes Kelly's own propensity to oversimplify and manipulate information to fit his mold, which he does with Wollstonecraft as well. It would take at least another book to argue that Paul's books in the Bible have more to say than how to behave, but here is just one rebuttal to demonstrate how far from the mark is Kelly's assumption. In the second letter to Timothy, Paul writes: "For God hath not given us the spirit of fear, but of power, and of love, and of a sound mind" (1:7). This is not about personal conduct. It is not even about what *we* do; it's about what *God* does. Furthermore, the verse has nothing to do with Kelly's theory of how conduct books inculcate middle class ideology to correct and challenge the higher and lower classes.

An example of how little information he includes about Wollstonecraft's life, when one needs to know enough about her in order to know her mind, is Kelly's discussion of the Bess/Bishop incident. He recounts it in one paragraph, discusses legal rights in the next paragraph, has Bess extricated, Fanny dead, and the women's schools failed—all in the following paragraph (26–27). This episode in Wollstonecraft's life takes other biographers entire chapters to cover. Granted, Kelly does not need to regurgitate what has already been written about Wollstonecraft, but certainly with his knowledge of Marxism and interest in class conflict and struggle, he could have identified various aspects of class conflict in what happened from 1784 to 1785, when Wollstonecraft was removing Bess from her domestic situation.

Here is another example of Kelly's reference to Wollstonecraft's life that he applies to his own theory instead of vice versa. In discussing Wollstonecraft's attraction to Fuseli, Kelly did very little research, or he includes very little research in his discussion. He relies only on what John Knowles wrote when

Knowles's work was extremely biased toward Fuseli and against Wollstonecraft. Since the incident had the potential for being embarrassing and derogatory for Fuseli, Kelly needed to evaluate Knowles's bias before he relied so heavily on what Knowles recounted regarding Wollstonecraft. Kelly quotes Knowles's sarcastic remarks and makes no commentary on them. For example, "Although Mrs. Fuseli had a right to the person of her husband."[1] and figures that, on Fuseli's part, Wollstonecraft's claim to him was purely a uniting of minds. At the center of Wollstonecraft's work, says Kelly, is the ideology that the "mind has no sex" (102), which may be an apt deduction of *Rights of Woman*, but Kelly fails to support the idea as it pertains to her interest in Fuseli. He deduces that the allure was simply "intellectual and cultural" (105), but without a convincing argument. How is the reader to understand what was going on in Wollstonecraft's mind and life when she proposed to Mrs. Fuseli that the three of them live together?

Kelly is correct to say Wollstonecraft argues that women have intellectual capacities equal to men and similar intellectual ambitions, which is what he probably means when he summarizes her ideology as "the mind has no sex." However, Wollstonecraft also complains that, in general, the intellectualism of most of the women in the eighteenth century is stunted because of poor education as well as the priority to attend to physical appearance in order to attract men so that men in turn will provide for them. Furthermore, to appear to be too intelligent threatens men. Ideally "the mind has no sex" or as E. P. Thompson describes her perspective: "She measured herself as an equal in the republic of the intellect." On the other hand, "Wollstonecraft was reminded by every fact of nature and of society that she was a woman. She was not a mind which has no sex, but a human being exceptionally exposed within a feminine predicament" (186). Thompson argues his claim with a quote from *Letters from Sweden:* "All the world is a stage, thought I; and few are there who do not play the part they have learnt by rote; and those who do not, seem marks set up to be pelted at by fortune; or rather as signposts, which point out the road to others, whilst forced to stand still themselves amidst the mud and dust" (186).

To Kelly's credit, his overview of conduct books, aside from the too-clever remark about St. Paul, is very useful and unique to the biographies although, as argued below, conduct books were more typical of the Victorian period, and courtesy books were more characteristic of the Neoclassical age, when the former had to do with character and upbringing and the latter had to do with social etiquette and civility. Kelly made a number of comments about Hester Chapone, comments that are particularly useful because Wollstonecraft does indicate that she respects Chapone but disagrees with her (*ROW* 189; ch. 5). Kelly also discusses Halifax, Fénelon, Pennington and Trimmer (29) and compares/contrasts them, in detail, to Wollstonecraft's *Thoughts*.

In her review Syndy McMillen Conger praises Kelly for "his extraordinary command of all the subjects he is called upon to address" (95). To Conger, Kelly was very knowledgeable of Wollstonecraft's contemporaries, and this is a strength of his biography over other biographies. The weakness is that he seemed to know less about Wollstonecraft's work and its criticism than do other biographers. His treatment of *Rights of Man* extends for 16 pages, but in them, he demonstrates his command of Burke and lack of command of Wollstonecraft (87–103). Since a comprehension of Burke is essential for working with *Rights of Man*, and in that several biographers do not offer the same depth, then Kelly's contribution is valuable. Nevertheless, his deliberation of *Rights of Woman* is too reductive, largely because he does not integrate the analyses of other historians and Marxists who have written extensively on *Rights of Woman*. And to argue that Wollstonecraft chose—as if she consciously chose—the "feminine style" of the conduct books with which to write her treatise, and that it is a call for revolution in female manners (83)—again is Kelly's attempt to force through his funnel a lot of information and perspectives that just cannot flow. In short, *Rights of Woman* addresses much more than culture and manners. Kelly contends that *Rights of Woman* is a "critique of 'woman' constructed for court culture and appropriated by the professional middle class cultural revolution through education in the broad sense, including socialization and culture" (108). His language, tinged with economics and Marxism, gives us something else to think about when reading *Rights of Woman*, but it is a forced argument that does not suffice. Kelly argues that the professional class, in which he situated Wollstonecraft, attacked both the British and French governments as well as the emulation of the lower classes of degenerate, corrupt "court culture" practiced by the upper classes (2–3). The professional class opposed the lower classes (including the rustic and the rural) because of their communal culture, which focused on communal labor production. It opposed the upper classes because of their courtly culture, which emphasized only fashion. In contrast, the middle class, so claims Kelly, prioritized the domestic, the family and friends (11–12); the professional class purposed to impose that culture, those forms on the other cultures (2). So, Kelly views *Rights of Woman* as an instrument of colonization. He does not factor in all the scriptural references in *Rights of Woman* that have nothing to do with class cultures. The morality and virtue that Wollstonecraft advocates are universal, non-gendered, not culture-specific and not peculiar to any class, such as when she refers to the "eternal rule of right" (204); she is asserting a biblical principle and not a class system or culture.

Even if Kelly placed her in a class, Wollstonecraft was anti-class and wanted an egalitarian world with freedom and opportunity for all, regardless of gender, race, religion, creed or class. If there were any class she admired, it was what Kelly called the lower class, but Wollstonecraft perceived it with an idealism equal to the Romantics like Joanna Baillie in her "A Winter Day," and in particular to Wordsworth as he described the "low and rustic life" in his Preface to the *Lyrical Ballads*. Rustics were unspoiled, more in tune with nature, conveyed "elementary feelings" and lived according to the "primary laws of our nature" (vii–viii). Although the rustics were considered a class, their values, the Romantics insisted, reflected the sensibility basic to all humanity. Class had nothing to do with it other than what class had effected by enticing them to material comforts and artificial manners meant to please, and seducing them away from healthy, wholesome and natural lifestyles that ensured harmony with each other, with nature, and with one's self. Kelly does not factor in this context of literary history.

Wollstonecraft called them country people and described a rustic scene. In Wollstonecraft's ideal world, the children in their clean clothes were gathered around a clean hearth with their mother who was suckling her baby. They were listening for the "scraping of the well known foot" approaching the door. That would be the father coming in from his day of labor to take care of his family, even though it was cold outside. The children and mother knew that he would take his seat next to the fire and generously caress them and they would return those caresses (*ROW* 232–33; ch. 9).

Kelly's historical perspective generates some novel ideas that he presents in his sixth chapter. As Conger observes, *French Revolution* was one work by Wollstonecraft that had not received much critical attention, so Kelly's extensive analysis of it through his expertise on the Jacobin Revolution does tender discourse in Wollstonecraft scholarship (95). Kelly meticulously works with the title of Wollstonecraft's book, exploring the meaning of every word in that title (154–55). His analysis of publications on the same subject by Wollstonecraft's contemporaries is very beneficial and shrewd. For example, he discusses Helen Maria Williams's *Letters* as feminine writing, meaning personal and subjective in contrast to detached and objective. Kelly describes Williams's treatment as "masculinization of the Revolution, breaking up families, destroying the domestic affections and wrongly excluding women from participation in the Revolution" (153–54). Scholars since Kelly have resisted the sort of essentializing of gendered writings that Kelly has identified. They would have reason to object to Kelly's simplification of Williams's writing and they certainly would counter with the part that women did play in the French Revolution. Kelly's book was published on the cusp of an outpouring of publications he did not anticipate that offered alternate ways of looking at the women of the French Revolution, such as Olwen H. Hufton's *Women and the Limits of Citizenship in the French Revolution* which came out the same year as did Kelly's book, Marilyn Yalom's *Blood Sisters: The French Revolution in Women's Memory*

(1995), Dominique Godineau's *The Women of Paris and Their French Revolution* (1998) and Lisa Beckstrand's *Deviant Women of the French Revolution and the Rise of Feminism* (2009), to name just a few.

Once Kelly attempts to convince that Wollstonecraft chose to write her book with a style betwixt and between the "sentimental, epistolary, obviously feminine discourse invented by Helen Maria Williams to feminize politics and the Revolution" (153–54), he gives us something more to think about, but fails to convince this reader that Wollstonecraft's "feminine discourse" was obvious. He would have succeeded more with his analysis of *French Revolution* by restricting himself to his expert historical contextualization of the Revolution and avoiding complicating and undermining his polemics with gender essentialization. Stilln a 27-page exploration of Wollstonecraft's little-known book is a noble contribution to Wollstonecraft scholarship.

So are the pages devoted to *Letters from Sweden* within the context of travel literature and of course through Kelly's evaluation of class dynamics (177–95). Exclusive of this and a brief study of *Maria*, he has very little to say about Wollstonecraft's life and does not attempt to go into much historical detail about Imlay—his books, his dealings in and out of America, his silver and gold dealings with the French that went awry in Scandinavia. Nor does he deal with Godwin's political theories. For a Marxist historian, this is surprising.

One commendation to which he is entitled is his theory that the revolutions of the 1790s were incited through paper (1). It is true that much blood was spilled, especially in France and America, to gain freedom, but revolutions began first by ideas put down on paper. Kelly's observation is ingenious, that the British debate about revolution took the form of writing, and writing was the major instrument for revolution, and "Wollstonecraft's Revolutionary feminism was a writing revolution, exemplified and conducted in writing" (1). Wollstonecraft and many other intellectuals pinned their hopes on the French Revolution as inspiring reform in Britain, but when they became disillusioned because of its outcomes, many became anti-Jacobins and warned about what would happen to Britain if it allowed the monarchy to be toppled and the government be run by the commoners. Since there were those like Wollstonecraft who embraced the ideas of the French Revolution and packaged egalitarianism for women with it, when the British turned against the French and their revolution, they also used its effects as reason to reject the kind of feminism advocated by Wollstonecraft—at least this is the way Kelly "reads" it (1) and thus gives us a new way to consider Wollstonecraft's life and works.

Chapter 11

JANET M. TODD'S
MARY WOLLSTONECRAFT:
A REVOLUTIONARY LIFE (2000):
THE "IMPUDENT AND IMPRUDENT"
WOLLSTONECRAFT

Arguably Janet Todd is the leading expert on Mary Wollstonecraft, with a quality of scholarship that is unsurpassed. In 2013 she was appointed Officer of the Order of the British Empire in honor of her contribution to scholarship and higher education.

Before she wrote *Revolutionary Life*, she produced *Mary Wollstonecraft: An Annotated Bibliography* covering critical and biographical entries from 1788 through 1975. A steady stream of criticism on Wollstonecraft has been published since the bibliography's first publication in 1976, and although Routledge has recently reprinted it, the work is outdated if one is looking for more contemporary criticism and biographies. However, the bibliography is still valuable for Todd's notes on books and articles published prior to 1975. Additionally, through Pickering & Chatto, Todd has produced scholarly editions of all of Wollstonecraft's works, including her articles in *Analytical Review*.

Todd's *Daughters of Ireland* (2003) contains very little biographical information on Wollstonecraft, but it certainly educates the reader as to the significance of that one year (1786–87), when Wollstonecraft was the governess to the Kingsboroughs, in forming Wollstonecraft's perceptions of the upper class that so profusely informs *Rights of Woman*. Caroline Fitzgerald, who would become Lady Kingsborough, descended from Old Celtic and Anglo blood, with an ancestor, the White Knight, whose battle wounds were bandaged with a white scarf by Edward III (4). She was the heiress of 75,000 acres, or 21 miles, of Cork and Limerick land and of Mitchelstown Castle. She married her cousin Robert and theirs was the largest fortune in Ireland (4).

Todd's book gives the reader a better understanding as to why Lady Caroline often invited Wollstonecraft and sometimes pressed her into joining her social gatherings and functions, even though Wollstonecraft was a "mere governess." When Wollstonecraft's *Thoughts on the Education of Daughters* was published, she was Lady Caroline's trophy. In the Wollstonecraft biographies, Lady Kingsborough's behavior seemed erratic and eccentric, but Todd's book explains how she came to be what she was, the kind of woman who showed more affection and attention on her dogs than to her children (89), the kind of woman who would spend more than five hours a day getting dressed (90), the kind of woman who fashionably lisped (90) and the kind of woman who spent £500 on a gown for Margaret that was the equivalent of 12 years of salary for a governess (117). Todd portrays Lady Kingsborough as a typical eighteenth-century aristocrat who expected the governess to replicate their mother's own characteristics, attitudes and behavior in her daughters. Todd's in-depth account helps one to appreciate Wollstonecraft's acrimony and target in *Rights of Woman*. It also reveals the extent to which Wollstonecraft's ideas about educating women were propagated by Margaret King, the oldest daughter in that family taught by Wollstonecraft.

As for *Revolutionary Life*, no matter how meticulous Todd was with her biographical information relating to Wollstonecraft, she was at a disadvantage by missing some information that would surface only after her work. Also, although discerning, Todd did borrow from the major biographers who preceded her but still repeated some of their errors. These were Godwin (1798), Paul (1878), Pennell (1885), George (1970), Nixon (1971), Flexner (1972), Tomalin (1974), Sunstein (1975), Tims (1976) and St. Clair (1989), when scholarship was not as rigorous as it would become in the 1990s. We should not dismiss earlier scholarship, but we must read it with skepticism and refrain from embracing what is said as truth until research validates it.

A Revolutionary Life includes claims that would have been strengthened by sources. For example, how did Todd know that when Wollstonecraft lived in Beverley, and because of the Beverley Minster, "she could not have avoided gaining some taste for religious beauty" (10)? Todd's details that follow to suggest such a propensity, create a scene that is very visual, but still fictive: A nine-year-old child doing what only a nine-year-old would do, and that was crawling under the seats in the choir and looking at the misereres. The artisans in the Middle Ages often carved caricatures of themselves and other commoners in their towns. These carvings were often kept hidden from view, and they were a way for artisans to put their individual stamps and signatures on their work. From these works we can learn a lot about daily life in mediaeval times, and of course they would invite a child's curiosity.

Todd describes "a man madly shoeing a goose" (10). Perhaps Todd saw this carving herself. To "shoe a goose" is a euphemism for a man who is drunk. He is so drunk or he is such a dimwit, he is ridiculously wasting his time trying to put shoes on a goose, and most likely the goose is not cooperating. It also was an expression that people used to indicate that someone was doing something that had very little purpose or value. For example, in Nicholas Breton's *Grinello's Fort* is this statement: "Yet I can do something else than shoe the goose for my living" (1604).[1] Or the *OED* gives this example from Thomas Nashe's *Unfortunate Traveller*: "Galen might goe shooe the gander for anie good he could doe" (1594).[2] In even earlier centuries Nashe referred to someone who meddled, such as Hoccleve's *Poems*: "Ye medle of al thing, ye moot shoo the goos" (1410).[3]

The second misericord that Todd mentions is a cat playing a fiddle for her kittens, which leads me to think that Todd saw the carving herself and misunderstood that the kittens were actually mice and that the carving reflects the English nursery rhyme, "Hey! Diddle, diddle, the cat and the fiddle." Thomas Tindall Wildridge describes the carving in his book on the Beverley misereres. With the fiddle playing attracting the mice to the cat, the suggestion from the carving is that one can get one's dinner through soft enticement (42).

Not as entertaining are Todd's slants of dislike toward Wollstonecraft. Todd is often critical of her, and even if the biographer tries to be fair-minded about the other people in Wollstonecraft's life, Todd often focuses on only the negative. Her composite portrait of Wollstonecraft is out of kilter for this reason. For example, she mentions that Wollstonecraft had light brown eyes with one lid slightly paralyzed, "giving her sometimes a mocking, leering look" (28). Compare this to Diane Jacobs's description: "her uncommon experience gave her an exotic charm—as did the slight squint, or *louche*, she'd developed in one eye" (244). Robert Southey refers to the same anomaly, but thinks "they are the most meaning I ever saw."[4] One fact, three different perspectives, which is another illustration that furthers my point that the biography is often more about the biographer than about the subject.

The most shocking divergence Todd takes, compared to other biographers, however, is her criticism of Wollstonecraft's orchestration of the dismantling of the Bishop family. As do other twentieth-century biographers, Todd realizes that Bess fell into an acute post-natal depression, which was not understood in the eighteenth century, but Wollstonecraft and other women in her century were aware that they often had to deal with depression or "melancholia" following childbirth, and that this was normal and something that would pass.[5] Although she does not document how she knows this, Todd speculates that Meredith wanted to be helpful by suggesting that he and Bess resume intercourse in the hope that that would lift her spirits. Todd probably deduces this from Wollstonecraft's comment in a letter to Everina that "B cannot behave properly" (Todd, *CL* 41).

Todd mentions that there was an Old Galenic notion that women should not participate in intercourse while they were lactating (45). They believed that intercourse spoiled the milk (Stone 427). It was also believed in Wollstonecraft's time that women were infertile while they lactated (McLaren 1–3). This is what Wollstonecraft means in *Rights of Woman* when she writes: "Nature has so wisely ordered things that did women suckle their children, they would preserve their own health, and there would be such an interval between the births of each child, that we should seldom see a houseful of babes."[6] Therefore, Wollstonecraft might have supposed that Bishop's attempt at intercourse would either spoil Bess's milk if she were breastfeeding or else cause her to become pregnant again. Other than considering her depression, Todd assumes that Bess was not nursing and did not have that excuse for rejecting Bishop (45). It is doubtful that Wollstonecraft would have been willing to be complicit in a scheme to separate mother from child when she was such a strong advocate of mothers bonding with their infants through nursing. Regardless, Todd reckons that the real reason Wollstonecraft acted so preemptively was that she feared Bess would become like their mother, trapped in an unhappy marriage and producing child after child (45).

What is interesting about Todd's account is that she presents Meredith Bishop as a kindly gentleman who was just trying to comfort his wife. There is no real evidence to the contrary. Wollstonecraft is never clear in her letters as to why Bess found her life so intolerable with Bishop, and Todd was not convinced that he had "ill-used" her (Todd, *CL* 39). Todd is sure that he became irate only after he had every reason to be irate—after his sister-in-law smuggled his wife out of the house while he was sick, without giving the couple the time that they would have needed to work through Bess's postpartum depression along with the suffering from whatever her additional mental illness (*Revolutionary* 46).

Todd's position is that Wollstonecraft did not like Bishop and was jealous of his power over her sister. When Bess began improving from her depression and started to indicate that being a wife and mother was not so bad, Todd claims that Wollstonecraft whisked her away because if one more day would pass, Bess would have been resolved to stay (49). This is a good example of how biographers fill in the gaps betwixt and between facts, but the fillers are not necessarily factual.

It is very likely that Bishop asked Wollstonecraft for aid in tending to and dealing with her sister. Since Bess was not nursing the child, it is not as if she needed her sister to come and attend to her household duties. Godwin was the first to suggest that Bishop invited her, and Flexner, Tims, Jacobs and Gordon assume that this was the case. Wollstonecraft might have barged in when she felt that her sister was in danger of losing her mind, but Bishop was not the brute that Wollstonecraft describes in the letters she writes *after* Bess and she have left. After all, he did loan money to Wollstonecraft *after* she took his wife. Bishop could have had both women arrested for breaking the law and could have had Bess committed to an insane asylum but, as Tims, stresses, he did neither (25). And certainly, Bess became more and more mentally unstable once she was in Wollstonecraft's hands (44), so that we have to wonder to what degree if any was Bishop the cause of her mental illness. Yet, *The Broadview Anthology* and numerous other publications attribute Bess's postpartum depression and unhappiness in marriage to Bishop's cruelty (100).

Kirstin Hanley, who published *Mary Wollstonecraft, Pedagogy, and the Practice of Feminism* in 2013, does not question Todd's account of the "rescue" and does not suggest any variations penned by other biographers. Instead of doing her own research, she builds upon Todd's account as if it were the Authorized Version. This is the danger of trusting only one biography. Hanley writes: "While biographical evidence suggests that there may have been motive for Wollstonecraft's intervention," where is that evidence? What evidence? Instead of providing that information, Hanley perpetuates the bias against Wollstonecraft by describing it in the very next sentence as "Wollstonecraft's unsolicited intervention." Hanley then cites Todd several times in order to make her own argument that Wollstonecraft's act "epitomizes the failure of feminism to recognize the individual needs, perspectives, and desires of those it seeks to 'rescue' from patriarchal control" (129), yet Hanley does not claim this to be her own argument, but Todd's instead. It is true that Todd states that Wollstonecraft's plan was "impudent and imprudent" (46), but she lists a number of reasons why Wollstonecraft thought it best to "rescue" her sister. For example, she feared that Bess' depression would become "permanent madness" (46). Todd emphasizes that depression and insanity ran in the family and was not necessarily caused solely by some patriarch tyrannizing women. A case in point was the mad brother (45). Todd also tells, as a matter of fact, that Wollstonecraft enjoyed being "centre stage" and thrilled at the "excitement" of the escapade (46).

Besides using Todd's *Revolutionary Life*, Hanley pulls out words and phrases from Todd's *Collected Letters* to manipulate her argument. Thus, Hanley asserts that Bess was married to "a man of 'passion' and 'malice,'" which "contributed to her depression after the birth of her first child."[7] She deduces this only because of Wollstonecraft's letter to Everina *after* they left Bishop (Todd, *CL* 44). Of course, he would be angry after he learned of his wife's decampment. Then in the next letter, she tells Everina that she has been in communication with Bishop to ask him for a loan of £20 to send to the Bloods to pay for their trip to Ireland. Apparently, Bishop gave it to her. In the next letter, she writes to Everina about Bishop's "malice" which, under the circumstances, should be no surprise. Yet, Wollstonecraft "smile[d]" at his "malice" (48) and felt elated that she delivered her sister from "this man's power" (48). Yet, there is nothing in these letters that indicate that Bishop was ever the passionate, malicious patriarch that drove Bess to the depression that Hanley divined. And Todd does not surmise it either.

Next Hanley appropriates the *"shameful incendiary"* reference from Wollstonecraft's letter (47), as if Wollstonecraft is boasting about her defiance of social mores. Wollstonecraft writes to Everina that she is sure that she will be accused of "the *shameful incendiary*" that she caused and that she will be vilified in the way Mrs. Brown was in Robert Lloyd's *Chit-Chat* for breaking up a home (47). What Hanley omits is Wollstonecraft's statement that she held "the marriage vow sacred" (48), and that she anguished over the entire business until she felt, led by God, that she was doing the right thing by removing Bess from Bishop (48).

After misrepresenting Wollstonecraft through relying so heavily on Todd and selective reading of Wollstonecraft's letters, and after misrepresenting Todd, Hanley concludes that "This episode, in conjunction with Wollstonecraft's treatment of women in *A Short Residence* [*Letters from Sweden*], also exemplifies how feminist arguments can enlist oppressive forces to objectify and script potentially problematic representations of women who fail to conform to a paradigm of 'reformable' womanhood" (130). Now Hanley's statement may very well be accurate, but to build it on such shoddy scholarship, especially in 2013, is disconcerting.

Of course, Todd—as well as any biographer—cannot be held responsible for how someone uses or misuses her information. However, it should be a sobering consideration that what a biographer and scholar do write most likely will be construed as fact and used in future arguments and research. They have the responsibility to be as accurate and objective as possible, knowing that what they put into print today will be quoted tomorrow. And they have the obligation to document their sources and warrant their grounds for claims.

Todd sympathizes with Bishop: "He had fulfilled the duties of a husband [...] He had cherished her and the baby. He had provided a comfortable home and allowed her to bring her bossy sister into it" (*Revolutionary* 50). He attempted reconciliation with his wife, conveying that he "would now endeavor to make Mrs B. happy," but Wollstonecraft mocks his sentiment and chastises George and Fanny and Fanny's beau, Hugh Skeys, for interfering and suggesting that the couple reconcile (Todd, *CL* 49). Todd's assessment is that Wollstonecraft was "now caught in a power struggle with Bishop and Skeys, husband and husband-to-be of two women she controlled. Both men recommended reconciliation. She knew she seemed a virago, but there was no help for it" (*Revolutionary* 55). Indeed, Todd does not portray Wollstonecraft as a heroine or even a positive feminist model.

The final note on the subject, and it is a final note that Todd found in Wollstonecraft's letter, is that baby Mary died (57). The silence implies guilt. Bishop never divorced Bess; Bess could never marry again (57). Wollstonecraft failed to live with Fanny Blood, alone, as, according to Todd, was Wollstonecraft's erotic desire, but Fanny was unhappy, too, as her beloved Skeys left for Lisbon without her (57).

Throughout, Todd is hard on Wollstonecraft, depicting her as a woman who was manipulative, nagging, wildly tumultuous, self-obsessed and often given to melancholy and depression. The most recurring perception of Wollstonecraft that Todd proffers is that she was domineering and controlling, such as this description of the relationship between Fuseli and Wollstonecraft: "No more than Jane Arden or George Blood did Fuseli care to be bludgeoned into behaving as Wollstonecraft wished" (156). When George Blood proposed to Everina, Wollstonecraft rejected it on her sister's behalf (173–74).

But at times, Todd tries to empathize. For example, Todd explains Wollstonecraft's outburst when she received a marriage proposal through Johnson as: "Such a huge reaction to what might have been indelicate but had been kindly meant argues how much marriage troubled her, how much she needed to believe herself superior to its blandishments. She was horrified to appear so universally needy, to seem a mere ordinary woman who would prostitute herself to be kept" (145). An assessment such as this does align with Wollstonecraft's abhorrence of marriage as an arrangement for women to be "legally prostituted" (*ROW* 137; ch. 4), but it does not explain why Wollstonecraft wrote to Everina, at a time when she felt stressed in taking care of Bess after leaving Bishop: "I almost wish for an husband—for I want some body to support me" (Todd, *CL* 44).

Todd intends to be realistic about who Wollstonecraft was and to paint her as a real person with all her shortcomings. Wollstonecraft was not just the icon of feminism she had come to represent to the twenty-first century. She was not just the author of several feminist books. Todd's portrayal of Wollstonecraft would be the most complete until Lyndall Gordon would rewrite the story in 2005, even though Todd's is better documented. Still Todd does repeat some of the mistaken assumptions Godwin made, especially about Wollstonecraft's religion, and she inserts her own assumptions throughout, which should be taken as just that, authorial assumptions and not necessarily fact. But with the volume of work Todd has produced on Wollstonecraft, she—along with Barbara Taylor and Myers—are to receive our gratitude for their efforts to make Wollstonecraft more visible and accessible to generations who have yet to learn much from Wollstonecraft's writing.

Chapter 12

MIRIAM BRODY'S *MARY WOLLSTONECRAFT: MOTHER OF WOMEN'S RIGHTS* (2000): A BEFITTING BETWIXT AND BETWEEN BIOGRAPHY

Mary Wollstonecraft: Mother of Women's Rights by Miriam Brody is a perfect example of biographical material that falls betwixt and between information from other biographies and contains a lot of betwixt and between information from other biographies, with the end result being a biography that is sometimes accurate and sometimes not. I almost did not include it in this study because, even though published by the prestigious Oxford University Press, it cannot be considered a scholarly work—but then, as I argued earlier, most of Wollstonecraft's biographies cannot be considered scholarly. Consisting of only 150 pages and most of them with pictures, it was designed to be one of the "Oxford Portraits" and, hence, not much more than a sketch of a famous person. Even so, most assuredly Oxford intended for that sketch to be accurate. Published in 2000, it represents a selective gleaning of biographical information that has been accumulating ever since Wollstonecraft died in 1797. Unfortunately, there is no documentation, making it difficult to ascertain the source of Brody's information and to judge the basis of her claims betwixt and between previous biographies and her own suppositions. Despite these limitations, her book is one of the more accurate of the biographies in regard to detail and the leanest in regard to bias. But it also suffers from a paucity that reflects myriad unsubstantiated assumptions and gaps, most likely drawn from the Wollstonecraft biographies that came before it.

Brody's subtitle demonstrates leanness. It makes no claim to Wollstonecraft as the mother of feminism, when "feminism" is such a broad term. Brody pares down the epithet to the most accurate that one can be about *Rights of Woman*; Mary Wollstonecraft was the "Mother of Women's Rights."

However, she does offer several unique details not found in any other biography. For example, she identifies Wollstonecraft's grandfather as a "master weaver," explaining that he would have bought thread for the journeymen who in turn would have their families in their homes spin it into cloth, and then the master weaver would sell the cloth. This was called the "putting-out" system of manufacture, and it predated factory work (10–11).

Another aspect that Brody took the time to clarify is the noisy and unsanitary atmosphere of Spitalfields when Wollstonecraft was a child which, Brody singularly reasons, is why her father wanted them to live in the country and for him to be a gentleman farmer (11). It is a nobler picture than we find in most of the biographies, including Tomalin's, which depicts the father at Barking as throwing away his inheritance on "both horse and bottle," proving "impatient and incompetent as a farmer," rejecting his wife's proposal that his children have a governess, as was expected of a family of his class, and irresponsibly moving on instead of persevering through failure (6). Janet Todd is just as scathing as Tomalin but then suggests a more comprehensive justification of her criticism. She asserts that Wollstonecraft's father had adequate resources to succeed in Barking because it was a fertile area. Even with the Enclosure Acts that were requiring farmers to be more efficient in the management of their lands, Todd accuses him of being too enthralled with his new life as landed gentry without attending to what had to be done to deal with the agricultural changes at the end of the century (*Revolutionary* 7–8). Maybe she is right, but Brody's description of him is more in keeping with Ruth Brandon's portrait (2008): "Edward Wollstonecraft, of course, did not set out to lose his inheritance. On the contrary, he hoped to propel himself up a class by abandoning his roots in trade to become a gentleman farmer" (45). He had every reason to believe that the time was ripe for him to make such a move; it was a period of great social mobility (Lorch 7). That he left London for the country to offer a healthier life for his children and to impel the entire family upward are worthy motives not often credited to him. Had he succeeded, Wollstonecraft would never have had to become a companion and a governess. Her father probably would not have turned into the tyrant he became, which, as Todd surmised, "would mark and mar her choice of lovers" and made her father "the embodiment of improper masculinity and weak despotic power" (*Revolutionary* 8). And then there would never have been *A Vindication of the Rights of Woman* that condemned male tyrants who "force all women, by denying them civil and political rights, to remain immured in their families groping in the dark" (*ROW* 73; ded.).

In those early, formative years, Wollstonecraft had a happy, healthy childhood. When they lived in Epping and then Barking, she remembered playing "happily with other children in the open air" (Brandon 45), followed by six happy years in Beverley. When she was 20 and living in the fashionable city of Bath, she wrote her old friend from Beverley that she missed the "agreeable" and "peaceful days" in the country (Todd, *CL* 20). Although she would make friends who would enrich her knowledge of books, religion and the world when her father moved them to Hoxton in London, it appears that it was when they returned to the city that the father lost his forbearance and temper, turned to drink and beat his wife and children (Godwin 46)

Brody is in agreement with most of the biographers that Wollstonecraft's father "had not inherited either his father's habit of hard work or his business sense" (14). Brody tempers her sketch of him by explaining the hardship on farmers because of the Enclosure Acts (14), but then she assumes that he should have been able to prosper with the capital he had, since other farmers in the region did, and the problem was that he was not "willing to accept the advice of a knowledgeable manager," and his temperament should have "been steadier and less self-indulgent" (14). The £10,000 he inherited, plus income from rental property in London, did make him what we would currently term a millionaire. Within two decades, he had so depleted his capital, that he was in debt, and neighbors were openly censorious, which Wollstonecraft said was justified (Todd, *CL* 23). Wollstonecraft wrote about her "father's violent temper and extravagant turn of mind" which caused so much of her own "unhappiness and that of the rest of the family" (23). Brody claims Wollstonecraft learned from him a "genteel snobbery that took the form of a lifelong hostility to making money from trade" (17), but the point would be more convincing had Brody provided grounds for this assumption. If Wollstonecraft had been snobbish, it was *against* gentility. In 1781 she wrote to Jane Arden: "I am particularly sick of genteel life, as it is called—the unmeaning civilities that I see every day practiced don't agree with my temper" (Todd, *CL* 29). And she had no delicacy about earning her living from writing reviews for Johnson.

On the other hand, Brody notes how self-conscious Wollstonecraft was when writing to Jane Arden (19). One reason was because she was distracted by having to care for her younger siblings (Todd, *CL* 10). Mostly she was sensitive about how little education she had received compared to Arden (8), whose father was a member of the Royal Society of London (18). To Brody, this self-consciousness demonstrated the low self-esteem that would plague her throughout her life, caused, according to Brody, because of the parents' preference for her older brother Ned and by the constant admiration of Bess, who was considered the family's beauty (21). These factors were mentioned by other biographers as well, but no one emphasizes that had not Wollstonecraft become aware of her lack of proficiency in writing, she might never had been motivated to improve, and improve to such an extent that she would write *Rights of Woman*.

One final point that Brody makes before leaving Wollstonecraft's youthful years is that she inherited moodiness from her father, whereas her mother was "passionless and plaintive" (22), assumptions made by other biographers. More research needs to be done about Wollstonecraft's mother. There has been too much building upon unfounded assumptions published by early biographers. By mooting her voice, by erasing her, by reducing her to just a "passionless and plaintive" woman would, were Wollstonecraft still alive, have provoked her to protest.

Also like many other biographers, Brody assumes that *Mary, A Fiction* is autobiographical. From it she deduces this about Wollstonecraft: "Could she have loved her father or mother, had they returned her affection, she would not so soon, perhaps, have sought a new world."[1] Brody deduces that Wollstonecraft was deprived of the love every child needs from parents. She does not comment on what Wollstonecraft means as "a new world." However, Michelle Faubert, who edited the Broadview edition of *Mary, A Fiction*, interprets it as meaning heaven (84n1). This is valid; Wollstonecraft often writes in her letters that she did not feel at home in this world and longed for heaven.[2] Had Wollstonecraft felt comfortable in her world, she would not have seen any reason to reform it. She would not have been driven to write her vindications for the purpose of trying to improve it.

A psychoanalytical thread runs through Brody's biography. Because of the difficult relationship with their parents, Wollstonecraft and her sisters found it very difficult to build healthy relationships with other people. "Having a young friend like Mary Wollstonecraft would have been work," Brody postulates from Wollstonecraft's demanding and moody letters to Jane Arden and her anxieties about Fanny Blood (28). She "idealized friendship" and held certain expectations of a perfect love that constantly disappointed her (28). Brody is not surprised that Bess wanted out of her marriage insofar as "no daughter of Edward and Elizabeth Wollstonecraft could move into married life without anxiety" (41), a condition that did not portend well for Wollstonecraft's own relationships with men.

Another marriage that cost Wollstonecraft a great personal price was Fanny's. A consideration unique to Brody's recounting of this part of Wollstonecraft's life is that Hugh Skeys had to bury Fanny at night and in secret. Portugal was a Catholic country, and Fanny was Anglican (49). In England, Nonconformists were treated the same way, but there the sanctioned religion was Anglican. In the 1780s and 1790s, European Catholics were stricter about prohibiting Protestants and others from being buried in consecrated ground. In England, burial of non-communicants in Protestant graveyards was decided by the incumbent cleric of the Church of England (Tarlow 45–47). Most Catholics were buried in family chapels and, if they were allowed burial in an Anglican churchyard, it was usually done at night (Houlbrooke 336). Given Wollstonecraft's anti-Catholic sentiments, this burial arrangement must have been galling.

Besides writing about Wollstonecraft's personal life, Brody does have things to say about her work. Brody considers *Mary, A Fiction* as "not a well-written book. It was uneven in narrative and unconvincing in characterization" and consistent with "novel of feeling" that was popular with the readers of the day (60). Brody provides no argumentation to justify this assessment but does underscore that, by publishing this novel, Wollstonecraft realized she no longer had to be a governess to earn her daily bread (60). *Thoughts* and *Mary* may have been just what Johnson needed to convince him to put Wollstonecraft on his staff as a regular reviewer for the *Analytical Review*. After that step came Johnson's commission for her to write a rebuttal of Burke's *Reflections on the Revolution in France*, which was one more stepping stone to her pièce de résistance, *A Vindication of the Rights of Woman*. Brody is right in stating that Wollstonecraft's "entire life had prepared her to make this argument" (78).

After discussing *Rights of Woman*, Brody treats Wollstonecraft's behavior toward Fuseli, and in this she makes a number of mistakes and erroneous assumptions that I have addressed in other parts of my book. Brody claims that Wollstonecraft told her sister that she was lonely. Wollstonecraft did write often to her sisters and friends that she was lonely and, although she had had several marriage proposals, Brody is probably right to say: "She had not yet discovered love between two like-minded persons who preferred each other to the rest of the world" (84). Brody is not clear as to Wollstonecraft's position on romantic love. In one paragraph, she argues that Wollstonecraft thought it a "noble sentiment" (Brody's phrase), and then in the next deduces from *Rights of Woman* that Wollstonecraft is warning that it would be better that a marriage be based on calm friendship instead of passion (85). The passage to which she refers reads:

> Were women more rationally educated, could they take a more comprehensive view of things, they would be contented to love but once in their lives; and after marriage calmly let passion subside into friendship—into that tender intimacy, which is the best refuge from care; yet is built on such pure, still affections, that idle jealousies would not be allowed to disturb the discharge of the sober duties of life, or to engross the thoughts that ought to be otherwise employed. This is a state in which many men live; but few, very few women. (205; ch. 6)

Wollstonecraft declares that "passion" is arbitrary, full of mischief, and easily extinguishable (205). Perhaps she was ambivalent about this herself. By the time she was involved with Imlay, she writes about her "sacred emotions, that are the sure harbingers of the delights I was formed to enjoy—and shall enjoy, for nothing can extinguish the heavenly spark" (Todd, *CL* 310).

But Brody is discussing Fuseli and applies Wollstonecraft's pre-Imlay theory of romance to the reason why she intellectually desired a platonic relationship with him, even if it required including his wife (85–87). Other biographers have made similar deductions, but mine differ: She was smitten by Fuseli because he flirted with her, and although other men had paid her similar attention, Fuseli was an intellectual radical, which attracted her and made him a worthy love interest. Furthermore, according to Tomalin, he was not married when they first met, although he was engaged (86). Additionally, she was now famous herself and most likely believed herself to be an equal in all respects to Fuseli.

Fuseli's biographer, John Knowles depicts him as a gentlemanly scholar who was friendly to Wollstonecraft only because he admired her talents, whereas Knowles depicts Wollstonecraft as a love-crazed, sexually deprived female whose "advances were not met with the affection which she had hoped to inspire in Fuseli" (162–66). Tomalin suggests that, since Fuseli was 47, he used Wollstonecraft to make his fiancé jealous and therefore more apt to go to the altar with him—or else that Wollstonecraft was simply one last fling to flatter his ego (85–86). Brody herself says Fuseli "was unwilling to break up his household on her behalf" (86). Tomalin questions Fuseli's conduct toward Wollstonecraft when considering what she calls his "steady stream of pornographic drawings, detailed but chilly in their eroticism" (83). And then there is the matter of his sending "graphic love letters" to Johann Kaspar Lavater, "recalling their earlier times together, even tempting Lavater when he was newly wed" (Sapiro 20–21).

Knowles claims that "Fuseli reasoned with her, but without any effect, upon the impropriety of indulging in a passion that took her out of common life" (167). Even before Godwin fell in love with Wollstonecraft, Godwin characterized Fuseli as "the most frankly ingenuous and conceited man" he had ever known."[3] Regardless, according to Knowles, she had "no resource [...] but to fly from the object which she regarded" to France (168), which is Brody's assumption as well (87), despite the fact that Wollstonecraft and the Fuselis and Johnson had already planned a trip to Paris to observe firsthand what was going on with the Revolution. In fact, in August 1792, the four of them had already gone as far as Dover, but upon hearing reports of great violence—most likely the arrest of King Louis XVI—the party turned back; but this was not Wollstonecraft's inclination (Jacobs 112) since, by November, she wrote William Roscoe that she would not be stopped in Dover again but would go to France even if she had to go alone (Todd, *CL* 206).

Wollstonecraft was appalled by what she witnessed. Brody pictures it for us: "Brave and upright, Jeanne-Manon Roland mounted the block, calling out to the goddess of liberty and asking how many had died in her name" (101). Wollstonecraft—the great champion of freedom and supporter of the French Revolution—had every reason to be concerned for own life while in Paris. Another English writer and outspoken proponent of liberty, Helen Maria Williams, who would be guillotined, had warned Wollstonecraft to burn her manuscript, *An Historical and Moral View of the Origin and Progress of the French Revolution* (Todd, *CL* 248). It is amazing that Wollstonecraft was able to send it to Johnson without detection. At the end of a letter to her friend Ruth Barlow, she writes about the decree of April 16, 1794, that all foreigners were to leave France or be taken prisoner. She cries, "My God, how many victims fall beneath the sword and the Guillotine!—My blood runs cold, and I sicken at thoughts of a Revolution which costs so much blood and bitter tears" (255). Brody describes the disillusionment that Wollstonecraft must have felt:

> The clatter of the two-wheeled tumbrels taking the condemned to execution; the warning clang of the tocsin, which were the bells announcing the tumbrels' approach; and the snap of the great ax of the guillotine—these were not the music of a rational society improving itself. (101, 103)

Wollstonecraft blamed the violence, not on the mob, but on the "monarchy and aristocracy [that] had corrupted the nation for so long" (103). Brody is somewhat correct in that in *French Revolution* Wollstonecraft did blame "absolute governments" and the "tyrants of the earth" and the indolent wealthy for what happened in France (508), but she wisely avoided condemning the monarchy in general lest she be guilty of treason in England.[4] Brody says, too, that Wollstonecraft believes France will heal itself and then be better off because of the Revolution (103), which hope Wollstonecraft does indeed express: After the removal of the "useless head" and old, ineffective order and its consolidation of a republican government "we may then look for a turn of mind more solid, principles more fixed, and a conduct more consistent and virtuous" (507–8).

Brody argues that Wollstonecraft threw over the conventional and biblical principles of marriage by managing to be married to Godwin while still remaining independent. This is Brody's reasoning: "Throughout her professional life she had claimed that the institution of marriage either oppressed women directly or smothered exceptional women who might be usefully engaged outside of housekeeping" (133). Wollstonecraft complains often about the state of marriages in her own society, forced upon people for reasons other than love, passion and compatibility. However, she does not condemn marriage; she condemns marriages that were forged and practiced by social vanity instead of virtue. In chapter 9 of *Rights of Woman* she describes her ideal marriage, and it is definitely a marriage.

Furthermore, if she were so keen on negating boundaries of marriage, why did she attempt suicide twice when Imlay ran roughshod over those boundaries? Surely, she experienced firsthand the suffering caused when one's partner refuses to be faithful and monogamous and committed.

As for the second part of Brody's comment about women being useful outside of housekeeping, she is right. Throughout *Rights of Woman* Wollstonecraft argues that God gave women talents and that they should use them for the betterment of humanity, and that these talents were the same that God gave to men. "How many women thus waste life away the prey of discontent," Wollstonecraft queries, "who might have practised as physicians, regulated a farm, managed a farm, managed a shop, and stood erect, supported by their own industry" (241; ch. 9). Working parents were still expected to prioritize their families. She does emphasize that fulfilling domestic responsibilities—for both genders—was also an obligation. Wollstonecraft also spoke of the fate that might make one a widow or cause a woman to remain single, and then pointed out the necessity of both situations for women to be able to earn a living. Whether married or single, women and men should have a good education and equal opportunity for vocations.

Brody's last chapter briefly mentions what, after Wollstonecraft's death, happened within the Godwin family and with her writing. She ends with this powerful statement: "Mary Wollstonecraft understood that ignorance and indifference erode liberty even faster than time erases granite. Her most important tribute, more long lasting than flowers and kind words, is the continuing campaign for women's rights, a call to arms that her brave writing announced to an astonished world" (150). Wollstonecraft would have been both pleased and dismayed to read such a statement: pleased that Brody was passing on the baton to continue the campaign for women's rights, and dismayed that in 2000, more than two centuries after she had sounded her own clarion, that gender equality still had not been guaranteed to all. Brody metaphorically mentions Wollstonecraft's gravesite, that when plans were being made to celebrate the bicentennial publication of *Rights of Woman*, the grave had fallen into great disrepair. Thus, Brody's allusions to granite and flowers challenge the upcoming generations not to settle for concessions made to women since Wollstonecraft threw down the gauntlet, but to continue the fight until women everywhere in every situation, do not have to accept being betwixt and between freedom but are indeed free.

Chapter 13

DIANE JACOBS'S *HER OWN WOMAN: THE LIFE OF MARY WOLLSTONECRAFT* (2001): NEVER JUST HER OWN WOMAN

Of all the biographies, *Her Own Woman: The Life of Mary Wollstonecraft* by Diane Jacobs, reads most nearly like a novel, while Lyndall Gordon's is the most enjoyable and accurate. Still, Jacobs fleshed out details that are both physical and psychological so that the reader is transported into scenes with an immediacy lacking in other biographies. Her sources were primarily letters instead of biographies or critical articles. In fact, if one scans her endnotes, one will find "Letter" and "ibid." over and over, with only rare references to other sources. *Her Own Woman* is not scholarly in that it does not often contextualize its narrative or substantiate its claims with scholarly sources, but the result is a clean, clear and pleasant read. Jacobs sometimes supplies useful information to support generalizations, but at other times she makes sweeping deductions without foundations.

The focus of Jacobs's biography seems to be on relationships. She rarely discusses Wollstonecraft or her works without addressing Wollstonecraft in relationship with someone. And the relationship she addresses more "carefully" than most is the one with Fanny Blood. Although several scholars have implied that Wollstonecraft had homoerotic desires for Fanny, and that the passion she felt exceeded traditionally acceptable boundaries for same-sex relationships, Jacobs writes: "Suddenly, Mary had a goal: to forge what the eighteenth century called a 'romantic friendship'" (27). An endnote to guide the reader to further reading or even to convince the reader that there was any such a thing that typified women-to-women relationships in the eighteenth century would have been helpful, but Jacobs obviously was not writing for academe. The book was published by Simon & Schuster for a broad audience. Nevertheless, her own explanation is useful. This is how she defines "romantic friendship": "a relationship between two women that could be as tempestuous as any love affair, but only rarely involved sex," and then she gives some examples of famous relationships of the day like Eleanor Butler and Sarah Ponsonby, the "ladies of Llangollen" (27), but without explanation.

Lady Eleanor Butler (1739–1831) hailed from an old and distinguished Irish family in County Waterford and rejected five marriage proposals (Armytage 328). Miss Sarah Ponsonby (1755–1831) was a member of a noble Anglo family and apparently rejected several "handsome offers" as well, and with Eleanor, "resolved on lives of celibacy" (710).[1] Despite the disapproval of their families, they eloped in 1778 to Llangollen in North Wales, where they bought a cottage, Plas Newydd, and had it refurbished in a Gothic style. Sir Walter Scott described their escape: "Lady Eleanor arrived (in Wales) in her natural aspect of a pretty girl, while Miss Ponsonby condescended to accompany her in the garb of a smart footman with buckskin breeches."[2] Although they wished to live in obscurity, they gained great notoriety and were flocked by visitors, including some very famous people, including Robert Southey, Josiah Wedgwood, Lady Caroline Lamb, Sir Humphry Davy and, most frequently, their close friend the Duke of Wellington (Castle 334)—as well as Edmund Burke, Lord Bessborough, Lord Castlereagh, The Duc de Montpensier, Lord Bolingbroke and William Wilberforce (Armytage 333). After meeting these two women, William Wordsworth, Anna Seward, Madame de Genlis and Sir Walter Scott, were so impressed that they wrote about them.[3] The couple became known as "the two most celebrated virgins in Europe," so labeled by Prince Pückler Muskaus, a famous artist in landscape gardening, who came to see their celebrated gardens.[4]

The two ladies of Llangollen wore the same costume without variation: stiff starched neckcloth and short powdered hair, men's black beaver hats, cravats, and jupons (short riding jackets), so they seemed very masculine from the waist up. However, below they wore petticoats, white stockings and low-cut shoes. They kept their bushy white hair cropped short.[5]

How has history recorded their relationship? The first record is a letter from Mrs. Tighe, Lady Betty Fowne's daughter, addressed to Mrs. Goddard, who was a friend of the Butler family: "The runaways are caught, and we shall soon see our amiable Friend again, whose conduct, though it has an appearance of imprudence, is, I am sure, void of any serious impropriety. There were no gentlemen concerned; nor does it appear to be anything more than a scheme of *romantic friendship*" (quoted in Casey 295; emphasis added). As long as there were no men involved—no heterosexual coupling—apparently, most people in the eighteenth century could not think that there would be anything sexual between a woman and another woman. Wollstonecraft did not share this naïvety, however. In *Rights of Woman* she warns that girls who sleep and wash together are very likely to be inclined to "nasty, or immodest habits" and behave improperly (215; ch. 7). The *General Evening Post* was not so naïve, either, when in a 1790 article it makes clear that Butler was the masculine partner to Ponsonby.[6]

An article in *Chambers's Edinburgh Journal* (1839) describes them:

> Their early choice of solitude, and preference of one another's society to that of the world, might have been ascribed to the common enthusiasm and romanticism of youth, but for the steadiness with which they adhered to their purpose in spite of all obstacles, and the enduring nature of their friendship—circumstances which showed unusual strength of character, and proved their resolves to be of a different kind from the many fleeting ones of a similar order, formed by other romantic pairs at the same period of life. With many oddities of temperament, Lady Eleanor Butler and Miss Ponsonby were assuredly very much superior, both in intellect and feeling, to the ordinary herd of mortals. (195)

More innocuous praise follows toward the end of the nineteenth century. *The Leisure Hour* (1877) remarks:

> It is probably impossible to find in written history a more remarkable instance of affection between two women, their virtues commanding the admiration of all the good, and their long lives being spent in cheerful usefulness and social enjoyment, although they chose to be in comparative seclusion. (711–12)

In 1880 Rev. John Prichard and a relative of Lady Eleanor wrote a short book on the two women, "who loved each other with an affection so true that they could never bear the idea of the separation which the marriage of either would necessitate. They, therefore, resolved on lives of celibacy" (*Account* 2). They were also honored with full romantic color in *The Red Dragon, the National Magazine of Wales* in 1882: "They were lovely and pleasant in their lives, and in their graves they are not divided" (Shindler 135).

In her article for *The Pall Mall Magazine* (1899), Fenella Armytage calls them "two eccentric ladies" (331) and asserts that "the unbroken friendship of these two women stands unrivalled among the stories of human life" (334). Armytage remarks that, after a hundred years, "their memory, their sayings and doings are still remembered" (336).

It would appear that the Victorians idealized their friendship and could not contemplate a sexual bond between women. After the turn of the century, the two were considered heroic for their independence. Theodora Roscoe, writing for the *Westminster Review* (1910), refers to them as "lady bachelors" (329). They were not like their contemporaries, Roscoe assures her readers in 1910, who "would often marry anyone to escape being classed under the category of 'Old Maids.'" She muses: "Present day girls prefer not to wear out their souls and bodies in a weary wait, with endless longings for something, we say 'something,' for, when desperate, anything in the shape of a male would serve their purpose, to release them from their one state of dependence, only to enter that of another" (328). Roscoe exalts the ladies as heroines of independence and encouraged her own sisters to embrace a similar spirit, but she adds very sadly that it was nearly impossible for women to have such an ideal existence as did Eleanor and Sarah unless they were as financially independent (330). In 1971 Susan Butler, a distant relative, praises her ancestor in similar terms: "They threw over their sheltered existence and became, not too self-consciously, the archetypes of female independence" (214).

By the middle of the twentieth century, the Llangollen ladies were understood to be the iconoclastic lesbian couple and appeared in nearly every book written in the past few decades that chronicled lesbian or gay or queer history. Still, writing for an encyclopedia of lesbian history, Lillian Faderman tries to put their relationship in a historic context. During the end of the eighteenth century, she says, women were expected to exude "sensibility, faithfulness, and devotion" but to remain chaste until they were married. Therefore, developing close same-sex friendships was very much encouraged, especially by patriarchy—by men who wanted women to bring those virtues into their marriages and could cultivate them in socially acceptable relationships, women with women (649). Faderman illustrates this practice by describing several eighteenth-century novels and other books that encouraged these relationships, such as Sarah Scott's *A Description of Millennium Hall* (1762), Mrs. Delaney's *The Autobiography and Correspondence of Mary Granville, Mrs. Delany* (written in the 1700s but not published until 1861), William Hayley's *The Young Widow* (1789), and Anne Hughes's *Henry and Isabella* (1788) (649).

Defining what Wollstonecraft felt for Fanny Blood (and the same may be said about her feelings for Jane Arden) as "romantic friendship" was a "safe" way to circumvent the sexual issues that intrigued other biographers regarding these relationships. "Romantic friendship" was a term that was common to describe the love between women in the eighteenth century. Because in general such friendships were understood to be platonic, and very few people believed them to be objectionable or a violation of social codes (Zimmerman 649).

Another topic that greatly interests Jacobs is Wollstonecraft's "lifelong tendency to depression, complaining to her sisters about 'gloom,' violent headaches, and 'nervous' fevers" (26). Unlike Janet Todd, with her *A Revolutionary Life*, Jacobs writes about Wollstonecraft as if she greatly admires her as well as empathizes with her. Wollstonecraft's battles were Jacobs's. Wollstonecraft's heartbreaks were Jacobs's. And the biographer allows the space needed to encourage her readers to share in these battles and heartbreaks. Most scholars note that Wollstonecraft often gave her income to her father and siblings as well as to the Blood family, but only a few point out that this experience impressed upon Wollstonecraft one of the main reasons women needed to be better educated: so that they could support themselves when men failed them.

Very few scholars vent hostility toward men on Wollstonecraft's behalf as does Jacobs. Here is one example, as Jacobs describes when Wollstonecraft's mother was dying: "For two years, Mary (with help from her sisters) devoted herself to caring for Elizabeth Wollstonecraft, while her father was off seducing a younger woman named Lydia[,] and Ned, now a married lawyer, rarely came around. [...] Once his wife was buried, Edward John lost no time proposing to his new lover, Lydia" (30). Although Godwin was the first to write about Wollstonecraft's father as a man who left much to be desired as a husband and a father, Jacobs attempts to capture what she imagines to have been Wollstonecraft's point of view toward him. It might have furthered Jacobs's criticism on behalf of Wollstonecraft had she added that Lydia was the housekeeper in the same house where his wife was dying (Sunstein 69).

Jacobs's narrative gives her readers a better sense of the fear and anxiety Wollstonecraft experienced in smuggling Bess out of Bishop's house, giving such details as Bess's filling a bag with dresses but forgetting the linen, and Wollstonecraft lying awake the first night of the escape, expecting to hear Bishop's carriage at any moment (34). The next day, "They ached in every muscle, and Mary's stomach roiled. Once Bess went deaf for hours, which was exactly how her earlier insanity had begun" (35). But Jacobs does not expend much time explaining or even theorizing why Mary felt it necessary to rescue Bess from her marriage. Jacobs makes this strange comment: "By taking action, she discovered the un-Christian joy of asserting her will. Against the male sex, no less" (35). Did Wollstonecraft really feel joy at separating Bess from her husband and child knowing the pain that it was going to cause all four of them, including herself in that she would have to support Bess? In contrast, Janet Todd makes this observation: "There was no suggestion of taking the baby, but the lack of any anxiety on Mary's part in separating mother and infant was extraordinary" (*Revolutionary* 49). If she had indeed felt joy because she was doing something that was right, why was it un-Christian? Jacobs does not explain. She says that Bess's baby died "probably of neglect." Yes, Mary Frances did die, but it was eight months later. She might have died of neglect but how does Jacobs know this? Jacobs covers Bess's marriage in barely four pages leaving out crucial information that can be found, instead, in an entire chapter devoted to the incident in Todd's *Revolutionary Life*.

Jacobs clearly has a feminist agenda in her biography, subordinating many details of Wollstonecraft's life to it. For example, about Bess's "bit[ing] her wedding ring to pieces," a detail that Wollstonecraft mentions in a letter to Everina, Jacobs adds her own commentary that the act was "a fitting farewell to domesticity" (34). She does not record how Bess pined for her baby and begged Wollstonecraft to let her return or any regrets that Wollstonecraft had.[7] In dramatic flair without explanation, Jacobs declares that *Rights of Woman* "was born the day Bess fled" (36). Jacobs presumes the reader will intuit the argument that supports the syllogism.[8] Jacobs treats Bess as a heroine "who sacrificed everything to leave an unhappy marriage" (99), but says nothing about what she did *not* sacrifice in order to create a happy marriage, nor what Bishop had to sacrifice with a wife who barely gave her marriage a chance to succeed.

Jacobs also has a tendency to extrapolate details from Wollstonecraft's writing to account for decisions she made in her life but, in so doing, often pulls them out of context. To justify Wollstonecraft's intervention in the Bishop marriage, Jacobs quotes the following phrases from *Rights of Woman*, with great misappropriation: "Neglected wives made the 'best mothers' and 'an unhappy marriage' was 'very advantageous to the family'" (266).

Jacobs does provide a useful discussion about Dissenters and the importance of their influence on Wollstonecraft. About Richard Price, Jacobs writes that "love of God meant attacking injustice" (38). This is an accurate assessment of Price and most Dissenters, who were devoted to improving the social conditions of their fellow man.

There was one Dissenter who did more to rescue Wollstonecraft from herself and her poverty than any single person in her life, and that was Joseph Johnson, her publisher, employer and friend. But Jacobs does not give much space to him. On the other hand, several biographers claim it was Johnson who persuaded Wollstonecraft to secure her independence through a career in writing, which was true; however, it was the Anglican biblical scholar, John Hewlett, who was the first to encourage Wollstonecraft to write down her ideas. Jacobs credits Hewlett for encouraging Wollstonecraft "to defy the tabu against professional female writers and pursue a literary career" (39). Sunstein, too, gives him credit, albeit insufficient for the role he played in convincing Wollstonecraft to earn her living from writing. But what neither Jacobs nor Sunstein notices is that it was through Wollstonecraft's religious convictions and the influence of fellow Christians (Richard Price, Joseph Johnson, and John Hewlett, to name the most influential) that encouraged her to contravene the traditional interpretation of Paul's edict in the Bible for women to remain silent and not exert any authority over men. She does this contravening through her writing.

Once finished with *Thoughts on the Education of Daughters*, Wollstonecraft gave the manuscript to John Hewlett who, in turn, gave it to Joseph Johnson, a man who was responsible for putting over 2,700 books into print (Jacobs 45). Not only did Johnson make it possible for Wollstonecraft to earn her living and support all her dependents from writing, and not only did he give her loans, but he provided a place for her to live. Jacobs's details here, however, are not as specific as they are in later biographers' renditions.

Jacobs also makes numerous sweeping statements such as this one about George Blood and Charles Wollstonecraft: "so perhaps both men were fed up with Mary's harsh judgments and relentless needs" (84). Jacobs neither explains nor supports this assumption. It is an irreconcilable charge for a feminist to make about another woman who had to struggle to earn money in a society hostile to women in the upper and middle classes taking employment. Wollstonecraft suffered poverty so that she could pay her father's incessant debts, support her sisters, and constantly bail out her brothers and George Blood. Had she not earned the right to be critical of slovenly and reckless men who leached off her, when making a living was the right and obligation of men a world that privileged the male?

Jacobs contributes well to the Wollstonecraft discourse with her treatment on bluestockings. "Though she was the first to explicitly demand equality for women," Jacobs asserts that Wollstonecraft "drew from a tradition of bluestockings" (99). She then furnishes some historical context about Mary Astell and Catharine Macaulay (99–101). Miriam Brody agrees that Wollstonecraft was a bluestocking (58), and E. Eger and Lucy Peltz include her in their book *Brilliant Women: 18th-Century Bluestockings*. However, Lyndall Gordon assures us that Wollstonecraft never attended any of the functions of the "Blue-Stocking Club," whose members were Mrs. Garrick (wife of the famous actor), Edmund Burke, Sir Joshua Reynolds, Fanny Burney, Hannah More and Horace Walpole (50–51). Susanne Schmid, in her book-length study of literary salons, does not consider Wollstonecraft a bluestocking in that she was more of a radical intellectual. The bluestockings, claims Schmid, did not want "to overthrow the societal order through their mode of living or their manner of writing" and did not "spread daring philosophical ideas" (34).

A detail to appreciate is Jacobs's note that John Adam's sister-in-law requested that Abigail get her a copy of *Rights of Woman* while she was in London (108).[9] Still, I would have liked to have read more evidence that supports Jacobs's claim that "Americans applauded" *Rights of Woman* (108).

Another truncation is Jacobs's treatment of Wollstonecraft's infatuation for Henry Fuseli; it is covered in only four pages (111–14), which barely does justice to this traumatic and puzzling time of her life. How could Wollstonecraft allow herself to be attracted to a married man, especially a flirt like Fuseli, when she had just finished writing *Rights of Woman*, which sharply criticized liaisons outside of marriage? She proposed the same alternate lifestyle a year later when Imlay told her that he would not give up his mistress (Sunstein 292). Why does Jacobs not address these issues?

Nevertheless, Jacobs's comment and discussion about England's attitude toward suicide is very useful: "England was called the suicide capital of the world because of its tolerance for self-killing—albeit on the grounds that anyone who didn't want to live was mad" (202).[10] One can understand the depth of despair Wollstonecraft felt with Imlay's rejection, but Jacobs does not explain how she could have abandoned her daughter Fanny other than to say, "Throughout her months in Paris, Mary had lived for her daughter, but now even Fanny could not tempt her from the longing to be done with the world" (201). Jacobs also passes too quickly over her thought about Wollstonecraft's "Anglican religion" that "condemned suicide, of course," stating, but not arguing: "For the past seven years the Enlightenment had been Mary Wollstonecraft's God" and it was in that literary environment that she accepted suicide as a "fine feeling" that was "ennobled in literature" (201).

Jacobs does not give as much credit to Fanny, who at the age of 22, followed her mother's example and swallowed laudanum, leaving this tragic note that Jacobs reproduces:

> I have long determined that the best thing I could do was to put an end to the existence of a being whose birth was unfortunate, and whose life has only been a series of pain to those persons who have hurt their health in endeavouring to promote her welfare. Perhaps to hear of my death will give you pain; but you will soon have the blessing of forgetting that such a creature ever existed as. (285)[11]

Jacobs's biography contains some gems, but there are many unsubstantiated claims and gaps to make this a reliable and useful biography on Wollstonecraft. Even if it were not intended for a scholarly audience, we readers do want to believe what biographies tell us about their subjects; do we not? Some of Jacobs's statements simply are in error or are highly questionable. Even so, that Jacobs brings to light Wollstonecraft's relationships that defined her contributes much to the composite Wollstonecraft. It is rather ironic that Jacobs titled her book, *Her Own Woman*, in that Jacobs seemed to prove just the opposite, that the woman was created by the people who influenced her life, and that she was never just "her own woman."

Chapter 14

CAROLINE FRANKLIN'S *MARY WOLLSTONECRAFT: A LITERARY LIFE* (2004): "THE EDUCATION OF AN EDUCATOR"

Caroline Franklin's biography is one of the sparest of the full-length biographies on Wollstonecraft. Franklin must have made the conscious determination to avoid duplication of what had been already published and to focus only on reconstructing Wollstonecraft's intellectual and political network that produced the emancipatory print culture of the late eighteenth century. Franklin perceives Wollstonecraft primarily as an autodidact, a term she attaches to Wollstonecraft and frequently repeats. Her objective is to identify those forces and people who educated Wollstonecraft, who, in turn, educated others through her writing.

On the first page of the first chapter, Franklin lets it be known that she is interested in Wollstonecraft's and Godwin's fascination with childhood and how its experiences form character. Although other writers were engaged in education reform and changes in the way that children were being raised in the eighteenth century, Wollstonecraft and Godwin—two social reformers who wrote mostly for adults—realized that reform had to begin with child-rearing. It was a revolutionary idea. The prevalent attitude in the seventeenth century was that children were born of sin, that sin was passed down from the parents to child, and that it was the parents' or nurses' or society's jobs to beat the sin out of them (Plumb 65). Prior to the Industrial Revolution, Britain persisted in somewhat a feudal state, where every member of society knew his or her place and relationship to those above and below. Working-class families, whether they made things or grew things, all worked together, including the children, generation after generation staying in the same geographical communities. With the Enclosure Acts of the late eighteenth century and the end of cottage industry, the physical and social mobility of England's lower classes—the largest part of the population—had a pronounced effect on their perception of children, especially with the rise of public schools and Sunday

Schools and their making education available to the masses. Stopping in the middle of that cataclysmic upheaval, and pondering the effect of environment instead of sin on the formation of human character, is what Franklin attributes to both Wollstonecraft and Godwin.

Franklin is to be commended for recognizing Wollstonecraft and Godwin in this way, but her understanding of Wollstonecraft's early childhood and what it teaches leaves much to be desired, because Franklin gathered her information mostly from the *Memoirs* of Godwin, who took most of his information from Wollstonecraft's written fiction.

Although Franklin may be accurate and perceptive in acclaiming Godwin for being a "pioneer of the burgeoning genre of biography" (2), she gives too much credit to him as a reliable biographer for Wollstonecraft. She quotes Godwin, who writes this about himself as the narrator of *Memoirs*: He "felt a curiosity to be acquainted with the scenes through which [his friends] had passed, and the incidents which had contributed to form their understandings and character."[1] Her point is that Godwin states that, throughout their relationship, he encouraged Wollstonecraft to share about the difficult times in her life. That exchange of information, to Franklin, authenticates Godwin's biography (2). However, the shortness of time, when they were unaware of how little time they would have together, added to the biases and gaps identified above, should make one little inclined to share Franklin's confidence in *Memoirs*.

Furthermore, Franklin's first quote from Godwin reads fully: "The writer of this narrative, when he has met with persons, that in any degree created to themselves an interest and attachment in his mind, has always felt a curiosity to be acquainted with the scenes through which they had passed, and the incidents that had contributed to form their understanding and character."[2] The primary focus of this second paragraph from *Memoirs* is on Godwin. Wollstonecraft—as just one of the persons who interested Godwin—is secondary. Although he listed some altruistic motives for writing *Memoirs*, such as expressing his "sympathy in their excellencies" (43), most of what he is saying is that he is writing the biography because Wollstonecraft interested *him*, she was an "attachment" to *him*, and *he* was curious about her.

Franklin repeats Godwin's statement that Wollstonecraft received little religious training in her youth (*Memoirs* 56). Franklin writes, without explanation or documentation, "Mary Wollstonecraft's family had been feckless not religious" (2). By page 13, however, Franklin asserts, without explanation or support, that "Wollstonecraft was strongly religious" and this is why Franklin thinks that Godwin writes that Wollstonecraft was always promoting the needs of others above her own.[3]

Another error Franklin makes is to assume that Wollstonecraft failed to receive love from either her mother or father. Franklin defends this assumption with a quote from Godwin:

> She experienced in the first period of her existence, but few of those indulgences and marks of affection, which are principally calculated to sooth the subjection and sorrows of our early years. She was not the favourite either of her father or mother. Her father was a man of quick impetuous disposition, subject to alternate fits of kindness and cruelty. In his family he was a despot, and his wife appears to have been the first, and most submissive of his subjects.[4]

The problem with Godwin's claim is that he deduces it from reading Wollstonecraft's then-unpublished novel, *The Wrongs of Woman; or Maria*.[5] Below Godwin's comment is a quote from *Maria* and Godwin's statement that he believes the novel is Wollstonecraft's rendering of "the first period of her own existence" (45). Franklin accepts Godwin's source of information about Wollstonecraft's childhood as coming from her fiction. Like several biographers before her, including Godwin, Franklin theorizes this because Wollstonecraft uses her own name, or one that approximates it, and her fiction draws from her life experiences (2). As I argue in more detail in my chapter on Lyndall Gordon, to assume that fiction is a non-fictitious reflection of an author's life is a non-sequitur unless one conducts the scholarly investigation of other sources in order to prove that it is otherwise. One might as well rely on the scholarly investigation to begin with.

Franklin next makes the assumption that Wollstonecraft went through her life needing maternal love because her mother preferred Ned and seemed to be very strict with her daughter but indulgent with her first son. The mother's preference, again, comes from Godwin (45), who deduces this about Wollstonecraft from *Maria* (211–12). There is no evidence that this was the case with the Wollstonecrafts, but even if it were true, Franklin should have supported her statement and might have explained that Wollstonecraft was also driven to find a surrogate father who would love her, which, I argue elsewhere in this book, was a strong psychological drive that might explain why she was desperate for men like Fuseli, Imlay and Godwin.

Regardless of the reasons, Wollstonecraft's family and friends were extremely important to her, with the major form of communication throughout her life being through letters. Although other biographers have commented on the profusion of Wollstonecraft's letter writing, Franklin regards Wollstonecraft as, literally, a woman of letters and by "letters"—she means "communicating with a network of like-minded friends" through written correspondence (viii).

Janet Todd, who collected many of Wollstonecraft's letters, recognizes that in her letters Wollstonecraft performs her various roles as "child, daughter, companion, friend, teacher, governess, sister, literary hack, woman of letters, lover, wife, rationalist and romantic" (*CL* ix). Although Todd, like Franklin, expresses how important these letters are as a form of "public authorship" (*CL* ix), Todd also sees that they are rife with self-pity, self-awareness, bossiness, priggishness and a host of other tones and emotions that surely portray Wollstonecraft more clearly but were never intended for public exposure. Franklin appreciates that all of her private letter writing made Wollstonecraft a skillful writer for the public in "the form of polemical epistle, advice book, travelogue, and conversational story which would remain central to her published works" (viii), a useful connection to make.

In her investigation of Wollstonecraft's education, Franklin identifies the influence of the Dissenters on Wollstonecraft, as do several other biographers, but Franklin emphasizes that their influence forged her into a latitudinarian Anglican (viii).[6] A more important and accurate point is that the Dissenters helped Wollstonecraft become a feminist,[7] for they modeled criticism of the establishment and welcomed women and their voice into their efforts to reform. Dissenters also showed their own intellectual independence through their publications and education, which also modeled for Wollstonecraft the value of both as opportunities and spiritual callings for her to be an author, an educator and a moralist (viii–ix).

Wollstonecraft was surrounded by a bounty of fellow intellectuals who expanded her knowledge and exchanged ideas. The Age of Enlightenment created for women public spaces, such as clubs, salons and meeting-places (Franklin viii), not to mention Joseph Johnson's table. Franklin explores the great influence of Johnson and Godwin and other writers and thinkers of several coteries that embraced Wollstonecraft as one of their own. This is one of the strengths of her biography, as she offers an in-depth treatment of the agencies that permitted the active exchange of ideas, and those ideas made their way into Wollstonecraft's work. When Wollstonecraft went to France, she joined the Girondin salon society, a group of thinkers who expounded their criticism and ideals through pamphlets. Jane Hodson has identified the end of the eighteenth century as a war of words, with over four hundred pamphlets on France published in Britain, which does not include "poems, ballads, periodical essays and novels."[8] Wollstonecraft learned the power of print to bring about reform, which would be the purpose of her writing *Letters from Sweden*. Franklin explains why a book about Scandinavia would have appealed to readers, with the premier attraction being the speculation that since the French Revolution had failed to bring about democracy, perhaps Sweden would be an "alternative model" (148). In addition, Franklin analyzes the "Bourgeois" group of writers to which Wollstonecraft belonged and identifies their criticism of feudalism and court culture, all the while separating themselves from the lower classes. Wollstonecraft's pedagogical works and stories for children, Franklin stresses, were designed to protect children and youth from the degeneracy of courtly society as well as the moral contagion of the lower classes (37). In *Original Stories*, there is no romanticizing whatsoever about the life of the lower classes, as one would expect a Romantic to do; instead, Franklin observes that the stories present the lower order as vulgar and filthy, but then Franklin seems to think the reason Wollstonecraft did this was to convict the rich of their selfish acquisition of material wealth at the expense of others (42–45).

Thus, Franklin considers a variety of groups of people who informed, and were informed by, Wollstonecraft's writing, resisting the tendency of several other biographers to portray her as only a feminist with a feminist agenda. Wollstonecraft's motivations and ideals for writing exceeded any single agenda. A good illustration of how Franklin's biography diverges from others is her treatment of the Bishop break-up. All Franklin says about Bess is "she suffered a severe post-natal breakdown with 'raving fit.' Wollstonecraft was galvanized into action, first in nursing her and then in organizing the secret flight of her sister from her husband" (12). Franklin adds that the experience would replay in *Maria*. Most biographers apportion at least an entire chapter on the escapade. Franklin gives very few details about her childhood, concluding on page two that the need for a mother's love would recur as a theme in her fiction (2).

On the other hand, she devotes the entire chapter 5—one of her seven chapters—to the events of the French Revolution and, especially, to its literary documentation and reactions to it. With high hopes for an emerging utopia, Wollstonecraft was in Paris and witnessed the escalating mob violence against what seemed to be indiscriminately designated enemies. She would have good reason to be concerned for her own life and registered as Imlay's wife so that she would be protected as an American in France. Franklin quotes Wollstonecraft's first literary response to what she was witnessing:

> About nine o'clock this morning, the king passed by my window [...]. I can scarcely tell you why, but an association of ideas made the tears flow insensibly from my eyes, when I saw Louis sitting with more dignity than I expected from his character, in a hackney coach going to meet his death [...]. I have seen eyes glare through a glass-door opposite my chair, and bloody hands shook at me [...]. I am going to bed—and for the first time in my life, I cannot put out the candle."[9]

She and Paine inclined to the sympathies[10] of the anglophile Girondins, who tried to stop the guillotine executions until the French Girondins themselves became victims of the blade. Franklin explains the differences between the Jacobins and the Girondins and then mentions, "Against this unpromising background, Mary Wollstonecraft fell head-over-heels in love with Gilbert Imlay" (124), and then gives a few paragraphs about Imlay and their relationship before she returns to the French Revolution and Wollstonecraft's writing about it. Franklin begins the next chapter with this insight:

> Though she temporized her political despair by taking the long view in her history of the French revolution, Wollstonecraft's ideals had been blasted by the Terror. She had got through by channeling all the force of her Utopianism into her relationship with Gilbert Imlay: envisioning it as an Edenic partnership of equals. (143)

Whereas most biographers provide at least one chapter exclusively on Imlay and make the French Revolution not more than a setting and the backdrop for the romance, Franklin portrays the Imlay affair as one of the outcomes of the French Revolution that impacted Wollstonecraft's life.

The claim Franklin makes, however, as to the reason Wollstonecraft did not marry Imlay is very difficult to accept without a convincing argument. She may have been correct in saying that Wollstonecraft expected "a sacred commitment to one another" (128). Franklin might have supported this by alluding to some of her letters to Imlay—for example, one that ends when Wollstonecraft is already troubled by Imlay's consistency: "I feel my fate united to yours by the most sacred principles of my soul" (Todd, *CL* 299). Then there is Wollstonecraft's highly cerebral, Romantic musings of how the two of them are not of the "common herd of eaters and drinkers and *child-begeters*" and through emotions and imagination, if he would only open her heart to him, they could live a life of "ineffable delight" and "exquisite pleasure" (*CL* 297). But that does not mean that she felt secure about not being legally married, as she did have to deal with the censorship of society in France and, even more severely, in England, which is why she argued that she did not want to return to England (284). Godwin says it was at Wollstonecraft's insistence, once she was pregnant with Mary, that they marry to avoid "the topic of vulgar discussion" by those around them. She did realize that there was going to be a public scandal anyway because she was supposed to be Mrs. Imlay, and Mr. Imlay was still alive (*Memoirs* 105).

With Wollstonecraft's religious conviction, biographers must be careful not to assume, as does Franklin (128), that Wollstonecraft was so willing to defy morality and reject the sanctity of a public declaration of marriage and a legal ceremony. Franklin also pulls a quote out of context when she implies that Wollstonecraft refused to marry Imlay because she would not have her soul "clogged [...] by promising obedience &c &c" (128).[11] This was actually Wollstonecraft's quoting Ruth Barlow in 1794 who teased her about "acquiring matrimonial phraseology," but managing to remain a woman strong and independent enough to carry out business details that involve Barlow and Imlay's business with a Norwegian shipper (*CL* 251). All of this needed to be explained and developed in Franklin's assumptions.

Notwithstanding the problems described above, Franklin's discussion of Wollstonecraft's philosophies of education within the milieu of pedagogical theory being published by other women is thorough and offers fresh insights. Franklin credits Wollstonecraft's *A Female Reader* as being the first elocution manual for women. Previously, elocution was thought essential for men to prepare them for their role in the public arena, but since women were not supposed to be involved with business or politics, no such manuals existed until Wollstonecraft published hers. All the women "author-educators" were "profoundly committed to professionalizing the maternal role of inducting literacy and training the next generation" (54). Franklin's chapter titled "'When the Voices of Children Are Heard on the Green': Mary Wollstonecraft the Author-Educator," by itself makes this biography worth reading.

Franklin seems to deliberately avoid what has been published before by jumping over information, but whatever she found that was not included in other biographies she presents. Hers is not a definitive biography. Unless one is familiar with the other biographies, or at least a biography like Todd's or Lyndall Gordon's that is more comprehensive, one will get a warped view of Wollstonecraft from Franklin. Her selection of detail is a leap and linger business. Whereas Franklin has very little to say about major events in Wollstonecraft's life, such as the death of Fanny, she is generous in supplying detail about Johnson's entertaining only on Tuesdays and Sundays and that the dinner was usually boiled cod, veal, vegetables and rice pudding. This was Wollstonecraft's university (58). She also allows a few pages to the history of Johnson's press and print shop and lists those who were published by him (59–62) and those books that Wollstonecraft reviewed (76–90). Unique among the biographies are Franklin's details about how much Wollstonecraft earned from her reviews. She received 2–3 guineas per sheet, and a sheet printed out 16 pages (64). After providing earnings by other women writers, Franklin figures that of the seven books Wollstonecraft published in three years, the income went to support her siblings. Franklin says that Johnson calculated that she needed £70 per year for this, but she does not cite her source. Janet Todd lists Johnson's figure of £200 she paid to them during her time in London, and that is probably where Franklin came up with her number.[12]

Unique among the biographers, too, is Franklin's convincing arguments as to the influence of Dr. Samuel Johnson as she compares *The Cave of Fancy* to *Rasselas* (although she got her idea from Basker).[13] She also reminds us that Wollstonecraft included five works by Samuel Johnson in *The Female Reader* (73).

Franklin takes a few positions that might invite debate, especially because she makes claims but does not support them. One is this assessment about a review Wollstonecraft wrote on de Staël's *Letters on the Works and Character of J. J. Rousseau* (1789), in which Wollstonecraft takes the opportunity to be critical of Rousseau. Geniuses like Rousseau are flawed, she argues, and in their attempt to "correct" human nature, only end up "transform[ing] a sublime mountain into a beautiful plain."[14] Franklin compresses an argument that scholars like Steven Blakemore have deliberated through entire books but fails to fairly represent the scholarship published on this subject. Franklin states that Wollstonecraft "elevates the Burkean masculine sublime (proto-Romantic) over the feminine beauty of order and regularity in aesthetics (Neoclassical)" (75). This concept did not originate with her. According to Blakemore, Burke's sexualized references of masculine sublimity with feminine beauty, found in *Enquiry, Speech on American Taxation,* and *Reflections* "angered Wollstonecraft, and so she begins *The Rights of Men* by describing Burke in the 'weaker' language of the beautiful while she uses the 'stronger' language of the sublime for herself" (27). He would not agree with Franklin's verdict that Wollstonecraft adopted Burke's sexual encoding of rhetoric.

Earlier, Blakemore identifies a deliberate effort by Wollstonecraft to subvert Burke's stereotypes by describing "both the Revolution and herself in the 'masculine' language of the sublime" and describing Burke and "the political order he defends in the 'feminine' language."[15] Gaura Shankar Narayan agrees that Wollstonecraft consciously redefines romanticism and initiates a "productive and desirable obfuscation of the gender divide" so that the Romantics should no longer be regarded as being either masculine or feminine (17). As a result, Wollstonecraft can be credited for the reclamation of sentimental literature as a popular form of romanticism that had been marginalized as "feminine" (contrary to Franklin's criterion), and thereby enabled it to rise in "status as a respectable, even canonical term" (17). Narayan assumes that sentimental literature is feminine and therefore inferior, or else that it is inferior and therefore feminine. Sentimental literature was not the exclusive domain of women writers[16] and, even if it were, a credible argument has been made that sentimental literature does have academic, historical and literary value.[17] These thoughts are just the tip of an iceberg of discussion on gendered linguistics but, strangely, Franklin equates the masculine with romanticism and the feminine with neoclassicism when, typically, those who do affix gender labels, invert those poles.

Claudia Johnson also notes that Wollstonecraft is critical of Burke's "politico-erotic effusions," and "pampered sensibility," and that Wollstonecraft accuses him and the fellow men of their society as being feminized and sentimental and therefore incapable of "self-command" much less leadership (*Equivocal* 7–8).[18] Even "men" who become soldiers are trained in "the school of finesse and effeminacy" instead of "fortitude," Wollstonecraft complains in *Rights of Woman* (236; ch. 9). Those who are sent to boarding school become "vain and effeminate" (253; ch. 12). In this sense, the effeminate male—who Wollstonecraft disdains in both *Rights of Men* and *Rights of Woman*—she finds archetypical of the eighteenth-century gentleman, but by doing so, she perpetuates the stereotype of feeling as being feminine and reason as masculine, with the former being construed as "other" at best, inferior at worst, and the latter implying the capability of maintaining authority and order.[19]

Another comment Franklin makes that is perplexing—not only because of its context, but also because of its lack of explanation—is that Wollstonecraft perceived her attempts at suicide as "revolutionary and heroic act[s] of will" (170). Franklin thinks this is apparently because Wollstonecraft declares, after her plunge into the Thames, her attempt at suicide was "one of the calmest acts of reason," and Godwin asserts that her determination to end her life was a "cool and deliberate firmness."[20] When a woman writes, after she realizes that she is alive when she fully expected to be dead, "I have only to lament, that, when the bitterness of death was past, I was inhumanly brought back to life and misery" (Todd, *CL* 327), how was the jump revolutionary and heroic? How could Godwin or Wollstonecraft's contemporaries view it in those terms? Wollstonecraft insists that she was accountable only to herself (327) and could care less about reputation, but who was going to raise her child? It might have been an effort to force Imlay to take responsibility for Fanny, because Wollstonecraft says in that same letter: "When I am dead [Was she contemplating or threatening another suicide attempt?], respect for yourself will make you take care of the child" (328). When did Fanny become "the child" instead of "our child" or "my child"? Regardless, Franklin's assessment of Wollstonecraft's efforts to commit suicide is problematic.

One last example that discredits some of Franklin's scholarship is her praising Wollstonecraft as being the first to depict domesticity and, in particular, the institution of marriage as an insane asylum and prison. Franklin declares, "The potent Gothicized image of the asylum/prison of the domestic interior has been going strong in feminist fiction ever since" (178). Again, that Gothic novels depicted "home" as dangerous and confining to women is not an original idea, so a citation would have been appropriate here. To claim that *Maria* was the first novel that conveys this theme is inaccurate. Kate Ferguson Ellis' book *The Contested Castle* is just one of several studies that deal with this theme as it was expressed in the novels of Walpole, Lewis and Radcliff, which predate Wollstonecraft.

Franklin contributed to the Wollstonecraft discourse blocks of information that are refreshing, interesting, useful and unique to the biographies. However, there are also numerous statements that should raise a red flag. If Franklin would have spent more time developing many of the claims she made, perhaps the claims would not be so questionable; but without substantiating them with argument and, at times, with citations for work she was borrowing from, the reader needs to "resist" assuming that Franklin is accurate and authoritative.

Chapter 15

LYNDALL GORDON'S *VINDICATION: A LIFE OF MARY WOLLSTONECRAFT* (2005): SOMETHING OLD, SOMETHING NEW, SOMETHING BORROWED, SOMETHING BLUE

Lyndall Gordon's 2005 book is the most readable and engaging of all the Wollstonecraft's biographies, and many of her theories, deduced from credible and reasonable evidence, are intuitive and convincing. Like Claire Tomalin, Gordon has garnered laurels for her literary biographies, written over an expanse of 38 years. She has won the British Academy's Rose Mary Crawshay Prize for her biography of T. S. Eliot, the James Tait Black Memorial Prize for her biography of Virginia Woolf, and the Cheltenham Prize for Literature for her biography of Charlotte Brontë. She was short-listed for the Duff Cooper Prize and Italy's Comisso Prize for her biography of Emily Dickinson. *Vindication of the Life of Mary Wollstonecraft* was a *New York Times* bestseller, long-listed for the Samuel Johnson Prize, selected by the *New York Times* as one of its 100 notable books of the year, and listed by the New York Public Library as one its top 25 books of the year (2005). Her biography of Eliot was selected by *The Independent* (a British online newspaper) as one of the "30 best biographies of the twentieth century."[1]

Nevertheless, one must read Gordon's version of Wollstonecraft with skepticism, for she includes many theories and details that have no support and that seem sensational and arbitrarily contrary, perhaps simply for the purpose of having something new to contribute to the mix for the sake of publication. New and true are not always the same.

Chapter 1 of Gordon's story of Wollstonecraft begins in medias res: "In December 1792 an Englishwoman at thirty-three crossed the Channel to revolutionary France" (1). Gordon makes two points from the get-go that establish her perspective of Wollstonecraft's life. First, she emphasizes that here was an Englishwoman travelling on her own; she was a woman with great independence, driven by intellectual and political curiosity, hopeful that the French Revolution would usher in a utopic new world. Not only was it not fashionable for women to travel alone, it was not safe. Courage was not something Wollstonecraft had in short supply. "Those who are bold enough to advance before the age they live in, and to throw off, by the force of their own minds, the prejudices which the maturing reason of the world will in time disavow," Wollstonecraft speculates in a letter to Mary Hays, "must learn to brave censure" (Todd, *CL* 410), which is to say, Wollstonecraft was a risk-taker.

Wollstonecraft was courageous and honest enough to see for herself what was happening in France. This is just one example of Gordon's success in delivering a new perspective. She eulogizes Wollstonecraft for not just being a "pioneer of women's rights," but for being "a pioneer of character" (3). She quotes from Virginia Woolf: "Every day she made theories by which life should be lived; and every day she came smack against the rock of other people's prejudices. Every day too—for she was no pendant, no cold-blooded theorist—something was born in her that thrust aside her theories and modelled them afresh."[2] What Gordon does extremely well in her biography is to strip away what has obfuscated who Wollstonecraft truly was and what she wrote, to reveal her philosophies, which were radical and prescient. Gordon cites so many of them with such refreshing insight, one wonders how earlier biographers missed them.

Not only was it radical for Wollstonecraft, as a single woman, and an unmarried woman yet at age thirty-three, to be traveling alone, and traveling alone to a country in the midst of a revolution, Gordon's second point is that while her fellow countrymen—with an emphasis on men—were retreating from France, Wollstonecraft brazenly charged into the Valley of Death.

Unlike the trend of most of Wollstonecraft's biographers, throughout Gordon's account she is a strong, disciplined woman whose major life decisions are not reactions to life's hard knocks but are calculated, deliberate and focused by a disciplined woman who refuses to be swayed by circumstances and by the stirrings and cries of her heart. Time and time again, Wollstonecraft either prides herself for being guided by reason or else chides herself whenever emotion clutters her ability to be rational. In fact, reason is so important to her, she mentions it 321 times in *Rights of Woman*.[3] Gordon's stipulated plan is to demonstrate "how her egotism and despair coexist with a pattern of extraordinary resilience. [...] This will not be a story of defeat" (4). This, too, is an approach radically different from those other biographers who portray Wollstonecraft as a victim. To them, her victimization began with her birth, unfavored because of her gender, deepened by parents with an array of psychological problems, and then perpetuated into adulthood with familial responsibilities and calamitous love affairs.

More than any other Wollstonecraft biographer, Gordon provides substantial, appropriate and interesting historical and social context. Helpful to the uninitiated is her brief survey of women's legal rights or lack thereof, on pages 10–11. While discussing Mr. Wollstonecraft's abuse of his wife, Gordon references Blackstone's *Commentaries on the Laws of England* (1765–69), explaining that married women were considered *feme-covert*. In other words, they were "covered," to use a biblical term,[4] or "hidden" in her husband. The Hardwicke Act of 1753 made it clear that women had no right to their own property, which Gordon discusses on page 11 but might have reminded the reader when she deals with Wollstonecraft's foiled efforts to recover her portion of an annuity that her brother kept for himself.[5] Women had no physical protection at home (11). Women had no rights to her own children or in securing a divorce, which Gordon might have mentioned when discussing Bess's flight from her husband. It would have helped explain why Bess and Wollstonecraft did not take the child with them. Without that information, the reader has to wonder why they deserted the baby, especially when the reader learns that she dies shortly afterward.

Although other biographers remark that Fanny Blood earned some money from her drawing, no one but Gordon supplies important information about it. Fanny drew, with scientific accuracy, wild flowers that were published in two volumes by William Curtis in *Flora Londinensis*. The purpose of his project was to give names to previously unidentified flowers, following the classification system by Linnaeus, and to identify their medicinal and other benefits. Curtis had a garden of over five hundred different species that Fanny would sketch in their various stages of growth (16–17). This is strikingly significant information that has been overlooked by previous biographers. Gordon presents Fanny as a young woman who was knowledgeable, fastidious and talented enough not only to earn money to support her family, but also to make a significant contribution to the advancement of science through her sketches. Gordon thought the experience with Fanny's flower drawings may have been the impetus for Wollstonecraft's creating the metaphor for herself as "an opening flower" and her intentions of becoming a "new genus" (17).[6] Wollstonecraft was fond of quoting from Thomas Gray's *Elegy Written in a Country Churchyard*, including: "Full many a flower is born to blush unseen / And waste its sweetness on the desert air," and therefore might have been influenced by Gray more than by Fanny. Wollstonecraft contradicted Gray's theme in a letter to Rev. Gabell in which she states her belief that God has a purpose for the "opening flower" or else He would never allow it to bloom in such a hostile climate as found on this earth.[7] Gordon's reference to a "new genus" has more validity in that Wollstonecraft was exposed to the lingo of Linnaeus through Fanny since her *genus* reference was made early in her career before she met scientists through Joseph Johnson. But a more important point Gordon might have made is perhaps that Fanny's unacknowledged contribution to science inspired Wollstonecraft to write in *Rights of Woman*, "what advances might not the human mind make"[8] if women (and men) were virtuous, well educated and free to make them?

Since in *Rights of Woman* Wollstonecraft vehemently decried her society's propensity to prioritize their external appearance, to have some idea of what that entailed is very useful. Gordon's description of women's dress on pages 24 and 25 helps explain how it was that women spent so much time on their toiletry. Gordon also inserts the interesting note that Wollstonecraft pressed the importance of hygiene in the prevention of disease—a revolutionary concept, as Gordon points out later, that would not be endorsed until the historical arrival of Florence Nightingale (119)—but that people instead preferred to cover up and disguise with cosmetics and colognes (24–25). Gordon might have taken this one step further to suggest that Wollstonecraft was equally concerned about society's disposition to disguise and conceal their immorality, human deformities and honest feelings, as she conveys often in *Rights of Woman*.[9]

Another tidbit Gordon shares that is invaluable is her discussion of birth control in the 1790s. This is relevant information because Godwin took measures to prevent Wollstonecraft's pregnancy, although they proved to be unreliable. Gordon speaks of condoms with a delightful reminder that Boswell called them "armour" and Casanova called them "English overcoats" (326). Godwin followed the "chance-medley system" which is a calendar-based form of contraception. Gordon alludes, with citation, to the codes in Godwin's diary to keep track, which was first deciphered by William St. Clair in his *The Godwins and the Shelleys: A Biography of a Family* (498). Apparently, Godwin's understanding of a woman's cycle was either not accurate or fail-proof, for by mid-November, Wollstonecraft was pregnant.

Although there are endnotes, Gordon fails to document much of her information and produces many statements that should raise questions as to their source and legitimacy. Others require a lot of searching if one wants to follow up or find evidence for the source, when a simple endnote would have been so useful—just like the above references to "opening flower" and "new genus," which were missing. Another example is Gordon's account of Wollstonecraft's sending an apology to Johnson for her misunderstanding of Fuseli's romantic intentions toward her. Gordon is intrigued that "this was the sole occasion when Johnson could offer Mary no comfort" (386). First, we do not know this to be true. Gordon bases this assumption on the lack of a letter, which proves nothing. A letter might simply be missing, and since Wollstonecraft saw Johnson nearly every day before she went to Paris, she did not need to write him. He certainly could have offered her some comfort or advice tête a tête. Second, Gordon's possible answer to her own question provokes even more questions. Gordon argues that Johnson was homosexual and therefore felt conflicted about Wollstonecraft's attraction to Fuseli when he himself was intimate with the artist (387).

About Wollstonecraft's religion, Gordon is ambivalent. She does mention that Wollstonecraft was christened at the Church of St. Botoph without Bishopsgate on May 20, 1759, where the Wollstonecrafts were members (6). Gordon says that Wollstonecraft received very little religious instruction, and that it was nature that awakened her spirit: "She had little religious teaching; it was the unspoilt natural world that woke her spirit" (9). Is this an echo of Godwin's unsubstantiated perceptions about his wife's religion? Godwin writes: "When she walked amidst the wonders of nature, she was accustomed to converse with her God [...]. In fact, she had received few lessons of religion in her youth, and her religion was almost entirely of her own creation" (*Memoirs* 56).[10]

Gordon also seems to borrow from *Memoirs* in which Godwin states that Wollstonecraft did not believe in "the doctrine of future punishments" and "notions of judgment and retribution" (*Memoirs* 56). His wife's view of God was that "He was amiable, generous, and kind" (56). So, Gordon writes, again without citation: "Her faith looked to a benevolent deity suggested by the sublimities of nature, a deity of forgiveness, not hell" (26). Not only does Gordon repeat details that are never substantiated by Godwin and are questionable, she does so without citation. It is a fickle appropriation of information because later, Gordon will return to the same page in *Memoirs* where Godwin avows that, although Wollstonecraft attended Dr. Price's sermons, she did not do so "with a superstitious adherence to his doctrines" (56). To this Gordon reasons that Wollstonecraft would have never used the word "superstition" to refer to any religion or doctrine (370).

Furthermore, if Gordon contends that Wollstonecraft's formative years were deprived of religious instruction, she shortly afterward contradicts herself by identifying the influence of the Rev. Mr. Clare and his wife as surrogate parents to Wollstonecraft when she was 15. Four years later Wollstonecraft had a romance with Rev. Joshua Waterhouse. Six years after that, she became friends with Dr. Richard Price, the pastor of Newington Green Unitarian Church. She was also friends with Rev. Mr. Bishop, the Master of the Merchant Taylor's School (17), and with Mrs. and Rev. Mr. James Burgh. On her way to Dublin to take her post as a governess, she met Rev. Henry Dyson Gabell who became a life-long friend and, shortly after that, Rev. John Hewlett who urged her to write a book and pursue a literary career in order to acquire a living. Because of Hewlett, she wrote *Thoughts on the Education of Daughters*, and even more significantly, he took the book to Joseph Johnson who published it. Thus because of him, her literary career commenced and so did her relationship with Johnson who would become the brother and father she never had (Todd, *CL* 166). Throughout her life, Wollstonecraft would maintain close friendships with Christians who were theological and biblical scholars and, as Gordon mentions, when in Bath, Wollstonecraft was a frequent attendant at St. George's Chapel, writing to Jane Arden, "I go constantly to the Cathedral. [...] I am very fond of the Service."[11] Gordon notes that many have considered Wollstonecraft an atheist, but the truth is that "she remained all her life in the established church" (26).

A statement Gordon makes that is unsubstantiated is "Her compassion for her mother became 'the governing propensity of her heart through life'" (9). It sounds good, and certainly serves a feminist agenda to assume this if Wollstonecraft often threw herself between her father and mother to take beatings intended for the mother (Godwin, *Memoirs* 46), she was motivated throughout her life to fight for the rights of women. But there are two scenarios not included in this formula. Gordon appropriates what she considers to be biographical material from *Mary, A Fiction*—as have other biographers before her—and reports that Wollstonecraft was "not the favourite of either parent" and that Mrs. Wollstonecraft favored the oldest son (6). If this were truly Wollstonecraft's situation, why did it not make her resentful of not only gender privileging but also of her mother's bias toward her? Could she have been detached enough to excuse her mother on grounds that she did not know any better and that that this was just the way of society and she should write about it as a general issue for all women?

Despite Mr. Wollstonecraft's violence and failure to be a proficient provider for the family, or maybe because of it, "To the day of her death her father was almost wholly supported by funds which she supplied to him" (Godwin, *Memoirs* 71). Of course, she could have done this out of a need for his approval or out of duty and could have done so with great resentment, but the point is, she was not always motivated by "compassion for her mother," as Gordon narrates.

As do several other biographers, Gordon extrapolates from Wollstonecraft's works information she believed to be autobiographical. Gordon and the others might be correct about some of these deductions, but an author's fiction and non-fiction are works that materialize from many different sources. They can come from autobiographical experiences, but they also germinate in the imagination and the subconscious, and from observation of others and study of history and so forth. The Mary and Maria of Wollstonecraft's fiction are not necessarily the replica of Mary Wollstonecraft, even if Godwin is the first to argue that one incident in *Maria* reflected Mary's actual experience. The fictional Mary has to sit "in the presence of her parents, for three or four hours together, without daring to utter a word," and this, as Godwin declares, is "copying the outline of the first period of her own existence," meaning Wollstonecraft (*Memoirs* 45). And then Gordon makes this statement: "It was not, then, unusual for Mary's early training to silence her voice. She was made to sit in silence for three to four hours at a time, when others were in the room" (6–7). There are several things wrong with this appropriation. First, Gordon does not document the source. She could at least have added an endnote that she is citing Godwin's *Memoirs*. Second, she makes an inductive leap, leaving out the business that this is what happened in *Maria* to the fictional Mary. Third, there is no documentation from either Gordon or Godwin that this actually happened to the real Wollstonecraft. Fourth, obviously Gordon's source was Godwin, but Godwin himself makes a mistake in his narrative. He argues that the mother was excessively hard on Wollstonecraft and showed partiality to the eldest son, supporting this assumption again from a fictional source, *Maria*. He quotes out of context by implying that the fictional character was being disciplined by both parents to be quiet. Instead, the Wollstonecraft context is that Mary often had to sit at the fireside, where both mother and child remained quiet in order not to upset the already out-of-humor father (*Maria* 212). Gordon misappropriates Godwin by using his argument to demonstrate that the mother was too severe with Wollstonecraft when the fictional passage demonstrates that both the mother and daughter were fearful of aggravating the father. Godwin misappropriates the passage to demonstrate that Wollstonecraft disagreed with the education she received as a child when both parents made her sit for hours without speaking. Neither Gordon nor Godwin make any effort to argue that this actually happened to Wollstonecraft.

Gordon also carelessly tosses around stereotypes. Here is one example: "Though Bess found Welshmen free from affectation, they had little to say—any man who could speak was sure to be Irish. As for her [Irish] employer, whom she called 'the miser,' he sat down to a dirty tablecloth on which reposed the remains of dead animals" (159).[12] Another is one of her delineations of Barlow and Imlay: As they

> plant themselves in corrupt old Europe, they appear as new-grown specimens from the New World. Barlow's appeal for Mary Wollstonecraft prepares her for Imlay, whom Barlow resembles: they are well-read Americans of the revolutionary generation; they come from the officer class in the War of Independence; and like many after the war they are opportunists. (165)

And one final example is her oversimplification of eighteenth-century America as a society that was very materialistic and defined manliness as having a passion for commerce (218).

There are a few different types of errors in Gordon's biography. Regarding Wollstonecraft's brother Henry, Gordon gives the credit to Janet Todd instead of Emily Sunstein[13] for the theory that he was mentally ill, which is why the family did not mention him (15). However, "In the last years of her life she did confide in Godwin, who kept the secret" (15), claims Gordon, and once again, I wonder how Gordon knew this, especially, as she observes that Godwin does not mention Henry's name in *Memoirs* (15), and especially, as Gordon also discovered, there were many things he did not know about Wollstonecraft when he wrote *Memoirs*.

Gordon makes some declarations about Wollstonecraft that are accurate, worth noting, and unique to her biography. For example, Gordon highlights that Wollstonecraft was the first woman to be a regular reviewer for a periodical for which she depended upon an income (137), thanks to the open-mindedness and generosity of Joseph Johnson. She pioneered a professional path for women to not only earn income from their writing of reviews, but these positions in turn made way for women to publish novels, including Edith Simcox, Fanny Fern and George Eliot, to name a few.

Gordon uniquely provides information about Fanny Blood's sister, Caroline. She became a prostitute after she was left behind when the family returned to Dublin, thanks to money Wollstonecraft was able to get from Bishop. Janet Todd wrote that Caroline was a "problematic Blood" and had been "picked up off the streets 'in a dreadful situation,'" but Todd did not include the context—that she did not accompany the family to Dublin (*Revolutionary* 130). Why Caroline did not accompany the family is not disclosed. She was arrested and then put into a parish workhouse, but the parish officers expected a half-a-crown a week for her maintenance. Mrs. Burgh applied for it from Wollstonecraft, and she paid it, and then pressed Caroline's father and brother for the rest of her life to send this fee (L. Gordon 156–57).[14]

This detail is significant on several levels. Once again it begs the question why Wollstonecraft felt compelled to provide not only for her own father's family but also for the Bloods. Was it because she was so desperate to have a family who loved her, and she attempted to acquire this love by taking care of them?[15] Another aspect of the possible answer is a crucial one: Because Wollstonecraft grew up in a dysfunctional nuclear family and adopted another family as her own—albeit just as dysfunctional—she came to define "family" in terms other than a biological mother, father and siblings. She found a mother in the form of Mrs. Burgh and both a father and responsible brother in Joseph Johnson, and she had an understanding that she was a sister to all women who suffered as she did from patriarchal oppression, as indicated in *Rights of Woman* when she addresses her readers as sisters (218; ch. 7). Her broad perception of "family" may also be the reason why she was willing to cohabitate with Fuseli, Imlay and Godwin, without being married to any of them.

As close as Wollstonecraft was to the Blood family, it also must have deeply affected her that one so dear would have had to resort to prostitution in order to survive financially. Wollstonecraft felt that prostitutes deserved both pity and disgust (*ROW* 208; ch. 2). Like most women during her time, they often had no way to survive other than to use their bodies to barter for their keep, a theme that threads its way through *Rights of Woman*. How this must have struck a chord that would reverberate in *Rights of Woman* as she referred to some marriages as legal prostitution (239; ch. 9) and understood that prostitution was often the only financial recourse available to women (136; ch. 4). However, Wollstonecraft did not call all marriage legal prostitution, as Gordon (32) and so many scholars claim she did in their works about Wollstonecraft. A simple search of "legal prostitution and Wollstonecraft" in *Google Books* brings up an astounding list that cite her as having described marriage as legal prostitution. This includes an assertion from Jessica Spector that "Wollstonecraft was the first to use the phrase 'legal prostitution' to refer to marriage," and she cites the source of this declaration as Wollstonecraft's biographer, "Clair [*sic*] Tomalin" (51n5).[16] This is astounding misinformation that demonstrates the domino effect of manipulating information about Wollstonecraft for an agenda instead of prioritizing integrity and accuracy. Spector's book was published in 2006; she should have consulted several other biographies more current than Tomalin's 1975 version because academic scholarship became more rigorous after the 1970s. In *Rights of Woman*, Wollstonecraft describes mercenary marriages as "legal prostitution" (239; ch. 9); she does not say that all marriages forced women into "legal prostitution." About marriage in general she has both positive and negative things to say, as she articulated her thoughts about it in her letters.

At 21, Wollstonecraft writes Jane Arden about her "pain and disappointment," the "dispensations of Providence," "misfortunes" and "afflictions" (Todd, *CL* 22). Later in the letter she talks about her frustration that her father purloined the fortune that had been settled on his children, but this was not the major source of the anguish with which she begins the letter. Neither is it her concern about Fanny, who obviously has consumption. She has experienced "acute feelings," and by them, she means that she was in love and hoped to marry. Young people have such high hopes that romance will lead to happiness, but they "must receive a great many stings before they are convinced of their mistake" (22) and a sting is exactly what Wollstonecraft was feeling, perhaps due to her relationship with Joshua Waterhouse.[17] It is possible but less likely she had hopes for a permanent relationship with Jane's brother John, but her hopes were dashed when he married Ann Barker in September 1779.

Regardless, at this time she refers to a positive outcome of romance as "a mere phantom; an empty name." Paradoxically, she next conveys that her brother Ned is happily married and that she hopes Jane's brother will know great joy in his recent marriage. Finally, she wants to know whether Jane has a beau. If so, Wollstonecraft will be happy "to hear that [Jane has] met with a sensible worthy man, tho' they are hard to be found" (Todd, *CL* 22–26). Although still in distress about her own recent disappointment in love, her attitude toward marriage and heterosexual relationships is positive.

Two years later she writes again to Jane Arden about marriage, as she congratulates Arden's sister on her marriage and says that her own sister Bess "has done well, and married a worthy man." She qualifies this, though, by warning about what transpires after the honeymoon:

> The joy, and all that, is certainly over by this time, and all the raptures have subsided, and the dear hurry of visiting and figuring aways as a bride, and all the rest of the delights of matrimony are past and gone and have left no traces behind them, except disgust:—I hope I am mistaken, but this is the fate of most married pairs.

She follows this with the announcement that she will never marry because she likes being free (38). Two years after that, there is the unfortunate suitor who gallantly offers to save Wollstonecraft through marriage. She is indignant at his proposal and accuses him of suggesting that she consider "*prostituting my person for a maintenance for in that point of view does such a marriage appear to me*" (174). Again, she is not rejecting marriage; she is contemptuous of the idea that a man could buy her through marriage.

Wollstonecraft's experience with Imlay would teach her to think that men do not stay in love as long as do women (231) and that they by nature struggle with fidelity (276) and are ruled by their appetites, which are never satiated (297); however, she celebrated the kind of marriage that is described in the Bible, the one based on self-denial. She writes:

> Ah! My friend, you know not the ineffable delight, the exquisite pleasure, which arises from a unison of affection and desire, when the whole soul and sense are abandoned to a lively imagination, that renders every emotion delicate and rapturous. (297)

This is not the language of a woman who is cynical about love and marriage.

There are two more choice tidbits that Gordon includes in her biography. She reminds us that in the late eighteenth century, "the woman as preacher was visible in society."[18] She might have elaborated through better research on this subject rather than simply alluding to George Eliot's aunt—the model for Dinah Morris in *Adam Bede*. Acknowledging the intellectual and spiritual qualities of his own mother, in 1761 John Wesley ordained the first of several women to preach. After Wesley's death in 1791, the church split on this (and other issues), with the American churches being more opened than the British. Still, Anna Howard Shaw, born in England but raised in the United States, where she received her theological degree in 1878 from the Boston University School of Theology, was denied ordination in the Methodist Episcopal Church. However, she was ordained in the Methodist Protestant Church, earned her M.D. in 1886, was active in the Sunday School Movement that provided education to the poor, chaired the Women's Christian Temperance Union, and became a strong suffragist who helped women get the vote in America. During World War I, Shaw headed the Women's Committee of the United States Council of National Defense, which coordinated industrial and farm production to support the war effort. She was the first woman to receive the Distinguished Service Medal.

Consequently, Gordon's assertion is slightly incorrect when she states that these women preachers believed they could speak about religious topics to a congregation, but that they "did not formulate this as a cultural expression" (145), meaning that they did not have an impact on culture. In particular the Quakers—men and women alike—were Christian activists with the conviction that they were called by God to do what they could to improve the human condition on earth, and they brought about much reform in prisons, insane asylums, factories and schools; and they were the leaders in the movement for women's suffrage.[19] Nevertheless, it was brilliant of Gordon to recall the radical move on Wesley's part to authorize a public sphere for women to have something of significance to say toward the improvement of the behavior of both men and women, and that this was a breakthrough for women to influence the culture and politics. Gordon reminds us that Wollstonecraft mixed often with Dissenters, and it is likely she would have been impressed and inspired by the history of the public activism of the Dissenting women.

The other interesting detail Gordon provides comes from Joan Smith's parallels between the Enclosure Acts (1750–1860) and the laws in place to enclose women's bodies, to prevent adultery and to ensure that property remained intact, inherited only by the proper son.[20] This is the cultural and political context of Wollstonecraft's life, which she acutely witnessed, as Gordon points out, through spousal abuse experienced by her mother and the bondage Bess felt in her marriage to Bishop (146).

Of all Gordon's theories, her account of the Wollstonecraft/Imlay affair is the most fascinating and unique, and certainly grants more depth to both of them. As mentioned above, several biographers fancied that Wollstonecraft left for France as a reaction to being rejected by Fuseli. The formation of a liaison with Imlay seems to happen so quickly after this, in most biographies, that Imlay seems to be either the object of a rebound or else her desire for Fuseli had been foreplay or else, as most biographers maintain, she was a woman past her prime desperate now for a husband. They often base this last assumption on excerpts from her joking letter to her friend William Roscoe on November 12, 1792, about her plans to go to Paris: She was a "spinster on the wing," and while in Paris, "I might take a husband for the time being, and get divorced when my truant heart longed again to nestle with its old friends."[21] These quotes are pulled out of context and totally ignore the part about getting divorced in order to be free to spend time with friends.

Gordon slows down the Wollstonecraft/Imlay affair. She astutely figures that Wollstonecraft's involvement with Imlay might not have happened had she not become involved with the Barlows. Wollstonecraft pursued a relationship with Joel Barlow in the hope that he would take her brother Charles with him to America to give him a new start. Barlow—as Gordon saw it—used her to persuade his resisting wife to leave London and join him in France, and that if he had not been so persistent in this vein, Wollstonecraft's path might not have crossed Imlay's (201–2).[22] The significance of such an observation is not a matter of "what if?" It iterates Wollstonecraft's commitment to provide for her siblings. Who is to say that as she pursued Barlow on Charles's behalf, she also pursued Imlay for the same reason, and she might have seen in him a way to support her two sisters? We know that these were driving motivations for her until she was deeply involved with Imlay, realized that he was not going to take them to America to start over, and understood that he could not or would not provide for her siblings, especially since he was ambivalent about taking care of her and his own child.

She met Imlay in March or April 1793 but, according to Gordon, *he* pursued her (204). By May, she was determined to leave France. There is nothing in her relationship with Imlay that indicates an intimacy that would have kept her there. Gordon supports this theory with these points: (a) Wollstonecraft acquired a position for Bess in Geneva and was going to join her, but Bess refused it. (b) If Wollstonecraft and Imlay were romantically involved, Imlay would have intervened with her plans in order to keep her in France with him. (c) If threatened with danger by being British in revolutionary France, Wollstonecraft planned to join Ruth Barlow at Meudon. (d) Gordon's last point is very convincing: After having just written *Rights of Woman* in which she so thoroughly and frequently lambasted sexual impropriety on biblical grounds, and as Gordon reminds us, she had known men who were flirts and who would have easily taken Wollstonecraft's virginity and then left her high and dry, why would have she participated in a sexual relationship with Imlay? (206)

All of this is persuasive and rings true about Wollstonecraft's character. The only thing lacking is that Gordon does not explain when Wollstonecraft became sexually active with Imlay. Gordon assumes that simply making love was a sacred act for Wollstonecraft, but if Wollstonecraft indulged in it outside of marriage, such an assumption contradicts Gordon's earlier thoughts on Wollstonecraft's commitment to chastity (213).

Gordon's biography does not end with September 15, 1797, the day that Wollstonecraft was laid to rest at Old St. Pancras, where she and Godwin had been married only five months before. Gordon recounts the history, reception and faults of Godwin's *Memoirs* and his subsequent marriage to Mary Jane Clairmont and the tragedies of Claire Clairmont, Fanny Imlay and Mary Shelley. This coverage is not, of course, unique to the biographies, but her chapter on the life of Margaret Kingsborough—as a "daughter" of Wollstonecraft is very valuable. It demonstrates the legacy Wollstonecraft left in someone in whom she greatly invested her philosophies of child raising and education. In fact, Margaret would pass on some of these ideas in her book *Advice to Young Mothers on the Physical Education of Children, by a Grandmother* (1823). Gordon relates that Gabriele Rossetti bought this book and followed it as a guide in raising his children, the three who would launch the Pre-Raphaelite Movement. Unfortunately, Gordon does not document her source, but the *Book Collector* records that Frances (Mrs. Rossetti) did buy the book when Dante was six months old. How amazing to think that Wollstonecraft's ideas influenced the way that three children were raised who, in turn, began the Pre-Raphaelite Movement.[23] And Margaret certainly followed Wollstonecraft's ideas in *Rights of Woman* when she dressed as a man so that she could study medicine at Jena in Germany and when she joined the Society of United Irishmen to end British rule of Ireland. The Shelleys spent time with her, and for several years, Claire Clairmont lived with her, so Wollstonecraft's spirit, through Margaret, was able to "mother" her child and Mary's stepsister.

Unfortunately, there was no one to reach out to Fanny when, 21 years to the exact day[24] after her mother's leap off Putney Bridge, she, too, killed herself, leaving behind a suicide letter that described her birth as having been "unfortunate" and that her "life has only been a series of pain to those persons who have hurt their health in endeavouring to promote her welfare" (quoted in Gordon 425). She was wearing her mother's stays. They were marked "M. W." (424).

Once again Gordon imparts detail that makes her biography so rich (and so frustrating when there is no supporting evidence, as there is none here).[25] That the child born to the "mother of feminism" took her own life wearing the very icon of bondage for women, stays (later known as a corset)—and not just any stays but those worn by her mother—succeeding where her mother did not in taking her own life when she found herself in a life that held out no hope for herself.

Chapter 16

JULIE A. CARLSON'S *ENGLAND'S FIRST FAMILY: MARY WOLLSTONECRAFT, WILLIAM GODWIN, MARY SHELLEY* (2007): "CON/FUSIONS OF FACT AND FICTION"

Julie Carlson's biography begins with this statement: "Why is it that the life stories of the Wollstonecraft-Godwin-Shelley family tend to fascinate readers even more than their written works?" (1). Her answer is that people have been enthralled with Wollstonecraft's "high drama": "unrequited passions for Fanny Blood, Henry Fuseli, and Gilbert Imlay and the psychic as well as geographical and literary extremes to which they took her" (1).

In the same year that Carlson published her biography, Janet Todd, after "many years" of having "been haunted by the figure of Wollstonecraft's eldest daughter, Fanny—the child who travelled with her mother through Norway, Sweden and Denmark and who featured so vibrantly in Mary Wollstonecraft's final works" (*Death* Preface), published a biography of sorts on Fanny Godwin, in the way that Carlson did; she deduced it from studying the writings of the Godwins and the Shelleys. She admits:

> To scour these [creative works, philosophical writings] for hints of life is considered bad form in biographies but what is distinctive in the lives of these extraordinary young people is their literariness, exactly their refusal to separate life from literature. They created themselves through the fictions of each other and wrenched life into serving fiction, their own and other people's. When living, Fanny felt the power of her mother's writings and in death was overshadowed in them. (Preface)

Her research found much betwixt and between, and Todd could not always discern whether contradictory texts were due to being secretive or bearing lies (Preface).

Similarly, in researching the lives and works of Wollstonecraft, Godwin and Shelley, Carlson discovered gaps between their novels and their biographies (3). She also found many contradictions between how these three defined "family" in their works and their practice (4). In her review of Carlson's book, Jacqueline Pearson suggests "The worst thing" is the title, noting the irony of it, since all the Godwin–Shelley group were notorious for their "ideological opposition to the family as an institution" (556). The title is ironic, but in that there is no other family in England that consisted of so many major writers, Carlson had a legitimate right to identify it as the "First Family of Writers."

Carlson takes yet another original approach in her biography. Granted, she is writing about not only Wollstonecraft but also Godwin and Mary Shelley, and to do this, she relays only that information that connects the three instead of spinning three separate biographies. That in itself has produced a different perspective on Wollstonecraft than what appeared before Carlson's publication in 2007. But her methodology is also different in that she insists the biographies and works of the three are "inextricable" (2) and "inseparable" (3), even if Carlson admittedly locates what she calls "slippages" or contradictions between what these three believed and defined in their works versus what they practiced. Carlson notes the "con/fusions of fact and fiction" in her study of their work, arguing that people whose lives are so bound up with reading and writing—as were Wollstonecraft and her husband and daughter—they lived their lives in such a way as to "blur [...] the boundaries between person and text" (3). It is an interesting sequitur to attempt to prove, namely that authors might be so devoted to the social issues, ideologies, purpose and mission that drive their writing, that they consciously live their lives according to their texts and vice versa.

Carlson asserts that the scandals of their lifestyles and the "dys/functions of family undermined their credibility as leading shapers of public opinion," when their devotion was to change public opinion through their writing (6). Susan Wolfson, in her review of Carlson's biography, summarizes Carlson's method of taking the private lives of the Godwins and Shelleys and "stressing the impersonal, transpersonal, and extrapersonal," thereby crossing 'boundaries between the private and public, person and person, the living, the dead, and the unborn" (E119).

Wolfson also praises Carlson's effort as does Wollstonecraft biographer Caroline Franklin, especially for her originality. In her attempt "to acknowledge that fluidity" of the biographical and the textual, which she "deems proto-psychoanalytical, Carlson identifies "experience and textualisation" that "entwined" the three writers (Franklin 291).

To accept Carlson's approach to Wollstonecraft, one must accept that there is a strong correlation between an author's life and the author's work. In his review of Carlson's work, Nicholas M. Williams argues that Carlson must have been familiar with Tilottama Rajan's theory of "autonarration." Explained in her *Romantic Narrative*, Rajan identifies a Romantic intergenre that she calls autonarration. Focusing primarily on Hays's *Memoirs of Emma Courtney*, Rajan notes where, when, and how the novel pulls from Hays's personal experience.[1] She says the Romantics tended to insinuate their personal lives into the text (93). These details she considers to be a deliberate insertion of "self-writing," but they are not autobiographical. It is "a form of self-writing in which the author writes her life as a fictional narrative," often leaping into his or her own text in the form of the personal "I" (96). Rajan argues that *The Wrongs of Woman* is an autonarration in its parallels between Maria and Darnford and Wollstonecraft and Imlay (96–97); the autobiography intrudes, but it is not purely autobiography because it is fiction; however, the fiction is not purely fiction because it is informed by the life of a real person—the author of the text (97).

It is an interesting theory, one that reviewer Williams endorses. It requires, as he says, "a nuanced reinterpretation of Maria's love for Darnford" as the reader is asked to consider a "coupled reading" (Williams's term; 259) or "double textualization of both life and fiction" (Rajan's term; xx). However, if one is to rely heavily on Godwin's writing to understand Godwin and Wollstonecraft, one will read his zealous opposition to marriage in several of his books and wonder why he decided to marry Wollstonecraft.

Additional questions quickly surface, such as what was Wollstonecraft's political or sexual agenda in becoming attracted to men like Fuseli or Imlay who could only break her heart? The only possible answer is that no matter how focused one might be about translating one's life to the page, the author has control only—and then maybe—of the world created by her pen. The opposite is not true. The author cannot control the world outside the printed page. Wollstonecraft really did want to die during her second suicide attempt, and she really did not want to die after giving birth to her second daughter.

Another series of questions arise as to Wollstonecraft's agenda for writing articles for Johnson at the beginning of her literary career. Was she not simply trying to become financially independent and providing for herself and her two sisters? When she forced herself to improve her comprehension of French and taught herself German and then translated texts that Joseph Johnson gave her, was it for high moral ground, social reformation or simply personal economics?

Carlson's statements should cause the reader to pause and ask, "Is that true?" One example is when she claims: "For both Wollstonecraft and Godwin aimed to make the domestic sphere more 'manly' by promoting disinterested conduct for women and men, an aim that frustrates feminists seeking to affirm the difference of Wollstonecraft" (12). Although the next few sentences are necessary to understand the second point about the feminists, there is no such person as "the feminist," as if feminists are all members of the same club, with the same mission and membership dues. The "manly" reference should sound an alarm and, by association, remind the reader of Benjamin Silliman's accusation that Wollstonecraft intended to expunge women of "every thing feminine, and to assimilate them, as fast as possible, to the masculine character" (23). It might also cause one to remember that infamous caricature of "Mrs. Godwin" engraved by John Chapman published in *Eccentric Biography*.[2] It is a sketch of Wollstonecraft from John Opie's 1797 portrait, except her face is replaced by masculine face with a man's hat, slightly cocked.

Wollstonecraft was sensitive to the bogey of masculine women during her time. In *Rights of Woman*, she makes "exclamations" against them and wonders who they are (76; introd.). There were Anne Bonny and Mary Read, notorious pirates who obviously transgressed gender lines. To be accused of being a transgressive "masculine woman" in the eighteenth century was a serious accusation. Women who acted like men were, in general, considered abhorrent and criminal, as conveyed in Henry Fielding's "The Female Husband or the Surprising History of Mrs Mary Alias Mr George Hamilton, who was convicted of having married a young woman of Wells and lived with her as her husband, taken from her own mouth since her confinement"; (1746) and Giovanni Bianchi's "Catherine Vizzani" (1751).

Wollstonecraft was familiar with Samuel Richardson's *Sir Charles Grandison* (1753). In 1790 she translated Maria van de Weken de Cambon's adaptation of Richardson's novel in that she quotes from it in her *The Female Reader* (1789) and refers to Lady G—(Grandison) in her 1788 novel *Mary: A Fiction*. Here is how the mannish Miss Barnevelt is described: "A lady of masculine features, and whose mind bely'd not those features, for she has the character of being loud, bold, free, even fierce when opposed; and affects such airs of contempt of her own sex, that one almost wonders at her condescending to wear petticoats" (Richardson 54).[3]

Carlson makes the following claim about Wollstonecraft and Godwin's "reformulations of family": "It invalidates the gendered associations of home and the tendency to perceive the 'privatizaton' of civic virtue, with its emphasis on civility, manners, and sociability, as indicating an advance for women (either in terms of increased respect or opportunities for them)" (12). Carlson is right that Wollstonecraft was critical of the games and plots of women to advance themselves into marriages and other forms of patriarchal favoritism, but she does reaffirm the belief that the ideal for women was very much "gendered associations of home" as she describes the wife/mother tending to her "smiling babes and a clean hearth" in chapter 9 of *Rights of Woman* (234). Instead of "the most artful wanton tricks," the woman possesses "maternal solicitude" and affection and devotes herself to domestic duty (235). Carlson ignores Wollstonecraft's prescriptions for domestic bliss.

The other social anomaly in the eighteenth (and nineteenth) century was the bluestocking, a term used to denote an intellectual woman. Wollstonecraft was often held up to ridicule for her mannish manner and lack of interest in domesticity. There was a famous Blue Stockings Club in London, originally begun by women, but which later included men. Members met at the house of the infamous Elizabeth Montagu in Hill Street, near Park Lane. Participants were Elizabeth Vesey, Anna Laetitia Barbauld, Ada Lovelace, Catharine Macaulay, Clara Reeve, Sarah Scott, Elizabeth Carter, Anna Williams, Harriet Bowdler, Edmund Burke, Sarah Fielding, Samuel Johnson, Frances Pulteney, Hannah More, Fanny Burney, Hester Chapone and Horace Walpole. Although often labeled a bluestocking, Wollstonecraft was not involved with these clubs (L. Gordon 50–51); she must have been too busy churning out articles for Johnson's *Analytical Review* to earn her bread and butter.

In *Rights of Woman* Wollstonecraft is ambivalent about gender roles. She agrees that women should not indulge in "hunting, shooting, and gaming" because they are manly sports (9); nevertheless, she makes this shocking statement, "all those who view [females] with a philosophic eye must, I should think, wish with me, that they may every day grow more and more masculine" (*ROW* 76; introd.). Volatile words indeed but, within her context, Wollstonecraft argues that both men and women needed to improve their "talents and virtues, the exercise of which ennobles the human character" (77).

Her friend Mary Hays wrote in her obituary for Wollstonecraft after her death:

> This extraordinary woman no less distinguished by admirable talents and a *masculine* tone of understanding, than by active humanity, exquisite sensibility, and endearing qualities of heart, commanding the respect and winning the affections of all who were favored with her friendship or confidence, or who were within the sphere of her influence, may justly be considered as a public loss (233; emphasis added).

Although "masculine" and "manly" were derogative words to describe women who transgressed gender boundaries, and were used by men and women in Wollstonecraft's day. She and Hays and others with shared hopes for equal education and vocation for women wore the words as badges of honor.

Carlson wants a more subversive Wollstonecraft than the one who actually existed. She makes numerous wild and false claims, that Godwin published all the illicit details of Wollstonecraft's personal history, which included her love for Fanny Blood, fantasized *ménage à trois* with the Fuselis, her bastard daughter, Fanny Imlay, two attempts at suicide out of despair over Gilbert Imlay, the intimate gynecological details surrounding her death, and, in so doing, ruined her reputation for generations. (24)

This is a sweeping generalization. There are many important details omitted by Godwin in each of these areas because he simply did not know them, as my chapter on Godwin points out, or else he would not have even thought of it, like suggesting a homoerotic relationship between Fanny Blood and Wollstonecraft.

"Even before they knew or loved each other," Carlson begins, with another assumption that she fails to support, "Wollstonecraft and Godwin each identified heterosexual love as a major impediment to their visions of social perfectibility." Here she explains but does not defend, that their goal was to preserve the independence of each in their relationship (24). Wollstonecraft did warn that "passionate heterosexual love" often got women into undesirable straits by deform[ing] the minds and prospects of women" (24), which would ring true in her own life when she fell in love with men who wrecked it.

Carlson makes a minor mistake in saying that *Rights of Woman* "delineates the extent of this training ['captivating a man'], claiming that it underlies the literary, religious, and pedagogical traditions of the West" (24–25). What about Wollstonecraft's references to "Mahometanism" and seraglios? Carlson advances another one of her hyperbolic statements in declaring Wollstonecraft's having a phobia about loving a man passionately, and then she cites Cora Kaplan's *Wild Nights,* Mary Poovey's *The Proper Lady*, and Tom Furniss's article on *Rights of Woman*. Indeed, anyone can make a case that all people have ambiguities about sexuality, but Carlson fails again to reconcile her statements with Wollstonecraft's life. If Wollstonecraft were troubled by a phobia about passion for men, then why was she so passionate for Waterhouse, Fuseli, Imlay, Godwin and possibly a number of other men? If this were one of the slippages that Carlson promised to identify, perhaps her statement would make more sense, but she does not discuss the phobia in any context.

An intriguing theory that Carlson offers commences with her statement that the lives of Wollstonecraft, Godwin and Mary Shelley were "bound up" with reading and writing (2), and that Carlson found them as illustrative of the "psychosocial dynamics of being and writer and the attractions, even sexiness, of a life devoted to mental pursuits" (2). This is a refreshing statement. Of course, one support she gives to this was Godwin's well-known statement about Wollstonecraft's *Letters from Sweden*: "If ever there was a book calculated to make a man in love with its author, this appears to me to be the book" (*Memoirs* 122). Their unconventional practices of lovemaking, says Carlson, paralleled their efforts to experiment with new forms of writing (26). Wollstonecraft's fictional heroines (Mary, Maria, Marquerite de Damville, Deoloraine) are thinking individuals in contrast to the idiots who populate some of the novels written by men during Wollstonecraft's time. Carlson reminds us of Claudia Johnson's observation that Wollstonecraft conscientiously strove to produce a new genre of literature by calling *Mary* a fiction instead of a "novel," "romance" or "history."[4] Carlson continues her convincing development of thesis that Godwin and Wollstonecraft knew marital bliss through their shared reading, discussion of books and writing.

Carlson's analysis of *Letters from Sweden* detects sycophancy, a softening of the "Amazonian temper,"[5] even though Carlson reminds us of Mitzi Myers's evaluation of Wollstonecraft, that she was a reviewer for the *Analytical Review*, a woman who disdained female posturing of subservience to men,[6] Carlson concludes that the melancholy in *Letters from Sweden* was deliberate; when combined with overt intelligence and "feigning surrender to men" (31), Wollstonecraft was sure of "effusions" that would garner positive attention (31). Her writing is "self-consciously performative," Carlson asserts; the purpose is to "to sympathize with female complaint if it adopts a sentimental rather than a strident tone" (31). In other words, Carlson finds Wollstonecraft's prose as conscientiously submissive in order to attract male readers. But Carlson seems to contradict this by citing many passages from *Letters from Sweden* that demonstrate that Wollstonecraft's women never surrender to men. Carlson defers to Saba Bahar's assertions that *Letters from Sweden* refuses to treat women as "objects of pity" but as agents who can claim their own victories, especially through the act of writing.[7] However, in fairness to Carlson, she questions Wollstonecraft's motives for writing *Letters from Sweden* and suggests that Wollstonecraft was unsure of her audience and intent (31), which is a reasonable admission. To be read and therefore to be paid, however, were essential motives behind *Letters from Sweden* as Wollstonecraft was thinking how she would support her child if Imlay would persist in rejecting his familial obligations.

Before leaving *Letters from Sweden*, coupled with commentary on Godwin's *Fleetwood; or, the New Man of Feeling* (1805), Carlson observes that they depict a variety of obstacles that get in the way of love and promote "writing as remedy" which is

> both representational and metadiscursive, in that each author not only employs writing to publicize how reading affects a fictional character's attitudes and approaches to love but also foregrounds the act of narration or composition and the necessary interaction between reforming

love and revising stories in novels and nonfictional texts. At the same time, within these texts each writer interweaves two arguments that accentuate love's publicity: love is a nonpersonal or transpersonal feeling, and writing influences the experience of being in love. For both, making love a less private, secret, and personal activity is a major step toward liberating women and men. (29–30)

Both writers came under severe attack for writing on issues that were not considered appropriate for polite society. For Wollstonecraft it was her advocacy of co-education, her proposal that sex education be taught to children, her criticism in *Rights of Woman* of widespread immoral sexual behavior, and her identification of prostitution of women in and out of marriage. For Godwin, it was his unabashed rejection of the conventions of marriage and his uncensored rendition of Wollstonecraft's life that included her two pregnancies outside of wedlock, her two suicide attempts, and explicit details of the childbirth that killed her.

With her excellent analysis of narration, Carlson identifies how *Maria* gives women voice through literary discourse. Beginning with Jemima's offering Maria books and writing supplies after Maria has been committed to an insane asylum by her ne're-do-well husband, Maria has the intellectual resources to keep herself sane. Although trapped in a heinous marriage and now in an asylum, she transcends her prisons through the keys of writing given to her by a sympathetic woman who was also no stranger to societal wrongs to women. Maria writes down her story and advice for her daughter and, in so doing, is Wollstonecraft's mouthpiece to generation after generation of daughters (30–37). Then Maria and Jemima tell each other their stories; they include atrocities and "misery and oppression, peculiar to women, that arise out of the partial laws and customs of society," Wollstonecraft explains in her preface. We are not to think that their stories are rare happenstance but instead are "the history [...] of woman."[8]

One charge that Wollstonecraft makes is that men in her time seemed to view women only as prostitutes, created for their own personal and capricious use. Venables married Maria in the first place because he saw her as his cash cow. On top of siphoning money from her uncle through her, he actually entered into an agreement with another man to receive a loan of £500 in exchange for "husband's rights" with his wife. Jemima spent most of her life on the streets as a prostitute, but even after she was taken in and loved by a "respectable" citizen, he treated her with sexual perversity as if she were his whore. Albeit a libertine who gave her little sexual respect, he was also an intellectual who facilitated her learning and strangely valued her feedback on his writing in progress. In exchange for sexual favors, Jemima gained knowledge and participated in his literary production, which gave her voice. Maria is similarly united in a heterosexual relationship via literary exchange. She read a fellow inmate's marginal notes in books that were loaned to her, and they enticed her to open her heart to him. Thus, the very act of reading and writing were "highly erotic activities and the best hopes for social reform" (Carlson 32). Carlson emphasizes that this romance that evolves through reading is instructive about the danger that can come from developing unrealistic expectations from novel reading that can lead to liaisons that do *not* have fairy tale endings (33). It is incumbent upon novelists to depict "less idealized or saccharine stories about love. Only by revealing the truth about the repression of women that must not be obscured by romance, can one use the pen to bring about political change" (36).

There are additional benefits to be had through reading novels like *Maria*. Although not intentional, the novel was left unfinished by Wollstonecraft's untimely death and thus allows readers to insert their own stories. Wollstonecraft did write a final chapter, but several chapters are missing before the final chapter. The last pivotal chapter puts Maria in front of an unsympathetic, patriarchal judge who will not sanction divorce for any reason and disbelieves her stories about her spousal abuse. In an unsettling, unromantic fashion, the novel reaches an impasse in which the "sanctity of marriage" is upheld, patriarch rule prevails and the woman is kept in her place, silent, poor and powerless.

Godwin provides Wollstonecraft's notes of her intentions for further plot developments that include additional acts of betrayal and oppression. Henry Darnford, the inmate in the insane asylum who was falsely confined, is released and for a time, it looks as if he and Maria will get to live happily ever after—but no, she is sued by her husband for infidelity, and he gains all her inheritance and assets. Darnford is unfaithful to her, as was Imlay to Wollstonecraft. Although pregnant, Maria attempts suicide. Then the last chapter gives Maria victory only through the resources of other women. Jemima never believed that Maria's daughter was dead and was determined to find her. In order to protect Maria's financial future, the uncle had bequeathed his fortune to her daughter, but Venables lied about her death, disposed of his wife, and claimed the money. But now the child—a daughter—has been restored to her mother, and Maria vomits up the laudanum as if she vomits all of the patriarchal poison she had taken throughout her life. In a family of only females, the novel ends with the only possible gender makeup that appears to be viable within such an oppressive social order that privileges men. At least that is how Laura Mandell reads the ending. She interprets both *Mary* and *Maria* as novels that are critical of heterosexual relationships and that resolve happily only in "queer families" (63–71). This is a position Carlson is right to dispute. That one can read Wollstonecraft as promoting a "female-only household and a proto-lesbian sensibility" (32) ignores details of Wollstonecraft's own life as she continued to pursue heterosexual relationships and was often equally frustrated with her relationships with women. It ignores the detail in *Maria* that it is a kindly uncle who supports Maria's decision to leave Venables. Although the uncle is a privileged male, he does not use his power for his own aims but bequeaths his money to Maria's daughter, making Maria the guardian, thus legally safeguarding the money from Venables. Carlson identifies *Maria* as a revolutionary attempting to portray love in terms of the misery that it can cause, and to suggest that readers must change "the grounds, or expectations, of happiness bother within marriage and outside of it" (37).

When Carlson attends to narratology, she is at her best. Her intertextual study offers insights unique among the bibliographies; however, some of her claims indicate that she is not as cognizant as she needs to be on previous biographies and scholarship published on Wollstonecraft. She relies too heavily on the betwixt and between texts to locate Wollstonecraft.

Chapter 17

ANDREW CAYTON'S *LOVE IN THE TIME OF REVOLUTION: TRANSATLANTIC LITERARY RADICALISM AND HISTORICAL CHANGE*, 1793–1818 (2013): "A SUBJECT OF GEORGE III"

As its title indicates, Andrew Cayton's book extends beyond what would be considered a biography. It offers a picture of Wollstonecraft that is very different from any other biography because it focuses more on the people in her life and the events that surrounded it.

Readers might assume that they are in for something different not only from the title but from the opening sentence: "Gilbert Imlay was a citizen of the United States, and Mary Wollstonecraft a subject of George III of Great Britain" (1). It definitely sets the stage for Cayton's agenda. Cayton is a historian and not a literary critic although his knowledge of eighteenth-century literature is prodigious. If he had intended to introduce his study like a biographer, he might have begun with the paragraph that ends his book:

> "The world we dwell in," observed Godwin in 1809, "is a curious object. It is an ever-shifting scene, and by some moralists has been compared to a *camera obscura*, that affords us the prospect of a frequented road." Nothing, he realized was more certain than that everything would change. Aware of his own mortality, conscious of the passing of others as well as the ebbing of his reputation, Godwin argued for the value of communing with "the Illustrious Dead" literally on their graves. The dead are "still with us," he insisted, "in their stories, in their words, in their writings, in the consequences that do not cease to flow fresh from what they did." As long as we engage with them, the dead are not really dead. They live, if only in our imaginations, because we wish them to be necessary to us. (333)

The analogy would have been an effective and appropriate opening for a biography. The camera obscura was first invented by a Chinese philosopher in the fifth century BCE, and Aristotle described it in the next. But the prototype for the twentieth-century camera was being developed in seventeenth-century Britain and became portable models in the eighteenth century but were not widely used (Ward 75–78) until Tom Wedgwood figured out how to copy paintings onto glass and then to moisten white paper with nitrate silver in order to capture an image (R. Litchfield 189–205).

The value of the reference of a camera obscura to biographical reproduction is readily apparent, but it is significant to our study in several other ways, especially in regard to Wedgwood. When the Wollstonecraft family moved to a farm in Laugharne, Wales, they became neighbors with the family of John Bartlett Allen at Cressely. The two eldest Allen daughters married the two eldest Wedgwood sons,[1] sons of the famous potter Josiah Wedgwood of Etruria who became a millionaire overnight when he began to turn out everyday, mass-produced dinnerware (Todd, *Revolutionary* 409).

Godwin became friends with Tom Wedgwood through a mutual acquaintance, Basil Montagu (1770–1851) (Meteyard 120). William Wordsworth lived with Montagu for several months and financially supported him for several years. He took Montagu's son at the age of five to live with him as a pupil in the West Country. Before leaving London, he introduced Montagu to Godwin, who proved to be a useful friend insofar as Godwin was chronically in dire straits because of debt, and Montagu was a barrister whose specialty was bankruptcy.[2] In early 1797, Montagu and Godwin took a walking tour of the Midlands and stopped at Etruria, the Wedgwood Estate. Montagu intended to propose to Tom Wedgwood's sister Sarah (Crosby 870) but, for whatever reason, they did not marry. Sarah never married, dedicating her life to abolition (Midgley 56). Montagu was constantly by Godwin's side during Wollstonecraft's last trial in life (*Memoirs* 117).

In 1797, Wollstonecraft made arrangements for Everina to secure employment with Tom's brother Josiah, as a governess to his two young children (Todd, *Revolutionary* 413). Emma Wedgwood, the youngest daughter (1808–96), would not have been born yet and therefore was not one of Everina's charges. Emma would be the first cousin to Charles Darwin and marry him in 1839 (H. Litchfield 441–42). Godwin knew Darwin's grandfather, Dr. Erasmus Darwin (Wardle 97–98).

It is ironic that Godwin employs the camera obscura reference in his own musings about the dead. In 1795 Wedgwood offered to send a copying machine of his own invention to Godwin, but Godwin declined the gift, apparently not wishing to be obligated to reciprocate in kind (R. Litchfield 29). It would have been a very useful gift for a writer. Apparently, Godwin did not have the same qualms about borrowing money from Wedgwood, for in 1797 he borrowed £50 in order to pay some of Wollstonecraft's debts (Barbour 150). Before Wedgwood's death in 1805 he borrowed £100 (Paul 141) in order to open a bookshop that sold school books (Meteyard 353–54).

Unique to Cayton's study is a portrait of Imlay in high resolution, constructed within Imlay's time and place in history. The first descriptor Cayton gives him is that he was "a slave to fancy"; "he lived a life shaped by his notions of the world as it could be rather than the world as it is" (55). "Fancy" is so intricately tied to romanticism that Jeffrey Robinson wrote an entire book on the subject: *Unfettering Poetry: Fancy in British Romanticism*, and is too broad a topic to cover in my project. "Fancy" and "imagination" have often been used synonymously with the understanding that the former is simply an archaic form of the latter. However, this was not how the Romantic perceived the two terms. Coleridge, for one, attempts to distinguish between the two in his *Biographia Literaria*. Briefly put, he describes imagination as a mystical force and faculty that draws from the beauty of nature and then creates new shapes and forms of beauty. Fancy is more a form of memory that is able to combine different things into different shapes.[3]

Imlay and Wollstonecraft shared "fancy"; they were both idealistic about the possibilities of recreating the world and reinventing their lives. Wollstonecraft put great stock in "fancy," using the word 29 times in *Rights of Woman*. Cayton was deliberate in his choice of words, and since "fancy" appears frequently in Wollstonecraft's works and letters, it is essential to understand what was meant by the term in the eighteenth century. His introductory statement about Imlay as "citizen of the United States" is Cayton's fancy of Imlay's fancy of himself. It exculpates Imlay of wrongdoing in his relationship and in his termination of the relationship with Wollstonecraft. With this persona of an American frontiersman and pioneer, Imlay comes across as a noble character of heroic portions, the kind of character that should appear in an epic poem. He "lived a life shaped by his notions of the world as it could be rather than the world as it was" (55), Cayton explains, as if to emphasize that the reality that Wollstonecraft perceived, and which defined her relationship with Imlay, did not coincide with the fancy Imlay perceived. Confirmation of this can be found in any number of letters Wollstonecraft wrote to Imlay, especially the ones in which she uses the word "fancy," such as "God bless you, my love; do not shut your heart against a return of tenderness; and, as I now in fancy cling to you, be more than ever my support" (Todd, *CL* 241).

Wollstonecraft was as caught up in the "fancy" of Imlay, as Imlay was of himself and his projection to others. She writes to her sister this description of "an American": "A most worthy man, who joins to uncommon tenderness of heart and quickness of feeling, a soundness of understanding, and reasonableness of temper, rarely to be met with— Having also been brought up in the interior parts of America, he is a most natural, unaffected creature" (*CL* 249). The truth is that Imlay was brought up in a town in New Jersey named after his family. He was in "the interior" as a surveyor for no more than one year. Wollstonecraft's fancy is that he will take her and her family to live on a farm in America, where they can begin tabula rasa with no debt and no class division (*CL* 277). Her greatest disappointment, this does not happen.

Cayton further describes Imlay as an idealist whose dream simply was not the same as Wollstonecraft's: "He lurched from possibility to possibility in a seemingly endless series of what his contemporaries called speculations or adventures. Most involved making money; all reflected an extraordinary imagination. Empowered to dream by revolution, Imlay never came to terms with reality" (55). Although Wollstonecraft often chided him for being so preoccupied in making money,"[4] she was enthralled with a man who followed his dreams. In a letter to him, she indicates that he imagined a life with her in America. He apparently "sketched" a "fire-side" scene with six children "clinging around [his] knees." His "picture" set her "fancy [...] instantly at work." They shared in unrestrained capacity to imagine and fancy and to be driven by them to create reality (Todd, *CL* 243). The major problem for Wollstonecraft was that Imlay's dream never kept him at the hearth for very long.

On the surface, Imlay may appear to be a "feckless male," Cayton suggests, but in truth he was

> a variation on a late-eighteenth-century man who assumed the importance of shape-shifting—adjusting his loyalty and accommodating his behavior—as circumstances demanded. Growing up in an era of global warfare, political revolution, and rapid economic change that undermined the authority of traditional institutions from households to monarchy, a cohort of ambitious provincials born in the middle of the century disassociated themselves from families and local communities and gambled on their ability to navigate through a fluid and uncertain world. The key to their lives was mobility, the ability move freely from possibility to possibility. Liberty to men such as Imlay and Brissot meant autonomy, and revolution the creation of a world in which men of merit became somebody by declaring themselves independent of any and all obligations, connections, and responsibilities, that, in their judgment and their judgment alone, inhibited that autonomy. (57–58)

This is an astute observation that Cayton renders, a perspective that no other biographer attempts, and yet, once one reads it, one must think of Daniel Boone, Davy Crockett, James Bowie, Lewis and Clark—all of them married, but where were their wives and children when they were hither and yon making history? Were there no women having adventures and contributing to the advancement of civilization? Where is their record?

In her seminal work, *Sensational Designs*, Jane Tompkins validates women's writing from the eighteenth and nineteenth centuries. Women did not go whale hunting, so no woman wrote *Moby Dick*. No woman had the freedom to traipse through the virginal woods with Native American Indians, so no woman wrote *The Deerslayer* (although we do have captivity narratives by women who were taken hostage by Native American Indians[5]). No little girls could go floating down the Mississippi River, so no woman wrote *The Adventures of Huck Finn* (although E. D. E. N. Southworth came close in *The Hidden Hand*). As Sir Walter Scott said of Jane Austen's *Emma*, he was able to "do" the "big Bow Wow strain," that is, write about high adventure, but he was unable to write with "exquisite truth" the way Austen does, which "renders ordinary common-place things and characters interesting" (114). Women writers and readers, says Tompkins, did not see the "world" as an important "territory" to conquer; they saw what they deemed was even more important, and that was the soul (165–66).

This argument is relevant to the irreconcilable differences between Wollstonecraft and Imlay, and exposes the gap in Cayton's treatment of the two. Wollstonecraft was "left in the dust" with a three-year-old child to support and a broken heart, while Imlay, as Cayton so poetically put it, "mounted his horse and rode off" (141). However, no one who writes about Imlay can tell us what he did after he, in Godwin's words, "like the base Indian, threw a pearl away, richer than all his tribe" (*Memoirs* 92). He was buried in New Jersey from whence he came. Very few people have ever heard of his two books much less read them. His name went down in infamy, whereas Wollstonecraft's name continues to be honored for her contribution of ideas.

Cayton subscribes to additional interesting perspectives on Imlay that are unique among the biographers. He reminds us that it was not only Wollstonecraft's reputation that was impeached by *Memoirs* (142). Perhaps because of the traditional double standard, we assume that only the woman suffered the ignominy of a bastard child, but Cayton thinks otherwise. He suggests that the reason we do not know much about Imlay is because the infamy destroyed his career and prevented him from securing any more "social and cultural capital he had enjoyed in 1793." He also hints that the reason Imlay vacillated so much in the relationship was because although he wanted his independence, he knew that Wollstonecraft was in the public eye, and abandoning her would have grave results on his own career (142).

Would we have ever heard of Imlay if not for his involvement with Wollstonecraft? Imlay was embroiled in schemes that were important road marks in American history, but he played an obscure and unsuccessful role in them and therefore does not appear in any textbook. If one looks him up in any encyclopedia, one finds very few statements about him that do not pertain to his relationship with Wollstonecraft.

Granted, Imlay published two books. Cayton thinks *The Emigrants* fell into "well-deserved obscurity" (55). However, the novel has much information to tell us about early America not found in other novels and textbooks. Still, hardly anyone reads it or Imlay's other work, *Topographical Description*. Furthermore, Cayton is mistaken when he says that Imlay published *The Emigrants* before he met Wollstonecraft (55). He is also mistaken in his statement that Wollstonecraft met Imlay in early April 1793 (55). Christopher Flynn sets the date of their meeting as November 1792 (55); whereas, Verhoeven and Gilroy claim December 1792 (xxviii). Flynn records *The Emigrants* as having been published in September 1793 (55); Amanda Gilroy lists March 1793 (192). The earliest review that I can find published on *The Emigrants* is the *Monthly Review* in August 1793; therefore, the September publication date is most likely accurate because publishers often sent early copies of books to be reviewed immediately prior to the authentic publication date. The next review is in *The Critical Review* in October. With there being no review around the March dates, one can deduce at least that Imlay was still working on the book when he was in a relationship with Wollstonecraft.[6] The dates are important because of the theory that several scholars, as well as myself, argue that Wollstonecraft co-authored the book.[7]

Cayton interjects a fresh idea, one for which he could have provided more elaboration, one that invites further commentary. About their impact, Cayton theorizes: "Wollstonecraft, Imlay, and Godwin did not change the world, at least not immediately. But they did participate in changing the ways in which English-speaking peoples understood change and the world because they focused on form as well as content" (10). What he means by that is that the three wrote novels in a different way and for a different purpose than what each had imagined. "In their view," Cayton explains, "a novel was an imagined personal history, a contingent narrative in which characters (and by extension readers), by learning something critical about themselves and one another, learn something critical about the world as a whole" (10). This, to Cayton, represents a revision of the then current "modes of discourse, especially the still relatively new genre of the novel, not only to make sense of their problems but also to link them to the experiences of thousands of readers and writers around the North Atlantic" (10). As such, this is another enduring contribution the three made (10). It is a pleasing claim but surely an exaggeration. Their predecessor, Daniel Defoe, for one, is more deserving of that credit, but further thought and development of Cayton's idea might produce a convincing argument.

There are several arguments that Cayton does make that are not accurate and/or not well substantiated. One relates to his comments on Wollstonecraft's view on marriage. Cayton states that the reason she did not want to marry Imlay was that she "spurned marriage because she rejected an institution that served the interests of men at the expense of women" (98). This does not correlate with what Wollstonecraft wrote just a few months before she met Imlay in *Rights of Woman*: "I respect marriage, as the foundation of almost every social virtue" (110). In a letter, she declares that she holds "the marriage vow sacred" (Todd, *CL* 48). If Cayton is correct that the French Revolution changed her way of thinking (190) and caused her to reject marriage, why was it her idea that she and Godwin marry? It is Godwin's contention that Wollstonecraft did not want to marry him because she was known as Mrs. Imlay, and since Imlay was still alive, there would be "vulgar discussion." Furthermore, it had been only six months since she "banished" Imlay from her mind and heart, and she thought it improper as well as injudicious to marry so soon after such a "trial" (*Memoirs* 105–6). Godwin claims that Wollstonecraft wanted to marry to avoid "vulgar discussion" about her and her exclusion from good society (105–6).

Elsewhere Cayton does posit a good question: "Why did an advocate of the rights of woman take up with an adventurer who possessed such a penchant for ignoring obligations?" (110). He attempts to answer this in several compelling ways until he misuses several phrases in a letter that she wrote to Imlay early in their affair. Cayton speculates that she "fancied" Imlay because he was not "the common run of men" who had "gross appetites" and had to be treated to "variety to banish *ennui*" (120). But these are exactly what Wollstonecraft accused Imlay of in that letter, asking him to combine his desire with "self-denial" (Todd, *CL* 297).

About Wollstonecraft's suicide attempts, Cayton claims that, in the eighteenth century, suicide was not considered an antisocial act (123). He also states that suicide was "common" among the middling and upper classes, which it was not. Neither was it "honored as a rational refusal to live at the mercy of others" (123).[8]

Despite these hiccoughs, Cayton's book contributes much to our understanding of Wollstonecraft's life. He realizes that Godwin's *Memoirs* paints himself as Wollstonecraft's hero, and that it is all self-congratulatory; "the plot of *Memoirs* leads inevitably to him" (169). Cayton also asks us not to be disappointed by all the gaps in the book, for Godwin wrote it in the style of the episodic novels common in the eighteenth century. In other words, we get a "handful of key episodes that revealed her character and its evolution over time" (168). In the discussion of *Memoirs*, Cayton gives us several gems, such as: Godwin's description of Wollstonecraft's father "foreshadow[s] Imlay, a restless, erratic, unhappy father unable to settle down" (169). This may be one of the reasons that she was attracted to Imlay against her better judgment. Cayton also infers from Godwin that even though Wollstonecraft was so disappointed in the French Revolution, it gave her a cause through which she could vent her personal frustrations over Fuseli and write an indictment against patriarchy for its culpability in failing to provide an adequate education for men and women, as evident in France (170).

Cayton's final statement about *Memoirs* is worth repeating here: "Its revelations about Wollstonecraft's private life sharply focused a discussion about the viability of a revolution taking place in the minds and hearts of individuals as well as on streets, battlefields, and the floors of Parliament and Congress" (209). Throughout his account of Wollstonecraft's life, Cayton sees revolution with effect. His elucidations of the implications and ramifications of such a revolutionary life are what make his biography extremely unique and rich. He does not just mention Richard Price and his influence on Wollstonecraft; he offers a full picture of him (43–44), as he does Fuseli (50–53) and Fanny Imlay Godwin (263–65), and so forth, as you would expect when discussing the importance of these key characters in Wollstonecraft's life. But he goes into great detail about the people who were more peripheral and yet influential in Wollstonecraft's formation, such as Burke (49–50), Barlow (65–73), Brissot (73–67, 91–92), Crèvecoeur (78–81), Cordorcet (81, 94–95), Amelia Alderson (149–50), Mary Hays (150–51, 199–203), Hannah More (190–93), Malthus (193–94), Adam Smith (194), Charles Lloyd (203–6), Elizabeth Hamilton (206–9), Elihu Hubbard Smith (213–17), Timothy Dwight (217–19), Sophia Courtland Westyn (233–35), Charles Brockden Brown (235–38), Maria James Reveley (242–44) and Mary Jane Clairmont (249–55), as well as the people who were influenced by Wollstonecraft. For every literary piece that Cayton mentions, he provides a plot summary and a critical dissection as to the work's relevance to Wollstonecraft. Of course, we would anticipate this about her work, but he also includes most of Godwin's works, even those after her death. He analyzes many works that one would rarely associate with Wollstonecraft, but he does make the connections.

Cayton liberally shares his superior knowledge of history and literature in his book, which greatly enriches the biographical canon on Wollstonecraft as well as on Godwin. It does not offer the intricate details, but it does give a broader picture than what we had before.

Chapter 18

CHARLOTTE GORDON'S *ROMANTIC OUTLAWS: THE EXTRAORDINARY LIVES OF MARY WOLLSTONECRAFT AND HER DAUGHTER* (2015): LIKE MOTHER, LIKE DAUGHTER

Charlotte Gordon had a brilliant idea when she produced a dual biography through which to identify the effect that Wollstonecraft had on her youngest daughter. Gordon noticed that even among those readers acquainted with Wollstonecraft and Mary Godwin Shelley (the author of *Frankenstein*), very few connected the two: "They viewed mother and daughter as unrelated figures representing different philosophical stances and literary movements. Shelley appears in the epilogues of biographies of Wollstonecraft, and Wollstonecraft in the introductory pages of lives of Shelley" (xv–xvi). Therefore, Gordon set out to examine the famous mother's imprint on her also famous daughter through Wollstonecraft's letters, journals, published works and biographies. She also studied Godwin's account/idealization and the views held by Shelley's contemporaries of Wollstonecraft. Actually, Gordon says that she took the opposite approach by attending to "the echo of Wollstonecraft in Shelley's letters, journals, and novels" (xvii), but her book pulls both ways. Her organizational plan is one chapter on Shelley, the next on Wollstonecraft followed by another on Shelley, and so on, each primarily but not always in chronological order, but with highlighted parallels between the two. She summarizes the affinity in her introduction:

> Both mother and daughter attempted to free themselves from the stranglehold of polite society, and both struggled to balance their need for love and companionship with their need for independence. They braved the criticism of their peers to write works that took on the most volatile issues of the day. Brave, passionate, and visionary, they broke almost every rule there was to break. Both had children out of wedlock. Both

fought against the injustices women faced and both wrote books that revolutionized history. (xvii)

With Gordon's thesis being to determine the intersections of the two women, she is quite successful, and her approach to meshing their biographical material is novel.

That said, however, much of what she presents about Wollstonecraft is haggard and redundant with what has been published already, unsupported by documentation, replete with errors made by previous biographers and diminished by a new set of errors. Notwithstanding these problems, she does offer a few compelling insights. One is her appreciation of Wollstonecraft's *Letters from Sweden*. Gordon identifies it as a "psychological journey, one of the first explicit examinations of an author's inner life" (342). She credits Wollstonecraft for being "among the first English writers to declare that the psychological journey was as important as the external, the self as worthy of exploration as a foreign land" (343). Writing this travelogue helped Wollstonecraft work her way out of despair about Imlay to arrive at a place of "self-acceptance, from desolation to a hard-won tranquility" (342). Gordon's recognition of its importance to letters and to Wollstonecraft's emotional healing is a significant study.

Gordon also notes the book's innovative "initiation of an artistic revolution" in which, six years prior to Wordsworth's preface to the *Lyrical Ballads*, Wollstonecraft "'vindicated' emotion, subjectivity, and psychological complexity," giving "the Romantics a new writing world" (342–43).

About Wollstonecraft's style, Gordon also reminds us that by the time she wrote *Rights of Woman*, she was "an experienced journalist." To Gordon this means that she "trained herself to catch and engage her readers, just as she liked to rally opinions back and forth across a table. She let cracks appear in her authorial armor on purpose, inviting readers to engage with her, just as she welcomed a good sparring match at a party" (179). One aspect of style that she would adopt is, as Gordon recognizes, "speaking with sincerity." It exasperated Godwin, whose writing was arranged and developed by logic (179).

Doubtlessly, most readers do not connect Wollstonecraft's experience with the *Analytical Review* in producing *Rights of Woman*, other than Mitzi Myers. She recounts that although Wollstonecraft was assigned to many different subjects, the majority of the assignments given to her by Johnson were "trash" or sentimental novels written about "artificial beings" with formula plots and "artificial feelings, cold nonsensical bombast, and ever varying still the same improbable adventures and unnatural characters."[1] Myers also emphasizes how writing the reviews for sentimental fiction "helped her to formulate her own special feminist stance, that particularly Wollstonecraft's blend of rational radicalism and precocious romanticism" (82). Gordon's theory of how Wollstonecraft's reviewing experiencing gave her the opportunity to work through her own notions of writing theory and feminist critique is worth considering.

Another significant insight is Gordon's perception that Wollstonecraft was "profoundly influenced by the *idea* of children. Wollstonecraft had directed most of her life's work toward the next generation, dreaming of what life might be like for them and how she could help them inherit a more just world" (xvi). However, later in her biography Gordon undermines this claim by discussing how short Wollstonecraft fell in this goal, with and without her own efforts. Wollstonecraft's work was first discredited by the public exposure of her private life in Godwin's *Memoirs* and then further disavowed during a period of anti-Jacobin movements beginning at the end of the 1790s. Next, Gordon contradicts this second stand by asserting that *Original Stories* was "a staple of the advice literature on the moral development of children for almost fifty years" (119). Not only does she not support this claim, she exaggerates. Gordon might have gotten the idea of its longevity of impact arguably from Mitzi Myers' essay, "Impeccable Governesses, Rational Dames, and Moral Mothers: Mary Wollstonecraft and the Female Tradition in Georgian Children's Books" in which Myers suggests that the heroine was "no one but a Georgian audience will much like" (40). Since Wollstonecraft's book was published in 1788, and if Myers's implication is that the novel did well only in the Georgian period, then its popularity would have evaporated during 1838 when the Victorian period began, fifty years after its publication. Nevertheless, although there were other people publishing their ideas about educating children—such as Maria Edgeworth, Hester Chapone and Hannah More—the eighteenth century was just igniting the modernization of education, but the actual reforms did not take place until the nineteenth century (Hans 209–12). To credit *Original Stories* as being a staple for fifty years is misleading.

This is not the only incident in which Gordon exaggerates and seems to either confuse or conflate the Georgian and Victorian periods. She uses the term "advice literature," which is relatively anachronistic. The term is used primarily to describe the major genre of the Victorian period and not before. Advice books were the number one best-selling books in Britain and America in the nineteenth century, important to socially mobile readers who, as they were moving up in society, could learn the proper way to behavior suitable for class. Especially in America and especially in the South, advice books comprised the highest sales in the 1800s for females to learn primarily proper British etiquette (Cogan 16). Mrs. Sarah Ellis published a series of books that were best-selling advice/conduct books on both sides of the Atlantic. They were *The Women of England* (1838), *The Daughters of England* (1842), *The Mothers of England* (1843), and *Wives of England* (1843).

Although it is true that there were conduct books in the eighteenth century—namely John Gregory's *Father's Legacy to His Daughters* (1761) as well as Hester Chapone's *Letters on the Improvement of the Mind* (1773), both discussed in *Rights of Woman*[2]—the genre was pronounced in the Victorian period and is usually associated with it. Books on etiquette were called courtesy books, beginning in the thirteenth century, peaking in the sixteenth century, evolving into preserving the proper behavior of the upper class in the seventeenth century and addressing the behavior of women in the eighteenth.[3]

Another problematic statement that is sweeping and not altogether accurate about Wollstonecraft's century is Gordon's implication that not only was it legal for a husband to beat his wife, it was common practice (xvii). Robert Shoemaker, and others, have supplied evidence of social pressure that made domestic violence unacceptable in the seventeenth and eighteenth centuries (106). He cites a pamphlet published in 1609 and again in 1682 that condemned wife beating, and through the early eighteenth century "society" urged civilized behavior where no one beats anyone (106). This attitude was promoted and publicized, especially in the popular periodicals the *Tatler* and the *Spectator* (Hunt 25–27). William Blackstone, an English judge famous for his *Commentaries on the Law of England*, writes:

> The husband also (by the old law) might give his wife moderate correction. [...] But this power of correction was confined within reasonable bounds, and the husband was prohibited from using any violence to his wife. [...] But with us, in the politer reign of Charles the second, this power of correction began to be doubted: and a wife may now have security of the peace against her husband; or, in return, a husband against his wife. Yet the lower rank of people, who were always fond of the old common law, still claim and exert the ancient privilege: and the courts of law will still permit a husband to restrain a wife of her liberty, in case of any gross misbehavior. (1:444–45)

Toward the second half of the eighteenth century, the legal profession was punishing many of the husbands who beat their wives. The social climate for the middling and upper classes was a demonstration of civilized order. To beat the wife, the husband, or the child was considered vulgar.

Women learned that they could get what they want by using their sexuality and by playing at being juvenile and coquettish. Although it was behavior that Wollstonecraft deplored, the arrangement was mutually entertained by both sexes,[4] so why was there any reason for beating one's spouse? Many marriages were mercenary or arranged because of familial interests or politics and, therefore, as Wollstonecraft objurgates, there was an understanding that romance and love could be found outside of the bonds of marriage, and that code of morality, as long as done discreetly, was tolerated.[5] Additionally, the upper classes were exerting their influence on judges and magistrates to protect women from wife beating (Clark 187). The intellectuals of the day embraced John Locke's idea of a social contract that supposed that individuals will naturally obey laws because the laws ensured their own rights and liberties. As some understood it, the Lockean contract ensured equal justice, but it also clashed with the social hierarchy ingrained in British society (191).

That is not to say that wife beating was not occurring, particularly among the lower and laboring classes (Foyster 72–73). In 1782, Francis Buller, a baronet and a judge, made the infamous ruling that a man could "thrash his wife with impunity provided that the stick was no bigger than his thumb" (Courtney 249)—an unfortunate and frequently cited statement, including referenced by Gordon (153), but it was not supported by the rest of the law system and by other judges during this this time in England.

Attitudes toward women changed drastically in the Victorian century, especially among the middle classes who embraced a gendered sphere divided by labor. This ideology pervaded novels, advice books, articles, lectures—like John Ruskin's lecture series that comprised *Sesame and Lilies*, first published in 1865. He echoed the message found in most of the didactic literature of the day: "The man's power is active, progressive, defensive. He is eminently the doer, the creator, the discoverer, the defender" (146). He is for war and cut-throat business and the "open world" full of "peril and trial," and he is to protect her from this (147). In contrast, "her intellect is not for invention or creation, but for sweet ordering, arrangement, and decision" (147), and her reign is in the "temple of the hearth" or the home (148). There was much social pressure to conform to these gender allocations, and as long as each did what he and she were expected, supposedly there would be domestic harmony.

Furthermore, in the Victorian period, wife beating was considered one of "the acts of the 'ruffian' class" (Tomes 341), and the number of spousal assaults in London dropped from 800 cases in 1853 to 200 in 1889, reflecting a similar decrease nationwide (330). Moreover between 1840 and 1882 men were being sentenced for assaults on women. In 1853, men could be imprisoned with hard labor for six months. The sentence was increased to one year in 1868, and then the Wife Beaters Act of 1882 sentenced men to the public pillory with flogging (340).

The problem with Gordon's incendiary statements about the legality of beating one's wife (xvii) as well as "She had no legal rights of any kind" (62) "[...] the best that lawmakers could do was to declare it illegal to beat one's wife with a stick that was thicker than a thumb" (153) is an oversimplification of the issue and an inaccurate depiction of the era. It is true that under the law of coverture, the identity of a married woman was subsumed by the husband, and she herself had very few legal rights to land property, even if she owned it when she entered the marriage (Brooks 364). Another right for women safeguarded her ownership of what was called "paraphernalia," which included her clothing and, importantly, her jewelry (2:435). Gordon does specify that it was the wife who "was not allowed to own anything," but without mentioning widows and single women, her sweeping statement may lead the reader to believe that, like the Bible, "wife" stood for any woman. Regardless, single and widowed women could own freehold land (Munroe 77). Therefore, it is not that she "had no legal rights of any kind." Further, the dower that women possessed—whether in the form of land or money—coming into the marriage, remained theirs in trust until the death of their husbands. Although a wife had no access to it while her husband was alive, neither did he. It was to be reserved for her if she outlived her husband (Blackstone 2:131–36). The same was true for jointure. Any property designated legally as joint estate shared by husband and wife or else estate limited to the wife became the wife's upon his death. While alive, the husband was "compelled by a court of equity to observe" as to how he was to manage it. In other words, he could not sell it and pocket the profits (2:136).

None of these concerns negate the reality that women did not have equal rights with men. Gordon is right in saying that a man could declare his wife insane and have her committed to an asylum (62) simply by his own signature without "sanity hearings" or professional evaluations (Koppelman xix). There was no law that said otherwise until 1891 (Foyster 254). Meanwhile, there was also the understanding in the eighteenth century that men who committed uxoricide were considered "very much unlike a husband and a man," but were often acquitted (Wiener 150–51). On the other hand, if a wife murdered her husband, she would be executed for treason (Jacob 724). Especially during the nineteenth century, when there was strong hegemonic pressure for gender conformity, "women were legally and involuntarily committed to insane asylums for expression of opinion, their religious beliefs, actions outside the scope of acceptable ladylike behavior of the day, or 'hysteria' determined to be caused inherently by their female bodily organs. These commitments were accomplished by fathers, husbands, and brothers" (Schonstein 16–17).

Gordon seemed to know more about the Victorian period than she did the time in which Wollstonecraft lived. Two examples go hand in hand and have to do with either a misleading or misled notion of attitudes toward women during the late eighteenth century. The first makes its first appearance on page 89 when Gordon maintains that Wollstonecraft was tackling the question of "the ideal woman."[6] "Was she the fainting maiden, easily fatigued and naïve?" Gordon asks and answers as she thinks Wollstonecraft would have answered: "No! She was a resourceful intelligent human being" (87). Gordon uses this term again by borrowing Godwin's definition from *Caleb Williams*: The "ideal female" is "the delicate frame of the bird that warbles unmolested in its native groves."[7] Why do people make such deductions from works of fiction? If Godwin truly believed this, then why did he become attracted to Mary Wollstonecraft who was anything but.

Gordon makes several additional uses of the term, especially in discussing Rousseau's portrayal of "the feminine ideal" (171–72, 237), and argues correctly that Wollstonecraft thought it nonsense that women were expected to act "Fragile in every sence of the word" and

> they [were] obliged to look up to man for every comfort. In the most trifling dangers, they cling to their support, with parasitical tenacity, piteously demanding succor; and their *natural* protector extends his arm, or lifts up his voice, to guard the lovely trembler—from what? Perhaps the frown of an old cow, or the jump of a mouse; a rat, would be a serious danger. In the name of reason, and even common sense, what can save such beings from contempt; even though they be soft and fair.[8]

The trouble here is not only how a woman should or should not behave; it is also about the man. Throughout *Rights of Woman*, Wollstonecraft criticizes the vanity, lack of virtue and the lack of reason displayed by both genders in the upper classes. There was not necessarily an ideal in the eighteenth century as there was a code of behavior, not expected, but permitted, tolerated and cultivated among these classes. If anything, Wollstonecraft is asking men and women to alter their behavior to conform to the moral code of the Bible. Much of the description of her notion of how one can find "true happiness," "contentment, and virtuous satisfaction, that can be snatched in this imperfect state, must arise from well regulated affections" (233; ch. 9). This is not an ideal; it is a biblical prescription couched in biblical rhetoric of how to enjoy domestic harmony. It is described in *Rights of Woman* in chapter 9, in an idyllic, Romantic snapshot of a woman surrounded by healthy children and with her suckling a baby at a "clean hearth," when the husband returns from a day of good labor in his provision for his family (234). This would become the ideology of domesticity that regimented Victorian society, but it contrasted to Wollstonecraft's observation of the typical parlor in the 1790s, of the upper classes and the middling sort that imitated them, where both spouses are indolent and have nothing to do with their children or the tending to their households.

The appeal for the "ideal woman" is not characteristic of the eighteenth century in literature. If anything, the Victorian ideology of domesticity was reactionary to a more prevalent previous era of lasciviousness. The latter half of eighteenth-century England experienced a drastic decline in religion, especially among the upper and middling classes, and along with it, a decline in morality (Smith 634). Beginning with Barbara Welter's widely quoted article titled "The Cult of True Womanhood: 1820–1860" first published in 1966, the term "ideal woman" and those like it became an area of major focus of the nineteenth century.

The second example is when Gordon says that if a man could not keep his "woman in check, [...] he was considered the subject of petticoat government" (xvii). The term "petticoat government" with its derogatory implications was popular in the early seventeenth and the nineteenth centuries. It is listed in the *OED* as first appearing in E. Ward's *London Spy* (1699; I.x.15).[9] In 1702 John Dunton wrote an exposition on the concept offering these definitions: "By Petticoat-Government, I mean when Good Women Ascend the Throne, and Rule according to Law, as is the case of the present Queen" (50)—which since she, being a woman, is highly virtuous and therefore it was very wise for Parliament, "knowing the Wisdom and Piety of English women," to put her on the throne (50). Then there is the petticoat-government of the woman who rules well her household, where a man should not "presume to direct their [*sic*], to order about Tarts, Puddings, Wines, and Kickshaws" (50–51). The worst kind is "when Bad Women usurp Authority [biblical language here] over their husbands, as in the case of Shrews" (51).

Quoting from Paul's letter to the Ephesians, Dunton warns that a "Husband who lets his Wife RULE, (except when she has a right to do so) deserves to wear the Petticoat, having renounc'd the Prerogative of his Sex" (6). It is not a matter that women are incapable of governing as demonstrated by Queen Anne; however, women are so virtuous, religious, and faithful, he likens them to angels (9). Men are lost without that rib bone that is represented by women: "They are the Guardians of our Infancy, the Life and Soul of our Youth, the Companions of our Riper Years, and the Cherishers of our Old Age. From the Cradle to the Tomb, we are wrapt in a Circle of Obligations to them, for their Love and good Offices" (9–11). If a "Masculine Spirit [inhabits] a Woman's Body" (13), apparently there it supplants this virtue. Moreover, women should be expending their virtues by being good mothers (22).

What an effort of equivocation and circumlocution to suggest when and where and how women should rule, without being definite about any gender divide, as no one was definite about such a thing, not then nor as the century evolved. By the time Wollstonecraft wrote *Rights of Woman*, being concerned about one's clothing, one's tiny waist, one's turn of leg, one's wig or coiffure, one's jewels, regardless of sex, this was what occupied most of the classes of leisure. Aristocrats and those imitating the aristocrats were dressing and acting as dandies. Being masculine in contrast to being feminine was simply not an issue for most of the upper classes until the Victorian period.

Another anachronism is Gordon's reference to "silly novels" (172). Although Gordon does not cite it, in *Rights of Woman* Wollstonecraft does honor a single "instance" of woman who read "chapters and psalms before breakfast, never touching a silly novel" (284; ch. 13). Regardless, like "petticoat government" and "ideal woman," "silly novels" was in vogue for the nineteenth century and was made particularly famous with George Eliot's 1856 essay, "Silly Novels by Lady Novelists," but it was not a term that was much used in Wollstonecraft's time.

Similarly, Gordon uses the term "scribbling women." This is another anachronistic term, a quote from Nathaniel Hawthorne in 1855 that became famous when, in 1910, it was published as part of a letter to his publisher. Hawthorne writes: "Besides, America is now wholly given over to a d—d mob of scribbling women, and I should have no chance of success while the public taste is occupied with their trash—and should be ashamed of myself if I did succeed."[10] When Fred Lewis Pattee writes his literary history of women's writing, *Feminine Fifties*, he introduces one of his chapter as "A D—d Mob of scribbling women" (110).[11]

Gordon refers to sentimental, formulaic novels that Wollstonecraft disdained as written by "scribbling women," citing Mitzi Myers's reference to the same (142–44, 565). The term did appear in a play that Wollstonecraft did see performed, but afterward, it was not repeated until Hawthorne made his complaint. Elizabeth Inchbald's 1791 play *Next Door Neighbours* has this line in the epilogue: "Whene'r we scribbling Women wield the Pen, Or dare invade the Rights of scribbling men [...]," some "will sicken and turn pale with jealousy" (63). Otherwise, in a letter to Everina, Wollstonecraft repines that she is not in a "scribbling vein" (Todd, *CL* 83). "Scribbling" was a word that Byron uses often in his letters, and although he did attach it once to "woman" (but not to "women") to disparage the writing of Anna Seward,[12] this was in 1811, and it was not quoted by others as Hawthorne's was and is. Like Wollstonecraft, Byron referred to his own writing as "scribbling."[13] The term, however, unfortunately used by Hawthorne, became the rallying cry for feminists beginning the 1970s for the egotistical discrimination—and yes, as Inchbald put it— jealousy of men toward the success women were experiencing in the popularity and sales of their novels. In reference to nineteenth-century sentimental novels, there are hundreds of references to the "scribbling women." In reference to women writing in the eighteenth century, I found only one and that was by Inchbald.

Aside from the anachronistic terms, there are two major concerns one should have about Gordon's portrayal of Wollstonecraft. First, too much of it is based on Godwin's *Memoirs*, and as I have argued before, Godwin's account cannot be considered a reliable source because of his bias, his brevity of relationship with Wollstonecraft, and his lack of gathering information from those who did know her well. Second is her lack of documentation and her flair for making unsubstantiated statements. Here is the first paragraph in her first chapter on Wollstonecraft with Gordon's claims on the left and my questions on the right:

Mary Wollstonecraft's childhood could not have been more different from her daughter's. Far from being the favorite Wollstonecraft was the invisible second child	Does this imply that Mary Shelley was the favorite in the Godwin/Clairmont household? How does Gordon know this? Is she, like other biographers, drawing on *Wrongs of Woman* with the narrator's brother having been "the idol of his parents"? If so, fiction is fiction and not necessarily a reliable basis for fact.[14]
In a family of seven	Does she mean seven children?
While Godwin was controlled and predictable	Where is the support for this?
Wollstonecraft's father was hot-blooded and capricious	Most biographers agree with this, but some attempt to sympathize with him. Where is Gordon's support for this claim?
An alcoholic	Support?
Who squandered his family's money	Support?
Edward Wollstonecraft brutalized his wife and children	Not all biographers think that he beat the children. What does Gordon mean by "brutalize"?
Mary's mother, Elizabeth, was so browbeaten (11).	Not all biographers agree with this deduction.

Some of these statements may be accurate, some of them are arguable, but since not one includes argument or documentation, their claims must be taken with a grain of salt.

In the next paragraph, Gordon states that Mary was more like her father with his "ferocious temper and his hatred of restrictions" (11). At least Gordon supplies some reasons to suppose this, but not one of her examples has support from evidence. For instance:

"She fought with her big brother when he tried to bully her" (11).	How does Gordon know this?
She "resisted her mother's rules"	What rules? When? How does Gordon know this?
She "began a lifelong insurgency against her father, using the very tools he had passed on to her: rage, stubbornness, and a deeply rooted sense of been entitled to a better life" (11).	This "sounds" good, but why does Gordon think that Wollstonecraft "began a lifelong insurgency against her father?" Where is there evidence of this? When does Wollstonecraft use "rage," especially toward her father?

The last point about entitlement really needs explanation and support.

Gordon is also prone to exaggerate or to manipulate information to support a theory that is impossible. For example, after claiming, correctly, that Wollstonecraft was sent to a wet nurse for the first year (11), and the wet nurse would have been in the country, Gordon writes, "The first four years of Mary's life were spent in an undistinguished house on Primrose Street" (12). Gordon concedes that "Four years is not long enough to make much of an impression, especially at the outset of life," which is true, but her point follows that "the Spitalfields way of looking at things, the Spitalfields jaundice, was passed down by way of her father." The "jaundice" was the "base injustices the poor suffered at the hands of the wealthy" (12). This implies that the Wollstonecrafts were poor and mistreated by the wealthy, but as Gordon notes, Mr. Wollstonecraft already felt entitled and although he had been apprenticed in the silk-weaving business, there is no indication that by the time he and his family were living on Primrose that he was doing any labor at all. Gordon mentions that the grandfather was wealthy and lived in a mansion on Fournier Street, so then why would the grandfather resent "the aristocrats who bought his gloves, gowns and cravats even though they had made him rich" (12–13)? Gordon adds, "Spitalfields silk weavers were famous for their hatred of the upper classes" (13). First, he made handkerchiefs and only handkerchiefs (Hostettler 141). Second, the laborers in Spitalfields often rebelled because of unfair economic situations, but the Wollstonecrafts *were* the upper class. Third, to discuss what happened in Spitalfields when Mary was six years old (15), when Mary and her family were actually living in Whale Bone is not apropos.

Like the other biographies on Wollstonecraft, Gordon's tenders some insight, and through her unique layering of mother and daughter, the reader does get to see Wollstonecraft in a diacritical way. It is a shame that so much information about Wollstonecraft, though, is redundant, reductive, unsupported, and at times simply wrong.

EPILOGUE

With two centuries of hindsight, one biographer attributes Wollstonecraft as "the first great champion of women's rights in the modern Western world" (Brody 6). Only a few days after Wollstonecraft's passing, her husband biographer etched in her gravestone in St. Pancras' churchyard this simple epitaph: "Mary Wollstonecraft Godwin: Author of 'A Vindication of the Rights of Woman'" (Jacobs 274). What a significant betwixt and between are the two.

"Vindication" was a popular word for books, articles, and pamphlets in the late eighteenth century in both England and the United States. Typing "Vindication" as a keyword in WorldCat, from 1780 to 1800, results in 2,480 hits. Here are a few examples: *A Letter from Edmund Burke, esq. in Vindication of His Conduct with Regard to the Affairs of Ireland* (1780); [...] *a Vindication of the Late Bishop Hoadly* (1790); and *Pursuit of Literature* [...] *A Vindication of the Work* [...]" (1800). Although the word was in popular usage in the Victorian period and appears in the titles of legal documents and theological treatises, apparently there was no longer the variety of subjects that needed vindicating as there had been in the previous century. Missing until 1792, when Wollstonecraft published *A Vindication of the Rights of Woman*, however, was a vindication for anything that had to do specifically with women.

Ever since her own vindication, Wollstonecraft would be betwixt and between people's opinion of her. As Miriam Brody puts it, "her readers either hailed her as one of the brave generation of rebels who were ending monarchies and building republics, or they scorned her as proposing ideas so ridiculous and outrageous they could not be taken seriously" (7). Prior to her publication, she and Fanny Blood enjoyed a friendship with Thomas Taylor (1758–1835), well-known for his lectures on Plato. Taylor had considered Wollstonecraft his "greatest favourite" (Yarrington 86), but immediately following the publication of *Rights of Woman*, he wrote a savage rebuttal in *A Vindication of the Rights of Brutes* (1792), with the hypothesis that if women were equal to men, then beasts were also equal to men. Even to a man who had respected her intellectual acumen, once Wollstonecraft declared women to be on equal intellectual footing, she fell betwixt and between what was estimable and what was aberrant.

Godwin had "author" etched on her gravestone, and this is how he identified her in the title of *Memoirs*. One might wonder why Godwin considered her an "author" instead of an "authoress." Is this not another betwixt and between issue? Most of her biographers refer to her as an "author," whereas most writers in the eighteenth and nineteenth centuries refer to her as an authoress. Surely, in days past, "authoress" carried a connotation that was not usually flattering when readers had different expectations based upon the gender of the writer of a work. William Enfield, a British Unitarian minister, was sensitive to this fact. In his review of *Rights of Woman* for the *Monthly Review*, he emphasizes that respect is due her: "In the class of philosophers, the *author* of this treatise—whom we will not offend by styling, authoress—has a right to a distinguished place" (198). Leslie Anne Walton Monstavicius contrasts Enfield's approbation with a two-part review written by Tobias Smollett for the *Critical Review*. She observes that Smollett attacked "Wollstonecraft's womanhood," which "becomes a critical issue not merely as a feminine use or misuse of rhetoric, or a womanly turn for romance in an otherwise 'manly' treatise, but as a concrete condition of her writing" (66). Smollett writes:

> But, as this is the first female combatant in the new field of Rights of Woman, if we smile only, we shall be accused of wishing to decline the contest; if we content ourselves with paying a compliment to her talents, it will be styled inconsistent with "true dignity," and as showing that we want to continue with the "slavish dependence."—We must contend then with this new Atalanta. (390)

The reference to Atalanta is relevant to women's studies. As the legend goes, King Lasus was so disappointed that his wife gave birth to a daughter instead of a son, he took the baby to a mountaintop and left her there to die. A bear found her and suckled and raised her. She grew up to be a fierce hunter and vowed to Artemis that she would never surrender her virginity. Once reunited with her father, she was coerced to marry so, to appease him, she agreed to marry any suitor who could beat her in a footrace. Many contenders died in the attempt, but Hippomenes asked the goddess of love, Aphrodite, to help him. Aphrodite was displeased with Atalanta because she declined love, so she gave him three sacred golden apples and told him to drop them, one at a time, to distract Atalanta. The plot worked; by stopping to pick up the apples that she could not resist, Atalanta lost the race and had to marry Hippomenes.

The feminist innuendos are obvious to us but apparently not to Smollett: (a) Atalanta was rejected by her father because she was female. (b) She was raised outside of human society and became a happy adult who was content not to marry. (c) Only when her father reentered her life was she forced to do something that she did not want, and that was to marry. A patriarch insisted that a woman had no business being alive if she refused to be some man's wife. Smollett condescendingly implies this when he suggests that "Miss Wollstonecraft" chose from one of the "batchelors" available (Smollett 390). (d) Men were miffed because Atalanta could beat them in a race. After all, being a woman, she was supposed to be weaker than they. Because she disproved their supposition, the realization of what women could do apparently was so threatening, it killed the men who challenged her. (e) A man defeated her through cunning conceit, tempting her with the apple in the way Eve was deceived in the Garden of Eden. (f) She was forced to lose her independence and her identity by becoming a man's wife. (g) Thus, androcentricity was fully restored to power.

In his patronizing criticism of Wollstonecraft's writing style, Smollett calls it "flowing and flowery" and her ideas and expressions full of "indelicacy" (141). He accuses of her lacking "decency and propriety," causing Monstavicius to conclude that it was Wollstonecraft's womanhood that was under attack: "The reviewer, galled by Wollstonecraft's lack of maidenly reserve, was quick to display on his own part the blushing modesty she lacks; his sensibilities, apparently, are so refined, he is unable, even in private, so much as to 'copy' her indelicacies" (67). She mentions this because Smollett claims that although he had planned to provide "a bouquet from the parterre" for the readers' inspection of Wollstonecraft's work, "we have blushed to copy in the closet, what she has openly published" (Smollett 141).

Monstavicius continues with her critique:

> His tactic effectually "unsexes" Wollstonecraft; not only does she fail to exhibit a degree of modesty proper to women, she fails to exhibit that proper to men. Her lack of womanliness has not, according to the reviewer, made her "manly," but rather has made her nothing—a creature who fails to abide by any moral standard, male or female. (67)

In *Rights of Woman* Wollstonecraft argues that men get to practice virtues and use their talents for noble industry and agency, unlike women, and since the term "woman" is "comprehensively termed mankind," she wished that all people—both men and women—would become "more and more masculine" (*ROW* 76; introd.). When writing Jane Arden, she boasts that her friend Fanny has a "masculine understanding" (Todd, *CL* 25). Therefore, to Wollstonecraft, to be "masculine" is to be adept and accomplished and rational; it is a worthy aspiration. Nevertheless, how terribly unfortunate it is that a strong woman like Wollstonecraft was put in a position in which she was unable to boast of the qualities that could and were demonstrated in women and instead had to encourage women to be more like men. Alas, she had a vision for women that was betwixt and between and could be possible only after another couple of centuries.

Meanwhile, it is Smollett's hope that we "shall leave miss [*sic*] Wollstonecraft at least to oblivion: her best friends can never wish that her work should be remembered" (141). He could not have been more wrong. There will be many more biographies written on Wollstonecraft, and as the gaps and contradictions in this volume indicate, there is need for more information, illumination and consideration of her life and her work.

In 1975 John Russell, in writing for the *New York Times*, asked why so many biographies had to be published on famous people. He complained that "there is a limit to the number of ways in which this patchwork can be reassembled." He, too, was wrong. There are many more patches that can be added to the work, and there is a full spectrum of colors in a person's life and works. Furthermore, the inclination is to patch in only certain aspects and another inclination is to patch in information in different ways, so that the patchwork is always changing. This process is not just subject to the proclivity of the biographer; the reader of the biography is equally disposed to process information in different ways from other readers. Furthermore, there is no limit to the ways in which people perceive another person, especially when they are looking for a hero or scapegoat.

Jüger Schlaeger observed how much the British, in particular, love biographies, as apparent in the popularity of the National Art Gallery (64). His theory is that all of us have a "pressing need for a reassertion of individualism" after the effects of post-modernism have so undermined and distorted any individual's right to self-identify (66). Biography, Schlaeger suggests, is "perpetually accommodating new modes of man, new theories of the inner self, into a personality-oriented cultural mainstream, thus always helping to defuse their subversive potential" (63). He sees it as a comfort to those of us who feel as if our lives in general are out of control, and that we have been forced to reject universal truths. We turn to biography because we "thirst for facts, experience, and identity in an age when they are threatened by a loss of authority" (67).

In the *New York Times* "Best Sellers," as of November 8, 2016, in the categories of print and e-book nonfiction and hardcover nonfiction, four out of the five bestsellers are biographies/autobiographies. The bibliography that follows includes an increase in "non-Western" names of scholars publishing in recent years. As more readers have greater opportunities to share their perspectives and priorities forged through their particular ethnic, cultural, social, political and religious backgrounds, we will see the emergence of yet more different portraits of Wollstonecraft.

Proof of this prediction is the biography *Alexander Hamilton*, which for more than a year was the number-one bestselling nonfiction paperback, thanks to the Pulitzer Prize–winning musical, *Hamilton*. Based on the biography, *Hamilton*, is the most commercially successful musical of all time. First Lady Michelle Obama decided it was "the best piece of art in any form" that she ever saw and that it is "a work of genius" ("Remarks"). What is remarkable about the musical is exactly what is happening and will continue to happen: Since people who were once marginalized are gaining fora and venues through which they can raise their voices and interpret history informed by perspectives steeped in their own culture and history, they are now recasting history and biography. The writer of the biography that inspired the musical is Ronald Chernow, who is Jewish. He has written biographies on Washington (for which he won the 2011 Pulitzer Prize for Biography and the 2011 American History Book Prize), and on Rockefeller (nominated for the 1998 National Book Critics Circle Award). Besides these, he wrote *The Warburgs: The Twentieth-Century Odyssey of a Remarkable Jewish Family*, which won the 1993 George S. Eccles Prize for Excellence in Economic Writing.

Lin-Manuel Miranda, of Puerto Rican descent, read Chernow's biography of Hamilton, which inspired him to write the musical that won, besides the Pulitzer, two Grammys, an Emmy, and three Tony awards (but a record-breaking 16 nominations), and a MacArthur "Genius" Award. The *New Yorker* summarized the stamp of diversity that makes the retelling of Hamilton so unique:

> Miranda portrays the Founding Fathers not as exalted statesmen but as orphaned sons, reckless revolutionaries, and sometimes petty rivals, living at a moment of extreme volatility, opportunity, and risk. The achievements and the dangers of America's current moment—under the Presidency of a fatherless son of an immigrant, born in the country's island margins—are never far from view. (Mead)

Hamilton reminded Miranda of his own father, Luis A. Miranda, Jr., who had been "an ambitious youth in provincial Puerto Rico, had graduated from college before turning eighteen, then moved to New York to pursue graduate studies" and climbed up the political ladder; "Miranda saw Hamilton's relentless brilliance, linguistic dexterity, and self-destructive stubbornness through his own idiosyncratic lens" (Mead). Thus, the biography of Hamilton became "an immigrant's story," and African-Americans portrayed America's founding fathers in ways that they could tell their American stories from their ethnic point of view, which had heretofore been told only by whites.

How much impact can another perspective have on revising history and making it more relevant to more groups of people? Before the musical, Hamilton was slated to be replaced on the $10 bill by some woman from American history. But because *Hamilton* is now so popular, the first secretary of the treasury will remain on the bill, and Harriet Tubman will replace Andrew Jackson (a slave owner) on the $20 bill (Calmes).

We have just as much need to raise social awareness of the inequality of women today as did Wollstonecraft more than two hundred years ago. Women have not yet reached full equality, even in the West, and they continue to experience horrific bondage in other countries. We have need to hear from Wollstonecraft. There will be more biographies written on her. There never will be just one Mary Wollstonecraft. Like a Picasso collage, who she was, what she believed, and what she wrote will always be slightly, more or less, betwixt and between what can be found in biographies and criticism that include biographical material on her.

NOTES

Introduction

1. As of February 2017.
2. According to Sandrine Bergès, during the 1920s Emma Goldman, the publisher of the journal, *Mother Earth*, was the first to hail Wollstonecraft as the mother of feminism (15). However, the first that I found to give her this title is Teodor Wyzewa in his chapter on Wollstonecraft, "The Mother of Feminism" (1909).
3. For an identification of biases evident in biographies, see David Novarr's *The Lines of Life: Theories of Biography, 1880–1970*.
4. C. Gordon 486–87. However, L. Gordon and most other biographers said he began a fortnight after his wife's death (366).
5. "She was in the habit of composing with rapidity," Godwin claimed in *Memoirs* (73) and then pointed out her errors (73, 76).
6. Southey wrote this in a letter to William Taylor on July 1, 1804. See Robberds 507.
7. See Janet Todd's annotated bibliography.
8. Columbia University Press would publish the most scholarship on Wollstonecraft. Alas, their priorities have since changed.
9. See the bibliography for a list of articles she published on Wollstonecraft in the 1970s.
10. Quoted in Green 136 from *New York Times Book Review* (July 13, 1975): 41.
11. I also argue the Romantic characteristics in her works in "The Romantic Essentials of Wollstonecraft" in my *The Essential Wollstonecraft*.
12. In a letter to Eliza, November 5, 1786 and again in a letter to Everina, March 25, 1878 (Todd *CL*, 88, 117 respectively).
13. Quoted in Wellington 40 from *FR* 121.
14. For an in-depth discussion of the perception of the feminine and masculine in *Rights of Woman*, see Barbara Andrew. For Wollstonecraft's treatment of both throughout several of her works, see Maunu and Brody.
15. As of February 2017.

1. WILLIAM GODWIN

1. The Charlotte Gordon account of the discord between Godwin and Wollstonecraft is probably accurate. See 174–80.
2. See C. Gordon 362–66.

3   Unless indicated otherwise, all references to Godwin's *Memoirs* are from the Broadview edition, edited by Clemit and Walker.
4   One month before they married, Godwin published his essay, "Of Cohabitation," (a copy of which is included at the back of Clemit and Walker's *Memoirs*). In it he writes, "Excessive familiarity is the bane of social happiness" (139).
5   See Paul's "Mary Wollstonecraft" 258.
6   Actually, the article denounced the *Analytical Review* as "anti-hierarchical and anti-monarchical" and by association, so was Wollstonecraft (174).
7   Johnson's letter is reprinted in *Memoirs*, Appendix C, 162–63.
8   About theories of Wollstonecraft's homosexuality see Foster 56–60 and Faderman, "Who Hid" 117. For a discussion of "grossly familiar" in *ROW*, see Yaeger 74–5.
9   The article is reprinted in Appendix D of *Memoirs* 179–81. For a discussion of its reception, see Myers's "Godwin's" 301n7.
10 Lloyd's poem, "Lines to Mary Wollstonecraft Godwin" was published in Lloyd and Lamb's *Blank Verse* (London: John and Arthur Arch, 1798). See Guest 103–6.
11 See Jerry Wallis's *The Oxford Handbook of Eschatology*. As for *The Book of Common Prayer*, even the wedding ceremony includes these words: "I require and charge you both (as ye will answer at the dreadful day of judgment, when the secrets of all hearts shall be disclosed [ ]." See "The Form of Solemnization of Matrimony." A copy of the 1752 edition is at https://books.google.com/books?id=ItkUAAAAQAAJ.
12 Quoted in Franklin 14. She cites the Abinger archive, Dep. c.604/1, which stores Godwin's private memoranda.

2. MARY HAYS

1   Letter to Everina, November 7, 1878 (Todd, *CL* 139).
2   According to Gordon's note, the letter is in the Abinger Collections, Dep. B. 227/8. See 598n485.
3   Quoted in L. Gordon 365 and C. Gordon 485, which were documented by letters of October 1797 in Abinger, Dep. B. 227/8.
4   Todd, *CL* 202nn463–64.
5   Todd, *CL* 209–11. *Letters and Essays* was first published by T. Knott, March 1793 (Todd, *CL* 211n488).
6   *The Castle on the Rock: or, Memoirs of the Elderland Family* (London: Symonds, 1798). It was translated into French the first year of its publication, *éliza, ou Mémoires de la Famille Elderland* (Paris: Chez Hautin, 1798). Her first novel was *Derwent Priory: or, Memoirs of an Orphan. In a Series of Letters* (London: Symonds, 1798), first serialized in *Lady's Magazine* 27 (January 96) to 28 (September 1797). Her fourth book was *Moreland Manor or, Who is the Heir?* (London: Longman, Hurst, Rees, and Orme, 1806). I was unable to learn anything else about this writer other than that she lived in Isleworth and that her husband must have been related to the Duchess of Kendall, who was the mistress to George I.
7   "bantling, n." OED Online. September 2016. Oxford University Press. http://www.oed.com.ezproxy.liberty.edu/view/Entry/15321?redirectedFrom=bantlings (accessed November 16, 2016).
8   See Byron's letter 27 to Mr. Becher, February 26, 1808 (10). A critic for the *American Monthly* called Coleridge's poetry, esp. *Christabel*, "Coleridge's bantlings," in a review

of Byron's *Childe Harold's Pilgrimage* (7). Coleridge's eldest son, Hartley Coleridge, wrote an essay for *Blackwood's Edinburgh Magazine* (1826) titled "Books and Bantlings." After that S. T. Coleridge compared Ruben's *Adoration of the Magi* (1634) to Raphael's painting, *Ansidei Madonna* (1505) and described the former as "a fac-simile of some real new-born bantling" (238).

9   To read more about Wollstonecraft's influence on *Emma Courtney* and its reception, see Gina Walker's *The Idea of Being Free* and Sloan's and Todd's chapters on the two (236–52). Walker's article on the "Two Marys" identifies Wollstonecraft's influence on other works by Hays as well.

10 Likewise, Harriet Jump distinguishes *Memoirs* as a model for future biographies, one which departs in content from those that preceded it ("Fond" 5).

11 See, Eberle 62–75, Kelly 80–125, Rendall 65, and Wallraven 62–67.

12 See Mellor 144–45.

13 See the obituary in *Monthly Magazine* 232–33.

14 See her article in *Annual Necrology* 412.

15 Quoted from *Annual Necrology* 416. It is a misquote from a letter that Wollstonecraft wrote to Everina after she helped her sister Bess leave her husband. The letter is dated January 1784 (Todd, *CL* 47–48). Paul reproduced a portion of it in *Mary Wollstonecraft* (xiv).

16 Letter from Mary Shelley to Mary Hays, April 20, 1836. See *The Love-Letters of Mary Hays* 246–47.

3. C. KEGAN PAUL

1   Quoted in Paul, *MW* xxvi–xxvii from *ROW* [CE: 255]; ch. 12.

4. ELIZABETH ROBINS PENNELL

1   Quoted in Clarke (118) from a letter from Paul to Pennell on January 19, 1884, in the Library of Congress, PC, Box 375.

2   Their lives at Sacred Heart in Torresdale were documented by a classmate, Agnes Repplier (1855–1950), in her book *In Our Convent Days* (1905). Pennell also wrote about it and the anti-Catholic sentiment in Philadelphia in *Our Philadelphia* (1914). See "Pennell Family Papers." The Pennells bequeathed all their work and information about Whistler and their cookbooks and many of their papers to the Library of Congress. The collection of personal correspondence, prints, memorabilia, and works is also extensive at the University of Pennsylvania.

3   Most of this information was acquired from a biographical sketch that is stored, along with 24 boxes of letters, at the Harry Ransom Center, University of Texas at Austin.

4   *Encyclopaedia Britannica.* 2016. "Joseph Pennell (American Artist and Writer)."

5   All quotes and references, unless otherwise noted, are from Pennell's 1885 publication of *Mary Wollstonecraft* at Project Gutenberg.

6   Quoted in Clarke (118) from a letter of Niles to Pennell, July 4, 1884 (Library of Congress, PC, Box 375).

7   This is from the 1890 version that is available at Gutenberg. The quote does not appear in the first edition.

8. "Therefore they are no more two, but one flesh. What therefore God has joined together, let not man put asunder" (Matt. 19:6).
9. See *The Victorian Governess Novel*, Cecilia Wadsö Lecaros (Lunds University Press, 2001) and Kathryn Hughes, The Victorian Governess (London: Hambledon and London, 2001).
10. Quoted in Pennell 122 from Paul v.
11. Quoted in Pennell 209 from Paul xl.
12. See David M. Craig. *John Ruskin and the Ethics of Consumption* (Charlottesville, VA: University of Virginia Press, 2006).
13. Appropriate quote from John Bradford (1510–55). When he was imprisoned in the Tower of London, shortly to be burned at the stake for being a Protestant heretic, he saw criminals being led to their execution at Tyburn, and exclaimed, "There, but for the grace of God, goes John Bradford" (Townsend xliii). He was martyred on July 1, 1555.
14. *ROW* 128[CE: 149]; ch. 4, for example.
15. Quoted in Pennell 184 from Paul xxxi–xxxii.
16. Godwin wrote that Wollstonecraft had said to Imlay, "If we are ever to live together again, it must be now, or we part for ever. You say, You [*sic*] cannot abruptly break off the connection you have formed. It is unworthy of my courage and character, to wait the uncertain issue of that connection. I am determined to come to a decision. I consent then, for the present, to live with you, and the woman to whom you have associated yourself." She explained the purpose of the proposal was for the sake of Fanny's needing the "affection of a father" (98).

5. RALPH M. WARDLE

1. As quoted in Neiman 433. The novel was titled *This Shining Woman: Mary Wollstonecraft Godwin, 1759–1797* (New York: Appleton, 1937).
2. Wardle provides a footnote that Mary never knew whether she was born in London on in Epping Forest. Wardle was unable to find that her birth was registered at Christchurch in Spitalfields, which definitely it would have been had she been born there. Therefore, it is very likely that she was born in Epping Forest (342n3).
3. Quoted in Wardle 62 from a letter to Everina, January 15, 1787 (Todd, *CL* 99).
4. Quoted in Wardle 62 from a letter to Everina, November 17, 1786 (Todd, *CL* 91).
5. Todd, *CL* 22–23, 28 and 30.
6. Quoted in 136 from a letter Johnson wrote to Dr. Taylor. See *Boswell's Life of Johnson*, 257n2.
7. See George's chapters 7 and 8.
8. See George 38–41.
9. Quoted in Boos 7 ("Biographies") from George 3.
10. Quoted in Boos 7 from George 3.
11. Quoted in Boos 7 from George 4.
12. Quoted in Boos 7–8 from George 170, emphasis added by Boos.
13. Quoted in Boos 7 from George 12.
14. She was a docent at the New Bedford Whaling Museum. An obituary tells that she lived to be 90. She died March 21, 2004. See http://www.southcoasttoday.com/article/20040323/NEWS03/ 303239998.

6. ELEANOR FLEXNER

1. Flexner quotes Wardle (1003) and Roper (37–38) in her appendix (273). Wardle arrived at his figure by totaling articles in the *Analytical Review* signed "M," "W," or "T," and deducing from style. Wollstonecraft wrote more than 30 reviews for any given issue (O'Neill 110). Marilyn Butler and Janet Todd studied all the reviews and selected 417 that they thought were Wollstonecraft's. They reproduced these reviews on *The Works of Mary Wollstonecraft*, vol. 7.
2. I am quoting myself here from my article "Edith Simcox's Diptych: Sexuality and Textuality" (66n2). The statistics came from Kathryn Hughes and Barbara Onslow.
3. Quoted in Jacobs 46 from a letter to George Blood of August 25, 1786 (Wardle *CL* 111–12).
4. Quoted in St. Clair 163n31 from an unpublished letter of November 15, 1796, from Johnson to Charles Wollstonecraft.
5. Quoted in St. Clair 163n31 from a letter to Everina of April 8, 1807. The letter is in the Abinger Manuscripts.
6. A thorough treatment of Wollstonecraft's theory of rhetoric is Chapter 5 of my *The Essential Wollstonecraft*.
7. Those who spent time were Thomas Paine, Helen Maria Williams and Gustav Graf von Schlabrendorf. Although Olympe de Gouges and Wollstonecraft never met (Kuhlman 383), Wollstonecraft was in Paris when De Gouges was arrested in the summer of 1793 and executed on November 3. Likewise, Wollstonecraft never met Louis XVI, and she did not attend his execution on January 21, 1793, followed by his wife's execution on October 16. She watched his arrest from her window (Todd, *CL* 216–17).
8. Quoted in Flexner 197 from "John Adams's Comments on Mary Wollstonecraft's French Revolution." See bibliography.
9. Wollstonecraft might have met the Adamses when they came to Newington Green in June of 1785 (C. Gordon 72) but, obviously, that predates her visit to France.
10. A friend of hers, Joel Barlow, while in Paris at the same time as Wollstonecraft, wrote his wife in a letter of April 1793 reprinted in Flexner 181. The original is in the Houghton Library at Harvard (Flexner 297n20).
11. See, in particular, "Plan for a Revolution in Louisiana," *Archives des Affaires Etrangères*. AHA Annual Report, 1896, 945–53 and *AHR* 491–4), citations provided by Flexner (297n21).
12. Turner was a professor of history at the University of Wisconsin and wrote a number of books and textbooks on American history. Although Flexner does not list the books she consulted by him, they must have included *Documents on the Relations of France to Louisiana, 1792–1795* (1898), *The Mangourit Correspondence in Respect to Genet's Projected Attack Upon the Floridas, 1793–1794* (1898), *The Policy of France Toward the Mississippi Valley in the Period of Washington and Adams* (1900?), and *Correspondence of the French Ministers to the United States, 1791–1797* (1903).
13. In a letter dated November 12, 1792 (Todd, *CL* 208). It is quoted in Janet Todd's introduction to *Vindications* (xxv), *Revolutionary Life* (251), and introduction to *Political Writings* xxii. It is also in Lyndall Gordon 180, Showalter 26 and Tomalin 119.
14. Quoted in Flexner 188–89 from a letter from Paris, dated August 1793. The letter has been reproduced in Paul 2–3.
15. "quickness, n." OED Online. September 2016. Oxford University Press. http://www.oed.com.ezproxy.liberty.edu/view/Entry/156447?redirectedFrom=quickness

(accessed November 16, 2016). Also "keep, v." and "to keep under. OED Online. September 2016. Oxford University Press. http://www.oed.com.ezproxy.liberty.edu/view/Entry/102776? redirectedFrom=keep+under (accessed November 16, 2016).

16   Quoted in Flexner 189–90 from Wollstonecraft's letter to Imlay from Paris, September 1793. The entire letter is in Paul 7–9.
17   Quoted in Flexner 190 from Wollstonecraft's letter to Imlay from Paris on December 1793. The entire letter is in Paul 13–15.
18   Quoted in Flexner 218 from the letter in Paul 207. See also Todd, *CL* 339.
19   Quoted in Flexner 192 from a letter to Imlay from Paris February 1794 in Paul 34–36.
20   In a letter from Mary Moody Emerson to Ruth Haskins Emerson, dated 20 January 1799 (24). Ruth would become the mother of Ralph Waldo Emerson, giving birth to him in 1803.

7. CLAIRE TOMALIN

1   For a history, see Holly Laird's *The History of British Women's Writing, 1880–1920*.
2   The exception was Margaret George's biography published by the University of Illinois Press.
3   See my chapter 4 about the influence of Dissenters in Wollstonecraft's thinking, in *Mary Wollstonecraft and Religion*.
4   Quoted in Wardle 147 from Tomalin 6.
5   John Opie painted her portrait in 1792 and in 1797.
6   Quoted in Tomalin 178 from Wollstonecraft's letter of February 19, 1975 (Todd, *CL* 284).
7   Quoted in Green 142 from Tomalin 23.
8   Quoted in 144 from Tomalin 109.
9   Quoted in Goodwin 108 from Knowles 170.
10 Jacobs, however, deduces from Wollstonecraft's letter that it was Imlay who held the "enlightened-libertine position," and was frequently lecturing her on "free-love principles" (199).
11 Quoted in Hampsey 100 from *ROW* 98; ch. 2.
12 In Polwhele's notes to his poem, "The Unsex'd Females" (16).

8. EMILY SUNSTEIN

1   Janet Todd identifies in 1956 William Gaunt as making the argument that Blake wrote "Mary" with Wollstonecraft in mind (*Annotated* 78, #453). G. E. Bentley, Jr., in 1979, offers even more convincing arguments than the obvious, pointing out very similar as well as verbatim language in *Maria*, which Godwin had published in 1798 (349–50).
2   L. Gordon 457n15. Godwin writes: "Three of her brothers and two sisters are still living; their names, Edward, James, Charles, Bess, and Everina" (5).
3   See "Smiley Face," at <www.ideafinder.com>.
4   Quoted in Sunstein 353, but Fanny's entire suicide letter is available in Dowden 328.
5   See Edward Shorter 19 and Frisch 60–62. The age of the first menarche depended upon that content.
6   Quoted in Sunstein 25 with Sunstein's emphasis, from *ROW* 215; ch. 7.
7   Quoted in Sunstein 173 from *ROW* 215; ch. 7.

8   While the family lived in Hoxton, Mr. Wollstonecraft apparently was guilty of some "misconduct" that resulted in a "keen blast of adversity" (quoted in L. Gordon 19). Gordon assumes this refers to a gross financial mistake and that the sisters were expected by duty to surrender their money to him. The only way they would have had money at this time was through an annuity—although Flexner and Todd had different theories about the mysterious annuity. Gordon's deduction is that this annuity was given the father with the understanding that it was a loan (19), but later had trouble collecting during what became the mysterious Roebuck Case (L. Gordon 78, 103).
9   Quoted in Sunstein 211 from *Rights of Woman* 107; ch. 2.
10 Quoted in Sunstein 211 from *Rights of Woman* 187; ch. 5.
11 Letter dated between October 20, 1782, and August 10, 1783 (Wardle *Letters* 79).
12 In a letter to Everina, November 7, 1787 (Todd, *CL* 139).
13 Wollstonecraft discusses Chapone's works in *ROW.* See 188; ch. 5.

9. MARGARET TIMS

1   She was married to Rembert Tims (1916–1972), according to her obituary at <http://obits.al.com/obituaries/mobile/obituary-preview.aspx?pid=142622681> (3 October 2013).
2   Her first publication was a play: *Many Happy Returns: A Play in One Act* (London: Frederick Muller, 1948). Before Wollstonecraft, she published *Jane Addams of Hull House, 1860–1935; a Centenary Study* (New York: Macmillan, 1961), which went through numerous reprints and publications. After that she published *Ealing Tenants LTD.: Pioneers of Co-partnership* (London: Ealing Local History Society, 1966). In the same year that she began to publish the first of a nine-volume set, *Poet's England* (London: Brentham Press, 1976–88). With Gertrude Bussey, she wrote *Pioneers for Peace: Women's International League for Peace and Freedom 1915–1946* (Syracuse University Press, 1993). Her last books were poetry: *Ver Poets' Voices: Thirtieth Anniversary Anthology* (1996), *Dust Devils Dancing: A Haiku Anthology* (1997) and *A View from a Death: Diana, Princess of Wales 1961–1997: An Anthology in Verse* (1998), all published by St. Albans: Brentham.
3   According to Lawrence H. Officer and Samuel H. Williamson, "Five Ways to Compute the Relative Value of a U.K. Dollar Amount, 1270 to Present," *MeasuringWorth*, 2016, Web, accessed November 12, 2016. Tims found the £10,000 figure in *Memoirs* 44, but also notes that Eleanor Flexner stipulates that most of the inheritance was in property and not cash (359n3). However, since the property generated rent, it was producing ready cash for Wollstonecraft.
4   *Shelley* 2:186. Tims observes that Godwin listed the moves as Beverley to Hoxton to Wales but, according to this letter, they went from Beverley to Wales and then to Hoxton (9–10).
5   For more on the Allens and Wedgwoods, see my chapter on Andrew Cayton. Cressely is a community in Pembrokeshire in Wales.
6   Quoted in Tims 37 from letter of July 25, 1785 (Todd, *CL* 58).
7   Quoted in Tims 32 from letter of November 12, 1785 to Bess and Everina from Fanny (Wardle, *Letters* 100–101).
8   Quoted in Tims 21 from letter of October 1782 to Jane Arden from Wollstonecraft (Cameron 2:983–84).
9   Quoted in Tims 22 from Todd, *CL* 38.
10 Quoted in Tims 26 from Todd, *CL* 44.

11 Todd thought there were two reasons that Wollstonecraft overreacted to Bess's situation, with the first being fear of insanity because of her brother who suffered it and the second being memory of how despicable was the marriage situation between her mother and father (*Revolutionary* 45). For a thorough discussion of Wollstonecraft and mental illness and insanity, see my chapter "Lucretia: Suicide in Eighteenth-century England" in *The Essential Wollstonecraft*, and "Wollstonecraft, the Melancholy: Her 'Melting Mood,'" in *Becoming Mary Wollstonecraft*.
12 See my chapter, "Wollstonecraft, the Liberator: "Misery Haunts This House": Did She Do Right by Bess?" in *Becoming Mary Wollstonecraft*.
13. Quoted in Tims 27 from letter of January 1784 to Everina from Wollstonecraft (Todd, *CL* 45).
14 For a thorough discussion on Joshua Waterhouse, see my "Wollstonecraft, Her Amours" in *Becoming Mary Wollstonecraft*.
15 For a thorough discussion on Neptune Blood, see my "Wollstonecraft, Her Amours" in *Becoming Mary Wollstonecraft*.
16 Quoted in Tims 106 from *ROM* 33.
17 Quoted in Tims 107 from *ROM* 37.
18 147–53, but she tells us more about Bess throughout the rest of her book as if struck by a special interest in her, and making this comment: "[Bess], it may again be noted in passing, was not nearly such a simpleton as she has sometimes been painted" (177).
19 I clear up the mystery in my chapter "Wollstonecraft, the Mother: Was the Mother of Feminism a Good Mother to Her Daughters?" in *Mary Wollstonecraft's War with Womanhood*.
20 Quoted in Tims 153 from Stiles 182. It is also quoted in Todd, *CL* 189n409.
21 For a short biography of Stiles's life, see Baldwin.
22 Quoted in Tims 164 from *Memoirs* 78.
23 I argue that Wollstonecraft was a co-author in my chapter "Wollstonecraft, the Utopian Dreamer: Topographical Untruths and Imlay's Literal Lies" in *Becoming Mary Wollstonecraft*.
24 Quoted in Tims 192 from *The Emigrants* 6.
25 Quoted in Tims 192 from *The Emigrants* 200.
26 See Goldin and Katz, and Collins.

10. GARY KELLY

1 Quoted in Kelly 105 from Knowles 165.

11. JANET M. TODD

1 See *The Free Dictionary by Farlex* on the Web for the word "futility."
2 "shoe, v." and "show the goose." OED Online. September 2016. Oxford University Press. http://www.oed.com.ezproxy.liberty.edu/view/Entry/178437?rskey=lc1jYp&result=3&isAdvanced=false (accessed November 16, 2016).
3 See Peter Richard Wilkinson, *Concise Thesaurus of Traditional English Metaphors* (Oxon: Routledge, 2008) 92.
4 In a letter to Joseph Cottle of March 13, 1797 (305).
5 See my chapter on melancholy in *Becoming Mary Wollstonecraft*.
6 Quoted in McLaren 3 from *Rights of Woman* 291; ch. 13.
7 Quoted in Hanley 129 from Todd, *CL* 44, 48.

12. MIRIAM BRODY

1   Quoted in Brody 23 from Wollstonecraft 84.
2   For example, in 1785 she writes to George Blood: "Church tell [sic] me I shall never thrive in the world—and I believe he is right—I every day grow more and more a proficient in that kind of knowledge which renders the world distasteful to me" (Todd, *CL* 61); and shortly after that, "If it had pleased Heaven to have called me home—what a world of cares I should have missed" (65).
3   Quoted in St. Clair (190) and in Jacobs (69) from a letter Godwin wrote to Knowles September 8, 1826, in the Pforzheimer Collection, reel 6 (Jacobs 294n31).
4   Godwin and Wollstonecraft's good friend Thomas Holcroft would stand trial for this very thing in 1794.

13. DIANE JACOBS

1   In the *Leisure Hour* (710), but according to the article, the writer is borrowing from "Irenaeus," an American writer for the *New York Observer*.
2   Quoted in "The Recluse Ladies of Llangollen" 194.
3   William Wordsworth wrote a poem titled "To the Lady Eleanor Butler and the Hon. Miss Ponsenby, Composed in the Grounds of Plas Newydd, near Llangollen, 1824." Ann Seward wrote some narrative on them (see "The Ladies of Lllangollen"), but also a long poem titled *Llangollen Vale* (1795). Madame de Genlis wrote "The Fair Recluses of Llangollen" (see Prichard, *Short Memoir* 6–9).
4   In Sawyer and Sawyer 26 from Anne Chambers, *Granuaile: The Life and Times of Grace O'Malley* (Dublin: Wolfhound Press, 1979): 77–78.
5   Arymtage 332, Pückler-Muskau quoted in Sawyer and Sawyer 26, and "The Ladies of Llangollen" 710.
6   Quoted in Sawyer and Sawyer (26) from the July 1790 issue, quoted in Mavor 27–28.
7   Wardle discusses her regrets (28).
8   See my chapter on Sunstein for a better discussion of the Bishop episode.
9   Her citation is Paul C. Nagel, *The Adams Women* (New York: Oxford University Press, 1987) 57.
10 She cited Roy Porter, *English Society in the Eighteenth Century* (Harmondsworth: Penguin, 1999) and Michael MacDonald and Terrence R. Murphy, *Sleepless Souls: Suicide in Early Modern England* (Oxford: Clarendon Press, 1990). I discuss the attitudes to suicide in "Lucretia: Suicide in Eighteenth-century England" in *The Essential Wollstonecraft*.
11 The letter was printed in the *Cambrian*, October 12, 1816 (3).

14. CAROLINE FRANKLIN

1   Quoted in Franklin 1–2 from *Memoirs* 44.
2   Quoted in Franklin from *Memoirs* 44.
3   Quoted in Franklin 13 from *Memoirs* 55.
4   Quoted in Franklin 2 from *Memoirs* 45.
5   211–12 or the beginning of chapter 7 in *Maria*.
6   In chapter 3 of my *Mary Wollstonecraft and Religion*, I dispute this claim.
7   Karen Offen's seminal article "Defining Feminism" provides a history of the term "feminism" and argues the complexity of its use. The word, *féminisme*, has often been

8   Hodson (1). On this subject Hodson footnotes Gayle Trusdel Pendleton's "Towards a Bibliography of the *Reflections* and *Rights of Man* Controversy," *Bulletin of Research in the Humanities* 85 (1982): 65–103 (65). See Hodson 1n1.
9   Quoted in full on 113 from a letter to Joseph Johnson, December 26, 1792 (Todd, *CL* 216–17).
10 For a thorough discussion of what "sympathy" meant in the eighteenth century and its power in print, see Fairclough's *The Romantic Crowd: Sympathy, Controversy and Print Culture*.
11 In a letter to Ruth Barlow, Wollstonecraft wrote that she is "acquiring the matrimonial phraseology without having clogged my soul by promising obedience &c" (Todd, *CL* 251).
12 See Janet Todd, *CL* 154n356. Her documentation is a letter from Johnson to Godwin, stored in Abinger MSS, Dep.b.210/3.
13 For more about Johnson's influence, see Basker's article.
14 Quoted in Franklin 75–76 from the review reproduced in Todd and Butler (7:136).
15 See Blakemore's full discussion of this in chapter 1.
16 See Mary Chapman and Glenn Hendler's *Sentimental Men*, which analyzes a history of male sentimentalism. Probably the most prolific of male sentimental writers was Charles Brockden Brown.
17 See Jane Tompkins's *Sensational Design*.
18 Quoted in Johnson "pampered sensibility" (7) from *ROM* (6).
19 For more analysis of Wollstonecraft's associations of the feminine versus masculine, see Susan Gubar's *Critical Condition* (137–46).
20 The Wollstonecraft quote on 170 is from her letter to Imlay (Todd, *CL* 327), and the Godwin quote (also on 170) is from *Memoirs* (97).

15. LYNDALL GORDON

1   See Lyndall Gordon's website at http://lyndallgordon.net/index.html.
2   Quoted in Gordon 3 from Woolf 159.
3   Besides the multiple references to "reason" in *Rights of Woman*, Wollstonecraft often writes about reason in her letters, urging herself and others to be governed by it. For example, in a letter to Jane Arden in 1781, she expresses her intentions to spend more time with Miss Blood, "follow[ing] the dictates of reason as well as the bent of my inclination" (Todd, *CL* 30). An example of her intention to let reason rule is conveyed in a letter to Everina in 1787. Her expectations with her sister were frequently blighted because "I too frequently, willing to indulge a delightful tenderness, forget the convictions of reason, and give way to chimerical hopes, which are as illusive, as they are pleasant" (107). This was concerning Everina's failure to respond

to Wollstonecraft's last three letters, but one has to wonder if she was not referring to her own proclivity to hope and expect for good things in general only to be constantly disappointed.

4   The biblical concept of "covering" can be found in 1 Corinthians 11:3–7:

> But I would have you know, that the head of every man is Christ; and the head of the woman is the man; and the head of Christ is God. Every man praying or prophesying, having his head covered, dishonoureth his head. But every woman that prayeth or prophesieth with her head uncovered dishonoureth her head: for that is even all one as if she were shaven. For if the woman be not covered, let her also be shorn: but if it be a shame for a woman to be shorn or shaven, let her be covered. For a man indeed ought not to cover his head, forasmuch as he is the image and glory of God: but the woman is the glory of the man. (KJV)

5   As Gordon explains it—and by no means is there a consensus about this mysterious annuity—when Mr. Wollstonecraft failed yet another time with his farm, he moved the family to Laugharne, Wales, but his debt had to be paid, and he apparently did so by using an annuity that was given to the girls, with an understanding that it was a loan. How it came about then that the annuity was being held by Roebuck & Henckell, insurance brokers, Gordon does not explain, but nearly every biographer mentions that Wollstonecraft was desperately hoping that her brother would win the Roebuck case and that her share would pay off all her debts, especially those to Mrs. Burgh, who loaned her money for the school. The biographers agree that Ned received the money, but he refused to share it with Wollstonecraft. According to Gordon, he did give a portion of it to Everina, but Flexner (267–68) and Todd (*Revolutionary* 25–26) had different theories.

6   The "opening flower" most likely refers to the metaphor she develops about herself in a letter to Everina, March 24, 1787; and shortly after that in a letter to Gabell, April 16, 1787 (116, 121, respectively). The genus reference is cited in n1 above.

7   Gray 2.55–56, quoted in a letter to Everina of March 24, 1787 (Todd, *CL* 116). She quotes from *Elegy* in a letter to Jane Arden (15) and to Imlay (232).

8   *ROW* 265; ch. 12.

9   One example is this statement about "idle superficial young men": "whose polished manners render vice more dangerous, by concealing its deformity under gay ornamental drapery" (*ROW* 87; ch. 1). Another concern that Wollstonecraft makes is that women are expected to conceal their affection for their husbands (92; ch. 2).

10 Quoted in 26. Gordon is using the edition of *Memoirs* edited by Richard Holmes (1987), but she rarely supplies page numbers. In order to have ready access, I supply page numbers from the edition edited by Clemit and Walker.

11 Quoted in Gordon 26 from letter to Jane Arden in the summer of 1781 (Todd, *CL* 33). I identify even additional Christians and go into more detail about their influence on Wollstonecraft in my chapter, "The Crafters of Wollstonecraft's Religion" in *An "Accountable Being": Mary Wollstonecraft and Religion*.

12 Quoted in Gordon 159 from letter of March 29, 1792 from Bess to Everina.

13 See Sunstein 36–38 who published in 1975 versus Todd, who published in 2000.

14 Gordon cites the letters exchanged by Wollstonecraft and the Bloods between November 1787 and December 1792 (Todd, *CL* 138–213).

15 See my chapter "Wollstonecraft, Her Amours: 'Melting into Love'" in *Becoming Mary Wollstonecraft*.

16. Other works include Maria Falco's *Feminist Interpretations of Mary Wollstonecraft*, Kelly Weisberg's *Applications of Feminist Legal Theory to Women's Lives* with her introduction to prostitution (187), and the latest work on *Rights of Woman: The Routledge Guidebook* by Sandrine Bergès.
17. See my chapter "Wollstonecraft, Her Amours: 'Melting into Love'" in *Becoming Mary Wollstonecraft*.
18. The connection between the woman preacher and Wollstonecraft was made by Dr. Isobel Rivers of St. Hugh's College, Oxford. See Gordon 473145.
19. Isichei and Stewart.
20. Smith's ch. 5 (L. Gordon 146).
21. Letter to William Roscoe November 12, 1792, from London (Todd, *CL* 206–8; 208).
22. Gordon quotes from letters from Barlow to his wife to wit: "Mrs W[ollstonecraft] was exceedingly disappointed to see me return without my dearest I told you before how she loves you [ ]," and "you would have been perfectly safe here [ ] Mrs W[ollstonecraft] is exceedingly affectionate to you" (April 5 and April 19, 1793; quoted in 202). Barlow refers to her as "Mrs." which was a customary address to a spinster.
23. Gabriele (an Italian scholar) and Frances Rossetti had four children: Christina, William Michael, Dante Gabriel and Maria Francesca (who became an Anglican nun). Gabriel and Michael were two of the seven founders of the Pre-Raphaelite Brotherhood in 1848 and Christina was considered an honorary member.
24. Wollstonecraft wrote her second suicide letter on October 10, 1795, made sure that her clothes were weighted down by rain water, and then jumped off the Putney Bridge. Fanny wrote her suicide note on the evening of October 9, 1816, and then took an overdose of laudanum that would have ended her life on October 10.
25. It is documented, however, in St. Clair 411–12. See also Marion Kingston Stocking, *The Clairmont Correspondence* 1:87.

16. JULIE A. CARLSON

1. See her chapter 3: "Unbinding the Personal: Autonarration, Epistolority, and Genotext in Mary Hays' *Memoirs of Emma Courtney*."
2. Figure 23 in *Eccentric Biography; or, Memoirs of Remarkable Female Characters, Ancient and Modern* (Worcester, MA: Library Company of Philadelphia, 1804). The artist is unknown.
3. For further reading about masculine women and what were called Sapphists (lesbians), see Kittredge and Donoghue.
4. Quoted in Carlson 26 from Johnson's *Equivocal Beings* 49.
5. This was Godwin's assessment of *Rights of Woman*, in his *Memoirs* (1798; 82). Carlson quotes it on 30.
6. Quoted in Carlson 31 from Myers, "Reviews" 82–91.
7. Quoted in Carlson 30 from Bahar 132–53.
8. From *Maria*, edited by Mellor and Chao, 247.

17. ANDREW CAYTON

1. Godwin, *Memoirs* 51. Clemit and Walker add this in a footnote: "In 1793 the eldest, Elizabeth (Bessy) Allen (1764–1846), married Josiah Wedgwood II (1769–1843) [ ]. Shortly afterward her sister Louisa Jane Allen (1771–1836) married John Wedgwood (1766–1844)" (51n1).

2   He worked for bankruptcy law reform throughout his career, and after Godwin's death, served as Accountant-General in Bankruptcy from 1835 to 1846 (Crosby 869–71).
3   To delve into this metaphysical exploration of the two concepts, begin with Coleridge's *Biographia Literaria*, chapters 4 and 10. Robinson illuminates and so does the first chapter of Rookmaaker's *Towards a Romantic Conception of Nature*. Difficult to read is Dugald Stewart's *Elements of the Philosophy of the Human Mind* (esp. 210–11), but because it was first published in 1792, its definition of "fancy," "imagination" and "sublimity" is time-appropriate to Wollstonecraft and Imlay. Also pertinent is Thomas Hobbes's definitions in his introduction to his translation (1686) of Homer's *Illiads* and his *The Elements of Law Natural and Politic* (1.10.4.36). James Engell's *The Creation Imagination* can help understand Stewart and Hobbes. For an excellent discussion of the use of "fancy" and its effect by eighteenth-century women writers, see Julie Ellison's "Female Authorship, Public Fancy."
4   Wollstonecraft begins a letter to Imlay with: "I just now received one of your hasty *notes*; for business so entirely occupies you." She warns that his "whirl of projects and schemes" will destroy him, his happiness, and hers as well (Todd, *CL* 277). In an earlier letter, she says point blank, "I hate commerce" (238).
5   See *A Narrative of the Captivity and Restoration of Mrs. Mary Rowlandson* (1682), Ann Eliza Bleeker's *The History of Maria Kittle* (1793), and Lydia Child's *Hobomok* (1824).
6   Despite the book's claim to have been written in America.
7   I argue that Wollstonecraft was a co-author in my chapter "Wollstonecraft, the Utopian Dreamer: Topographical Untruths and Imlay's Literal Lies" in *Becoming Mary Wollstonecraft*.
8   Please see my chapter on suicide which disputes his assertions: "Lucretia: Suicide in Eighteenth-century England" in *The Essential Wollstonecraft*.

18. CHARLOTTE GORDON

1   "Reviews" 87. Myers writes: "Although Wollstonecraft reviewed books about children, education, women, travel, and even boxing, fiction—sentimental fiction in particular—seems to have been her niche" (83) The "trash" comment is quoted in Myers, "Reviews" 84 and comes from a letter to Johnson, July 1788 (Todd, *CL* 156). "Artificial beings," (quoted in 86) comes from Wollstonecraft's reviews (97n13), but it also is found in *Rights of Woman* (77; introd.)
2   Wollstonecraft is very critical of Gregory's ideas in *Rights of Woman* in chapters 2, 7. In chapter 2 she is deferential toward Chapone although she disagrees with some of her theories.
3   For a more in-depth treatment, see Berberich, Bryson, and Carré.
4   In *Rights of Woman*, Wollstonecraft discusses women's "propensity to tyrannize" and use "cunning" (since they lacked physical strength), "which leads them to play off those contemptible infantine airs that undermine esteem even whilst they excite desire" (80; introd.). Women use their "persons" in order to purchase their "maintenance" (150; ch. 4).
5   "A husband," Wollstonecraft asserts, "cannot long pay those attentions with the passion necessary to excite lively emotions, and the heart, accustomed to lively emotions, turns to a new lover" (142; ch. 4). She discusses faithless husbands and faithless wives in the Dedication, for one place (72).

6   Gordon addresses this again on 179 as she described Godwin's notion of the "ideal female."
7   Quoted in 179 from Godwin 50.
8   "What nonsense!" comes from *Rights of Woman* (97; ch. 2), and my longer quote comes from the same (139; ch. 4).
9   "petticoat government, n." OED Online. September 2016. Oxford University Press. http://www.oed.com.ezproxy.liberty.edu/view/Entry/242337?redirectedFrom=petticoat+government (accessed November 16, 2016).
10 The letter was sent to D. Ticknor on January 19, 1855 (1:75).
11 The seminal article on the issue that nineteenth-century male writers had with female authors is Nina Baym's "Melodramas of Best Manhood," but see her other work about this. Also excellent are Ann Douglas Wood's "The 'Scribbling Women' and Fanny Fern" and Jane Tompkins' *Sensational Designs*.
12 The actual quote is: "I have heard nothing of Miss Milbanke's posthumous buffooneries, but here is Miss Seward with 6 tomes of the most disgusting trash, sailing over Styx with a Foolscap over her periwig as complacent as can be.—Of all Bitches dead or alive a scribbling woman is the most canine" (132). The letter was dated November 17, 1811.
13 One example is in a letter to his publisher John Murray dated April 26, 1814: "I can't, for the life of me, add a line worth scribbling; my 'vein' is quite gone. [ ]" (249).
14 *Wrongs of Woman, or Maria* 212.

BIBLIOGRAPHY

Adams, John. "John Adams's Comments on Mary Wollstonecraft's French Revolution." *Bulletin of the Boston Public Library*, 4th Series, 5, no. 2 (January–March 1923): 4–13.
Anon. Excerpt from the *Anti-Jacobin Review* 1 (July 1798): 94–99. Repr. in *Memoirs of the Author of A Vindication of the Rights of Woman*, edited by Pamela Clemit and Gina Luria Walker, 172–78. Peterborough, ON: Broadview Press, 2001.
———. "Rossetti Family Books." *The Book Collector* 22, no. 1 (1973): 217.
[Aldis, Charles]. "A Defence of the Character and Conduct of the Late Mary Wollstonecraft Godwin, Founded on Principles of Nature and Reason, as Applied to the Peculiar Circumstances of her Case; in a Series of Letters to a Lady." *The Monthly Review* 45 (December 1, 1804): 447–44. http://ezproxy.liberty.edu/ login? url=http://search.proquest.com.ezproxy.liberty.edu/docview/ 4675389?accountid=12085.
Andrew, Barbara. "The Psychology of Tyranny: Wollstonecraft and Woolf on the Gendered Dimension of War." In *Bringing Peace Home: Feminism, Violence, and Nature*, edited by Karen J. Warren and Duane L. Cady, 118–32. Vancouver, WA: Hypatia, 1996.
Apetrei, Sarah. *Women, Feminism and Religion in Early Enlightenment England*. Cambridge: Cambridge University Press, 2010.
Armytage, Fenella F. "The Ladies of Llangollen." *The Pall Mall Magazine* 19, no. 79 (May 1893–September 1914): 328–37. http://ezproxy.liberty.edu/login?url= http://search.proquest.com/docview/6340983?accountid=12085.
Austen, Jane. *Pride and Prejudice*. 1813. London: Bentley, 1853. https://books.google.com/books?id=kQ0mAAAAMAAJ.
Ayres, Brenda. *Mary Wollstonecraft and Religion*. Forthcoming.
———. "Edith Simcox's Diptych: Sexuality and Textuality." *Women in Journalism at the Fin de Siècle: Making a Name for Herself*, edited by Elizabeth Gray. London: Palgrave Macmillan, 2012, 53–70.
———. *The Essential Wollstonecraft*. New York: Palgrave Macmillan, 2017.
———. *Frances Trollope and the Novel of Social Change*. Westport, CT: Greenwood Press, 2001.
———. *Becoming Mary Wollstonecraft*. Forthcoming.
———. *Silent Voices: Forgotten Novels by Victorian Women Writers*. Westport, CT: Praeger, 2003.
Bahar, Saba. *Mary Wollstonecraft's Social and Aesthetic Philosophy: "An Eve to Please Me."* Houndmills: Palgrave, 2002.
Baltzell, E. Digby. *The Protestant Establishment Revisited*, edited and introduction by Howard G. Schneierman. New Brunswick, NJ: Transaction, 2001.
Barbour, Judith. "Mary Shelley: Writing/Other Women in Godwin's 'Life.'" In *Mary Wollstonecraft and Mary Shelley*, edited by Helen M. Buss, David Lorne MacDonald and Anne McWhir, 139–57. Waterloo, ON: Wilfrid Laurier University Press, 2001.

Barker-Benfield, G. J. *Abigail and John Adams: The Americanization of Sensibility*. Chicago: University of Chicago Press, 2010.

Basker, James G. "Radical Affinities: Mary Wollstonecraft and Samuel Johnson." In *Tradition in Transition: Women Writers, Marginal Texts, and the Eighteenth-Century Canon*, edited by Alvaro Ribeiro and James G. Basker, 41–55. Oxford: Oxford University Press, 1995.

Baudelot, Christian, and Roger Establet. *Suicide: The Hidden Side of Modernity*. Cambridge: Polity Press, 2006.

Baym, Nina. "Again and Again, 'The Scribbling Women.'" In *Hawthorne and Women: Engendering and Expanding the Hawthorne Tradition*, edited by John L. Idol, Jr. and Melinda M. Ponder, 20–35. Amherst, MA: University of Massachusetts Press, 1999.

———. "Melodramas of Beset Manhood: How Theories of American Fiction Exclude Women Authors." *American Quarterly* 33, no. 2 (Summer 1981): 123–39. doi:10.2307/2712312.

———. "Rewriting the Scribbling Women." *Legacy* 2, no. 2 (Fall 1985): 3–12. http://www.jstor.org/stable/25678934.

Beasley, Chris. *What is Feminist?: An Introduction to Feminist Theory*. London: Sage, 1999.

Benson, Jackson J. "Steinbeck: A Defense of Biographical Criticism." *College Literature* 16, no. 2 (1989): 107–16. www.jstor.org/stable/25111810.

Bentley, G. E., Jr. "'A Different Face': William Blake and Mary Wollstonecraft." *Wordsworth Circle* 10, no. 4 (Autumn 1979): 349–50. *The Romantic Era Redefined*. http://asp6new.alexanderstreet.com.ezproxy.liberty.edu/romr/romr.object.details.aspx?id=1002130362&searchurl=1G7E0.

Berberich, Christine. *The Image of the English Gentleman in Twentieth-Century Literature: Englishness and Nostalgia*. London: Routledge, 2016.

Bergès, Sandrine. *The Routledge Guidebook to Wollstonecraft's A Vindication of the Rights of Woman*. Oxon: Routledge, 2013.

Berghahn, Volker, and Simone Lässig, eds. *Biography Between Structure and Agency: Central European Lives in International Historiography*. New York: Berghahn Books, 2008.

Besant, Sir Walter. *London in the Eighteenth Century*. London: A & C Black, 1902. Hathi Trust. http://hdl.handle.net/2027/mdp.39015046339589.

Black, Joseph et al., eds. "Mary Wollstonecraft, 1759–1797." In *The Broadview Anthology of British Literature: The Age of Romanticism*, 2nd ed., 4:100–104. Toronto: Broadview Press, 2010.

Blackstone, William. *Commentaries on the Laws of England in Four Books*. Vols. 1 and 2. London: Strahan and Woodfall, 1793. https://books.google.com/books?id=tP1BAAAAYAAJ.

Blake, William. "Mary." In *The Poetical Works of William Blake*, edited by John Sampson, 280–82. London: University of Oxford, 1905. https://books.google.com/books?id=I1QJAAAAIAAJ.

Blakemore, Steven. *Intertextual War: Edmund Burke and the French Revolution in the Writings of Mary Wollstonecraft, Thomas Paine, and James Mackintosh*. Cranbury, NJ: Associated University Press, 1997.

Boos, Florence. "The Biographies of Mary Wollstonecraft." *Mary Wollstonecraft Journal* 1, no. 2 (April 1973): 6–10.

———. *Mary Wollstonecraft: Mother of Women's Rights*. Oxford: Oxford University Press, 2000.

Boswell, James. *Boswell's Life of Johnson*. 6 vols. Edited by George Birkbeck Hill. Vol. 5. New York: Bigelow, Brown, 1786. https://books.google.com/books?id=C_FGAQAAIAAJ.

Braithwaite, Helen. *Romanticism, Publishing and Dissent: Joseph Johnson and the Cause of Liberty*. Basingstoke, Hampshire: Palgrave Macmillan, 2003.

Brandon, Ruth. "Mary and Her Sisters: The Problem of Girls' Education." In *Governess: The Lives and Times of the Real Jane Eyres*, 41–92. New York: Walker, 2008.

Brody, Miriam. *Mary Wollstonecraft: Mother of Women's Rights*. Oxford: Oxford University Press, 2000.

———. "The Vindication of the Writes of Women: Mary Wollstonecraft and Enlightenment Rhetoric." In *Feminist Interpretations of Mary Wollstonecraft*, edited by Maria J. Falco, 105–24. University Park: Penn State University Press 1996.

Browning, Robert. "Mary Wollstonecraft and Fuseli." In *The Poetic and Dramatic Works of Robert Browning*. 6:206. Boston: Houghton Mifflin, 1889. https://books.google.com/books?id=NrEzAQAAMAAJ.

Bryson, Anna. *From Courtesy to Civility: Changing Codes of Conduct in Early Modern England*. Oxford: Clarendon Press, 1998.

Buhle, Mari Jo. *Feminism and Its Discontents: A Century of Struggle with Psychoanalysis*. Cambridge, MA: Harvard University Press, 1998.

Burgh, James. *"Of Knowledge."* In *The Dignity of Human Nature, or, A Brief Account of the Certain and Established Means for Attaining the True End of Our Existence*. 1754. 4 books. Bk. 3:129–217. New York: James Oram, 1812. https://books.google.com/books?id=wXoxAQAAMAAJ

———. *Thoughts on Education Tending Chiefly to Recommend to the Attention of the Public, Some Particulars Relating to that Subject; Which Are Not Generally Considered with the Regard Their Importance Deserves*. 1747. Boston: Rogers and Fowle, 1749. http://docs.newsbank.com.ezproxy.liberty.edu/openurl?ctx_ver=z39.88-2004&rft_id=info:sid/iw.newsbank.com:EAIX&rft_val_format=info:ofi/fmt:kev: mtx:ctx&rft_dat=0F2FD2B5007B0818&svc_dat=Evans:eaidoc&req_dat=8A8B718A23D24E09993EC67C59F3D21D.

Burke, Edmund. *Reflections on the Revolution in France: and on the Proceedings in Certain Societies in London Relative to That Event*. 2nd ed. London: Dodlsey, 1790. https://books.google.com/books?id=TtUuAAAAMAAJ.

Butler, Susan. Review of *The Ladies of Llangollen*, by Elizabeth Mavor. *Journal of the Butler Society*. 1, no 3. (1971): 214.

Byron, Lord George Gordon. *Byron's Letters and Journals*. Edited by Leslie Marchand. Vol. 2 Cambridge, MA: Belknap Press of Harvard University Press, 1973.

———. *The Life, Letters, and Journals of Lord Byron*. Edited by Thomas Moore. London: Murray, 1860. *Hathi Trust*. http://hdl.handle.net/2027/coo.31924086046285.

———. *The Works of Lord Byron, in Verse and Prose. Including His letters, Journals, etc*. Edited by Fitz Green Halleck. Hartford: Silas Andrus & Son, 1846. https://books.google.com/books?id=P5A-AAAAYAAJ.

Caine, Barbara. *English Feminism, 1780–1980*. Oxford: Oxford University Press, 1997.

Calmes, Jackie. "Change for a $20: Tubman Ousts Jackson." (April 20, 2016). *The New York Times*. http://www.nytimes.com/2016/04/21/us/women-currency-treasury-harriet-tubman.html?_r=0.

Cameron, Kenneth Neill, *Shelley and His Circle, 1773–1822*. Vol. 1 of 4 vols. Carl H. Pforzheimer Library. New York: Carl and Lily Pforzheimer Foundation, 1961.

Carlson, Julie Ann. *England's First Family of Writers: Mary Wollstonecraft, William Godwin, Mary Shelley*. Baltimore: Johns Hopkins University Press, 2007.

Carré, Jacques. *The Crisis of Courtesy: Studies in the Conduct-Book in Britain, 1600–1900.* The Netherlands: E. J. Brill, 1994.

Cary, Elisabeth. "John Adams and Mary Wollstonecraft." *The Lamp* 26, no.1 (February 1903): 35–40. https://books.google.com/books?id=3kcDAAAAYAAJ.

Casey, Elizabeth Owens. *Illustrious Irishwomen, Being Memoirs of Some of the Most Noted Irishwomen from the Earliest Ages to the Present Century.* Vol. 2. London: Tinsely Bros., 1877. https://books.google.com/books?id=9EoDAAAAYAAJ.

Castle, Terry. "'The Ladies of Llangollen' [Eleanor Butler (1739–1829) and Sarah Ponsonby (1755–1831)]." *The Literature of Lesbianism: A Historical Anthology from Aristotle to Stonewall.* New York: Columbia University Press, 2003. 334–39.

Catlin, George E.C. Introduction. In *The "Rights of Woman," by Mary Wollstonecraft, & "The Subjection of Women," by John Stuart Mill.* Edited by Ernest Rhys Science, i–xxxix. London: Dent, 1929.

Cayton, Andrew. *Love in the Time of Revolution: Transatlantic Literary Radicalism & Historical Change, 1793–1818.* Chapel Hill: University of North Carolina Press, 2013.

Chalmers, William. "Godwin (Mary)." In *The General Biographical Dictionary*, 16:51–55. London: Nichols, Son, and Bentley, 1814. https://books.google.com/books?id=SexHAAAAMAAJ.

Chapman, Mary, and Glenn Hendler, eds. *Sentimental Men: Masculinity and the Politics of Affect in American Culture.* Berkeley and Los Angeles: University of California Press, 1999.

Chapone, Hester. Letter V: "On the Regulation of the Heart and Affections." In *Letters on the Improvement of the Mind*, 58–110. London: J. Walter, 1790. https://books.google.com/books?id=h5QDAAAAQAAJ.

Clark, Anna. "Humanity or Justice? Wifebeating and the Law in the Eighteenth and Nineteenth Centuries." In *Regulating Womanhood: Historical Essays on Marriage, Motherhood and Sexuality*, edited by Carol Smart, 187–206. London: Routledge, 1992.

Clark, Sir James. *The Influence of Climate in the Prevention and Cure of Chronic Diseases.* 2nd ed. London: John Murray, 1830. https://books.google.com/books?id=fXM_AAAAcAAJ.

Clarke, Meaghan. *Critical Voices: Women and Art Criticism in Britain, 1880–1905.* Aldershot: Ashgate, 2005.

Clemit, Pamela. "Self-Analysis as Social Critique: The Autobiographical Writings of Godwin and Rousseau." *Romanticism* 11 (1205): 161–80.

———, and Gina Luria Walker, eds. *Memoirs of Mary Wollstonecraft.* 1798. Peterborough, ON: Broadview Press, 2001.

Cogan, Frances B. *All-American Girl: The Ideal of Real Womanhood in Mid-Nineteenth-Century America.* Athens, GA: University of Georgia Press, 1989.

Coleridge, Hartley. "Books and Bantlings." In *Essays and Marginalia*, edited by Derwent Coleridge, 1:84–92. London: Moxon, 1851. https://books.google.com/books?id=vBILAAAAYAAJ.

Coleridge, S. T. *Biographia Literaria; or Biographical Sketches of My Literary Life and Opinions.* 2 vols. London: Rest Fenner, 1817. https://books.google.com/books?id=EO85AAAAcAAJ.

———. *Specimens of the "Table Talk" of the Late Samuel Taylor Coleridge.* 2 vols. Edited by Henry Nelson Coleridge, vol. 1. London: Murray, 1835. https://books.google.com//books?id=5xglAAAAMAAJ.

Conger, Syndy McMillen. Review of *Revolutionary Feminism: The Mind and Career of Mary Wollstonecraft*, by Gary Kelly. *Eighteenth-Century Fiction* 6, no. 1 (October 1993): 94–95. doi:10.1353/ecf.1993.0029.

Courtney, William Prideaux. "Buller, Francis." *Dictionary of National Biography*. Edited by Leslie Stephen, 7:248–49. London: Smith, Elder & Co., 1886. https://books.google.com/books?id=OyR6nQEACAAJ.

Crafton, Lisa Plummer. *The French Revolution Debate in English Literature and Culture*. Westport, CT: Greenwood Press, 1997.

Crosby, Mark. "Montagu, Basil." In *The Encyclopedia of Romantic Literature*, edited by Frederick Burwick. Chichester, 869–71. West Sussex: Blackwell, 2012.

Culley, Amy. "'The Little Hero of Each Tale': Mary Wollstonecraft's Travelogue and Revolutionary Auto/biography." In *British Women's Life Writing, 1760–1840: Friendship, Community, and Collaboration*, 173–188. Basingstoke, Hampshire: Palgrave Macmillan, 2014.

Darcy, Jane. "Philosophical Biography (1): Godwin's *Memoirs* of Mary Wollstonecraft." In *Melancholy and Literary Biography, 1640–1816*, 105–172. Palgrave, 2013.

Denlinger, Elizabeth. "Exemplary Women: Mary Wollstonecraft, Hannah More, and Their Worlds." In *Before Victoria: Extraordinary Women of the British Romantic Era*, edited by Elizabeth Denlinger, 22–37. New York: Columbia University Press, 2005.

Detre, Jean. *A Most Extraordinary Pair: Mary Wollstonecraft and William Godwin*. Garden City, NY: Doubleday, 1975.

Dickens, Charles. *Oliver Twist*. Philadelphia: Lea & Blanchard, 1839. https://books.google.com/ books?id=8nYmAAAAMAAJ.

Donoghue, Emma. *Passions Between Women: British Lesbian Culture, 1668–1801*. New York: HarperPerennial, 1996.

Douglas [Wood], Ann. "The 'Scribbling Women' and Fanny Fern: Why Women Wrote." *American Quarterly* 23 (Spring 1971): 3–24. doi:10.2307/2711584.

Dowden, Edward. *The Life of Percy Bysshe Shelley*. London: Kegan Paul, Trench, Trübner, 1896. https://books.google.com/books?id=5lBAAAAAYAAJ.

Dubos, René, and Jean Dubos. *The White Plague: Tuberculosis, Man, and Society*. Boston: Little, Brown & Co., 1996.

Dunton, John. *Petticoat-Government. In a Letter to the Court Lords. By the Author of the Post-Angel*. London: E. Mallet, 1702. Dunton Homesite Archive. http://www.treeshaker.com/dunton/john_bookseller/1702_petticoat.htm.

Durant, W. Clark. Preface. *Memoirs of Mary Wollstonecraft*, by William Godwin. New York: Haskell House, 1927. xxv–xlvi. https://books.google.com/books?id=ZgAL73FanKwC &pg=PR3.

Eberle, Roxanne. "Legions of Wollstonecrafts." In *Chastity and Transgression in Women's Writing* 55–75. Basingstoke: Palgrave Macmillan, 2002.

Eger, E., and Lucy Peltz. *Brilliant Women: 18th-Century Bluestockings*. Culemborg, The Netherlands: Centraal Boekhuis, 2008.

Eliot, George. "Silly Novels by Silly Novelists." *Westminster Review* 66, no. 130 (October 1856): 442–61. http://ezproxy.liberty.edu/login?url=http://search.proquest.com.ezproxy.liberty.edu/docview/8117171?accountid=12085.

Ellis, Kate Ferguson. *The Contested Castle: Gothic Novels and the Subversion of Domestic Ideology*. Champaign, IL: University of Illinois Press, 1989.

Ellis, Mrs. Sarah. *The Daughters of England: Their Position in Society*. London: Fisher, 1842. https://books.google.com/books?id=bTNTAAAAcAAJ.

———. *The Mothers of England: Their Influence and Responsibility*. London: Fisher, 1843. https://books.google.com/books?id=VEThyNiwmmoC.

———. *The Wives of England: Their Relative Duties, Domestic Influence, & Social Obligations*. London: Fisher, 1843. https://books.google.com/books?id=GzQEAAAAYAAJ.

———. *Women of England: Their Social Duties, and Domestic Habits*. London: Fisher, Son & Co., 1838. https://books.google.com/books?id=jRASAAAAYAAJ.

Ellison, Julie. "Female Authorship, Public Fancy." In *Cato's Tears and the Making of Anglo-American Emotion*, 97–122. Chicago: University of Chicago Press, 1999.

Elwood, Anne. "Mrs. Mary Wollstonecroft [sic] Godwin." In *Memoirs of the Literary Ladies of England from the Commencement of the Last Century*, 2 vols., edited by Anne Elwood, 1:125–54. London: Colburn, 1843. https://books.google.com/books?id=FXtJAQAAMAAJ.

Emerson, Mary Moody. *The Selected Letters of Mary Moody Emerson*. Edited by Nancy Craig Simmons. Athens, GA: University of Georgia Press, 1993.

Emerson, Oliver F. "Notes on Gilbert Imlay, Early American Writer." *PMLA* 39 (1924): 406–39. doi:10.2307/457192.

Enfield, William. Review of *A Vindication of the Rights of Woman: With Strictures on Political and Moral Subjects*, by Mary Wollstonecraft. *Monthly Review* 8 (June 1792): 198–209. http://ezproxy.liberty.edu/login?url=http://search.proquest.com.ezproxy.liberty.edu/docview/4654510?accountid=12085.

Engell, James. *The Creative Imagination: Enlightenment to Romanticism*. Cambridge, MA: Harvard University Press, 1981.

Faderman, Lillian. "Romantic Friendship." In *Lesbian Histories and Cultures: An Encyclopedia*. Edited by Bonnie Zimmerman, 648–50. New York: Taylor & Francis, 2000.

———. "Who Hid Lesbian Theory?" *Lesbian Studies: Present and Future*, edited by Margaret Cruikshank, 115–21. Old Westbury, NY: Feminist Press, 1982.

Fairclough, Mary. *The Romantic Crowd: Sympathy, Controversy and Print Culture*. Cambridge: Cambridge University Press, 2013.

Fant, Joseph Lewis, III. "A Study of Gilbert Imlay (1754–1828): His Life and Works." Order No. 8505062, University of Pennsylvania, 1984. In PROQUESTMS ProQuest Dissertations & Theses Global, http://ezproxy.liberty.edu/login?url=http://search.proquest.com.ezproxy.liberty.edu/docview/303305422?accountid=12085.

Farber, David, and Beth Bailey. *The Columbia Guide to America in the 1960s*. New York: Columbia University Press, 2001.

Faubert, Michelle. Introduction. In *"Mary, A Fiction" and "The Wrongs of Woman, or Maria," by Mary Wollstonecraft*, 11–50. Peterborough, ON: Broadview Press, 2012.

Ferguson, Moira, and Janet Todd. *"Mary Wollstonecraft: An Assessment."* Boston: Twayne, 1984. Twayne's English Authors Series 381. Accessed November 17, 2016. http://p2048-ezproxy.liberty.edu.ezproxy.liberty.edu/login?url= http://go.galegroup.com.ezproxy.liberty.edu/ps/i.do?p=GVRL&sw=w&u=vic_liberty&v=2.1&it=r&id=GALE%7CCX1575000019 &asid=4ca7e26dbb199c8279525d3cb0ef8601.

Flexner, Eleanor. *Mary Wollstonecraft: A Biography*. Baltimore: Penguin, 1973.

Flynn, Christopher. *Americans in British Literature, 1770–1832: A Breed Apart*. Aldershot: Ashgate, 2008.

Foster, Jeannette. *Sex Variant Women in Literature*. 1956. Baltimore: Diana Press, 1976.

Fox, Margalit. "Emily Sunstein, 82, a Biographer and Scholar, Dies." *The New York Times* (April 27, 2007). http://www.nytimes.com/2007/04/27/books/27sunstein.html?ref=books.

Foyster, Elizabeth. *Marital Violence: An English Family History, 1660–1857*. Cambridge: Cambridge University Press, 2005.

France, Peter, and William St. Clair, eds. *Mapping Lives: The Uses of Biography*. New York: Oxford University Press, 2003.

Franklin, Caroline. *Mary Wollstonecraft: A Literary Life*. Basingstoke, Hampshire: Palgrave, 2004. http://site.ebrary.com.ezproxy.liberty.edu/lib/liberty/detail.action?docID= 10262940.a.

———. "Julie A. Carlson, *England's First Family of Writers: Mary Wollstonecraft, William Godwin, Mary Shelley*." *Romanticism* 14, no. 3 (December 2008): 291–92. Academic Search Alumni Edition. EBSCO*host*.

Fraser, Arvonne S. "Becoming Human: The Origins and Development of Women's Human Rights." *Human Rights Quarterly* 21, no. 4 (November 1999): 853–906. http://heinonline.org.ezproxy.liberty.edu/HOL/Page?handle=hein.journals/hurq21&div=41&start_page=853&collection=journals&set_as_cursor=0&men_tab=srchresults#.

Fredman, Alice Green. Review of *Mary Wollstonecraft: A Biography*, *The Life and Death of Mary Wollstonecraft*, and *A Different Face: The Life of Mary Wollstonecraft*, by Eleanor Flexner, Claire Tomalin and Emily W. Sunstein, respectively. *Keats-Shelley Journal* 25 (1976): 135–49. http://www.jstor.org/stable/30213178.

Frisch, Rose E. *Female Fertility and the Body Fat Connection*. Chicago: University of Chicago Press, 2002.

Furniss, Tom. "'Nasty Tricks and Tropes': Sexuality and Language in Mary Wollstonecraft's '*Rights of Woman*.'" *Studies in Romanticism* 32, no. 2 (1995): 177–209. http://ezproxy.liberty.edu/login?url=http://search.proquest.com.ezproxy.liberty.edu/docview/223457068?accountid=12085.

Gaine, Mike. *Harmless Lovers?: Gender, Theory, and Personal Relationships*. Oxon: Routledge, 1993.

Gaunt, William. *Arrows of Desire: A Study of William Blake and His Romantic World*. London: Museum Press, 1956.

Giffard, John (or Misospludes). "To the Editor." *Anti-Jacobin Review* 5, no. 19 (January 1800): 91–94. http://ezproxy.liberty.edu/login?url=http://search.proquest.com.ezproxy.liberty.edu/docview/5196649?accountid=12085.

Gilroy, Amanda. "Espousing the Cause of Oppressed Women": Cultural Captivities in Gilbert Imlay's *The Emigrants*." In *Revolutions & Watersheds: Transatlantic Dialogues 1775–1815*, 191–206. Amsterdam: Rodopi, 1999.

Godwin, William. Excerpt from "Essay of History and Romance." 1797. In *Political and Philosophical Writings of William Godwin*, 7 vols., edited by Mark Philp, 5:292–95. London: Pickering & Chatto, 1993. Repr. in *Memoirs of the Author of A Vindication of the Rights of Woman*. Edited by Pamela Clemit and Gina Luria Walker, 143–46. Peterborough, ON: Broadview Press, 2001.

———. "On Cohabitation and Marriage." Excerpt from *An Enquiry Concerning Political Justice, and Its Influence on General Virtue and Happiness*. 7 vols. 1793. In *Political and Philosophical Writings of William Godwin*, edited by Mark Philp, 3:55–56. London: Pickering & Chatto, 1993. Repr. in *Memoirs of the Author of A Vindication of the Rights of Woman*, edited by Pamela Clemit and Gina Luria Walker, 136–38. Peterborough, ON: Broadview Press, 2001.

———. *Memoirs of the Author of A Vindication of the Rights of Woman*. 1798. Edited by Pamela Clemit and Gina Luria Walker, 43–122. Peterborough, ON: Broadview Press, 2001.

———. *Memoirs of the Author of "A Vindication of the Rights of Woman*." London: Johnson, 1798. 2nd ed. https://books.google.com/books?id=7msEAAAAYAAJ.

———. *Memoirs of Mary Wollstonecraft* [*with Supplementary Material* by W. Clark Durant]. New York: Haskell, 1927. https://books.google.com/books?id=74KIbV_ucbAC.

———. "Of Cohabitation." From *The Enquirer. Reflections on Education, Manners, and Literature.* 1797. In *Series of Essays. Political and Philosophical Writings of William Godwin*, 7 vols., edited by Mark Philp, Pt. 1, 5:118–21. London: Pickering & Chatto, 1993. Repr. in *Memoirs of the Author of A Vindication of the Rights of Woman*, edited by Pamela Clemit and Gina Luria Walker, 139–43. Peterborough, ON: Broadview Press, 2001.

———. "Of History and Romance." In *Political and Philosophical Writings of William Godwin*, 7 vols, edited by Pamela Clemit, vol. 5. London: Pickering & Chatto, 1993.

———. *Things as They Are; or, The Adventures of Caleb Williams.* 1794. London: Penguin, 1988.

Goldman, Emma. 1981. "Mary Wollstonecraft: Her Tragic Life and Her Passionate Struggle for Freedom." *Feminist Studies*, 7: 114–21. http://ezproxy.liberty.edu/login?url=http://search.proquest.com.ezproxy.liberty.edu/docview/1295939331?accountid=12085.

Goodwin, Albert. Review of *The Life and Death of Mary Wollstonecraft*, by Claire Tomalin. *Literature and History* 1 (March 1975): 108–11. http://ezproxy.liberty.edu/login?url= http://search.proquest.com.ezproxy.liberty.edu/docview/1303911276?accountid=12085.

Gordon, Charlotte. *Romantic Outlaws: The Extraordinary Lives of Mary Wollstonecraft and Her Daughter Mary Shelley.* New York: Random House, 2015.

Gordon, Lyndall. *Vindication: A Life of Mary Wollstonecraft.* New York: HarperCollins, 2005.

Gosse, Edmund. Review of *Mary Wollstonecraft. Letters to Imlay. With Prefatory Memoir*, by C. Kegan Paul. *The Academy* 346 (December 21, 1878): 573–74. http://ezproxy.liberty.edu/login?url=http://search.proquest.com.ezproxy. liberty.edu/docview/8084490?accountid=12085.

Gray, Thomas. *Elegy Written in a Country Churchyard*, edited by John Martin. London: John Van Voorst, 1839. https://books.google.com/books?id=fx9kAAAAcAAJ.

Grenby, M. O., *The Child Reader, 1700–1840.* Cambridge: Cambridge University Press, 2011.

Grimshaw, Jean. "Mary Wollstonecraft and the Tensions in Feminist Philosophy." *Socialism, Feminism, and Philosophy: A Radical Philosophy Reader*, edited by Sean Sayers and Peter Osborne, 9–14. London: Routledge: 1990. *eBook Collection (EBSCOhost).*

Gubar, Susan. "Feminist Misogyny; or, The Paradox of 'It Takes One to Know One.'" In *Critical Condition: Feminism at the Turn of the Century*, edited by Susan Gubar, 135–52. New York: Columbia University Press, 2000.

Guest, Harriet. "Remembering Mary Wollstonecraft." In *Unbounded Attachment: Sentiment and Politics in the Age of the French Revolution*, 88–122. Oxford: Oxford University Press, 2013.

Gunther-Canada, Wendy. *Rebel Writer: Mary Wollstonecraft and Enlightenment Politics.* Dekalb, IL: Northern Illinois University Press, 2001.

Hampsey, John C. *Paranoia & Contentment: A Personal Essay on Western Thought.* Charlottesville, VA: University of Virginia Press, 2004.

Hanley, Kirstin. *Mary Wollstonecraft, Pedagogy, and the Practice of Feminism.* New York: Routledge, 2013.

Hans, Nicholas. *New Trends in Education in the Eighteenth Century.* London: Routledge, 2001.

Haraszti, Zoltán. *Adams and the Prophets of Progress.* Cambridge, MA: Harvard University Press, 1952.

Harrison, Mark. *Disease and the Modern World: 1500 to the Present Day.* Cambridge: Polity, 2004.

Hawthorne, Nathaniel. *Letters of Hawthorne to William D. Ticknor, 1851–1864.* Vol. 1. Newark, NJ: The Carteret Book Club, 1910. https://books.google.com/books?id=mpUIAQAAIAAJ.

Hays, Mary. *Appeal to the Men of Great Britain.* 1798. Charleston, SC: BiblioBazaar, 2010.

———. *Female Biography; Or Memoirs of Illustrious and Celebrated Women of All Ages and Countries*. Vol. 6. London: Phillips, 1803. https://books.google.com/books?id= BcQCAAAAYAAJ.

———. Preface. *Letters and Essays, Moral and Miscellaneous*. v–vi. London: Thomas Knott, 1793. https://books.google.com/books?id=gzpcAAAAcAAJ.

———. *Love-Letters of Mary Hays*. Edited by Annie F. Wedd. London: Methuen, 1925.

———. "Mary Wollstonecraft, Author of *A Vindication of the Rights of Woman*." *Annual Necrology for 1797–1798*, 1:411–60. London: Phillips, 1800. https://books.google.com/books?id =qPsLAAAAYAAJ.

———. *Memoirs of Emma Courtney*. 1796. New York: Griffith, 1802. https://books.google.com/books?id=94UgAAAAMAAJ.

———. "Memoirs of Mary Wollstonecraft." *The Annual Necrology for 1797–1798*. Vol. 1. London: Phillips, 1800. 411–60. https://books.google.com/books?id=94UgAAAAMAAJ.

———. "Deaths in and near London." *Monthly Magazine* 4, no. 22 (September 1797): 232–35. http://ezproxy.liberty.edu/login?url=http://search.proquest.com.ezproxy.liberty.edu/docview/4479814?accountid=12085.

———. Review of *The Castle on the Rock, or Memoirs of the Elderland Family, by the Author of Derwent Piory*. *The Analytical Review* 27, no. 4 (April 1798): 418–19. http://ezproxy.liberty.edu/login?url=http://search.proquest.com.ezproxy.liberty.edu/docview/5289091?accountid=12085.

———. *The Victim of Prejudice*. 1799. Edited by Eleanor Ty. 2nd ed. Peterborough, ON: Broadview, 1985.

Hobbes, Thomas. *The Elements of Law Natural and Politic*. 1640. Whitefish, MT: Kessinger Pub., 2004.

———, trans. *The Illiads and Odysses of Homer*. 11 vol. 1675. Vol. 10. London: Longman, Brown, Green, and Longmans, 1846. https://books.google.com/books?id= xr5fAAAAMAAJ.

Hodson, Jane. *Language and Revolution in Burke, Wollstonecraft, Paine, and Godwin*. Aldershot: Ashgate, 2007.

Holmes, Richard. "Biography: Inventing the Truth." In *The Art of Literary Biography*, edited by John Batchelor, 15–25. Oxford: Clarendon Press, 1995.

———. *Godwin on Wollstonecraft: The Life of Mary Wollstonecraft by William Godwin*. New York: HarperCollins, 2010.

———, ed. *Memoirs of the Author of "The Rights of Woman."* Harmondsworth: Penguin, 1987.

———. "A Philosophical Love Story." In *Sidetracks: Explorations of a Romantic Biography*, 195–266. New York: Vintage Books, 2000.

———. "The Proper Study." In *Mapping Lives: The Uses of Biography*, edited by Peter France and William St. Clair, 7–18. Oxford: Oxford University Press, 2002.

Honan, Park. "Theory of Biography." *Novel* 13, no. 1 (Autumn 1979): 109–20. doi:10.2307/1344955.

Hopkins, Gerard Manley. "Binsey Poplars." 1879. In *Poems of Gerard Manley Hopkins Now First Published*, edited by Robert Seymour Bridges, 40. Oxford: Humphrey Milford, 1918.

Hostettler, John. *Dissenters, Radicals, Heretics and Blasphemers: The Flame of Revolt That Shines Through English Literature*. Sherfield, Hampshire: Waterside Press, 2012.

Houlbrooke, Ralph Anthony. *Death, Religion, and the Family in England, 1480–1750*. Oxford: Oxford University Press, 1998.

Hughes, Kathryn. *George Eliot: The Last Victorian*. New York: Cooper Square Press, 2001.

Hunt, Margaret. "Wife-Beating, Domesticity, and Women's Independence in Eighteenth-Century London." *Gender and History* 4, no. 1 (1992): 10–33.
Inchbald, Elizabeth. *Next Door Neighbours: A Comedy; in Three Acts*. Dublin: P. Byrne, et al., 1791. https://books.google.com/books?id=OnACAAAAYAAJ.
Isichei, E. *Victorian Quakers*. London: Oxford University Press, 1970.
Jacob, Giles. "Treason." *A New Law-dictionary: Containing, the Interpretation and Definition of Words*, London: E. and R. Nutt, et al. 1729. https://books.google.com/books?id=2sZLAAAAcAAJ.
Jacobs, Diane. *Her Own Woman: The Life of Mary Wollstonecraft*. New York: Simon & Schuster, 2001.
James, Henry. *William Wetmore Story and His Friends: From Letters, Diaries, and Recollections*. Vol. 1. 2 vols. Boston: Houghton, Mifflin & Co., 1903. https://books.google.com/books?id=Q6Q5AAAAMAAJ.
James, Henry Rosher. *Mary Wollstonecraft: A Sketch*. New York: Ardent Media, 1932.
Jebb, Camilla. *Mary Wollstonecraft*. Chicago: F. G. Browne, 1913.
Jenkins, Annibel. *I'll Tell You What: The Life of Elizabeth Inchbald*. Lexington, KY: University Press of Kentucky, 2003.
Jennings, Judi. *Gender, Religion, and Radicalism in the Long Eighteenth Century: The "Ingenious Quaker" and Her Connections*. Aldershot: Ashgate, 2006.
Johnson, Claudia. *Equivocal Beings: Politics, Gender, and Sentimentality in the 1790s, Wollstonecraft, Radcliffe, Burney, Austen*. Chicago: University of Chicago Press, 1995.
———. "Mary Wollstonecraft's Novels." In *Cambridge Companion to Mary Wollstonecraft*, edited by Claudia L. Johnson, 189–208. Cambridge: Cambridge University Press, 2002. doi:10.1017/CCOL0521783437.011.
Johnson, Samuel. No. 84. *The Idler* (November 24, 1759): 90–91. In *Works of Samuel Johnson*, edited by Arthur Murphy, 339–42. https://books.google.com/books?id=mcFEAAAAYAAJ.
Jones, Vivien. "The Death of Mary Wollstonecraft." *Journal for Eighteenth-Century Studies* 20, no. 2 (September 1997): 187–205. doi:10.1111/j.1754-0208.1997.tb00213.x.
Jump, Harriet. "'A Fond Partiality'; Mary Wollstonecraft's Anonymous Defender." *The Charles Lamb Bulletin* 109 (January 2000): 5–10.
———. Introduction. *Mary Wollstonecraft*. In *Lives of the Great Romantics III: Godwin, Wollstonecraft and Mary Shelley by Their Contemporaries*, 5:107–16. London: Pickering & Chatto, 1999. http://asp6new.alexanderstreet.com. ezproxy.liberty.edu/romr/romr. object.details.aspx?id=1004178907&tocurl=MCB9.
Kanner, Barbara Penny. Review of *Revolutionary Feminism: The Mind and Career of Mary Wollstonecraft*, by Gary Kelly. *American Historical Review* 99, no. 1 (February 1994): 229–30. *MasterFILE Premier, EBSCOhost*.
Kaplan, Cora. "Mary Wollstonecraft's Reception and Legacies." In *Cambridge Companion to Mary Wollstonecraft*, edited by Claudia L. Johnson, 246–70. doi:10.1017/CCOL0521783437.014
———. "Wild Nights: Pleasure/Sexuality/Feminism." *Signs; Journal of Women in Culture and Society* 5, no. 4: 631–60.
Kelly, Gary. *Revolutionary Feminism: The Mind and Career of Mary Wollstonecraft*. Basingstoke: Macmillan, 1992.
———. *Women, Writing, and Revolution 1790–1827*. Oxford: Oxford University Press, 1993.
Kendall, Mrs. A. *The Castle on the Rock, Or, Memoirs of the Elderland Family*. London: John Rice, 1799.

———. *Derwent Priory: or, Memoirs of an Orphan; in a Series of Letters*. London: Symonds, 1798. https://books.google.com/books?isbn=1170006760.

———. *Tales of the Abbey: Founded on Historical Facts*. 1800. London: Wogan and Colbert, 1801. *Hathi Trust Digital Library*. http://hdl.handle.net/2027/njp.32101068971405.

Kittredge, Katharine. *Lewd & Notorious: Female Transgression in the Eighteenth Century*. Ann Arbor: University of Michigan Press, 2003.

Knowles, John, ed. *The Life and Writings of Henry Fuseli*. Vol. 1. 3 vols. London: Colburn and Bentley, 1831. https://books.google.com/books?id=Av41AAAAMAAJ.

Koppelman, Susan, ed. and introd. *The Other Woman: Stories of Two Women and a Man*. New York: Feminist Press, 1984.

Koutsantoni, Katerina. *Virginia Woolf's* Common Reader. Farnham: Ashgate, 2009.

Kuhlman, Erika. "Women's Rights Activists: A. Wollstonecraft, Mary (Mary Wollstonecraft Godwin)." *A to Z of Women in World History*. New York: Facts on File, 2002. 382–83.

"The Ladies of Llangollen." *The Leisure Hour, January 1877–October 1903*, no. 1350 (November 10, 1877): 710–12. http://ezproxy.liberty.edu/login?url=http://search.proquest.com.ezproxy.liberty.edu/ docview/3421462?accountid=12085.

Laird, Holly, ed. *The History of British Women's Writing, 1880–1920*. Vol. 7. London: Palgrave Macmillan, 2016.

Laird, Susan. *Mary Wollstonecraft: Philosophical Mother of Coeducation*. New York: Continuum International Pub, 2009.

Landberg, Ferdinand, and Marynia F. Farnham. *Modern Woman: The Lost Sex*. New York: Crosset & Dunlap, 1947.

Lässig, Simone. Introduction: "Biography in Modern History—Modern Historiography in Biography." *Biography Between Structure and Agency: Central European Lives in International Historiography*, edited by Volker Berghahn and Simone Lässig, 1–26. New York: Berghahn Books, 2008.

Leighton, Angela. *Victorian Women Poets: Writing Against the Heart*. Charlottesville, VA: University Press of Virginia, 1992.

Linford, Madeline. *Mary Wollstonecraft*. New York: Haskell House, 1932.

Litchfield, Henrietta Emma, ed. *Emma Darwin, Wife of Charles Darwin: A Century of Family Letters*. 2 vols. Vol. 1. Cambridge: Cambridge University Press. 1904 https://books.google.com/ books?id=Eg4_AAAAYAAJ.

Litchfield, Richard Buckley. *Tom Wedgwood, the First Photographer: An Account of His Life, His Discovery and His Friendship with Samuel Taylor Coleridge*. London: Duckworth, 1903. https://books.google.com/books?id=SSsLAAAAYAAJ.

Lloyd, Charles. "Lines to Mary Wollstonecraft Godwin." 1798. Repr. in *The Broadview Anthology of Literature of the Revolutionary Period 1770–1832*. Edited by David L. Macdonald and Anne McWhir. Peterborough, ON: Broadview Press, 2010. 858–60.

Looser, Devoney. "Mary Wollstonecraft, 'Ithuriel,' and the Rise of the Feminist Author-Ghost." *Tulsa Studies in Women's Literature* 35, no.1 (Spring 2016): 59–91. doi:10.1353/tsw.2016.0002.

Lorch, Jennifer. *Mary Wollstonecraft: The Making of a Radical Feminist*. New York: Berg, 1990.

Lucas, E.V. Introduction. *Mary Wollstonecraft's "Original Stories."* London: Frowde, 1906. https://books.google.com/books?isbn=1465543546.

Lynn, Loretta. *Loretta Lynn: Coal Miner's Daughter*. Chicago: Henry Regnery, 1976.

Macdonald, David L., and Anne McWhir, eds. "Mary Wollstonecraft, 1759–1797." *The Broadview Anthology of Literature of the Revolutionary Period 1770–1832*. Peterborough, ON: Broadview Press, 2010. 374.

Malkin, Benjamin Heath. "On the Female Character." In *Essays on Subjects Connected with Civilization*. London: Dilly, 1795. 257–285. https://books.google.com/books?id=A6BYAAAAcAAJ.

Malmgreen, Gail. Introduction. *Religion in the Lives of English Women, 1760–1930*, edited by Gail Malmgreen, 1–10. Bloomington, IN: University of Indiana Press, 1986.

Mandell, Laura. "Bad Marriages, Bad Novels: The 'Philosophical Romance.'" In *Recognizing the Romantic Novel: New Histories of British Fiction, 1780–1830*, edited by Jillian Heydt-Stevenson and Charlotte Sussman, 49–77. Liverpool: Liverpool University Press, 2008.

Marshall, Peter H. *William Godwin*. New Haven, CT: Yale University Press, 1984.

Matthew, Patricia. "Biography and Mary Wollstonecraft in *Adeline Mowbray* and *Valperga*." *Women's Writing* 14, no. 3 (December 2007): 382–98. *Humanities International Complete*, EBSCO*host*.

Maunu, Leanne. "Mary Wollstonecraft's Nation-Building Project." In *Women Writing the Nation: National Identity, Female Community, and the British-French Connection, 1770–1820*, 145–87. Cranbury, NJ: Rosemont, 2007.

Mavor, Elizabeth. *The Ladies of Llangollen: A Study in Romantic Friendship*. London: Michael Joseph, 1971.

Mazel, Ella. *Ahead of Her Time: A Sampler of the Life and Thought of Mary Wollstonecraft*. Lexington, MA: Bernel Books, 1995.

McClelland, J. S. *A History of Western Political Thought*. London: Routledge, 1996.

McInnes, Andrew. "Imagining Mary: Representations of Wollstonecraft in the Works of Mary Hays and William Godwin." In *Wollstonecraft's Ghost: The Fate of the Female Philosopher in the Romantic*, 22–59. London: Routledge, 2017.

McLaren, Dorothy. "Martial Fertility and Lactation 1570–1720." In *Women in English Society, 1500–1800*, 1–24. London: Methuen, 1985.

Mead, Rebecca. "All About the Hamiltons: A New Musical Brings the Founding Fathers Back to Life—with a lot of Hip-Hop." *New Yorker* February 9, 2015. http://www.newyorker.com/ magazine/2015/02/09/hamiltons

Mellor, Anne K. "Mary Wollstonecraft's *A Vindication of the Rights of Woman* and the Women Writers of Her Day." In *The Cambridge Companion to Mary Wollstonecraft*, edited by Claudia L. Johnson, 141–59. Cambridge University Press, 2002. doi:10.1017/CCOL0521783437.009.

Mennell, Stephen. *All Manners of Food: Eating and Taste in England and France from the Middle Ages to the Present*. 2nd Ed. Urbana, IL: University of Illinois Press, 1996.

Meteyard, Eliza. *A Group of Englishmen (1795 to 1815) Being Records of the Younger Wedgwoods and Their Friends*. London: Longmans, Green, 1871. https://books.google.com/books?id=IRsMAAAAYAAJ.

Midgley, Clare. *Women Against Slavery*. New York: Routledge, 1992.

Moers, Ellen. "Vindicating Mary Wollstonecraft." *The New York Review of Books* (19 February 1976). http://www.nybooks.com/articles/1976/02/19/vindicating-mary-wollstonecraft/.

Monsam, Angela. "Biography as Autopsy in William Godwin's *Memoirs of the Author of 'A Vindication of the Rights of Woman*.'" *Eighteenth-Century Fiction* 21, no. 1 (Fall 2008): 109–30. doi:10.1353/edv.0.0029.

Monstavicius, Leslie Anne Walton. "The New Heloise: Reforming Heterosexuality in the Novel, 1760–1900." Diss. University of California, Berkeley, 2008. http://ezproxy.liberty.edu/ login?url=http://search.proquest.com.ezproxy.liberty.edu/docview/304696185?accountid=12085

Moore, Jane. *Mary Wollstonecraft*. Aldershot: Ashgate, 2012.

Mulvey, Laura. "Visual Pleasure and Narrative Cinema." *Screen* 16, no. 3 (Autumn 1975): 6–18.

Munroe, Jennifer. *Gender and the Garden in Early Modern English Literature: Women and Gender in the Early Modern World*. Aldershot: Ashgate, 2008.

Myers, Mitzi. "Godwin's *Memoirs* of Wollstonecraft: The Shaping of Self and Subject." *Studies in Romanticism* 20, no. 3 (Fall 1981): 299–316. doi:10.2307/25600307.

———. "Impeccable Governesses, Rational Dames, and Moral Mothers: Mary Wollstonecraft and the Female Tradition in Georgian Children's Books." *Children's Literature* 14 (1986): 31–59. *Project MUSE*, doi:10.1353/chl.0.0638.

———. "Mary Wollstonecraft's Literary Reviews." In *The Cambridge Companion to Mary Wollstonecraft*, edited by Claudia L. Johnson, 82–98. Cambridge: Cambridge University Press, 2002. doi:10.1017/CCOL0521783437.006.

Myers, Sylvia Marcstark. *The Bluestocking Circle: Women, Friendship, and the Life of the Mind in Eighteenth-Century England*. Oxford: Clarendon Press, 1990.

Narayan, Gaura Shankar. *Real and Imagined Women in British Romanticism*. New York: Peter Lang, 2010.

Nehring, Cristina. *A Vindication of Love: Reclaiming Romance for the Twenty-First Century*. New York: HarperCollins, 2009.

Neiman, Fraser. Review of *Mary Wollstonecraft: A Critical Biography*, by Ralph M. Wardle. *The William and Mary Quarterly*. 9, no. 3 (July 1952): 434–35. doi:10.2307/1916994.

Nicholes, Eleanor Louise. "Mary Wollstonecraft, 1759–1797." In *Shelley and His Circle, 1773–1822*, 4 vols., edited by Kenneth Neill Cameron, 1:39–66. Carl H. Pforzheimer Library. New York: Carl and Lily Pforzheimer Foundation, 1961.

Nitchie, Elizabeth. "An Early Suitor of Mary Wollstonecraft." *PMLA* 58, no. 1 (March 1943): 163–69. doi:10.2307/459038.

Nixon, Edna. *Mary Wollstonecraft: Her Life and Times*. New York: Dent, 1971.

Novarr, David. *The Lines of Life: Theories of Biography, 1880–1970*. West Lafayette, IN: Purdue University Press, 1986.

Oates, Stephen B. "The Johnson Biographies." *The Texas Observer* (3 June 1983): 18–23. doi:10.2307/42862124.

Offen, Karen. "Defining Feminism: A Comparative Historical Approach." *Signs*, vol. 14, no. 1, 1988, pp. 119–57. www.jstor.org/stable/3174664.

O'Neill, Daniel L. *The Burke-Wollstonecraft Debate: Savagery, Civilization, and Democracy*. University Park, PA: Pennsylvania State University, 2007.

Onslow Barbara. *Women of the Press in Nineteenth-Century Britain*. London: Macmillan, 2000.

Pattee, Fred Lewis. *The Feminine Fifties*. New York: D. Appleton-Century, 1940.

Paul, C. Kegan. *Mary Wollstonecraft: Letters to Imlay, with Prefatory Memoir by C. Kegan Paul*. London: C. Kegan Paul, 1879. https://books.google.com/books?id=EDNDnQEACAAJ.

———. *William Godwin: His Friends and Contemporaries*. Boston: Robert Bros., https://books.google.com/books?id=srA9DQEACAAJ.

Pearson, Jacqueline. Review of *England's First Family of Writers: Mary Wollstonecraft, William Godwin, Mary Shelley*, by Julie A. Carlson. *Modern Language Review* 104, no. 2 (April 2009): 556–57. http://www.jstor.org/stable/25654885.

Pennell, Elizabeth Robins. "A Century of Women's Rights." *Fortnightly Review* 48, no. 285 (September 1890): 408–17. http://ezproxy.liberty.edu/ login?url=http://search.proquest. com.ezproxy.liberty.edu/docview/2434548?accountid=12085.

———. *Life of Mary Wollstonecraft.* Boston: Roberts Brothers, 1884. https://books.google.com/books?id=j4RnAAAAMAAJ.

———. Prefatory Note. *A Vindication of the Rights of Woman.* By Mary Wollstonecraft. London: Walter Scott, 1884. vii–xxiv. https://books.google.com/books?id=3GgWoIUt91UC.

———. *Mary Wollstonecraft.* 1884. Boston: Roberts Brothers, 1890. http://www.gutenberg.org/files/22800/22800-h/22800-h.htm.

———. "Pennell Family Papers." Penn Libraries at the University of Pennsylvania. http://dla.library.upenn.edu/dla/ead/detail.html?id=EAD_upenn_rbml_MsColl50.

Polwhele, Richard. *The Unsexed Females.* 1798. http://xtf.lib.virginia.edu/xtf/view?docId=legacy/uvaBook/tei/PolUnse.xml.

Poovey, Mary. *The Proper Lady and the Woman Writer: Ideology as Style in the Works of Mary Wollstonecraft, Mary Shelley, and Jane Austen.* Chicago: University of Chicago Press, 1984.

Preedy, George. *The Shining Woman: Mary Wollstonecraft Godwin, 1759–1797.* New York: Appleton, 1937.

Prichard, John. *A Short Memoir of the Ladies of Llangollen.* Llangollen: Hugh Jones, 1887.

———, and Eleanor C. Butler. *An Account of the Ladies of Llangollen.* Llangollen: H. Jones, 1880. https://books.google.com/books?id=9XoHAAAAQAAJ.

Rajan, Tilottama. "Framing the Corpus: Godwin's 'Editing' of Wollstonecraft in 1798." *Studies in Romanticism* 39, no. 4 (Winter 2000): 511–31. http://ezproxy.liberty.edu/login?url=http://search.proquest.com.ezproxy.liberty.edu/docview/223462863?accountid=12085.

———. *Romantic Narrative: Shelley, Hays, Godwin, Wollstonecraft.* Baltimore, MD: Johns Hopkins University Press, 2010.

Rauschenbusch-Clough, Emma. *A Study of Mary Wollstonecraft and the "Rights of Woman.* New York": Longmans, 1898. https://books.google.com/books?id=TXtDAAAAIAAJ.

"The Recluse Ladies of Llangollen." *Chambers's Edinburgh Journal* 389 (July 13, 1839): 194–95. http://ezproxy.liberty.edu/login?url= http://search.proquest.com.ezproxy.liberty.edu/docview/2557968?accountid=12085.

"Remarks by the First Lady at 'Hamilton at The White House' Student Workshop." The White House: Office of the First Lady Press Release. March 14, 2016. https://www.whitehouse.gov/the-press-office/2016/03/14/remarks-first-lady-hamilton-white-house-student-workshop.

Rendall, Jane. *The Origins of Modern Feminism: Women in Britain, France, and the United States, 1780–1860.* Hampshire: Macmillan, 1985.

Riverol, Armando. *Live from Atlantic City: The History of the Miss America Pageant.* Bowling Green, KY: Bowling Green State University Popular Press, 1992.

Richardson, Samuel. *The History of Sir Charles Grandisoni*, vol. 1. 7th ed. London: John Donaldson, 1776. https://books.google.com/books?id=4nJdAAAAcAAJ.

Robberds, J. W., ed. *A Memoir of the Life and Writings of the Late William Taylor […] Containing His Correspondence of Many Years with the Late Robert Southey*." Vol. 1 of 2 vols. London: John Murray, 1843. https://books.google.com/books?id=iDkLAAAAYAAJ.

Roberts, William. *Memoirs of the Life and Correspondence of Mrs. Hannah More.* Vol. 1. New York: Harper, 1836. 2 vols. *Hathi Trust.* http://hdl.handle.net/2027/uc1.b3141114.

Robinson, Henry Crabb. *Books and Their Writers.* Edited by Edith Morley. London: J. M. Dent & Sons, 1938.

Robinson, Jeffrey C. *Unfettering Poetry: Fancy in British Romanticism.* New York: Palgrave Macmillan, 2006.

Robinson, Victor. *William Godwin and Mary Wollstonecraft*. New York: The Altrurians, 1907. *Hathi Trust*. http://hdl.handle.net/2027/mdp.39015080473625.

Rookmaaker, H. R., Jr. *Towards a Romantic Conception of Nature: Coleridge's Poetry up to 1803: A Study in the History of Ideas*. Philadelphia: John Benjamins Publishing Co., 1984.

Roper, Derek. "Mary Wollstonecraft's Reviews." *Notes and Queries* 5 (January 1958): 37–38.

Roscoe, Theodora. "Modern Ladies of Llangollen." *Westminster Review* 174, no. 3 (September 1910): 328–30. http://ezproxy.liberty.edu/login?url= http://search.proquest.com.ezproxy.liberty.edu/docview/8129190?accountid=12085.

Rousseau, John Jacques. *Emile, Or on Education*. Sioux Falls, SD: Nu Vision Publications, 2007. September 21, 2013.

Rusk, Ralph L. "The Adventures of Gilbert Imlay." *Indiana University Studies* 10, no. 57 (1923): 3–26.

Ruskin, John. *Sesame and Lilies: Two Lectures Delivered at Manchester in 1864*. 2nd ed. London: Smith, Elder & Co., 1865. https://books.google.com/books?id= YJBRAAAAYAAJ.

Sapiro, Virginia. *A Vindication of Political Virtue: The Political Theory of Mary Wollstonecraft*. Chicago: University of Chicago Press, 1992.

Sawyer, Dr. Roger, and Roger Sawyer. *We Are But Women: Women in Ireland's History*. New York: Routledge, 1993.

Schmid, Susanne. *British Literary Salons of the Late Eighteenth and Early Nineteenth Centuries*. New York: Palgrave Macmillan, 2013.

Schornstein, Sherri L. *Domestic Violence and Health Care: What Every Professional Needs to Know*. Thousand Oaks, CA: Sage Publications, 1997.

Schlaeger, Jürgen. "Biography: Cult as Culture." In *The Art of Literary Biography*, edited by John Batchelor, 57–71. Oxford: Clarendon Press, 1995.

Scott, Walter. *Journal of Sir Walter Scott*. Ed. W. K. Anderson. Oxford: Clarendon Press, 1972.

Seward, Anna. "The Ladies of Llangollen." In *A Swan and Her Friends*, edited by Edward Verrall Lucas, 260–94. London: Methuen, 1907. https://books.google.com/books?id= 119bAAAAMAAJ.

———. *Llangollen Vale. Llangollen Vale, with Other Poems*. London: G. Sael, 1796. 1–11. https://books.google.com/books?id=LL5EcubW70MC.

Shindler, Robert. "The Ladies of Llangollen." *The Red Dragon* 2 (August–December 1882): 129–35. https://books.google.com/books?id=XWIEAAAAQAAJ.

Shoemaker, Robert B. *Gender in English Society 1650–1850: The Emergence of Separate Spheres?* Oxon: Routledge, 2013.

Shorter, Edward. *A Social History of Women's Encounter with Health, Ill-Health, and Medicine*. 1982. New Brunswick, NJ: Transaction, 1991.

Showalter, Elaine. "Amazonian Beginnings: Mary Wollstonecraft." In *Inventing Herself: Claiming a Feminist Intellectual Heritage*, 21–40. New York: Scribner, 2001.

Sigerman, Harriet, ed. *The Columbia Documentary History of American Women Since 1941*. New York: Columbia University Press, 2003.

Sigillito, Gina. "Mary Wollstonecraft." In *The Daughters of Maeve: 50 Irish Women Who Changed World*, 14–18. New York: Kensington, 2007.

Silliman, Benjamin. *Letters of Shahcoolen, a Hindu Philosopher Residing in Philadelphia; to His Friend El Hassan, an Inhabitant of Delhi*. Boston: Russell and Cutler, 1802. http://docs.newsbank.com.ezproxy.liberty.edu/openurl?ctx_ver=z39.88-2004&rft_id=info:sid/iw.newsbank.com:EAIX&rft_val_format=info:ofi/fmt:kev:mtx:ctx&rft_dat= 104404B7E897EC08&svc_dat=Evans:eaidoc&req_dat=8A8B718A23D24E09993EC67C59F3D21D.

Sloan, Margaret Kathryn. "Mothers, Marys, and Reforming 'The Rising Generation': Mary Wollstonecraft and Mary Hays." In *Mentoring in Eighteenth-century British Literature and Culture*, edited by Anthony W. Lee, 225–44. Farnham, Surrey: Ashgate, 2010.

Smith, Goldwin. "The Prospect of a Moral Interregnum." *The Atlantic Monthly* 44 (November 1879): 629–42. https://books.google.com/books?id=lR_ZM4LzxpYC.

Smith, Joan. *Moralities: How to End the Abuse of Money and Power in the 21st Century.* New York: Allen Lane/Penguin Books, 2002.

Smollett, Tobias George. Review of *A Vindication of the Rights of Woman: With Strictures on Political and Moral Subjects*, by Mary Wollstonecraft. *The Critical Review* 4 (April 1792): 389–98. http://ezproxy.liberty.edu/login?url=http://search.proquest.com.ezproxy.liberty.edu/docview/4351648?accountid=12085.

———. *The Critical Review* 5 (June 1792): 132–41. http://ezproxy.liberty.edu/login?url=http://search.proquest.com.ezproxy.liberty.edu/docview/4353763?accountid=12085.

Southey, Robert. *The Life and Correspondence of Robert Southey.* 6 vols. Edited by C. C. Southey, vol. 1. London: Longman, Brown, Green, & Longmans, 1849. https://books.google.com/books?id=8aEvAAAAIAAJ.

Spector, Jessica. *Prostitution and Pornography: Philosophical Debate About the Sex Industry.* Redwood City, CA: Stanford University Press, 2006.

St. Clair, William. "The Biographer as Archaeologist." In *Mapping Lives: The Uses of Biography*, edited by Peter France and William St. Clair, 219–52. Oxford: Oxford University Press, 2002.

Sterling, John. "The State of Society in England." In *Essays and Tales: Fragments from the Travels of Theodore Elbert*, edited by Julius Charles Hare, 2:25–33. London: Harrison, 1848. https://books.google.com/books?id=BMM_H_WuyAAC.

Stewart, Dugald. *Elements of the Philosophy of the Human Mind.* 1792. 7 vols. In *The Works of Dugald* Stewart, vol. 1. Cambridge: Hilliard and Brown, 1829. https://books.google.com/books?id=VxtSAAAAMAAJ.

Stewart, W. A. C. *Quakers and Education: As Seen in Their Schools in England.* London: Epworth Press, 1953.

Stocking, Marion Kingston, ed. *The Clairmont Correspondence: Letters of Claire Clairmont, Charles Clairmont, and Fanny Imlay Godwin, and Marion Kingston Stocking.* 5 vols. Baltimore: Johns Hopkins University Press, 1994.

Stone, Lawrence. *The Family, Sex and Marriage: in England 1500–1800.* London: Weidenfeld and Nicolson, 1977. http://quod.lib.umich.edu.ezproxy.liberty.edu/cgi/t/text/text-idx?c=acls;idno=heb01414.

Sunstein, Emily. *A Different Face: The Life of Mary Wollstonecraft.* Boston: Little, Brown & Co., 1975.

Sutherland, Kathryn. "Writings on Education and Conduct: Arguments for Female Improvement." In *Women and Literature in Britain, 1700–1800*, edited by Vivien Jones, 25–45. Cambridge: Cambridge University Press, 2000.

Swift, Simon. "Mary Wollstonecraft's Religious Characters." In *Called to Civil Existence. Mary Wollstonecraft's "A Vindication of the Rights of Woman,"* edited by Enit Karafili Steiner, 131–54. Amsterdam: Rodopi, 2014.

Tarlow, Sarah. *Ritual, Belief and the Dead in Early Modern Britain and Ireland.* Cambridge: Cambridge University Press, 2011.

Taylor, Barbara. *Eve and the New Jerusalem: Socialism and Feminism in the Nineteenth Century.* London: Virago Press, 1983.

Taylor, George Robert Stirling. *Mary Wollstonecraft: A Study in Economics and Romance.* New York: John Lane, 1911. https://books.google.com/books?id=-jlNq_4098gC.
Taylor, Thomas. *A Vindication of the Rights of Brutes.* London: Pall Mall, 1792. *Philaletheians.* December 5, 2014.
Thompson, Edward Palmer. "Mary Wollstonecraft." *The Essential E. P. Thompson.* New York: The New Press, 2001. 185–91.
Tims, Margaret. *Mary Wollstonecraft: A Social Pioneer.* London: Millington, 1976.
Todd, Janet M., "The Biographies of Mary Wollstonecraft." *Signs* 1, no. 3 (Spring 1976): 721–34. http://www.jstor.org/stable/3173151.
———. *Daughters of Ireland: The Rebellious Kingsborough Sisters and the Making of a Modern Nation.* New York: Ballantine, 2003.
———. *Death and the Maidens: Fanny Wollstonecraft and the Shelley Circle.* London: Profile Books, 2007.
———. "Frankenstein's Daughter: Mary Shelley and Mary Wollstonecraft," *Women and Literature* 4, no. 2 (1976): 18–27. *Humanities International Complete,* EBSCO*host.*
———. "The Language of Sex in *A Vindication of the Rights of Woman.*" *Mary Wollstonecraft Newsletter* 1 (1973): 10–17. EBSCO*host.*
———. *Mary Wollstonecraft: An Annotated Bibliography.* Babingdon, Oxon: Routledge, 1976, 2012.
———. "The Polwhelan Tradition and Richard Cobb." *Studies in Burke and His Time* 16 (Spring 1975): 271–78.
———. *A Revolutionary Life.* London: Weidenfeld and Nicholson, 2000.
———, ed. *The Collected Letters of Mary Wollstonecraft.* New York: Columbia University Press, 2003.
Tomalin, Claire. *The Life and Death of Mary Wollstonecraft.* New York: Harcourt, 1975.
Tomes, Nancy. "'A Torrent of Abuse.' Crimes of Violence Between Working-Class Men and Women in London, 1840–1875." *Journal of Social History* 11 (Spring 1978): 328–45. http://www.jstor.org/stable/3786818.
Tompkins, Jane. *Sensational Designs: The Cultural Work of American Fiction, 1790–1860.* Oxford: Oxford University Press, 1985.
Townsend, Aubrey. "Biographical Notice." In *The Writings of John Bradford,* xi–xiii. Cambridge: Cambridge University Press, 1853. https://books.google.com/books?id=iWsJAAAAQAAJ.
Tuchman, Barbara W. "Biography as a Prism of History." In *Biography as High Adventure: Life-Writers Peak on Their Art,* edited by Stephen Oates, 93–103. Amherst, MA: University of Massachusetts Press, 1986.
Tuttle, Lisa. *Encyclopedia of Feminism.* New York: Facts on File, 1986.
Tyson, Gerald P. "Joseph Johnson, an Eighteenth-Century Bookseller." *Studies in Bibliography* 28 (1975): 1–16. http://www.jstor.org/stable/40371608.
Unsigned review of *Memoirs of the Author of the* "Vindication of the Rights of Woman." By William Godwin. *British Critic* 12 (September 1798): 228–33. http://ezproxy.liberty.edu/login?url=http://search.proquest.com.ezproxy.liberty.edu/docview/4811332?accountid=12085.
Unsigned review of "Paul's Mary Wollstonecraft." *The London Quarterly Review* 53, no. 105 (October 1879) 257–58. http://ezproxy.liberty.edu/login?url= http://search. proquest. com.ezproxy.liberty.edu/docview/2518937?accountid=12085.
Unsigned review of *Childe Harold's Pilgrimage, Canto III,—Prisoners of Chillon, and Other Poems,* by Lord Byron. *American Monthly Magazine and Critical Review* 1, no. 1 (May 1817): 3–12. https://books.google.com/books?id=8VpFAAAAYAAJ.

Unsigned review of *The Emigrants, or the History of an Expatriated Family, being a Delineation of English Manners, Drawn from Real Characters* 11 (August 1793): 468–69. http://ezproxy.liberty.edu/login?url=http://search.proquest.com.ezproxy.liberty.edu/docview/4652995?accountid=12085.

———. *The Critical Review* 9 (October 1793): 155–58. http://ezproxy.liberty.edu/login?url=http://search.proquest.com.ezproxy.liberty.edu/docview/4357479?accountid=12085.

Unsigned review of *Mary Wollstonecraft: Letters to Imlay. With Prefatory Memoir*. By C. Kegan Paul. *British Quarterly Review* 138 (April 1879): 494–95. http://ezproxy.liberty.edu/login?url=http://search.proquest.com.ezproxy.liberty.edu/docview/6580160?accountid=12085.

———. *Examiner* 3705 (1 February 1879): 147–48. http://ezproxy.liberty.edu/login?url=http://search.proquest.com.ezproxy.liberty.edu/docview/9062143?accountid=12085.

Verhoeven, W. M. *Gilbert Imlay: Citizen of the World*. London: Pickering & Chatto, 2009.

———, and Amanda Gilroy, eds. Introduction. *The Emigrants* by Gilbert Imlay. 1793, ix–xlix. New York: Penguin, 1998.

Walker, Gina Luria. *The Idea of being Free: A Mary Hays Reader*. Peterborough, ON: Broadview, 2006.

———. "The Two Marys: Hays Writes Wollstonecraft." *Called to Civil Existence: Mary Wollstonecraft's "A Vindication of the Rights of Woman,"* edited by Enit Karafili Steiner, 49–70. Amsterdam: Rodopi, 2014.

Wallis, Jerry L., ed. *The Oxford Handbook of Eschatology*. Oxford: Oxford University Press, 2008.

Wallraven, Miriam. *A Writing Halfway Between Theory and Fiction: Mediating Feminism from the Seventeenth to the Twentieth Century*. Würzburg, Germany: Verlag Königshausen & Neumann GmbH, 2007.

Ward, Gerald W. R. "Camera obscura." *The Grove Encyclopedia of Materials and Techniques in Art*, 75–78. Ithaca, NY: Oxford University Press, 2008.

Wardle, Ralph M., ed. *Collected Letters of Mary Wollstonecraft*. Ithaca, NY: Cornell University Press, 1979.

———, ed. *Godwin & Mary: Letters of William Godwin and Mary Wollstonecraft*. Lawrence, KS: University of Kansas Press, 1966.

———. "Mary Wollstonecraft, Analytical Reviewer." *PMLA* 62, no. 4 (December 1947): 1000–1009. doi:10.2307/459145.

———. *Mary Wollstonecraft: A Critical Biography*. 1951. Lincoln, NE: University of Nebraska Press, 1967.

———. Review of *The Life and Death of Mary Wollstonecraft*, by Claire Tomalin. *The Wordsworth Circle* 6, no. 3 (Summer 1975): 147–51. http://ezproxy.liberty.edu/login? url=http://search.proquest.com.ezproxy.liberty.edu/docview/1300165154?accountid=12085

Waters, Mary A. "'The First of a New Genus.' Mary Wollstonecraft as a Literary Critic and Mentor to Mary Hays." *Eighteenth-Century Studies* 37, no. 3 (2004): 415–34. doi:10.1353/ecs.2004.0037.

Weisberg, Kelley D., ed. *Applications of Feminist Legal Theory to Women's Lives: Sex, Violence, Work, and Production*. Philadelphia: Temple University Press, 1996.

Wellington, January "Blurring the Borders of Nation and Gender: Mary Wollstonecraft's Character (R)evolution." In *Rebellious Hearts: British Women Writers and the French Revolution*, edited by Adriana Craciun and Karl E. Lokke, 33–61. Albany: State University of New York Press, 2001.

Welter, Barbara. "The Cult of True Womanhood: 1820–1860." *American Quarterly* 18, no. 2, Pt.1 (Summer 1996): 151–74. doi:10.2307/2711179.

White, Norman. "Pieties and Literary Biography." In *The Art of Literary Biography*, edited by John Batchelor, 213–25. Oxford: Clarendon Press, 1995.

———. *Hopkins: A Literary Biography*. 1992. Oxford: Clarendon Press, 1995.

Wiener, Martin J. *Men of Blood: Violence, Manliness, and Criminal Justice in Victorian England*. Cambridge: Cambridge University Press, 2004.

Wildridge, Thomas Tindall. *The Misereres of Beverley Minster: A Complete Series of the Seat-Carvings in the Choir of the Church of St John Beverley*. Hull: J. Plaxton, 1879. https://books.google.com/books?id=pEMIAAAAQAAJ.

Williams, Helen Maria. *Letters Written in France, in the Summer 1790, to a Friend in England, Containing Various Anecdotes Relative to the French Revolution*. 4th ed. London: T. Cadell, 1794. https://books.google.com/books?id=pf5HiMDsMoUC.

Williams, Nicholas M. Julie A. Carlson, *England's First Family of Writers: Mary Wollstonecraft, William Godwin, Mary Shelley*. *Nineteenth-Century Literature* 63, no. 2 (2008): 258–63. doi:10.1525ncl.2008.63.2.258.

Wolfson, Susan J. Review of *England's First Family of Writers: Mary Wollstonecraft, William Godwin, Mary Shelley*. *Modern Philology*. 107, no. 4 (May 2010): E117–120. *Academic Search Alumni Edition*. EBSCO*host*.

Wollstonecraft, Mary. *An Historical and Moral View of the Origin and Progress of the French Revolution*. London: Joseph Johnson, 1794. https://books.google.com/books?id=089IAAAAcAAJ.

———. *Letters Written in Sweden, Norway, and Denmark*. London: Johnson, 1796. https://books.google.com/books?id=4hJbAAAAcAAJ.

———. *Maria; or The Wrongs of Woman*. Edited by William Godwin. London: Johnson, 1798, posthumously. https://books.google.com/books?id=QjWYDAEACAAJ.

———. *Mary, a Fiction*. In *"Mary, a Fiction" and "The Wrongs of Woman, or Maria,"* edited by Michelle Faubert, 73–148. Peterborough, ON: Broadview, 2012.

———. *Original Stories from Real Life; with Conversations, Calculated to Regulate the Affections, and Form the Mind to Truth and Goodness*. Illust. William Blake. London: Joseph Johnson, 1788; 1791; 1796. https://books.google.com/books?id=e3c4AAAAMAAJ.

———. *Thoughts on the Education of Daughters: With Reflections on Female Conduct, in the More Important Duties of Life*. London: Johnson, 1787. https://books.google.com/books?id=hVIJAAAAQAAJ.

———. *A Vindication of the Rights of Woman*. London: Joseph Johnson, 1792. http://oll.libertyfund.org/titles/126.

———. *The Wrongs of Woman, or Maria*. In *"Mary, a Fiction" and "The Wrongs of Woman, or Maria,"* edited by Michelle Faubert, 149–289. Peterborough, ON: Broadview, 2012.

Woodberry, George Edward. *Mary Wollstonecraft*. *Atlantic Monthly* 46 (December 1880): 843–46. https://books.google.com/books?id=eV4CAAAAIAAJ.

Worthen, John. "The Necessary Ignorance of a Biographer." In *The Art of Literary Biography*, edited by John Batchelor, 227–44. Oxford: Clarendon Press, 1995.

Woolf, Virginia. *The Second Common Reader*. 1929. New York: Harcourt, 1960.

Wordsworth, Williams. Preface. *Lyrical Ballads: With Pastoral and Other Poems*. 3rd ed. Vol. 1 of 2 vols. London: Longman and Rees, 1802. https://books.google.com/books?id=BAsUAAAAQAAJ.

Wyzewa, Teodor. *Some Women: Loving or Luckless*. Trans. C. H. Jeaffreson. London: John Lane, 1909. https://books.google.com/books?id=nHlCAAAAIAAJ.

Yarrington, Alison. "Anne Seymour Damer: A Sculptor of 'Republican Perfection.'" In *Bluestockings Displayed: Portraiture, Performance and Patronage, 1730–1830*, edited by Elizabeth Eger, 81–99. Cambridge: Cambridge University Press, 2013.

Yaeger, Patricia. "Writing as Action: *A Vindication of the Rights of Woman*." *Minnesota Review* 29 (Fall 1987): 67–80.

Yeazell, Ruth Bernard. *Fictions of Modesty: Women and Courtship in the English Novel*. University of Chicago Press, 1991.

Zaw, Susan Khin. "The Reasonable Heart: Mary Wollstonecraft's View of the Relation Between Reason and Feeling in Morality, Moral Psychology, and Moral Development." *Hypatia* 13, no. 1 (Winter 1998): 78–117. http://www.jstor.org/stable/3810608.

Zimmerman, Bonnie. *Lesbian Histories and Cultures: An Encyclopedia*. Vol. 1. New York: Garland, 2000.

INDEX

abolition 194
Adams, John 81, 157
advice books 114, 162, 203, 205
Alderson, Amelia 41, 69, 96, 200. *See* Amelia Alderson Opie
America xiv, xvi, 5, 16, 20, 37, 61, 65, 70, 81, 82, 84, 104, 105, 106, 122, 123, 134, 163, 166, 175, 179, 180, 195, 196, 198, 203, 209, 213, 217, 234, 236, 237, 238, 242, 246, 247, 249, 250, 251
Analytical Review xv, 31, 34, 65, 78, 135, 147, 187, 189, 202, 241
Anglican 27, 28, 30, 92, 93, 146, 156, 158, 162, 174
Anti-Jacobin Review 16, 19, 39, 70, 233, 239
Apetrei, Sarah ix, 9
Arden, Jane xiv, 68, 78, 80, 98, 112, 118, 141, 145, 146, 154, 174, 177, 178, 215
Arden, John xiv, 79, 145
aristocracy 11, 47, 80, 149, 205, 207, 209, 211
atheism 43
Austen, Jane 47, 90, 197
Ayres, Brenda
  Becoming Mary Wollstonecraft ii, 233
  Frances Trollope and the Novel of Social Change 89
  Mary Wollstonecraft and Religion 233, 251
  Silent Voices 89
  The Essential Wollstonecraft ii, 233

Bahar, Saba 189
Baillie, Joanna 133

bantlings 35
Baptist 113
Barbauld, Anna Laetitia 30, 41, 187
Barker-Benfield, G. J. 81
Barking xiv, 54, 144
Barlow, Joel 82, 123, 175, 180, 200
Barlow, Ruth 82, 123, 165, 180
Bath xiv, 68, 80, 87, 145, 174
Beverley xiii, xiv, 118, 119, 136, 137, 145, 251
Bible, King James 27, 28, 40, 57, 59, 60, 61, 63, 70, 83, 109, 118, 130, 132, 149, 156, 171, 174, 178, 181, 206, 207, 208
birth control 74, 106, 127, 172
Bishop, Mary Elizabeth Frances (niece) xv, 21, 98, 99, 121, 140, 141, 155, 156, 171
Bishop, Meredith xiii, xiv, xv, 21, 37, 40, 46, 57, 58, 68, 95, 98, 99, 111, 112, 114, 120, 121, 130, 137, 138, 139, 140, 141, 155, 156, 163, 173, 176, 179, 213
Blackstone, William 171
Blake, William 30, 73, 103, 104, 234, 239, 251
Blakemore, Steven 166, 234
Blood family xiv, xv, 57, 112, 139, 155, 171, 176, 177
Blood, Caroline 176
Blood, Fanny xiv, xv, 10, 17, 21, 22, 37, 56, 58, 70, 75, 80, 87, 93, 94, 95, 114, 119, 130, 140, 141, 146, 151, 154, 167, 171, 176, 183, 188, 213, 215. *See* Fanny Skeys
Blood, George xiv, 62, 93, 94, 107, 126, 140, 141, 157

Blood, Neptune xiv, 121
bluestockings 157, 187. *See* intellectualism
boarding schools 20, 29, 30, 98, 167
Bonnycastle, John 30
Boos, Florence ix, 7, 17, 72, 73, 75, 86, 234
Bournemouth xvii
Bowdler, Harriet 187
Brandon, Ruth 144
breastfeeding 80, 133, 138
Brissot, Jacques Pierre 82, 196, 200
Brody, Miriam ix, 21, 55, 101, 112, 113, 143–50, 157, 213, 235
Brontë, Anne 49, 59
Brontë, Charlotte 59, 97, 169
Brontë, Emily 44
Browning, Robert 124
Burgh, James 29, 31, 93, 173, 235
Burgh, Mrs. Hannah xv, 29, 30, 80, 93, 176
Burke, Edmund xv, 22, 122, 147, 152, 157, 166, 187, 200, 213, 234
   Reflections on the Revolution in French xv
Burney, Fanny 96, 157, 187
Butler, Eleanor 151–54, 236
Byron, Lord 3, 35, 209, 235, 250

Calvinism 28, 159
Cambon, Maria van de Weken de xv
camera obscura 193, 194
Carlson, Julie A. ix, 9, 79, 183–92
Carlyle, Thomas 56
Catholicism 75, 146
Cayton, Andrew ix, 9, 14, 193–200
Chapman, John 94
Chapone, Hester 41, 80, 114, 131, 187, 203, 204
child rearing 3, 159
childhood 37, 44
Christianity 27, 56, 70, 93, 106, 107, 156, 174, 179
Christie, Rebecca 15
Christie, Thomas 125
Church of England. *See* Anglican
Clares 173
Clairmont, Claire 181, 248
Clairmont, Mary Jane 200, 210
Clare, John xiv

Clare, Mrs. xiv, 80
Clares 79
class 11, 12, 59, 80, 99, 129, 130, 132, 133, 159, 207
Clemit, Pamela ix, xi, 17, 18, 233, 236, 239, 240
conduct books 130
Conger, Syndy McMillen 132, 133
Conrad, Joseph 50
consumption 58, 119, 177
Cowper, William 30
Curtis, William 171

Darcy, Jane 18
Darwin, Erasmus 30, 194
Dawson, Sarah xiv, 10, 28, 68, 80
de Staël, Baroness 80, 166
death 28, 33
Denlinger, Elizabeth 8, 66, 237
depression 56, 67, 87, 113, 120, 121, 137, 138, 139, 141, 154
Detre, Jean ix, 7, 8, 71, 90, 237
Dickens, Charles ii, 45, 47, 54, 56, 59, 61, 90, 97, 237
Dissenters 30, 93, 99, 156, 162, 179, 241
divorce 21, 47, 171, 191
dolls 53, 54, 55
domesticity 11, 22, 53, 65, 74, 80, 85, 87, 105, 118, 150, 156, 167, 186, 187, 207, 208
dress 54, 55, 61, 68, 172
dropsy xiii, 68
Durant, W. Clark 17, 117, 239

Edgeworth, Maria 41, 78, 96, 203
education 2, 3, 22, 28, 30, 36, 46, 47, 54, 73, 74, 79, 92, 95, 96, 111, 123, 126, 131, 132, 135, 145, 150, 159, 160, 162, 165, 175, 179, 181, 187, 190, 200, 203
effeminacy 11, 153, 167
Eliot, George 31, 44, 48, 78, 97, 176, 179, 209, 241
Eliot, T. S. 169
Elwood, Anne ix, 5, 6, 238
   Memoirs of the Literary Ladies of England 5, 238
Enclosure Acts 66, 144, 145, 159, 179
Enfield xiv

Enfield, William 30, 214
Enlightenment 8, 36, 158, 162, 233, 235, 238, 240
Epping Forest xiii, 66, 144
ERA 74
eroticism 148
Evangelicalism 16, 83
exercise 53, 54, 55, 144

fallen women 61
family 156, 176, 184, 186, 207
fancy 195, 196, 238, 246
Farnham, Marynia F. 65
Faubert, Michelle ix, 146, 251
feminism 1, 7, 9, 14, 71, 74, 75, 95, 100, 101, 105, 118, 129, 134, 139, 141, 143, 182, 219n.2
feminist 118, 130, 141, 155, 162, 214
feminists 16, 72, 73, 76, 86, 87, 89, 95, 101, 185, 209
Ferguson, Moira 129
Fern, Fanny 31, 176, 237
Fielding, Henry 63
Fielding, Sarah 187
Flexner, Eleanor ix, 7, 71, 72, 75, 77–88, 89, 90, 92, 93, 98, 99, 100, 104, 105, 114, 117, 136, 138, 238, 239
Fordyce, Dr. James 23
Forster, Johann Reinhold 30
France xiv, xvi, 11, 12, 15, 20, 22, 34, 37, 47, 48, 55, 58, 60, 61, 70, 73, 76, 80, 81, 82, 90, 91, 95, 124, 125, 126, 134, 148, 149, 158, 162, 163, 164, 169, 170, 172, 180, 200, 235, 239, 241, 244, 246, 248, 251
Franklin, Caroline ix, 27, 78, 159–68, 184, 239
Fredman, Alice Green ix, 7, 72, 85, 86, 90, 94, 97–100, 101, 114, 115, 239
free love 16, 101
French xv, 11, 16, 20, 24, 76, 78, 81, 91, 132, 134, 163, 185, 244
French Revolution xvi, 11, 16, 17, 60, 80, 81, 129, 133, 134, 149, 162, 163, 164, 170, 199, 200, 237
Furniss, Tom 188
Fuseli, Henry 6, 12, 22, 30, 37, 41, 47, 52, 62, 69, 72, 83, 85, 87, 95, 100, 101, 107, 114, 124, 130, 131, 141, 147, 148, 157, 161, 172, 173, 177, 180, 183, 185, 188, 200, 235, 243
Fuseli, Sophia xvi, 47, 62, 69, 131

Gabell, Ann 121
Gabell, Henry 109, 121, 122, 171, 173
Gaskell, Elizabeth 55, 97
genius 17, 18, 25, 26, 39, 49, 52, 217
Genlis, Stephanie de 80, 152
gentility. *See* aristocracy
gentry 12, 66, 77, 118, 144
George, Margaret 7, 8, 67, 72, 73, 136
Georgian 91
Gilroy, Amanda 198, 250
Girondins 162, 163, 164
Godwin, Fanny. *See* Fanny Imlay
Godwin, William ix, xvi, xvii, 4, 7, 9, 13, 14, 15–32, 34, 36, 38, 39, 41, 43–57, 62, 63, 69, 70, 71, 73, 74, 75, 81, 85, 86, 87, 95, 96, 100, 105, 108, 110, 112, 126, 134, 148, 149, 150, 159, 160, 161, 162, 167, 172, 173, 174, 175, 176, 177, 183, 184, 185, 186, 187, 188, 189, 190, 191, 193, 194, 197, 198, 199, 200, 201, 202, 207, 210, 213, 219n.5, 233, 235, 236, 237, 238, 239, 240, 241, 242, 243, 244, 245, 246, 247, 248, 249, 251
  works
    Caleb Williams 207, 240
    Enquiry Concerning Political Justice 23, 239
    Fleetwood 189
    Memoirs xi, xvi, xvii, 4, 5, 15, 16, 17, 18, 20, 22, 23, 24, 25, 28, 30, 31, 32, 33, 34, 36, 44, 51, 53, 54, 55, 63, 69, 70, 75, 81, 96, 103, 105, 107, 110, 112, 113, 117, 119, 124, 129, 136, 138, 141, 155, 160, 161, 164, 167, 173, 174, 175, 176, 181, 185, 188, 189, 194, 197, 199, 200, 203, 210, 213, 219n.5, 233, 236, 237, 238, 239, 240, 241, 244, 245, 249, 250
    Posthumous Works xvii, 53
Goodwin, A. 100, 101
Gordon, Charlotte ix, 4, 34, 55, 201–11, 219n.4

Gordon, Lyndall ix, 3, 4, 31, 34, 55,
    105, 110, 121, 141, 151, 157,
    161, 169–82
Gosse, Edmund 49
governess xv, 10, 11, 20, 21, 37, 59, 68,
    93, 123, 135, 136, 144, 147, 162,
    173, 194
Gray, Thomas 171
Gregory, Dr. John 23
Guest, Harriet 26
guillotine 60, 149, 163
Gunther-Canada, Wendy 9

Hamilton, Elizabeth 96
Hampsey, John C. 101
Hanley, Kirstin 139, 140
Hardwicke Act 171
Hawthorne, Nathaniel 209
Hays, Mary ix, 5, 7, 15, 28, 30, 33–41,
    68, 69, 96, 101, 107, 170, 185,
    187, 200, 240, 241, 244, 246,
    247, 250
  works
    "Memoirs of Mary Wollstonecraft" 5,
      33, 36, 39, 41, 241
    *Appeal to the Men of Great Britain,
      An* 34, 36
    Female Biography 5, 34, 36, 41, 241
    Letters and Essays 34
    Memoirs of Emma Courtney 36, 185, 241
    Victim of Prejudice, The 36
Henry, Thomas 30
Hewlett, John 29, 30, 31, 51, 68, 70, 113,
    156, 173
Holcroft, Thomas 30
Holmes, Mark 3
Holmes, Richard ix, 2, 3, 75
Homes, Ann 69, 122, 123
homosexuality 108, 109, 151–54, 183, 192
Hopkins, Gerard Manley 31, 241
Hoxton xiv, 105, 119
Hoxton Academy 56
hysteria 112, 206

Imlay, Fanny xvi, xvii, 15, 20, 48, 69, 85,
    95, 181, 183
Imlay, Gilbert xi, xvi, 5, 6, 12, 14, 15,
    20, 22, 34, 37, 38, 39, 41, 44, 45,
    48, 49, 56, 60, 61, 62, 63, 69, 70,
    72, 81, 82, 83–85, 86, 87, 95, 97,
    99, 101, 107, 108, 110, 124, 125,
    126, 134, 148, 150, 158, 161, 163,
    164, 165, 167, 175, 177, 178, 180,
    181, 183, 185, 188, 189, 191, 193,
    195–99, 200, 202, 238, 239, 247,
    248, 250
Inchbald, Elizabeth 209, 210
insane asylum 55, 105, 114, 119, 139, 167,
    190, 191
insanity 105, 114, 115, 139
intellectualism 2, 8, 30, 36, 37, 56, 74, 75,
    76, 79, 93, 99, 104, 105, 111, 114,
    121, 122, 129, 131, 134, 148, 157,
    159, 162, 170, 187, 190, 205, 213
Ireland xiii, xiv, xv, 10, 20, 41, 60, 80,
    91, 96, 100, 109, 135, 139, 152,
    173, 175, 176, 181, 213, 242, 247,
    248, 249

Jack the Ripper 91
Jacobinism 9, 16, 70, 101, 133, 134,
    164, 203
Jacobs, Diane ix, 55, 107, 113, 119, 137,
    138, 148, 151–58, 213, 242
James, Henry R. 7
Jewsbury, Geraldine 78
Johnson, Joseph ix, xv, 3, 14, 15, 20, 27,
    30, 34, 37, 62, 68, 70, 73, 78, 79,
    92, 95, 99, 110, 113, 114, 141, 145,
    147, 148, 149, 156, 162, 165, 166,
    172, 173, 174, 176, 185, 187, 189,
    202, 234, 235, 239, 242, 244, 245,
    249, 251
Johnson, Samuel 12, 28, 30, 70, 71, 169,
    187, 234, 242
Jordan, Dorothea 60, 90
Jump, Harriet ix, 9, 17, 18, 41, 242

Kanner, Barbara 8, 129
Kaplan, Cora ix, 67, 76, 129, 188
Kelly, Gary ix, 8, 11, 12, 34, 129–34,
    236, 242
Kelly, Mary 91
Kendall, Mrs. A. 34–36
    Castle on the Rock, The 34, 242
    Tales of the Abbey 35

King, Lady Caroline xv, 10, 12, 68, 80, 109, 135, 136
King, Margaret, Countess of Mount Cashell 136, 181
King, Viscount xv, 10
Kingsboroughs 21, 59, 68, 78, 96, 135
Knowles, John 62, 63, 130, 131, 148, 243

Laird, Susan ix, 9
Lamb, Lady Caroline 152
Landberg, Ferdinand 65
latitudinarianism 162
Laugharne xiv, 194
Lavate, Johann Kaspar 148
Leavenworth, Mrs. 123
Lecky, William 96
Linnaeus, Carl 171
literary canon 1, 8, 89
Llangollen 152–54, 233, 235, 236, 243, 244, 246, 247
Lloyd, Charles 26, 101, 200
Lloyd, Robert 140
Locke, John 205
London iv, xiii, xiv, xv, xvi, 15, 20, 28, 30, 37, 49, 74, 75, 77, 78, 80, 91, 123, 124, 144, 145, 157, 165, 180, 187, 194, 205, 208, 233, 234, 235, 236, 237, 238, 239, 240, 241, 242, 243, 244, 245, 246, 247, 248, 249, 250, 251, 252
Lorch, Jennifer 66

Macaulay, Catharine 36, 41, 80, 157, 187
Malkin, Benjamin Heath 73
Malthus, Thomas 30
marriage 3, 11, 21, 23, 37, 40, 41, 46, 47, 48, 49, 52, 55, 57, 60, 62, 68, 69, 71, 87, 95, 98, 99, 106, 107, 108, 110, 111, 112, 119, 120, 121, 126, 138, 139, 140, 141, 146, 147, 149, 150, 152, 153, 155, 156, 157, 164, 167, 177, 178, 179, 181, 185, 186, 190, 191, 192, 199, 205, 206
Marshall, Peter 4, 33, 56, 244
Marxism 9, 130, 132, 134
Mary Wollstonecraft Journal 7, 75, 234

masculine 12, 22, 24, 34, 35, 36, 61, 79, 81, 94, 111, 133, 152, 153, 166, 167, 186, 187, 209, 215
McInnes, Andrew 5
Mellor, Anne 36
ménage à trois xvi, 22, 62, 63, 69, 100, 101, 188
Methodism 179
Mill, John Stuart 97, 236
misogyny 73
Mitchelstown Castle 135
Moers, Ellen ix, 75
Mohamedism 188
Montagu, Basil 194
Montagu, Elizabeth 187
More, Hannah 41, 96, 157, 187, 200, 203, 237, 246
motherhood 54, 65, 86
mothers xv, 1, 10, 38, 53, 54, 68, 73, 88, 124, 133, 138, 143, 156, 176, 179, 181, 182, 183, 186, 191, 201, 211, 219n.2
Myers, Mitzi ix, 9, 15, 18, 21, 129, 141, 189, 202, 203, 209, 245

narrative technique 6, 35
Necker, Jacques xv, 27, 78
Nehring, Christina 9
Neiman, Fraser 74
neoclassicism 1, 8, 9, 131, 166
Newington Green xv, 30, 70, 91, 92, 93, 99, 173
Newington Green Unitarian Church xv
Newton, John 30
Nicholson, William 30
Nightingale, Florence 172
Nitchie, Elizabeth ix, 68
Nixon, Edna ix, 7, 8, 71, 90, 136, 245
NOW 74

Oates, Stephen 14, 245, 249
Ogle, George 11, 109
Opie, Amelia. *See* Amelia Alderson
Opie, John xvi, 41, 69, 94, 96, 186

Paine, Thomas 15, 30, 123, 163, 234
pantheism 27

parents 29, 43, 159, 173, 174, 175, 210
passion 5, 8, 12, 28, 38, 39, 60, 67, 139, 147, 148, 149, 151, 183, 188
patriarchy 67, 89, 106, 118, 154, 176, 186, 191, 200, 214
Paul, C. Kegan ix, xi, 5, 6, 7, 34, 43–50, 51, 60, 62, 136, 240, 245, 249
　Letters to Imlay xvii, 18, 43, 49, 51, 240, 245, 250
　William Godwin 245
Pennell, Elizabeth Robins ix, 5, 6, 7, 43–50, 51, 52, 53, 54, 56, 58, 59, 60, 61, 62, 63, 69, 75, 136, 245
　Life of Mary Wollstonecraft 51, 52, 54, 56, 57, 58, 59, 60, 61, 62, 63, 69
　Mary Wollstonecraft Godwin 53
Pennell, Joseph 51, 52
Percival, Thomas 30
petticoat government 208
plants 33, 113, 171–73
Polwhele, Richard 7, 102, 246
Polygon, The xvi, 16
Ponsonby, Sarah 151–54, 236
Poovey, Mary ix, 108, 129, 188
Portugal 70, 75, 119, 146
　Lisbon xv, 21, 29, 75, 141
postpartum depression 21, 68, 120, 138, 139, 140
Preedy, George R. 65
Price, Richard xv, 26, 27, 30, 91, 92, 93, 156, 173, 200
Priestley, Joseph 28, 30
prison 112, 125, 167, 179, 190
prostitution 5, 39, 41, 47, 103, 104, 141, 176, 177, 190
Pulteney, Frances 187
Putney Bridge xvi, 6, 38, 48, 181. *See* Mary Wollstonecraft suicide

Quakers 51, 179

Radcliffe, Anne 41
Rajan, Tilottama 18, 25, 26, 185, 246
Rauschenbusch-Clough, Emma ix, 7
religion 61
Reveley, Mary 69
Richardson, Samuel xv, 78, 83, 186

Robinson, Mary 60
Rolan, Jeanne-Manon 149
romance 191
romanticism 8, 9, 79, 83, 133, 163, 164, 166, 185, 195, 207, 234, 237, 238, 239, 241, 242, 244, 246, 247
Roscoe, William xvi, 148, 180
Rousseau 23, 45, 166, 207, 236, 247

Salzmann, Christian xv, 27, 78
Sand, George 44, 61
Sapiro, Virginia ix, 2, 8, 13, 148, 247
Scandinavia xvi, 25, 38, 48, 60, 84, 95, 134, 162, 165
Scott, Sir Walter 152, 197, 247
sensibility 12, 19, 24, 26, 39, 58, 74, 115, 122, 133, 154, 166, 187, 192
sentimentality 114, 166, 209
septicaemia xvi
seraglios 188
Seward, Anna 152, 209
sex 108, 112, 152, 153, 172
sex object 80, 105
sexual revolution 14, 89, 101, 103, 106, 107, 115, 118, 126
Shaw, Anna Howard 179
Shelley family 183, 184
Shelley, Mary Godwin xvi, xvii, 22, 41, 43, 104, 105, 126, 164, 181, 201
Shelley, Percy Bysshe 43, 184, 201
Shelley, Percy Florence xvii, 43
Silliman, Benjamin 186
Simcox, Edith 31, 176, 233
Skeys, Hugh xv, 58, 119, 120, 140
slavery 40, 122
Sloan, Margaret 36
Smollett, Tobias 63, 214, 215, 216
Somers Town 15, 16
Southey, Robert 4, 137, 152, 219n.6, 246, 248
Spitalfields xiii, 66, 77, 91, 144, 211
spousal abuse 67, 138, 171, 174, 205
St. Botolph without Bishopsgate xiii, 27, 77, 173
St. Clair, William 1, 136, 172
St. Pancras Church xvi, 16, 20, 150, 181, 213
Stiles, Ezra 123

INDEX 259

suffragettes 16, 65
suicide xvi, xvii, 4, 6, 20, 22, 38, 39, 48, 61, 63, 84, 95, 101, 108, 126, 150, 158, 167, 181, 185, 188, 190, 191
Sunday School 160, 179
Sunstein, Emily ix, 7, 20, 55, 60, 85, 89, 92, 93, 100, 103–15, 119, 136, 156, 176, 238, 239, 248
Swift, Simon 29

Talleyrand-Périgord, Charles-Maurice de 24, 76, 78
Tarleton, Banastre 61
Taylor, Barbara ix, 9, 29, 66, 101, 141
Taylor, George Robert Stirling ix, 7, 9, 75
Thackeray, William 97
The Emigrants 125, 126, 198, 239, 250
Thompson, E. P. 131
Tims, Margaret ix, 1, 4, 78, 117–27, 136
Todd, Janet ix, xi, 7, 8, 13, 17, 28, 33, 68, 75, 85, 86, 92, 99, 100, 104, 105, 112, 113, 114, 115, 117, 122, 129, 135, 144, 154, 155, 162, 165, 176, 183, 194, 219n.7, 238, 249
  Collected Letters of Mary Wollstonecraft xi, 12, 13
Tomalin, Claire ix, 7, 20, 71, 85, 89, 104, 114, 115, 117, 136, 144, 148, 169, 177, 239, 240, 249, 250
Tompkins, Jane 89, 197
Tooke, John Horne 30, 74
Topographical Description 198
travelogue 162, 202
Trimmer, Sarah 28, 131
Tuchman, Barbara 2
tyranny 67

Unitarianism xv, 92, 113, 173, 214

Verhoeven, Wil 198
Victorian ii, vii, 2, 5, 6, 9, 16, 18, 43, 44, 45, 46, 47, 48, 49, 51, 55, 56, 57, 58, 59, 60, 61, 63, 86, 89, 91, 95, 96, 131, 153, 203, 204, 205, 206, 207, 208, 209, 213, 233, 241, 242, 243, 251
Voltaire 22, 96

Wakefield, Gilbert 30
Wakefield, Priscilla 30, 96
Walker, Gina 33, 36
Walkington xiv
Walpole, Horace 187
Walworth xiv
Wardle, Mary E. 73
Wardle, Ralph ix, xi, 6, 7, 8, 65–76, 78, 85, 86, 90, 94, 98, 100, 117, 121, 194, 245, 250
  works *Collected Letters of Mary Wollstonecraft* xi, 73
  Godwin and Mary 73
  Letters of William Godwin 250
Waterhouse, Joshua xiv, 68, 121, 126, 173, 177, 188
weaker vessel 12, 24, 60
Wedgwood, Josiah 152, 194
Wedgwood, Sarah 194
Wedgwood, Thomas 118, 194, 195, 243
Wellington, Jan ix, 11
Wesley, John ix, 179
West, Jane 34, 96
Whale Bone xiii
Wilberforce, William 152
William, Anna 187
Williams, Helen Maria 133, 134, 149, 251
Wollstonecraft Everina (sister) xiv
Wollstonecraft family 160, 161, 174, 176, 210, 211
Wollstonecraft, Bess (sister) xiii, xiv, xv, 19, 20, 21, 30, 40, 41, 46, 55, 57, 58, 68, 94, 95, 98, 99, 105, 106, 111, 112, 113, 114, 115, 120, 121, 122, 124, 126, 130, 137, 138, 139, 140, 141, 145, 146, 155, 156, 163, 171, 175, 178, 179, 180. *See* Bess Wollstonecraft Bishop
Wollstonecraft, Charles (brother) xiv, 78, 105, 180
Wollstonecraft, Edward (grandfather) xiii, xiv, 66, 77, 110, 118, 144, 145
Wollstonecraft, Edward Bland (Ned) (brother) xiii, 20, 55, 66, 77, 105, 145, 155, 161, 174, 178

Wollstonecraft, Edward John (father) xiii, xiv, 5, 13, 19, 20, 30, 47, 51, 56, 66, 67, 68, 70, 76, 77, 82, 84, 85, 86, 93, 110, 111, 112, 118, 120, 123, 126, 144, 145, 146, 155, 157, 161, 174, 175, 177, 199, 210, 211
Wollstonecraft, Elizabeth Dickson (mother) xiii, xiv, 19, 20, 51, 54, 55, 57, 67, 68, 70, 84, 86, 95, 108, 111, 138, 146, 155, 161, 174, 175, 210, 211
Wollstonecraft, Everina (sister) xiv, xv, 17, 20, 28, 33, 40, 80, 84, 95, 105, 106, 109, 112, 121, 122, 124, 137, 139, 140, 141, 156, 194, 209
Wollstonecraft, Henry (brother) xiii, 55, 105, 114, 115, 118, 119, 176
Wollstonecraft, James (brother) xiv, 105
Wollstonecraft, Lydia (stepmother) xiv, 155
Wollstonecraft, Mary
  autodidactic 79
  birth xiii
  brothers 20, 53, 54, 55, 157
  burial xvii
  Catholicism 75, 146
  childhood 19, 51, 54, 67, 119, 144, 146, 160, 163, 210
  death 4, 28, 31, 34, 48, 53, 55, 95, 150
  depression 56, 67, 87, 120, 121, 137, 138, 139, 141, 154
  girls' school 10, 21, 70, 120, 130
  narrative technique 24, 33, 34, 79, 86, 90, 122, 147, 215
  parents 27, 40, 44, 55, 57, 68, 70, 111, 145, 146, 170
  religion 2, 3, 9, 10, 13, 26, 27, 28, 29, 30, 31, 32, 36, 39, 40, 41, 43, 46, 48, 49, 52, 53, 57, 60, 63, 72, 83, 86, 87, 88, 92, 93, 106, 107, 108, 109, 115, 118, 130, 132, 136, 140, 141, 145, 146, 149, 150, 156, 158, 160, 164, 171, 173, 174, 179, 188, 195, 206, 208, 216
  romance 68, 69, 121, 126, 148, 164, 173, 177, 180, 188, 205, 214
  sex 6, 15, 37, 39, 41, 72, 73, 75, 87, 96, 97, 101, 103, 107, 108, 109, 112, 115, 141, 148, 154, 166, 172, 181, 185, 188, 190, 204
  sisters 10, 11, 19, 20, 21, 46, 54, 86, 93, 94, 121, 124, 146, 147, 154, 155, 157, 180, 185
  suicide xvi, 20, 70, 158, 167, 199
  temperament 92, 94, 111, 118, 120, 140, 145, 146
  works
    "Hints" xvii
    Cave of Fancy, The xi, xvii, 113, 165
    Elements of Morality xv, 27, 46, 78
    Female Reader, The xi, xv, 165, 166, 186
    Historical and Moral View of the Origin and Progress of the French Revolution, An xi, xvi, 11, 80, 81, 133, 134, 149, 164, 233, 251
    Letters Written During a Short Residence in Sweden, Norway, and Denmark xi, xvi, 25, 131, 134, 140, 162, 183, 188, 189, 202, 251
    Mary, a Fiction xv, 19, 36, 55, 109, 146, 147, 174, 186, 189, 238, 251
    Of the Importance of Religious Opinions. *See* Necker, Jacques
    On the Importance of Religion Opinions 27
    Maria xi, xvi, xvii, 24, 25, 36, 41, 57, 63, 70, 86, 96, 99, 108, 134, 161, 163, 167, 174, 175, 185, 189, 190, 191, 192, 210, 235, 238, 251
    Original Stories from Real Life xi, xv, 28, 92, 163, 203, 243, 251
    Thoughts on the Education of Daughter xi, xv, 10, 29, 30, 70, 78, 107, 123, 130, 131, 136, 147, 156, 173, 235, 251
    Vindication of the Rights of Men, A xi, xv, xvi, 22, 67, 122, 126, 132, 166, 167
    Vindication of the Rights of Woman, A xi, xv, xvi, 5, 8, 12, 13, 22, 23, 24, 25, 26, 27, 30, 34, 35, 36, 39, 40, 45, 46, 47, 53, 54, 59, 60, 62, 63, 67, 68, 71, 73, 74, 75, 76, 78, 79, 80, 83, 86, 87, 88, 90, 93, 96, 99, 101, 107, 108, 109, 110, 111, 115, 122, 123, 124, 131, 132, 133, 135, 136, 138, 141, 143, 144, 145, 147, 150,

152, 156, 157, 167, 170, 172, 176, 177, 180, 181, 186, 187, 188, 190, 195, 199, 202, 204, 207, 209, 213, 214, 215, 234, 236, 238, 239, 244, 246, 248, 249, 250, 251, 252
Young Grandison xv
womanhood 105, 215
women's liberation 4, 72, 74, 103, 115, 118

Woolf, Virginia ix, 6, 16, 76, 169, 170, 233, 243, 251
Wordsworth, William 133, 152, 194
World War I 179
World War II 65, 67, 71, 73

Yonge, Charlotte 46

Zaw, Susan Khin ix, 9